RE-INVENTING
CONSTRUCTION

Editors: Ilka & Andreas Ruby
Design: Leonard Streich, Julian Schubert, Elena Schütz
Copy editing: Jessica Bridger, Uta Hoffmann, Christine Moran, Sue Pickett
Proof reading: Sue Pickett, Christine Moran
Translations: Daniel Wentz, Rory O'Donovan

A CIP catalogue record for this book is available
from the Library of Congress, Washington D.C., USA.

Bibliographic information published by
Die Deutsche Bibliothek.
Die Deutsche Bibliothek lists this publication
in the Deutsche Nationalbibliographie; detailed
bibliographic data is available online at
http://dnb.ddb.de

This work is subject to copyright.
All rights are reserved, whether the whole or part of
the material is concerned, specifically the rights of translation,
reprinting, re-use of illustrations, recitation, broadcasting,
reproduction on microfilms or in other ways,
and storage in data banks.

For any kind of use, permission of the copyright holder
must be obtained.

© 2010 Ruby Press, Berlin
© 2010 Holcim Foundation for Sustainable Construction, Zürich
© The contributors for their texts and images

Printed in Germany
ISBN 978-3-9813436-2-5
http://www.ruby-press.com
http://www.holcimfoundation.org

RE-INVENTING CONSTRUCTION

Edited by Ilka & Andreas Ruby

With an Illustrated Index
Compiled by Something Fantastic and Written by Jessica Bridger

Acknowledgement

The book you hold in your hands evolved from a debate-platform, the International Holcim Forum for Sustainable Construction on *Re-inventing Construction*, that took place in April 2010 at the Universidad Iberoamericana in Santa Fé, Mexico City. For three days 270 specialists from 39 countries—architects, urban planners, engineers, scholars, business and government representatives—met in workshops, lectures, and on guided tours to exchange and expand their views on the ways in which construction could be re-invented. Unlike a conference proceedings publication, this book does not just document the Forum literally, but develops it further. It features both a selection of papers given at the Forum in Mexico-City, as well as a number of additional essays by experts in the field whom we have specially solicited to contribute to the book. We thank all authors for the energy and care invested in the production of their valuable contributions.

We would like to express our sincere gratitude to the Holcim Foundation for Sustainable Construction for its ongoing commitment to the discourse in architecture and urbanism. With this Forum in Mexico-City the Holcim Foundation has continued a series of discursive events and publications that was initiated with *Basic Needs* at the Swiss Federal Institute of Technology (ETH Zurich) in 2004 and followed by *Urban_Trans_Formation* at Tongji University in Shanghai 2007, which gave rise to a similar publication (*Urban Transformation*, edited by Ilka & Andreas Ruby, Berlin: Ruby Press, 2008). The 4th International Holcim Forum is scheduled to take place in 2013, at the Indian Institute of Technology Bombay in Mumbai, India.

In particular we would like to thank Rolf Soiron, Chairman of the Board of Directors of Holcim Ltd and Chairman of the Advisory Board of the Holcim Foundation as well as Hans-Rudolf Schalcher, Member of the Management Board and Head of the Technical Competence Center of the Holcim Foundation. We would also like to thank the members of the academic committee of the 3rd Holcim Forum: Hans-Rudolf Schalcher, Hansjürg Leibundgut, Holger Wallbaum, and Marc Angélil. We are specifically indebted to Marc Angélil, Member of the Management Board and of the Technical Competence Center of the Foundation, as well as Edward Schwarz, General Manager of the Holcim Foundation. Their tremendous support and invaluable advice has been very instrumental in the production of this book.

Ilka & Andreas Ruby, Berlin 2010

TABLE OF CONTENTS

Ilka & Andreas Ruby
Introduction
Toward a Gay Science of Construction 10

REDUCE CO_2

Forrest Meggers
Reduce CO_2 20

Amory B. Lovins
Saving the Climate Saves You Money
How Buildings Can Use Energy Intelligently by Integrative Design 25

Werner Sobek
Architecture Isn't Here to Stay
Toward a Reversibility of Construction 34

Sheila Kennedy / KVA
Going SOFT
Design Strategies for a New Materiality of Energy 46

Bjarke Ingels / BIG
The Joys of Ecolomy
How to Make Sustainability a Haven of Hedonism 55

Forrest Meggers, Hansjürg Leibundgut
EOL, COP, PVT, TABS and LowEx
How to Reduce CO_2 Emissions with New Construction Technologies 67

Tobias Wallisser / LAVA
Conditioning the Desert
How to Create Usable Outdoor Public Space in Masdar City 84

Something Fantastic
An Illustrated Index of Re-inventing Construction A-H 95

TAKE ON COMPLEXITY

Hans-Rudolf Schalcher
Take on Complexity 123

Kazuhiro Kojima / C+A
In Favor of Flow
How to Naturally Ventilate a University Campus Building in Tropical Vietnam 127

Michel Rojkind / Rojkind Arquitectos
Building on Speed
Realizing the Nestlé Chocolate Museum in Ten Weeks Without Construction Documents 134

Francisco Pardo / at103
Challenge the Standard
Reinventing Typologies and Programs for Housing and a Fire Station in Mexico City 146

Jeanne Gang / Studio Gang Architects
The Cook, the Prospector, the Nomad and their Architect
Three Approaches to Building with Local Resources 163

Anne Lacaton, Jean-Philippe Vassal / Lacaton & Vassal Architects
Buy One, Get One Free
Doubling the Space for the New Architecture School in Nantes 175

Peter Swinnen, Johan Anrys / 51N4E
Squaring the Circle
Building a Tower the Tirana Way 188

Minsuk Cho / Mass Studies
Best Used Before
The Asian City and the Quest for a Time-specific Architecture 201

Something Fantastic
An Illustrated Index of Re-inventing Construction H-P 217

MINE THE CITY

Ilka & Andreas Ruby
Mine the City 243

Marc Angélil, Cary Siress
Re: Going Around in Circles
Regimes of Waste 248

Keller Easterling
Architecture to Take Away
The Subtraction of Buildings as a New Construction Economy 265

Michael Sorkin
Big Apple, Homegrown
Feeding New York in New York 275

Dickson Despommier
The Hanging Gardens of the 21st Century
Agriculture Going Urban with Vertical Farms 286

Ada Tolla, Giuseppe Lignano / LOT-EK
Pimp my World
How to Construct New Environments by Re-using Old Ones 296

Dirk Hebel
The Vernacular Rediscovered
Applying Local Construction Technologies and Materials in Ethiopia 310

Something Fantastic
An Illustrated Index of Re-inventing Construction P - Z 325

STIMULATE STAKEHOLDERS

Chrisna du Plessis, Holger Wallbaum 355
Stimulate Stakeholders

Jeremy Rifkin
The Empathy Principle
Creating Biosphere Consciousness Through a Communication and Energy Revolution 358

Anne-Julchen Bernhardt, Jörg Leeser / BeL Associates
The Settler is King
How to Democratize Home Ownership with Do-it-yourself Building Techniques 366

Elinor Ostrom, Harini Nagendra
Governing the Commons in the New Millennium
A Diversity of Institutions for Natural Resource Management 380

Jose Castillo
The Promise of Neza
Building a City for 1.2 Million Inhabitants One House at a Time 388

Livia Corona
The Mexican Dream
Bottom-up Customization of Generic Tract Housing in Mexico 404

Christian Roth, Sascha Zander / Zanderroth Architects
Architecture without Developers
Building Groups as a Catalyst for Better Housing 419

Cary Siress
Sustaining what?
The Discourse of Sustainability in Need of Re-invention 433

INTRODUCTION

Toward a Gay Science of Construction

By Ilka & Andreas Ruby

Re-inventing construction, the title of this book, appears both obvious and obscure. The meaning of construction seems so obvious that any attempts to define it appear almost redundant: It's building! But building requires design and planning—hence there is a build up to construction. And since buildings usually are not built for the sake of building alone, the singular act of construction is carried on in processes of use, appropriation, transformation, and even demolition of buildings. In many ways, construction is much more than a mere act of production, it is a multilayered process of re-organizing matter, taking place in a variety of scales and time frames.

The book unfolds this differentiated understanding of construction in four chapters focussing on four central issues: *Reduce CO_2* investigates how architecture and urbanism are affected by the shift from fossil to renewable energy production. *Take on Complexity* explores how architecture can embrace the relentless specificity of a particular project without simplifying its complexity to tried and tested models. *Mine the City* describes our built environment as a man-made mine filled with material assets which are only waiting to become ressources of future building. *Stimulate Stakeholders* finally identifies the various agents, interest groups, and users who are instrumental in current processes of transformation in construction.

In the following we will identify a series of critical themes which circumscribe a discursive horizon for all contributions.

1. Invention versus Re-invention

There is without any doubt a lot of actual invention in construction today, and it is occurring on levels as diverse as these: construction techniques, materials, building services, but also programming techniques, new financing models, and development methods, to name but a few. There is almost no area of construction that is excluded from contemporary research, be it empirical, heuristic, technology-driven, or artistic in nature. This blissful spirit of innovation may well be stimulated by the fact that the construction industry has been rather resistant to innovation. While almost all other industries thrive on ever accelerating innovation cycles, the bulk of construction today to a large extent relies on building technologies invented during the time of the first and second industrial revolutions. This does not mean that there has not been any progress and research in construction, on the contrary. But as new technologies and building techniques introduce alternatives to established ones, the powerful lobbies of the latter have a vital interest in fighting the emergence of the former. Still today different national building cultures distinguish themselves by the influence of specific industrial interest groups who favor particular construction technologies over others. Invention interferes with these patterns of interest by offering alternatives. Invention, therefore, is never just a technical issue; in as much as it increases choice, invention is clearly a political matter.

Despite all our excitement about the 'new' that invention brings about, we should not forget that newness can easily turn into a lure. The 'new' was Modernism's favorite fetish and ideological strategy to claim sovereignty over the past. We know now that this pretension came at a high price—the deliberate suppression of huge amounts of knowledge embodied and cultivated by hundreds and thousands of years of architectural practice. Many inventions that marked the progress of building in the 19th and 20th century were only different solutions to problems that had already been dealt with successfully in times past. The invention of air conditioning, for example, was certainly not the first solution to adapt extreme air temperature and humidity to human comfort levels. It was one of the first *technical appliances* that could be produced and commercialized as a commodity, and thus enabled a whole industry to start off and trigger a corresponding market. The marketing of air-conditioning as a supreme technological solution could, however, only be successful because innumerable pre-industrial techniques of climate control that had been exercised and refined by vernacular building cultures—evaporative cooling, wind towers, and so on—had been abandoned through concerted efforts, driven by the illusion that energy presented no value and would be available forever. Now that traditional energy sources are no longer as abundant, we are beginning to realize the hubris of that belief and start to rediscover a pre-industrial world of knowledge so obligingly suppressed in the name of a progress, which in actual fact has led us in a gridlock. And Kazuhiro Kojima shows in his contribution for this book (see page 127), a design for a University Campus in Vietnam, the architectural surplus of such a rediscovery of natural air-conditioning techniques.

To fight the entropy of knowledge, contemporary research on construction must focus on both the discovery of new invention and the re-discovery of old inventions, which have either been forgotten or consciously suppressed. And in as much as the re-discovery of a forgotten invention succeeds in increasing the range of possibilities we can choose from, re-invention contributes as much to the production of knowledge as does invention. What has prevented this sustainable use of knowledge to take full effect so far is a distorted notion of authorship that has emerged more and more urgently in the past decade. In the software industry, for example, an increasing number of corporations are attempting to patent elements of software programs, which, if carried through, would effectively immobilize the dynamic of innovation of the Internet, which thrives on copy-and-paste processes. It seems obvious that the world would have never reached its present state of technological development if this limitation of the use of existing knowledge had been applied throughout history. Had the anonymous inventor of the wheel protected it with a patent right—which is nothing else than the right to exclude others from making, using, offering for sale or selling the invention—then the process of civilization would likely have occurred differently. Unbound by any such arbitrary protection, the wheel became one of the most influential inventions throughout the history of mankind. Its fundamental use value for the entire society being so plainly apparent it in a way belongs to no one—and maybe that would be a favorable condition for all inventions the use of which we wish to see maximized.

This schism is also reflected in one of the most important political projects of our time, the project of the commons. It proposes a way to share the resources and products of the world by waiving exclusive individual ownership or user rights. The commons would stimulate a production of knowledge, which would free us from having to invent the wheel all over again, allowing instead the re-use of an existing solution that has proven to solve a problem satisfactorily and efficiently. However, the implementation of the concept of the commons in highly developed economies seems rather unlikely, because it threatens the very foundations of economic systems based on private property. However, the fact that the 2009 Nobel Prize in Economic Sciences was awarded to Elinor Ostrom for her groundbreaking research on the Commons (see her contribution in this book page 380), as well as the constantly increasing influence of related projects such as the Creative Commons License on the distribution of knowledge, hints at the considerable transformative potential of this model.

2. New Synergies between Architecture and Engineering

Today the concept of the commons is not only relevant as an alternative model in managing shared resources. It could also inspire a different spirit for knowledge production in the construction sector, in particular for the two disciplines of architecture and engineering. Although today both depend on each other more than ever, their relationship is still charged by the reverberation of a disciplinary rivalry in the 19th century that surfaced in the famous polemic between the Écoles des Beaux-Arts and the new Écoles Polytechniques. The idea of architecture being in charge of design, while engineering would only serve its realization, was already out of date then. The most important innovations in construction in the 19th century were achieved by a new cast of movers and shakers, who were dealing with the actual construction of emerging typologies: Paxton, a gardener turned builder, laid the foundations of greenhouse constructions; Eiffel, an engineer, broke the ground for novel steel truss constructions, tested in bridges and monuments; and Hennebique, also an engineer, invented reinforced concrete. It was inventions like these that were to revolutionize the language and logic of modern architecture.

Today we can witness a similar divide between engineers and architects in regard to the quarrel over sustainability. While engineers in general take on the challenge of rethinking the production of our built environment according to criteria and parameters imposed by climate change and shrinking fossil energy resources, architects often denounce sustainability as a subject extrinsic to architecture.[1] But this is a distorted notion of sustainability. For what is sustainability in architecture, urbanism, and urban planning if not the methodical effort to adapt the production of our built environment to better correspond to the urgencies of our time? Maybe sustainability is only our version of the very project that drove modern architecture to adapt itself to the conditions of industrialization at large. And as architects experimented with new materials such as concrete, steel, and glass, they clearly generated a new esthetics with a very distinct iconicity and, not least of all, new notions of space. But they could only discover these new horizons of architecture because they did not deny the paradigm of industrialization as something extrinsic to architecture. They accepted it as the evolutional eye of the needle, which architecture had to pass through in order to fulfill new performative demands, imposed on construction by unprecedented growth. In the same way architects have to understand sustainability today as the eye of the needle that architecture has to pass through in order to respond appropriately to the present condition which is characterized by the slowing growth rates, shrinking resources, and severe climate change. Architects need to embrace sustainability as a systemic thinking that becomes a seamless layer of design.

3. Paradigm Change in the Discourse on Sustainability

Purely engineering-based approaches to sustainability usually suffer from an exclusive confidence in numbers while disregarding architecture's non-quantifiable reality layers. If energy saving as the sole goal justifies the construction of monstrously thick insulated walls with minutely small and inoperable windows as we can experience in the "passive house"[2], then the energy saving comes at a price way too high. One of the prime achievements of 20th-century architecture was to improve the relationship between man and his environment by dematerializing the boundary between interior and exterior space. If that boundary was to be rematerialized to medieval scales, creating imprisonment rather than inhabitation, something was fundamentally wrong with the rationality behind this new ecologically correct discourse.

But luckily for everyone involved, there are now increasingly more enlightened engineers who support their fellow architects in their critique of the passive house, arguing that energy saving alone is not efficient enough if we don't specify the kind of primary energy we are using (see the contributions of Werner Sobek page 34, as well as the one by Forrest Meggers and Hansjürg Leibundgut page 67). We need to drastically reduce fossil energy, as we are running out of fossil resources, which need to be reserved for other end uses, such as pharmaceuticals. But we have endless regenerative energy available, which we can use to supply the energy demands of buildings. If it is true, as most energy experts predict, that our societies will make this transition from fossil to renewable energy sources in the course of the next 20 to 30 years, we will have more energy at our disposal than we can spend.

On an architectural level this paradigm shift will replace the "passive house" with active buildings and urban systems that generate all the energy they need based on renewable resources. The "passive house" stands for a mechanistic response to climate change. It took into account only those properties of architecture that can be represented in spreadsheets such as the input and output of energy—it is a purely quantitative approach. But the discourse of sustainability needs to embrace qualities as well or else architecture will be drowning in numbers. The "active house" represents such a qualitative approach. It is a differential response to climate change that includes qualities of space which are not easily quantifiable, but vital for the quality of life provided by buildings.

In the face of this radical change to come, the present environmental policies of Western countries known to be among the vanguard of a new ecological awareness such as Germany and Switzerland display a fatal cultural jetlag from the old energy paradigm. Billions of Euros are budgeted for programs to retrofit existing building stock with extra insulation to reduce heat loss. But as soon as our society's energy demand will be covered by renewable sources, this massive operation will suddenly loose its meaning and reveal its principal beneficiary: the industry supplying the insulation material.

This massive insulation attack on architecture may serve as an example of waste produced in the name of energy saving. The transition from a fossil to a post-fossil society allows us to embrace a more fruitful way to deal with surplus—the art of spending. It will take serious unlearning to overcome decades of intellectual indoctrination in the name of shortage and abdication, but we should find helpful advice in of the writings of the French philosopher and anthropologist Georges Bataille, namely his major oeuvre *La Part Maudite* (The Accursed Share)[3], as Marc Angélil and Cary Siress remind us in their contribution (see page 248). Drawing on the works of Max Weber[4] and Marcel Mauss[5], Bataille had devised a radical critique of all conventional economy. According to him all societies produce more riches than they need for their own reproduction, hence there remains a surplus. Bataille argues that one can distinguish societies by how they have dealt with this surplus. Various so-called primitive societies invented ritual acts to get rid of the surplus, such as the sacrifice to the Gods or the Potlatch. Capitalist economies by contrast save the surplus to reinvest it in the cycle of production, generating what Marx described as the accumulation of capital. Despite this proliferation of wealth, our societies constantly struggle with shortage and scarcity. Bataille suggests that this discrepancy might not arise if we re-learned how to *spend* the surplus. It might indeed be that after a century-long obsession of architecture with reduction as both an esthetical and philosophical principle, the innovators of our built environment today have to come to terms with notions such as excess and expenditure, two central concepts of Bataille's theory. Bjarke Ingels' call for a hedonistic approach to sustainability (see his contribution in the book page 55) points exactly in this direction, as well as Lacaton & Vassal's practice of systematically producing more space than was requested in the brief (see their contribution in the book page 175).

4. The Transition from Central to Distributed Production of Energy

The shift from fossil to renewable energy production incurs a second shift, which might further increase the operative ties between architects and engineers: the shift from a central to a distributed mode of energy production. The bulk of renewable energy today is still generated in central production facilities, which require large and costly distribution networks to transport the energy to the end user. Most of these centralized renewable energy production facilities, such as solar thermal power plants, are using the same generator technology as conventional power plants. Their dependence on heavy industry requires high initial investments to set up the facilities, which make these technologies rather unaffordable for the very countries, which would benefit most from them—for example Northern

Africa. Therefore it is not surprising that Desertec, the biggest project for a solar-thermal parabolic trough power plant system in the Sahara desert, is developed almost exclusively by an alliance of European heavy industry corporations, banks, and energy corporations[6] with only a minute participation of national businesses from the local context.

As agonizing dinosaurs of the passing age of industrialization, these centralized power plants will indeed restrain the break-through of a distributed energy production in North Africa.

On the other hand, distributed energy is produced locally by a variety of small-scale facilities located at or near the places of their consumption, turning villages and houses into micro power plants in their own right. As the energy is consumed at the place of its generation, distribution networks are no longer needed, which further reduces the cost of initial investment considerably. Distributed energy thrives on the same logic as mobile telephone communication which within only a few years has managed to connect the entire African continent, after decades of repeated failure to install a conventional terrestrial telephone system.

While there is almost a consensus in the scientific community about the need for this system change from fossil to renewable energy, there is a fundamental methodological dissent about how this change can be brought about best. Current debates reveal an unforgiving division between two radically opposed approaches: systemism[7] versus incrementalism. Systemism aims to implement change by radically renewing the operating systems of our built environment. Incrementalism seeks change in a pragmatic way, working towards it slowly and over time by locally patching existing systems wherever parts of them can be optimized. While systemists believe that the system can only be transformed by reconfiguring its underlying structure as a whole, incrementalists are convinced that many small changes will ultimately yield a qualitative change, and therefore transform the system at large in the end as well.

5. Index of Re-inventing Construction

The division between systemism and incrementalism is clearly recognizable in the contributions in this book, sometimes even within a single contribution. As editors we did not want to reconcile this tension, as it is a productive academic discourse of two equally legitimate approaches that should be pursued at the same time. As opposed to the fundamentalism of an either-or, we believe in the pragmatism of the both-and, searching in the footsteps of Paul Feyerabend's *Against Method*[8] for a gay science of construction to correct the cliché of construction being dull with a dose of healthy Nietzschean heresy. The spirit of this search is emblematically expressed in the *Illustrated Index of Re-inventing Construction* that forms a counterweight to the essays part of the book, which appears in three batches placed between its four chapters. Compiled by *Something Fantastic*, a Berlin-based architectural practice run by Julian Schubert, Elena Schütz and Leonard Streich, this index gives a non-exhaustive overview of inventions and reinventions in the area of construction that are available, albeit often not very known. The entries of the index encompass idiosyncratic techniques, technologies, and typologies, materials that challenge the standard in construction. Many of them are not contemporary, but belong to a century-long tradition of construction and often have existed for the longest time only in textbooks and technical references—useful anomalies that have often been repressed for no reason. Many of them are only practiced in particular areas in the world, while they would principally be applicable elsewhere too. By grouping these scattered bits of knowledge in the index we hope to increase the knowledge base and therefore the freedom of choice of a truly contemporary practice of construction. The illustrated index can obviously only be a beginning. In order to turn it into a powerful and growing resource, we have launched an online-version of it—accessible at www.whatwow.org—where users can upload their own entries and thus, assisted by careful editorial selection, contribute to an ongoing discourse on re-inventing construction. Calling for the active participation to all players in the construction who are dedicated to its re-invention, we seek to create a reference to the most powerful dictionary project of the enlightenment—*Didérot's Encyclopédie ou Dictionnaire raisonné des sciences, des arts et des métiers*. Although mainly initiated and directed by Didérot, the Encyclopédie was a collective project from the start. Didérot had assembled a group of researchers, famous minds such as d'Alembert, Montesquieu and Voltaire as well as more anonymous experts, to go out into the world and catalogue the knowledge of their times. The ambition of the index is slightly more modest: it aims to register that kind of knowledge on construction that transgresses the boundaries of the norm, and in so doing, could play a vital role in pushing its envelope.

1.) A paradigmatic example of this thinking is this statement by Viennese architect Wolf Prix: "Sustainability denies iconicity, and it is therefore impossible to generate an esthetics out of sustainability. There is no vital esthetic of sustainability." See Wolf D. Prix, "Vom Werden und Entstehen. Über Räume und Gedankenräume," *Süddeutsche Zeitung*, 20.6.2009. In the German original the quote reads as follows, "Nachhaltigkeit verleugnet Zeichenhaftigkeit und daher ist es nicht möglich, aus diesem Begriff Nachhaltigkeit ‚Ästhetik' zu generieren. Eine lebendige Ästhetik der Nachhaltigkeit gibt es nicht."
2.) The idea of the *Passivhaus* was invented by Bo Adamson and Wolfgang Feist in 1988. It reduces heating energy by a series of specific construction principles: the building's envelope is made as airtight as possible with extra-thick insulation layers, triple glazing. To minimize heat loss, manual ventilation through windows is discouraged. The exchange of air is realized by way of a controlled internal ventilation system. The *Passivhaus-Institut* in Darmstadt has issued a set of rules that buildings have to fulfill in order to be certifed as passive houses. With currently around 25,000 certified buildings in Europe, the passive house has become a de-facto standard for ecological architecture.
3.) Georges Bataille, *The Accursed Share, Volume 1: Consumption*, New York: Zone Books, 1991.
4.) Max Weber, *The Protestant Ethic and "The Spirit of Capitalism"*, London: Penguin Books, 2002.
5.) Marcel Mauss, *The Gift: The Form and Reason for Exchange in Archaic Societies*, London: Routledge, 1990.
6.) Desertec's most important investors are: Siemens, ABB, Abengoa Solar, Cevital, M+W Zander Group, MAN Solar Millennium, Schott Solar, E.ON, RWE, EdF, Enel, Red Eléctrica, Deutsche Bank, and HSH Nordbank.
7.) We borrow the term systemism from Eric Bunge, see: Eric Bunge, "Systemism: The Alternative to Individualism and Holism." *The Journal of Socio-Economics* 29, 2000, pp. 147-157. While Bunge uses the term to grasp the behavior of social systems at large, we imply the term in order to describe systemic change in the production of the built environment.
8.) Paul K. Feyerabend, *Against Method: Outline of an Anarchistic Theory of Knowledge*, London: New Left Books, 1975.

REDUCE CO_2

It is amazing how society tends to overlook the environmental impact of buildings. Smokestacks, tailpipes, and garbage are all out in the open to see, but behind the esthetics of even the most beautiful building lies a silent demon. That demon is the generation of CO_2 emissions due to inefficient building operation, excessive material demand, and creation of unnecessary waste.

Buildings play a significant role in generation of anthropogenic CO_2 emissions. In fact, buildings are directly or indirectly responsible for over half of all global CO_2 emissions. This is remarkable considering the wide variety of solutions available in the building sector to reduce energy consumption and CO_2 emissions. There are many ways that we can reduce CO_2 with technology to zero emissions.

Not only that, but buildings provide some of the lowest hanging fruit when it comes to the cost of reducing CO_2 emissions. By utilizing integrated design and more intelligent systems, zero emission buildings would be a reality without significant extra costs. New design methods, analysis tools, and technologies are being researched and created all over the globe to facilitate this necessary shift to zero emission buildings. In some places the social and political obstacles for implementation may be high, but nevertheless, the

2010 MEXICO CITY MANIFESTO:

Bearing in mind the responsibility to future generations and the environment, all building processes require the immediate development and realization of Triple Zero technologies to be applied during production, life-cycle and decomposition:

- Maximize renewable resources:
  Zero fossil energy
- Maximum environmental restoration:
  Zero emissions
- Maximize recycling:
  Zero waste

Our target must be the development of comprehensive strategies to ensure the transition from current practices to the complete implementation of these technologies by 2020.

Mexico City, April 17th, 2010

Hansjürg Leibundgut
Forrest Meggers
Werner Sobek
Mike Schlaich
Menghao Qin
Masanori Shukuya
Sheila Kennedy

Érica Ferraz de Carlos, Jamilur Reza Choudhury, David Dominguez, Daniel Irurah, Vanderley M John, Yolanda Kakabadse, Sam Leung, Patricio Mardones, Matthias Mast, Ivett Flores Núñez, Juan Felipe Ordonez, Julian Schubert, Harald Sternberg, Viviana Strassberger, Christian Volkmann, Lynette Widder, Prima Wijaya

same advancements are theoretically possible when professionals, the general public, and policy makers are properly addressed.

By exploring these facts in depth in a dedicated workshop of the 3rd Holcim Forum for Sustainable Construction in Mexico City with an international team of experts we have generated a manifesto statement about reaching zero emissions in the building sector.

The manifesto sets out a significant challenge, but one that is possible to achieve. First, in order to maximize renewable resources we have to improve the distribution and availability of renewable energy technologies. This includes not just the production of wind and photovoltaic systems, but also the integration and implementation of these into buildings and the urban fabric. Also, these systems are by no means the only method of implementing renewable systems. Ground source heat and geothermal energy have huge potential in the building sector, and there are many new methods of capturing passive solar energy as heat, as well as passive wind energy for more efficient ventilation. New theories considering the concept of exergy demonstrate the wastefulness of the combustion of high-energy-content fossil fuels, and when implemented in practice will lead to the paradigm shift necessary to achieve the first goal of the manifesto and eliminate fossil fuel use in buildings.

Eliminating fossil fuel-based energy will be a huge step toward zero emission buildings, but it will only contribute to reducing operational emissions. In order to achieve the second goal of zero emissions we also have to consider the significant indirect emissions of buildings. These are caused by the material resources consumed by the building sector which have an associated grey energy. Grey energy is the energy that is necessary to produce a building material; it's a kind of energy that is embodied by the building. Only if we factor in the grey energy of a building can we actually start to think about how to minimize the subsequent "grey emissions" of buildings. This includes finding new ways to construct strong lightweight buildings with minimal material demand. Along with that there are ways to redesign the materials themselves, such as the use of new lightweight concretes with reduced and/or reformulated concrete moving toward zero net emissions. Only by taking into account the full production cycle of materials and the actual resource demands placed on the environment can zero emissions be achieved for buildings.

Nevertheless, most buildings and virtually all building components do not last forever, so even if the creation and operation of a building has zero impact, that benefit is squandered when the building cannot be deconstructed without harmful impacts. Recycling components is one important aspect, but before the components can be recycled they first have to be deconstructed and separated. This is where the design for end-of-life becomes essential. What are currently viewed as waste streams must be addressed so that they are capable of being recycled (and not downcycled) back into the product stream or harmlessly reabsorbed as nutrients (not pollution) into the environment. There are already systems available that are designed to eliminate waste. A wide variety of systems provide ways to capture and utilize storm water and grey water. Interior components like carpets are now made to be separable for recycling. Building mechanical systems are made accessible so that the components can be easily remanufactured or refurbished in new systems. Rooms are given flexible designs so that when one function of a building potentially ends, there can be a smooth transition to another. Also, new design tools are allowing even structural components to be redesigned so that raw materials can be more easily removed at the end-of-life. With this last goal of the manifesto, the paradigm shift toward design for end-of-life, we are able to account for the full impact of the building through its lifecycle, and guide all the necessary changes to reach our overall goal of zero emissions.

This may seem like a lot to accomplish within our aggressive timeline, but we are not policy makers, we are just possibility makers. We know what technology is available and what techniques can be implemented, and therefore we are simply stating what can be done. Hopefully, by propagating this knowledge, we can make this possibility a reality.

Forrest Meggers

About the author: Forrest Meggers is a researcher in the Building Systems Group at the ETH Zurich under Prof. Dr. Hansjürg Leibundgut. Meggers has a BSE in Mechanical Engineering and a MSc in Environmental Engineering from the University of Iowa where he researched sustainable building design. He is also a LEED Accredited Professional and served on several committees for the USGBC. He is author of many papers on low exergy building systems. In fall 2011, he will take on the leadership role in a team of researchers to evaluate the potential of low exergy systems in hot and humid climates as a part of the Future Cities collaboration between the ETH and Singapore.

Saving the Climate Saves You Money

How Buildings Can Use Energy Intelligently by Integrative Design

AMORY B. LOVINS

Imagine a world where everyone has abandoned oil, coal, and nuclear energy in favor of alternatives that work better and cost less. Efficient use and renewable energy could solve many of the world's greatest problems without making new ones. That world is available, practical, and profitable now.

Politicians and the media often administer a stupid multiple-choice test about energy policy. Plainly stated, it asks: would you rather die of climate change, oil wars, or a nuclear holocaust? The appropriate answer, seldom offered, is: none of the above. This is possible when we use energy in a way that saves money. Climate change, oil dependence, and nuclear proliferation would be solved, not at a cost but at a profit, because saving fuel costs less than buying fuel. It seemed that most of the negotiators at the Copenhagen Climate Summit in 2009 forgot that efficiency is cheaper than fuel. Instead of discussing costs, burdens, and sacrifice, the discourse there should have been about profits, jobs, and competitive advantage. This could potentially sweeten the politics so much that any remaining resistance to climate protection would melt faster than the glaciers.

In 2008, the consulting firm McKinsey & Company did a study showing how to cheaply cut global emissions of greenhouse gases by 70% by 2030. Our research at Rocky Mountain Institute (RMI) using integrative design and new technologies shows even bigger and more profitable savings are possible. However, the first question is really whether we have enough time to implement these solutions. If the energy used to make a dollar of real GDP keeps drifting down by just 1% a year, then carbon emissions would triple by 2100. Yet cutting this "energy intensity" by 2% a year would stabilize emissions. Cutting it by 3 or 4% a year would reduce emissions enough to avoid triggering further climate chaos. Even the United States has routinely cut its energy intensity 2 to 4% a year for decades. China cut its energy intensity more than 5% a year for a quarter-century, and after a few years' lapse, has nearly regained that pace. Many big companies are making billions of dollars in profits by substituting efficiency for fuel, cutting their energy intensity by 6 to 16% a year. Clearly a 3 to 4% reduction should be feasible—especially because most of the growth is in countries like China and India, which can more easily build their infrastructure right the first time rather than fix it later.

About 70% of U.S. electricity is used in buildings, and 30% in industry. Two decades ago, RMI looked at roughly one thousand technologies for saving electricity. We measured their cost and performance and found out that about three-quarters of all the electricity used then could be saved, at an average cost of 0.01 USD per kilowatt-hour in today's dollars. That's cheaper than *operating* a coal or nuclear station, even if the station and the grid were free. Since we did that study, the efficiency technologies have improved faster than they have been applied, so now the potential savings are even bigger and cheaper.

Yet even more important than these better technologies are new ways to *combine* technologies through what at RMI we call "integrative design." Most people think efficiency is about gadgets, equipment, and devices. That is like thinking that the best way to make a tasty meal is to use the best ingredients, toss them in a pot, and then hope some kind of magic happens. Actually, efficient systems, like a good meal, are the result of whole-system design. You have to use a good recipe that tells you how to combine the right ingredients in the right sequence, manner, and proportions, so that a skilful chef can make something really tasty.

An example of integrative design in action is my house. I live at about 2,165 meters above sea level, in the Colorado Rockies, where temperatures can sometimes dip to minus 44 °C. There can be frost on any day of the year, and there can be midwinter cloud cover for over a month. Despite these challenging climatic conditions, the house is fossil-fuel-free and combustion-free, it's probably a net energy exporter, and it's about 99 % heated with passive solar energy, using no conventional heating or cooling equipment. The interior is like a tropical jungle, where we've harvested 35 banana crops so far. In 1984, the house saved 99 % of the energy for heat and hot water and 90 % of the household electricity typical of a home of the same size and location. We have just retrofitted the house with the technologies of 2010, which are even better. Integrative design allows multiple benefits from single expenditures. In my house hardly any element has fewer than three functions; many have 5 to 8; the central arch has 12 functions, but only one cost. Integrative design works in big or small buildings, in old and new buildings, and in any climate—even in Bangkok. With reduced construction cost, integrative design has been used to eliminate air conditioning, yet provide greater comfort, at temperatures up to 46 °C.

RMI brought integrative design to the current retrofit of the Empire State Building. It's expected to save 38 percent of the building's energy use with a three-year payback. The 6,500 windows are being remanufactured in a temporary "window factory" on a vacant floor. They are being transformed into "superwindows," which are almost perfect at letting light in without unwanted heat. Combined with better lights and office equipment, this cuts the peak-cooling load by a third. As a result the old chillers can be made smaller and renovated in place, rather than expanded and replaced. This saves 174 million USD in capital costs and cuts the payback time for the retrofit and renovation to three years.

Another example is the renovation of Deutsche Bank's famous twin towers in Frankfurt, Germany. It's expected to cut the heating load by two-thirds, the electricity use by more than half, and the carbon emissions by 98 %. The use of ceilings with radiant cooling has increased ceiling heights, and every office has operable windows. The space efficiency has risen by 20 %, and in one of the towers the mechanical systems could be optimized to free up an entire floor for new uses. Altogether Deutsche Bank gained space for 600 more employees because all of the mechanicals in the building were optimized to take up less space. Buying renewable power will make the building nearly carbon-neutral. If this kind of deep retrofit is undertaken when the building's façade or major equipment is being renovated anyway, these improvements can be cost-effective, and in some cases because of energy savings, they can even cost less than zero.

1: The private house of Amory B. Lovins. Even under the climatic conditions of the Colorado Rockies the house is fossil-fuel-free and combustion-free. Heated to about 99% with passive solar energy, it needs no conventional heating or cooling equipment.
2: The interior is like a tropical jungle, where you can even harvest bananas.

That was the case with a 19,000 m² Chicago office tower. Chicago is hot and humid in the summer and very cold in the winter. A new glass curtain wall needed to be built because the glazing seals were starting to fail, something that happens every 20 years. Instead of replacing the façade with the same kind of dark heat-absorbing glass, replacing it with "superwindows," even in the early 1990s let in six times more visible light and reduced unwanted heat by 90 %. Daylighting could then be directed deep into the building, without glare. After improving lighting and office-equipment efficiency too, the peak-cooling load would go down by 77 %. By replacing the old chlorofluorocarbon-containing mechanical system with a new CFC-free design that is four times smaller and four times more efficient, enough capital cost can be saved (compared to normal renovation of the big old system) to pay for the other improvements. So, at a slightly lower cost than a typical renovation, which saves nothing, our approach could save three-quarters of the energy currently used in the building and greatly improve comfort.

In conventional practice, the more you save, the more it costs you. In conventional thinking, you invest in efficiency only up to a certain threshold. For instance, insulation is usually added to a house only until extra energy savings don't justify it. That's the cost-effectiveness limit where most people stop. However, if investment is continued beyond this limit, you reach a point where suddenly the marginal cost goes down. In my house, by using twice the "cost-effective" level of insulation, I no longer needed the furnace, pipes, pumps, ducts, fans, wires, controls, or fuel supply arrangements, so I saved 99 % of the normal heating energy while reducing the construction cost by 1100 USD. Therefore optimizing the building as a system, instead of the insulation as a component, yields expanding returns on investments in efficiency.

The same principles apply in industry. RMI has lately redesigned more than 30 billion USD worth of facilities in 29 diverse sectors. Recent projects range from refineries to chemical plants to ships to high-tech manufacturers. For example, we helped a computer chipmaker find ways to save two-thirds of its next fabrication plant's energy consumption and half of its capital cost while eliminating all 22,000 tons of chillers. We also worked with a data center that saved up to 75 % of the energy it usually consumed, without any software improvements, at normal cost; fully following our recommendations, which the client didn't allow, would have saved about 95 % of the energy and half the capital cost—again with no chillers. Our latest mine design uses no fossil fuels and no grid electricity; it runs on gravity—very reliable. However, none of these advanced retrofits would have been necessary if the original designs had been done properly in the first place.

An important efficiency opportunity is that three-fifths of the world's electricity runs motors, and half of that electricity runs pumps and fans. We can save about half of all motor energy with a one-year payback by integrating 35 retrofit improvements to the drive system, 28 of which are free byproducts of the first 7. But first we should improve the devices that use the motors' torque. Pumps are the biggest single use of motors. A Dutch engineer redesigned a typical industrial pumping loop to use at least 86% less pumping energy just by using fat, short, straight pipes rather than thin, long, crooked pipes. American engineer Peter Rumsey did a retrofit using this kind of pipe construction for the Oakland Museum of California, with larger pipe diameters, few and easy bends, and other smart changes that saved three-quarters of the pumping energy.

Making big energy savings can be inexpensive, in both industry and in buildings, and as in cooking, you must do the right things in the right order. For example, to provide comfort in a hot and humid climate, the goal is to keep the people cool—not the building, which has no nervous system. Many things can be done to expand the range of conditions in which people feel comfortable. A ceiling fan nets 5°C. of high-end comfort. Sitting on a net or mesh chair instead of insulating upholstery keeps people several degrees cooler. Passive cooling can be used, and there are many techniques for this, often perfected by traditional cultures. In the United States, passive-cooling methods can sufficiently cool almost anywhere; you can even do it in the heat of Dallas, Texas. Some old buildings even in places like hot and humid New Orleans are comfortable without air conditioning because of shading, proper massing, and simple ceiling fans. For situations with high humidity, active, non-refrigerative cooling can be used, perhaps combining a desiccant or absorption air-dryer with a direct/indirect evaporative cooler. That gives up to 100 units of cooling per unit of electricity. Even a big refrigerative air-conditioning system can be made three times more efficient, and coolth storage and controls can be used if there's anything left to store and control. But nowhere in the world is refrigerative air-conditioning actually required for comfort if cheaper, more efficient options are chosen first.

At RMI, we advocate using very efficient lighting systems with a lot of daylighting and good controls, efficient office equipment, and efficient windows. In severe climates, my home's best windows insulate like 22 sheets of glass, but look like two and cost less than three, thanks to specialized films. The windows sort light from heat, and can be tuned to each side of the building, eliminating the need for perimeter heating even in places like Calgary or Stockholm. Carefully chosen roof surfaces can reject solar energy and better radiate away heat as infrared rays. This greatly reduces the cooling load, so the cooling system, if there is one, can become much smaller and extremely efficient. Mainly because of the savings on mechanicals, total capital cost will go down by about 3 to 4 %.

To achieve these levels of efficiency, whether in buildings, factories or vehicles, inefficiency must become unacceptable. There can be no rules of thumb or rote actions used. Things must be actually measured and analyzed. This means no *infectious repetitis*: we cannot just copy and paste old drawings and details. And instead of using an incremental, component-centric approach, whole systems must be optimized for multiple benefits. If designers would be paid for what they save, not for what they spend, that would have a salutary effect on design.

Finally, while we're learning to save most of our electricity, there is a little-noticed revolution going on in how it is produced. Wind, solar, and other renewable energy sources are increasing their share of electricity production explosively around the world. Renewables, aside from large-scale hydroelectric power, plus combined-heat-and-power now make 18 % of the world's electricity, versus nuclear power's 13 %. In 2008, these "micropower" sources, which get their economies not from giant units but from mass production, produced about 91 % of the world's new electricity. All renewables now provide half the world's new generating capacity and get the majority of the world's power-plant investments. Coal, gas, and nuclear plants have been pushed into the minority and have shrinking market shares. They have become too costly and entail too much financial risk to attract investors in comparison to renewables. In 2007, China, Spain, and the United States each added more wind power than nuclear capacity added worldwide. The U.S. added more wind power in 2007 than it added coal power in the previous five years combined.

In 2009, China doubled its wind power for the fourth year running, and over 70 % of new European capacity was renewables. In spring 2010, China is passing its 2020 windpower target. Around the end of 2010, worldwide, renewables, other than big hydro, will have more global capacity than nuclear, and around 2014/2015, will pass nuclear in output too. In 2009, those distributed renewables received 131 billion USD of private capital investment and added 52 billion watts of power. Nuclear received no private capital investment, and lost capacity for the second year. Electricity output is now growing so much faster from solar cells than from nuclear that nuclear may never catch up. The micropower revolution is increasingly led by China. Distributed and mainly renewable sources of electricity are walloping central thermal plants in the world market; even China's nuclear program, the world's most ambitious, remains seven times smaller in capacity and growth rate than China's distributed renewables, and the gap is widening. Nuclear power's inability to raise private capital, despite subsidies exceeding 100% in the U.S., mean that it has no prospects in market economies, and indeed, every one of the 60 reactors under construction worldwide was centrally planned. Energy security and climate protection can be achieved better, faster, and cheaper by efficiency, renewables, and micropower.

There are even more ways to generate power in an environmentally sound and economically advantageous fashion. Running existing combined-cycle gas plants more, and the existing coal plants less, became generally profitable starting in 2009 and could eliminate about a third of U.S. coal-power production. Industrial and building cogeneration, tri-generation, heating and cooling with renewables, and geothermal are usually profitable. Power from ocean waves, tidal currents, and solar thermal are becoming so. Just putting photovoltaics on 3% of U.S. structures could displace all U.S. coal-fired electricity on an annual basis. That's initially costlier than a new coal plant, but won't be by the time that coal plant could be built.

Increased efficiency frequently makes it cheaper to adopt renewable power. In California, a firm now called SunPower put over a hectare of photovoltaics on the roof of the Alameda County Jail in 2001. They made the roof white, to reflect solar heat, and the building itself was made more energy-efficient. On the hottest afternoons, when the solar cells produce a lot of electricity, the jail therefore has more net surplus to export. This can be sold back to the grid at peak pricing levels. Thus, the solar power would have made money with no subsidies.

Traditionally, power companies relied on giant coal and nuclear plants, and augmented these with giant gas plants. Efficient use and renewable energy sources remained modest. Until recently, utility companies were rewarded for selling more electricity. Many regulators are now changing the rules to reward cutting electricity use, giving the consumer and the utility the same incentive: savings. The result of this, in places where this reform is in effect, is that the market is shifting massively towards efficiency, renewables, and combined heat and power. Renewables, combined heat and power, and efficiency save about 2 to 20 times more carbon per U.S. dollar, and 20 to 40 times more carbon per year, than nuclear power. The marketplace winner is thus also the most effective climate solution. Acknowledging nuclear power's market collapse and helping countries harness modern options for reliable and affordable energy can also help end energy poverty and curtail nuclear proliferation—thus making the world richer, fairer, cooler, and safer.

Currently, we run advanced industrial societies by burning the rotted remains of primeval swamp goo and dinosaur droppings. If we combine the electricity revolution with the comparable oil revolution[1], the way we use and produce energy can be changed fundamentally. Fire, the first primeval energy source, will be re-invented. The easiest way to do this is to have every way to save or to produce energy compete fairly, at honest prices, regardless of its type, size, technology, location, or ownership.

The strategies and examples summarized here rest on detailed practical experience and empirical evidence. They reflect where the smarter energy companies are heading in their co-evolution with civil society. A few governments are helping; most struggle to keep up; some even stand in the way. A lot of old thinking still holds sway—not all the fossils are in the fuel. But if anything outlined here sounds too good to be true, remember this comment by Marshall McLuhan: "Only puny secrets need protection. Big discoveries are protected by public incredulity."[2]

1.) www.oilendgame.com
2.) McLuhan, Marshall and Barrington Nevitt. *Take Today: The Executive as Dropout*. Harcourt Brace Jovanovich, New York, 1972, p. 92.

About the author: Physicist Amory Lovins, consultant to business and government leaders, is Chairman and Chief Scientist of Rocky Mountain Institute (www.rmi.org) on energy (including buildings) and its links to economy, environment, development, and security. He has written 29 books and received the Blue Planet, Volvo, Onassis, Nissan, Shingo, and Mitchell Prizes, MacArthur and Ashoka Fellowships, 11 honorary doctorates, and the Heinz, Lindbergh, Right Livelihood, National Design, and World Technology Awards. Amory Lovins has been a member of the Advisory Board of the Holcim Foundation since its inception 2004.

Architecture Isn't Here to Stay

Toward a Reversibility of Construction

WERNER SOBEK

Frankly, I can no longer stand the word sustainability. Architects brag about making sustainable buildings as if this was something special, whereas by now sustainability should be as essential as fire safety and structural stability. I hope that in five years it will no longer be necessary to speak explicitly of sustainable construction. Throughout my career as an architect and engineer, I have always treated sustainability as an integrated aspect of architecture and construction, not as an additional or optional gimmick.

If we begin to look at the role the building industry plays in sustainability, we find that more than 50 percent of the natural resources used worldwide are consumed by the building industry alone. The building industry is also responsible for 50 percent of the total waste produced, and accounts for more than 35 percent of the total energy consumption in the world. When we look closely at resources, and resource consumption, it is quite obvious that there must be a reduction in the amount of material and energy used in buildings. I use the terms *Material-*

leichtbau, *Strukturleichtbau*, and *Systemleichtbau* to support the explanation of my ongoing examination of what it means to reduce the amount of material used in buildings, thereby making them more sustainable, and more resource efficient.

The term *Materialleichtbau* (building with lightweight materials) refers to materials that have an optimum ratio between a material quality, like strength or stiffness, and the specific weight of the material. The stronger and the lighter the material is, the less material you need to use. *Materialleichtbau* focuses only on materials. *Strukturleichtbau* (building with lightweight structures) refers to structures that have the minimum weight possible relative to specific structural demands. It is not about materials but rather about structural systems. A structural system is a monofunctional system, optimized for carrying loads, and this is its only purpose. Lastly, *Systemleichtbau* (building with lightweight systems) refers to lightweight and multifunctional systems. For example, an aircraft wing is a beautiful and simple example of *Systemleichtbau*. It is aerodynamic and very lightweight, it can withstand a lot of bending and torque, and it also functions as a large tank for jet fuel.

The Station Z Memorial project is an example of the application of the principles of *Materialleichtbau*, *Strukturleichtbau*, and *Systemleichtbau* in an architectural context. Designed by architect HG Merz in cooperation with my office, it is located at the site of the former concentration camp Sachsenhausen, which is a national monument. The client asked for a waterproof covering, to span a remarkable distance of 40 m, over the crematorium of the concentration camp. Spanning such a long distance would require a lot of structure using more typical engineering principles. Because of the deep sadness of the place, we felt that there shouldn't be any piece of "architecture" visible, only minimal structure, and no details. We used a roof support structure consisting of steel lattice girders fabricated from standard rectangular box sections, with metal grating and perforated metal sheeting affixed on the outside and inside of the frame, cladding it on both sides. A membrane of transparent glass fiber/PTFE fabric was then stretched over the structure and made airtight, and then a vacuum was created between the membrane and the structure, to bind both pieces together. Hence, the entire interior and exterior skin of the structure is not bolted, not glued, and not clipped; it is held perfectly in place by virtue of only the air pressure difference. Only a small pump was needed to create the vacuum, and the energy to run the pump is equivalent to the energy generated by $8\,m^2$ of photovoltaic cells. The Station Z project allowed us to explore building techniques that could make it possible to easily and completely disassemble a huge building within minutes. By simply releasing the vacuum, the entire project can be disassembled and the materials can be separated out into approximately 1,000 tons of steel and 500 kg of fabric.

However, progressive projects like the Station Z Memorial are not the norm in construction, architecture, and engineering. There are diverse reasons for the slow adoption of sustainable building design, and a notable laggardness on the part of most industry players. A main reason is that we simply lack a sound foundation. Only very few people today manage to construct buildings that follow the simple triple-zero principle of zero energy consumption, zero emissions, and zero waste during construction, operation, and demolition. We lack even basic things like data calculation methods and basic knowledge about sustainable building design. We know today, for example, how to measure the weight of a building and how that weight can be reduced, but we don't really know how to measure and reduce the grey energy that goes into a building. We have no methods for the design and construction of truly recyclable buildings. The list of missing knowledge is long.

The reason for this missing knowledge begins with unfavorable shifts in research practices and budgets. This has resulted in a lack of resources and infrastructures to disseminate knowledge and to do the actual inventing and innovation that is required. The construction industry ceased conducting research long ago, and the universities began addressing the issue too late and with insufficient intensity. Governments are requiring and supporting sustainable construction, but the necessary organizational and technical interfaces are missing between the technical, commercial, and government players. The various parties have too little exchange with each other. It is obvious that the design tools and methods that we urgently need will have a markedly interdisciplinary character, because today individuals can no longer independently master the complex, multidisciplinary problems and interconnections at the level required to achieve excellent results. The introduction of sustainability concerns requires that individual designers take into consideration complex issues such as maintenance, repair, and recycling. It requires the complete integration of energy conservation, emissions reduction, and many other aspects. This cannot be achieved through traditional sequential design processes; instead, integrated and interdisciplinary design must become the new standard.

We must counteract the specialization and compartmentalization that has occurred in the allied design and construction professions. The thematic and spatial separation of the training of engineers and architects severely limits a mutual understanding of the language and the approaches of these two very closely allied professions. Integrated design requires a change in our way of training architects and engineers. Because more interdisciplinary collaboration is required at all levels, I have been involved in the creation of an additional interface, the SIS. This platform, the only one of its type in the world, links industry with academics. We aim to establish a basis for sustainable construction and to find practical solutions. Interdisciplinary work and integrative thinking should be used to answer questions such as: How can we take the recycling of a building into consideration from the initial phases of design? It is in these initial phases that we must begin the radical changes that will follow.

We must consider waste production and recycling as early as possible in the design process. In central Europe, the construction industry produces 50 to 60 % of the waste in the waste stream. A mandatory recycling rate of even 15 % percent would bring the construction industry to a standstill. In comparison, the German car industry has a recycling rate of at least 85 %, and some cars made by Mercedes-Benz can have 95 % of their components recycled. Valuable materials can be reclaimed for reuse by recycling, such as steel, aluminium, and copper. These same materials can be reclaimed and recycled from buildings. Normally, as architects and engineers, we don't consider the fact that in a central European office building, there are many important materials to be recovered. One ton of stone from a profitable Chilean copper mine contains 100 units of copper ore; in a central European office building, one ton of material contains at least 40 units of copper ore. Buildings can be mined for materials during the recycling process — in amounts significant enough to be financially lucrative.

When recycling isn't considered early in the design process there are significant barriers to even the simplest reclamation of material. Primarily this is because it is hard to separate materials from one another; the better the materials are bonded together, the better for the architect, because he must guarantee that the building will not fall apart. But the better the building materials are bonded together, the harder they are to recycle. However, one can do things in other ways; there are different ways to deal with the necessity for the structural integrity of the building and the integrity of the architect's reputation. This involves building with things like velcros, magnets, click and snap fasteners; all essentially displacing and replacing more traditional building techniques. It is completely possible to use alternative methods and to depart from the typical solutions. The Station Z Memorial project is proof of this, as is my own home, R128, in Stuttgart.

2

3

4

1: (Previous pages) Built to protect the remains of the crematorium at Sachsenhausen Concentration Camp, the Station Z Memorial by Werner Sobeck is made from a glass fiber / PTFE skin, vacuum sealed over steel structural components.
2: The lack of overt formal or ornamental gestures was intended as a recognition of the somber location and history.
3-4: The steel grating is visible as light shines through the semi-transparent skin. The building can be disassembled easily, and broken down into component parts.

ARCHITECTURE ISN'T HERE TO STAY

R128 is the embodiment of my personal manifesto. It conforms to my triple zero principle, and it has the qualities of *Materialleichtbau*, *Strukturleichtbau*, and *Systemleichtbau* underlying its design, materials, and construction. Made completely from glazed elements, it is like living in a "soap bubble" of three-dimensional transparency. As there are few buildings with this degree of transparency, it is new and somewhat mystifying to many people. At first, many people think the house looks very chic but that living in it must feel somehow cold, as if one was living in a machine. But the many guests who have stayed in the house often say—openly and honestly after just a few hours—that they would like to live in such a house. Having learned from this experience, I continue to advocate architectural designs that deviate from conventional norms of all kinds.

R128 is sustainable and environmentally neutral. However, it is not a so-called "passive house." The passive house concept is a reaction to calls for sustainable buildings. It answers that call by adding insulation, by making the windows smaller and more efficient, and by making the building airtight. But this is not enough. And while solving some problems, the "passive house" creates others, e.g. with regard to recyclability, but also with regard to esthetics.

The environment of a passive house is not the kind of environment I want to live in, and that is why I designed a house like R128. It is the opposite of a passive house; instead it is an active house, with active technology, which collects the solar energy that naturally shines on the building. The solar energy on our planet is 10,000 times more than the energy we need globally. Storing and releasing that energy, as it is needed, is a simple thing. However, making every building embody principles like those in R128 will take time, and require different and complex thinking to achieve.

It isn't only the principles behind the design and construction of buildings that must change. Unsuitable processes are probably the greatest hindrance to achieving sustainable construction. Let's say that you have an ideal design team of 40 people that works on designing a building for one and a half years and then documents everything in a set of specifications, numbering several thousand pages. This document is then sent to contractors who are supposed to understand everything within a few weeks and offer a firm price for constructing the building. This can never work—here an entire industry is fooling itself! The contractors will either look for omissions in the specifications so that they can request change orders later or they will propose an alternative solution, to work around the specifications. Once construction begins, many things will be done differently

5

6

7

5-7: The R128 house was built in 2000 as a completely recyclable building. It produces no emissions and is self-sufficient in heating energy requirement. The completely glazed building has high-quality triple glazing panels, featuring a k-value of 0.4. The electrical energy for the house is provided by solar cells. Assembled by means of mortice-and-tenon joints and bolted joints, the modular construction can be easily dismantled.
The heat energy radiated into the building by the sun is absorbed by water-filled ceiling panels and transferred to a heat storage from which the building is heated during the winter by reversing the process of heat exchange in that the ceiling panels function as heat radiators; additional heating is not needed.

than planned. Changes and special proposals will be worked out and executed at once. In the end, you have a building that deviates from the original design in innumerable ways—and the building is no longer correctly documented. In 20 years no one will know exactly what was done or which specific products were used. In this scenario, how are we supposed to make any progress toward recycling? This process is the status quo today; what we need is a radical change.

This change is only possible if everyone who will be involved in a building project is included as early as possible in the design phase. Determining costs should also be done in a process that leads to increasingly precise specifications—contractors should never have to quote a price without fully understanding what they are expected to deliver. At a certain point in the design process, everyone must agree to stop making changes. It's what we call "design freeze." In addition to that simple idea, the construction records—plans, document sets and so on—must correspond with what is actually built. My office tries to achieve such a freeze in our projects, but we are not always successful. However, it is our normal procedure to draw on the expertise of other companies involved in the project, during the design phase, and to get them on board early, with a full understanding of the project. However we recognize that because of significant differences between architecture, engineering, construction, and other fields, the pace of change is slow.

In the construction industry, there is a completely different set of conditions in comparison to sectors where there is a much faster innovation cycle. For example, there are four billion cell phones in the world, and hardly any of them are more than three years old. The innovation cycle for buildings is much slower. This is partially because of the overall investments—it would be easy to ruin a builder with a single project; that's why we are obliged to exercise great care in our work, and that leads to a certain sort of conservatism. I'm not talking about backwardness—which I hold as scandalous because backwardness typically functions at the expense of the environment and society. But I have sympathy for people who have an aversion to high-risk construction projects. Sometimes we also have to deal with senseless regulations that slow innovation and progress. For example, in some small towns in Germany gable roofs are mandatory. However this building feature, from the 14th century, is inadequate to meet a wide variety of current requirements. But the main problem is that most companies in the construction industry are not capable of constructing a building such as R128. Thus, a qualification system of mandatory quality standards for building contractors must be developed, standards that contractors must meet in order to participate in the market. In addition, the market must change. But because change means that many who were successful under the status quo will no longer be part of the process, many players oppose new ways. Still, my office will continue to create our prototype buildings and hope that they spark new development.

Our desire for radical change does not entail the reduction of comfort, or any extreme economization. R128 is a large house, and my office is also composed of large spaces. I attempt to create habitable environments that improve people's performance, including their intellectual performance. Our surroundings must support the birth of ideas. Smaller is not necessarily better. We have enough space on the Earth — just compare domestic area with desert area! If you consume materials and energy sparingly, and construct fully recyclable buildings, then you can easily afford a grand scale of space. I would like a brilliantly built environment in which one feels good, which allows ample space for creativity, and which is breathtakingly beautiful. I'm not talking about some sort of absurd luxury, but I'm not in favor of an esthetic of renunciation either. The question that remains is: How should the built environment be conceived? Many people still consider the high-rise building a sin, but the real sin is the one- or two-family house. We must build with much greater density and with breathtaking beauty.

Beyond the simple consideration of the creation of generous and beautiful spaces, that are also sustainable, I advocate solutions that address simple issues of human comfort, and not a "back to nature" return to spare and spartan conditions. Non-sustainable construction is associated with our heightened expectations of indoor temperature, quiet, and other comforts. In a simple house built of wood, paste, and straw, you will never achieve constant temperature and humidity levels, a high degree of fire resistance and acoustic insulation, or the robust finishes and surfaces that we take for granted and expect in today's world. Today everything must function optimally, and this requires the coordination of many disparate things. The new complexities have led to the problem of too many parts and too many suppliers. However, the notion of going "back to nature" has no future; such notions romanticize the past and misjudge the current requirements for our built environment. As our expectations rose, so did our sensitivity to comfort and our need for efficiency; on the other hand, our susceptibility to sickness declined — people live longer. Understandably, we do not want to give up these advancements. Reduced comfort would not be accepted socially — today when the temperature in an office building rises above 26 °C, the tenant can claim a rent reduction on the grounds of a supposed reduction in the performance level of his staff! The building of the future is therefore not characterized by a return to more simplicity in the sense of "back to nature," but by simplicity within high complexity.

I think that though I am very tired of the word "sustainable," I am seeing progress toward the principles behind that word becoming an integral part of architecture, engineering, and construction. The timescale might be long, but in the end I think that the buildings I design are ultimately ephemeral architecture. Ephemeral means the architecture could last one day or 1,000 years. I think we, as architects and engineers—similar to anyone involved in creating things of some duration—cannot predict what the upcoming generations will need and love. The buildings we design today should therefore have the ability, at the very least, to leave the planet respectably.

Text documentation: Marius Leutenegger

About the author: Werner Sobek is an engineer and architect. Since 1994 he has been Professor at the University of Stuttgart, where he heads the Institute for Lightweight Structures and Conceptual Design (ILEK). ILEK tests and pushes the limits of feasibility in engineering and architecture. Sobek has also been Mies van der Rohe Professor at the Illinois Institute of Technology in Chicago since 2008. In 1992 he founded the company group Werner Sobek. The company group specializes in lightweight construction, high-rise construction, building shell engineering, and the design of sustainable buildings.

Going SOFT

Design Strategies for a New Materiality of Energy

SHEILA KENNEDY / KVA

Although technology performance has dominated recent discussions around renewable energy, the mass adoption of clean energy does not depend on technology alone. A hard look at the "soft" issues of clean energy shows clearly that system cost, inscription (or not) into existing building industry markets and channels of mass-distribution, familiarity to consumers, and cultural perceptions and habits will be deciding factors in the implementation of distributed energy. In the United States, efficient polycrystalline glass solar roof panels face three significant barriers to widespread adoption. Purchase costs are high, and more than 50 percent of total system costs are in rooftop installation, labor and inverters[1]. Once installed on the roof, it is hard for the homeowner to "use" solar energy since domestic appliances and wiring in the United States runs on 110 AC; the energy generated by the panels is DC, and the sale of clean energy grid tie sales is not mandated at the federal level. While the DC electrical energy can be inverted to AC, this adds cost, complexity and inefficiency.

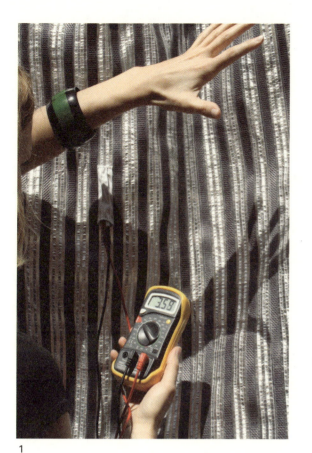

1

1-2: Measuring the power yield from a thin-film photovoltaic. The material is promising for many architectural applications. The power yield of the fabric varies due to the composition of the thin-film photovoltaic fabric. Shown are configurations that generate from 29.9 watts to 82.8 watts. The fabric is instrumental in the SOFT HOUSE concept.

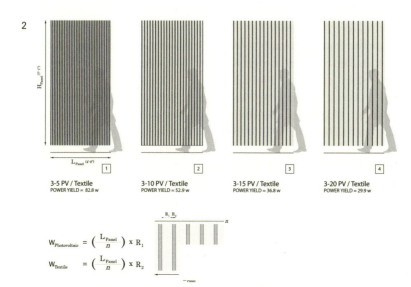

2

| 3-5 PV / Textile | 3-10 PV / Textile | 3-15 PV / Textile | 3-20 PV / Textile |
| POWER YIELD = 82.8 w | POWER YIELD = 52.9 w | POWER YIELD = 36.8 w | POWER YIELD = 29.9 w |

$$W_{Photovoltaic} = \left(\frac{L_{Panel}}{n}\right) \times R_1$$

$$W_{Textile} = \left(\frac{L_{Panel}}{n}\right) \times R_2$$

The less visible embodied or "grey" energy in the typical domestic solar installation must also be considered if carbon emissions are to be reduced. Significant carbon emissions are created in the production chain of glass-based solar panels, due to manufacturing footprints that require high heat (energy) processes in specialized clean room buildings (high grey energy). Once made, weight and breakage contribute to additional carbon emissions related to fuel in transport, particularly as China and India export inexpensive glass panels. Today, it takes a homeowner more than two years to "amortize" the embodied energy *already spent* in the production of a silicon glass panel[2]. If carbon emissions are to be reduced, a dilemma is posed: Can the manufacture of "clean energy" in the future be traded against for carbon emissions in the present?

In contrast to the typical glass-based solar panels, flexible thin-film photovoltaics (PV) create opportunities for architects to re-consider the materiality of energy in designs that emphasize an overall ecology of energy generation, grey energy and operational energy. While less "efficient" than glass-based solar technologies, thin-film PVs yield a very small carbon footprint, as they are manufactured with high volume, low heat and low carbon roll-to-roll and deposition processes. The average greenhouse gas emissions from thin-film PV production, excluding transport (40 g CO_2/kWh), are less than 50 percent of equivalent power silicon panels, and less than five percent of the emissions of petroleum, coal or natural gas energy sources[3].

When energy generation becomes materialized, it becomes a subject of architecture. Flexible energy harvesting materials enjoy the resiliency of being soft. These material qualities offer to energy technology a conceptual flexibility in the design of soft building components with integral energy harvesting capabilities, that can adapt to different circumstances and cultures of use. Soft materials can also be stealthy—and sometimes subversive. They have an ability to be disarming and persuasive; they exert influence through their ability to be integrated by design into familiar architectural elements and materials[4], and their suitability for mass production.

In the SOFT HOUSE project by KVA Matx, the domestic practice is used harvest energy so that it can be integrated into an existing consumer market and cultural patterns of use. The domestic curtain is transformed into a set of energy harvesting textiles, which can move to accommodate the changing spatial needs of living and working at home. A central curtain under a skylight can be lowered to create an instant room or raised to form a soft chandelier that defines space in an open living area with solid-state lighting. Perimeter curtains move horizontally along the southern building envelope on a standard track. Since track and curtain are always linked, the track is a strategic choice for distributing domestic renewable DC electrical power harvested by the curtain.

The principles of the SOFT HOUSE energy network are simplicity, adaptability, and intelligent cooperation among individual contributing elements. Mechanics are simple. It is not hard to move a curtain; the thin-film solar materials and textile host are flexible and lightweight. As the textile surface engages space, it also reflects heat, shades sunlight, and provides the house with an additional layer of insulation along the window surface. The curtain is transformed, while still retaining its traditional passive capacities and formal qualities of furling, flow, translucency and movement — qualities that then become associated with the photovoltaic technology.

SOFT CITIES, the urban exploration of the SOFT HOUSE concept, is bound by both the limitations and advantages of pliable organic photovoltaic materials (OPVs). This class of photovoltaic materials presents a paradoxical paradigm that pairs inefficient energy conversion, in relation to conventional solar panels with abundance, in a high throughput, low carbon manufacturing process. Where conventional solar materials are evaluated by the standard industry metric of "peak efficiency", OPV's have a broad solar aperture and make energy — inefficiently — all day long, so a new metric of "total energy accrued per day" must be introduced into design considerations.

To take advantage of the material's flexibility, the SOFT CITIES design re-configured the printable OPV structure, creating long, thin pliable solar strands to maximize material flexibility and minimize the number of electrical connections required to aggregate harvested energy. Using computer-driven 3D knitting machines, the solar strands are integrated into a textile surface — creating a hybrid, which is architecture, mobile furnishing, and infrastructure. Mass production of the retractable roof top canopy design was prioritized. This shifts the unlimited resource model of centralized electrical infrastructure to a discrete, mass-manufactured product form for solar energy, one that provides lighting and is ready to use upon purchase.

The IBA Hamburg SOFT HOUSE Smart Materials Housing project, with Jan Knippers Advanced Engineering and Solites Climate Design, explores a carbon negative sustainable energy concept for the Wilhelmsburg Island district based on a town house typology. The project combines a panelized, engineered wood construction, which sequesters carbon with a lightweight flexible CIGS solar cladding that

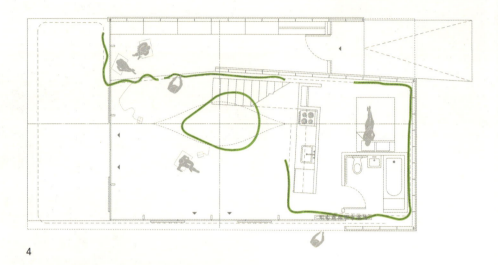

4

5

3: (Previous pages) The SOFT HOUSE uses the typical domestic curtain, as transformed by the use of thin-film photovoltaics into a productive element. Visible in the SOFT HOUSE model are interior, exterior, and rooftop curtains, for the harvest of solar energy. When combined with LEDs, the curtains can become a light source.
4: Diagram showing curtains in green, with tracks for alternate positioning shown in dashed lines.
5: All of the curtains can be dynamically configured to suit a range of functional, esthetic and programmatic demands.
6-7: Model of rooftop panel and structural modifications necessary for thin-film photovoltaic utilization.
8: Aerial visualization of rooftop thin-film photovoltaics, as imagined in widespread urban usage.

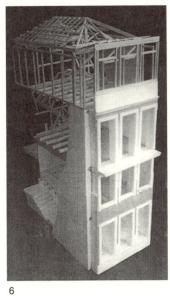
6

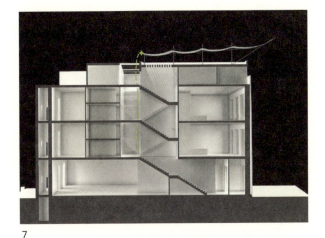
7

8

harvests energy and provides a beneficial climate buffer in summer and winter. Like plant leaves, the flexible solar cladding is organized in linear strips that turn open to provide views, harvest sunlight for energy throughout the day, and create a dynamically changing façade that establishes the public identify of the architecture.

The interior dwelling units utilize a system of movable smart curtains and tracks. These provide a low voltage DC distribution "ring" that is optimized for LED lighting with smart controls. This new domestic landscape of movable, space-making curtains brightens the dark winter months and can be configured to enclose and augment floor-based radiant heating or cooling. It is also playful and engaging—allowing people to make new connections between the "interior weather" of the domestic sphere and that of the exterior climate. LED lighting in the movable curtains can be programmed via open source software to illuminate as the wind blows, creating an ambient interior expression of the external windy environment of Hamburg. SOFT HOUSE living offers residents the freedom and flexibility to adapt their homes to fit their personal lifestyle and comfort zones.

1.) Balance-of-system (BoS) costs, including inverters and installation labor (15%) account for more than half the cost of a PV system, according to a 2010 Solar PV Balance of System Initiative Report by the Rocky Mountain Institute, USA.
2.) MIT Professor Marc Baldo has calculated that a polycrystalline Si panel requires over two years of use to amortize the high costs of the embodied energy in its manufacture (excluding the grey energy used in transport and installation.)
3.) Fthenakis, V., et al. (2008). "Emissions from Photovoltaic Life Cycles." *Environmental Science & Technology* 42.6 (2008): 2168–2174.
4.) For the political argument, see Nye, Joseph S., Soft Power; NY: *Public Affairs*, 2004
5.) Contreras, Migual A., et al. "19.9%-efficient ZnO/CdS/CuInGaSe2 solar cell with 81.2% fill factor." *Progress in Photovoltaics: Research and Applications* 16 (2008). In 2008 the National Renewable Energy Laboratory demonstrated that modifications to the CIGs surface achieved 19.9% efficiency. Typical sustained efficiencies for CIGs thin films currently range from 11% to 13%.

About the author: Sheila Kennedy is Professor of Architecture at the Massachusetts Institute of Technology (MIT) and Principal of KVA (www.kvarch.net). Kennedy directs MATx, an interdisciplinary materials research unit at KVA that accelerates the use of sustainable digital materials in architecture, urbanism, and the design of responsive building components. KVA's SOFT HOUSE won the IBA-Hamburg competition in 2010; KVA's Law School building for U Penn and KVA's Public Ferry Terminal in Manhattan are currently under construction. KVA has received AIA Design Excellence Awards, Progressive Architecture Awards, Industrial Design Excellence Awards, among others.

The Joys of Ecolomy

How to Make Sustainability a Haven of Hedonism

BJARKE INGELS / BIG

The issue of sustainability is a dominant theme now, and especially in relation to design. But there is a moral undertone in a lot of the talk surrounding sustainability, a protestant-like implication that life has to hurt in order to be good. You aren't supposed to take long showers because it isn't good for the environment; you aren't supposed to fly because airplanes are bad for the environment. Gradually one gets the idea that sustainable life must be less fun than normal life. On the other hand, sustainability has become hip and unavoidable. You can't submit anything to a competition today without supplying information about how 'green' your project is. Of course this also has its virtues, such as establishing climate change and sustainability as major subjects of design. But by formulating our environmental problems mostly in terms of political correctness, the discourse on sustainability deprives architects of finding answers to our climate challenge through design.

You may describe today's environmental problems as political, economical, or ecological—but we see them essentially as a design challenge. We are convinced that we need to find a way to organize all the activities of our society so that we can keep doing what we want to do without having to deny ourselves the freedoms that technological development has given us. A sustainable society should not be built upon frugal and ascetic behavior but rather on innovative design solutions. We believe that through the combined effort of manufacturers, developers, investors, foundations, workers and residents, both public and private, engineers, and architects, we could design a society that works like a perpetual motion engine. Our cities, our buildings, everything we make, can be designed in a way that allows us to drive as much as we want, to have an air-conditioned room, or take a 45-minute shower without harming the planet. Now, more than ever, design can improve human life.

Architectural projects should arise from the given conditions of society. They should not be driven by a single architect's supposedly superior knowledge about how people should live, or what the city should be or what the right esthetic is or isn't. Design needs to be a process of curation rather than the act of a superior creator. Designers have to attempt an almost impossible summersault, without stepping on anybody's toes, to please everyone. That increases the demands on architecture, and it also forces architecture into a more exciting way of operating than heroically, but no less stupidly, disregarding fundamental constraints such as relating to your context or staying within a budget. To Mies van der Rohe's motto 'less is more' we would retort 'yes is more'. Essentially, architects should say 'yes' to all of the different aspects of a project. Following the discourse on sustainability, and aware of the threat posed by climate change, we think you can address all of those issues sustainably in architecture.

Architecture is a means through which we can address today's ecological concerns in a way that is also economically sensitive and sensible, because architecture is capable of harnessing multiple inputs. Sustainability in the current discourse is too much about ecology, and not enough about economy. We believe that there is a fundamental misunderstanding that pits ecology against economy, in a relationship akin to 'good vs. evil'. Ecology and economy are not diametric opposites but rather two sides of the same coin. Ecological initiatives will only prosper in the real world if they work as viable economic models. Business models based on wearing down our national resources are not viable for long-term growth. Economy and ecology need to merge into *ecolomy*. In economy, waste is worthless. In ecology, there is no waste. In *ecolomy*, the waste of one is the food of another. The engine of *ecolomy* builds a hedonistic kind of sustainability, a society where the more energy you spend, the more energy you make. Rather than getting more sustainability for our money, we want to get more money from our sustainability.

Our project *Little Denmark* (LDK) uses precisely this idea of *ecolomy* to create a model Denmark with an energy bill of zero by designing a series of interconnected loops that feed output back into the consumption loop as input. All of Denmark would be like a single household where no resource is wasted, and no by-product a dead end—a society in ecolomical symbiosis. With the systematic application of renewable energy sources, and with hydrogen as an energy exchange currency, we designed an ecosystem of programs with complementary consumption patterns.

The idea of turning all of Denmark into an economical and ecological ecosystem seems utopian because of its magnitude. All concrete proposals will appear like abstract principles because we can't grasp them. Therefore, we have boiled the components of Denmark down to the size of an architectural project: all programs compressed proportionally into a 100,000 m² urban block—like a biopsy of the Danish urban tissue. At this scale the challenge becomes as tangible as any other commission: solve the program and keep count of the flow of resources and energy, just as we do with the square meters and the construction costs in a typical project.

We began by asking what it would take to supply all of Denmark with renewable energy. If we relied on the sun we would have to cover all of the Storstrøms islands with solar cells. If we relied on biogas we would need the manure from a pig farm the size of the greater metropolitan area of Copenhagen. A wind farm of 75 x 75 km of windmills could keep us covered. However, all systems rely heavily on one massive centralized enterprise. We quickly realized that betting on one energy source didn't seem like a wise choice. Better to combine multiple inputs and outputs like a chain! The principles of *ecolomy* become easy to grasp when we translate their abstract general concepts to LDK. It can harness the waste heat and energy of its population, to insert it directly back into the system. For instance, in architecture 90 percent of our energy is spent on heating or cooling buildings. But while houses spend energy on heating, offices do so on cooling. Houses benefit from the sun and benefit from the passive solar heat gain. Clearly, the needs of one could be fulfilled by the other if they were married in a symbiotic relationship. A supermarket spends most of its electricity on refrigerators. A refrigerator essentially moves heat from one place to another. Normally, the undesirable heat

USE
1# ~~REDUCE, REUSE,~~ RECYCLE

HIT THE ROAD
2# ~~STAY CLOSE TO HOME~~

MAXIMIZE HYDROGEN
3# ~~MINIMIZE~~ USE OF ~~COMBUSTION~~ ENGINES

PRODUCE ENERGY WHILE DRIVING
4# ~~REDUCE FUEL CONSUMPTION~~

SUPPORT YOUR OWN HOUSEHOLD WITH ENERGY
5# ~~SUPPORT GOVERNMENT REGULATION WITH POLITICAL CHOICES~~

6# SUPPORT THOUGHTFUL INNOVATIONS **!!!**

THE MORE YOU USE — THE MORE YOU GET
7# ~~PRIORITIZE~~

WASTE
8# ~~VOTE~~

Don't ✓
9# FEEL GUILTY

ENJOY MORE
10# ~~ENJOY WHAT YOU HAVE~~

1

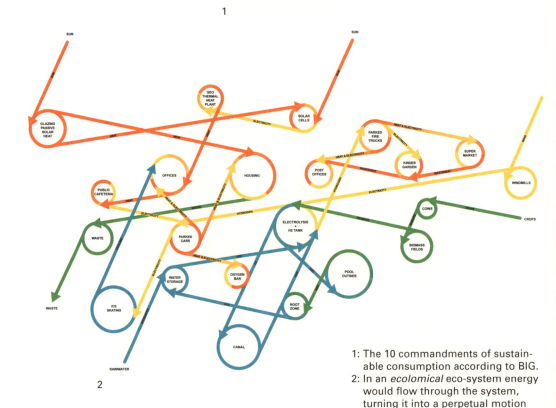

2

1: The 10 commandments of sustainable consumption according to BIG.
2: In an *ecolomical* eco-system energy would flow through the system, turning it into a perpetual motion engine.

is released into ambient air. If this waste heat is used to heat a swimming pool, for example, a medium size supermarket could heat an entire public pool—for free. We can knit together a network of different programs that would reach an equilibrium of complementary energy supplies and demands, where energy would flow through the system like a perpetual motion engine. For LDK we followed the natural propensity of each program and have organized the entire 100,000 m² block so that each program claims its optimum position in the whole scheme. That optimum location has been determined by solar orientation, urban adjacencies, proximity to symbiotic neighbors, and requirements for access, scale, sunlight, views, etc.

The testing ground for our project LDK is a site between Amager City, Ørestad Nord and the open fields of Amager Fælled. We connected the site into the surrounding urban fabric with shortcuts. These shortcuts, when subtracted from the site, give us the form of the building footprints. The logic of this is simple and elegant. There is no need for us to search for some sort of formalistic strategy for the buildings: the simple triangular shapes left over helped to inspire us to use the form of a pyramid for the buildings. In *ecolomy*, logic is king, and therefore superficial decisions are solved by a higher power.

The form and orientation of each pyramid was decided by a solar optimization study. Towards the south, the sun is relatively high in the sky, giving a rather inclined angle of almost 45 degrees. To the east or west, the sun angle is incrementally lower, making the optimal façade more vertical. To the north, there is never direct sun, so vertical façades make perfect sense. Applied to our site, crisscrossed by shortcuts, the formula produced a cluster of tilting pyramids of various sizes—the optimal building envelope for maximum solar heat gain.

Each pyramid contains a mix of programs. The programs were arranged within the pyramids in the most suitable place for their requirements and most advantageous adjacencies, in relationship to the solar conditions particular to each pyramid. Office space sits in a 10-m-deep zone on the north-facing slopes of the buildings. This takes advantage of the relatively cool and shaded condition of north-facing façades, and eliminates some of the need to cool offices for comfortable daytime use. Housing is placed in a 7-m-deep zone on the sunnier façades. This provides good daylight conditions, sunshine, views, and passive solar heat gain. In addition, the terraces become even more enviable and viable for all kinds of program. One could even imagine urban vertical gardening! The deeper spaces, in the pyramid centers, are useful for large public spaces, commercial spaces, and

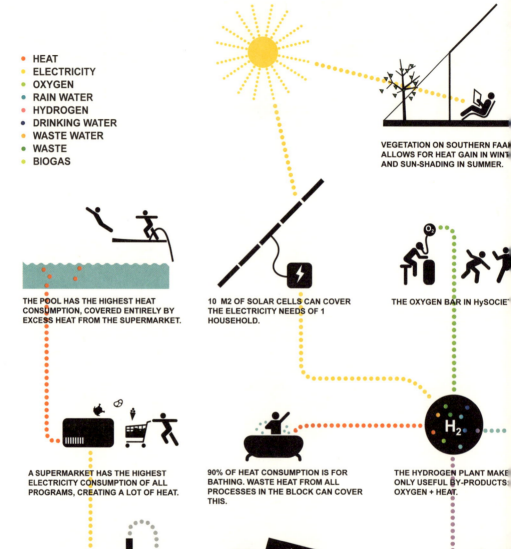

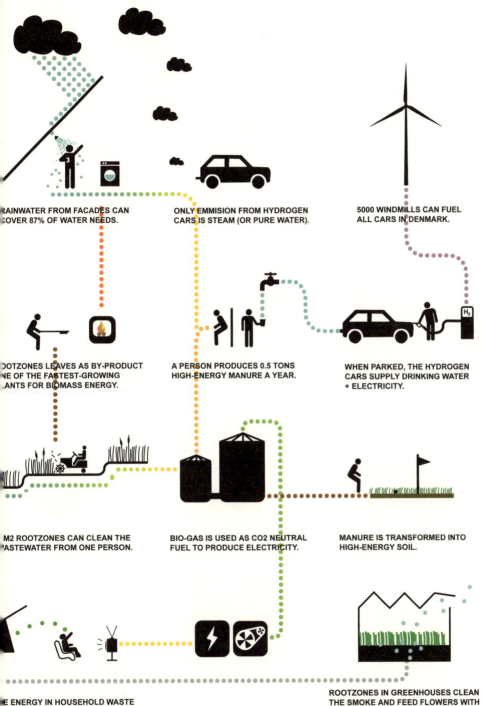

3: System of flows in *Little Denmark*. Interconnected loops feed output back into the consumption loop as input.

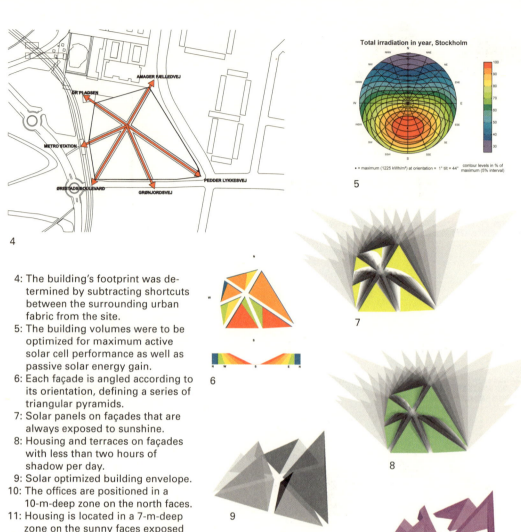

4: The building's footprint was determined by subtracting shortcuts between the surrounding urban fabric from the site.
5: The building volumes were to be optimized for maximum active solar cell performance as well as passive solar energy gain.
6: Each façade is angled according to its orientation, defining a series of triangular pyramids.
7: Solar panels on façades that are always exposed to sunshine.
8: Housing and terraces on façades with less than two hours of shadow per day.
9: Solar optimized building envelope.
10: The offices are positioned in a 10-m-deep zone on the north faces.
11: Housing is located in a 7-m-deep zone on the sunny faces exposed to the sun.
12: Public programs and parking occupy the large interior volumes.
13: Work spaces are facing north, living spaces are facing the sun and hybrids of public spaces, businesses, and parking are found in the interior of the pyramids.
14: Each pyramid has a specific character and identity due to the placement of programs.
15: Library Parking Slopehouse: A continuous spiral of bookstacks unites the entire library collection. Inside the 3-m-thick floor is space for technical installations and cars. Terrace houses on the south serve as the roof of the library. A tree on each terrace provides shade in the summer, while allowing passive solar energy gain in the winter.

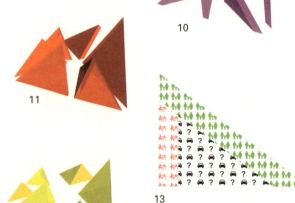

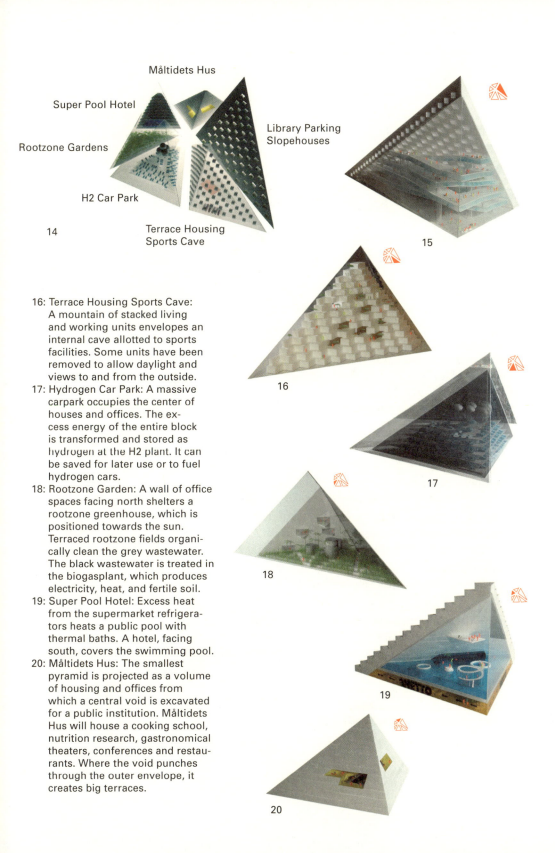

16: Terrace Housing Sports Cave: A mountain of stacked living and working units envelopes an internal cave allotted to sports facilities. Some units have been removed to allow daylight and views to and from the outside.

17: Hydrogen Car Park: A massive carpark occupies the center of houses and offices. The excess energy of the entire block is transformed and stored as hydrogen at the H2 plant. It can be saved for later use or to fuel hydrogen cars.

18: Rootzone Garden: A wall of office spaces facing north shelters a rootzone greenhouse, which is positioned towards the sun. Terraced rootzone fields organically clean the grey wastewater. The black wastewater is treated in the biogasplant, which produces electricity, heat, and fertile soil.

19: Super Pool Hotel: Excess heat from the supermarket refrigerators heats a public pool with thermal baths. A hotel, facing south, covers the swimming pool.

20: Måltidets Hus: The smallest pyramid is projected as a volume of housing and offices from which a central void is excavated for a public institution. Måltidets Hus will house a cooking school, nutrition research, gastronomical theaters, conferences and restaurants. Where the void punches through the outer envelope, it creates big terraces.

parking. Each pyramid has a specific character and identity due to the placement of program: libraryparking slopehouses, terracehousing sportscave, "måltidets hus," H2 carpark, superpool hotel, rootzone gardens.

LDK can be a model project. It sets up a system and a flow through ecology and energy, which engages multiple programs at multiple scales for universal benefit. The pyramids stand for more than their own sum total, and the concepts illustrated make clear principles that can be used in other applications. This is exactly what we need, to guide the narrative of sustainable living. It is also what we need so that we can develop sustainable ways of living that don't feel like a punishment for the sins of the past. We believe in progress, not penance. This belief comes from the human capacity for innovation and the ability to always find a way. It is not because the engineers and architects of the past were evil that our cities aren't sustainable: they simply didn't know about the consequences of greenhouse gas emissions and other hazards, environmental and social. Architecture and architectural thinking are a way of organizing, a way of analyzing, and a way of turning that organization and analysis into action. What defines architecture, as opposed to many other disciplines, is the need to directly intervene. We are tasked with understanding the city and trying to understand the functions of a specific institution in order to host it, but we also have to *do* something, there is always the necessity of intervention. It's quite easy with contemporary technology to create buildings that have a positive energy output. It's just a question of doing it.

Our office is interested in the idea of a pragmatic utopia. We envision projects like LDK as small steps in the evolution of a utopian ideal. The pragmatic utopian approach is an evolution rather than a revolution. In LDK, we had the chance to create a fragment of the city, and within that fragment we tried to realize a small piece of utopia. It isn't the end goal but it's a step on the way.

We like the notion that life evolved according to Darwin, and that life is always adapting to change. Through mutation, all forms of life gradually evolved. But when we, as 'evolved monkeys,' invented technology and architecture, we reversed this relationship. We started manipulating our surroundings, the environment, even life itself. We altered conditions to fit the way we wanted to live. With this reversal, humans, not nature or evolution, claimed the power to create the world. That comes with the responsibility of establishing equilibrium between the forces we exert on the planet and the forces already present. Evolution in our current context is highly dependent on technological and architectural evolution.

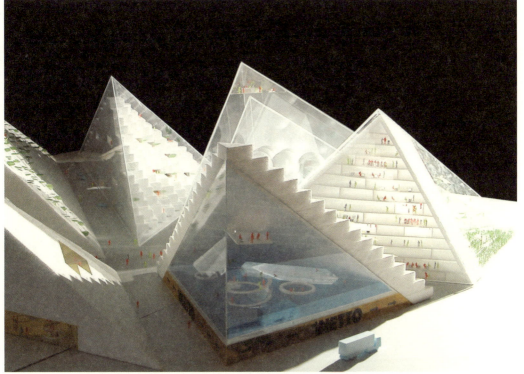
21

22

21-22: Little Denmark reduces the components of Denmark to the size of an architectural project: all programs are compressed proportionally into a 100,000 m² urban block.

BJARKE INGELS

With the arrival of global climate change we are slowly assuming the responsibility that was given to us the second we started messing with the planet instead of just adapting to the conditions we found.

About the author: Bjarke Ingels started BIG (Bjarke Ingels Group) in 2005 after co-founding PLOT Architects and working at OMA. Through a series of award-winning design projects and buildings, Bjarke Ingels has developed an international reputation as a member of a new generation of architects who combine shrewd analysis, playful experimentation, social responsibility and humor. Bjarke has been active as a Visiting Professor at Rice University's School of Architecture and Columbia University's Graduate School of Architecture, Planning and Preservation. Bjarke is currently Visiting Professor at Harvard University.

EOL, COP, PVT, TABS and LowEx

How to Reduce CO$_2$ Emissions with New Construction Technologies

FORREST MEGGERS AND HANSJÜRG LEIBUNDGUT

Buildings are a fundamental part of human life and culture as well as of society itself. Yet in our technically highly advanced age, buildings have in many ways been neglected. Construction has not reached the level of highly integrated performance that is found in, for instance, the IT and automotive industries. A building is still designed as the sum of separate parts. Since buildings have a significant environmental impact there is an extraordinary potential and need for improvement.

Nevertheless, there have been significant advances in building construction and operation, and some aspects are becoming increasingly integrated. But for a variety of reasons, these changes are proceeding much too slowly. Firstly: buildings have a long life span. Once something is implemented it stays for quite some time. Secondly: buildings represent a conglomeration of systems and materials from a wide variety of fields, ranging from the mechanical and material sciences, to design and architecture, to construction and contraction. Lastly: the ecological impact of buildings on the environment is frequently given less priority than esthetic beauty or the acceptance and comfort of the users or occupants. This is not to say that beauty and comfort are not important, but rather that the buildings' impact on the environment must also be an integral part of good building design.

Today, architects and engineers are designing and constructing buildings that will last for decades or even centuries, and any CO_2 emissions resulting from them will be unsustainable long term. Buildings are directly or indirectly responsible for over half of the greenhouse gas emissions. Unfortunately, many studies consider only the direct emissions from residential and commercial buildings, which represent only a small slice of the pie. But it is a fact that buildings consume 2/3 of all electricity, produce the majority of wastewater and 2/3 of global waste. A significant portion of industrially generated energy and forestry production result directly from building demand; its demand easily accounts for 50 percent. If architects and engineers act quickly and change the current technologies and design practices towards zero emission during all states of a building—from creation, to operation, and then to dismantling—we will play a huge role in mitigating the climate change problem.

Climate change is not an issue for academics and/or politicians alone, it has also become a priority for architects, engineers, and anyone participating in the shaping of our built environment. Together, we need to develop multifaceted solutions which address the political and industrial realities. This will require that antiquated attitudes and practices be replaced by environment-conscious practices and technologies.

Limits of Past Solutions

This is not the first time that the impact and urgent reduction of the energy consumption of buildings has been addressed. Already in the 1970s a substantial demand to reduce the energy consumption in buildings was made. This in turn initiated a number of important energy conservation programs that still exist today. The combined issues of climate change and secure energy supply provide the incentive for further work in this sector. But we must take heed not to fall into a rut. Many good ideas have already been executed in the past, but we must go further and develop new technologies and tools to get there.

Unfortunately a large number of the ideas and practices of the past, both good and bad, are deeply rooted in today's fundamental practices, generating obstacles for these new potential innovations. Making real and urgently needed progress will require innovative concepts and the commitment to go against accepted routines. For instance, the ways in which we build with steel and concrete have to be drastically rethought, because the production of steel and concrete are very energy-intensive processes. Cement production alone accounts for five percent of the global CO_2 emissions.

One attempt to improve the energy efficiency of buildings was the concept of *Passivhaus* [passive house]. Despite its merits, the *Passivhaus* concept is based on the wrong and commonly adopted notion that the demand for heat is bad, rather than analyzing the actual primary energy input to supply that demand, and the resulting CO_2 emissons. This is resulting in excessively thick walls and the employment of enormous amounts of material in order to achieve insulation-levels that are in fact unnecessary—just resulting from a single-minded focus on heat reduction. Take into consideration the material input that goes into creating a 50-cm-wall (Figure 1) and imagine the difficulty of deconstructing and recycling this wall. Unfortunately the *Passivhaus* concept overlooks these considerations, leading to excess emissions from the construction (and demolition) of these otherwise high-performance buildings.

Instead of focusing on the heat or cooling demand of a building (as in the *Passivhaus*), we need to focus on the amount of primary energy required to provide this demand, and on wether that primary energy can be or is supplied by renewable energy. Following this approach, we can independently reduce the negative environmental impacts of CO_2 and other emissions resulting from the common use of primary energy from fossil fuels. The minimization of CO_2 emission can be achieved with innovative techniques and technologies that concentrate less on just heating and cooling demand. At the same time, it allows for structures that are less material-intensive to be built. The combined result is a more strategic reduction of CO_2 emission to meet national and international goals (Figure 2).

Along with a better understanding of the influence of building energy concepts on material consumption, there must also be a better understanding of the energy flows in buildings. Building energy analysis has, up until very recently, only focused on simple energy balances to estimate the heat demand and the primary energy that must be supplied to achieve the desired comfort levels. The energy balance simply accounts for the heat being lost or gained by the building and equates this directly to the energy input needed to supply the requisite heating or cooling. This leads to a problem. Although an energy balance is a valid way to account for the amount of energy moving in and out of each part of a building energy system, it does not account for the quality of each of those energy flows. Energy flows that are at higher temperatures are more valuable than others at lower temperatures, and this is not accounted for in a simple energy balance alone. These temperature differences will affect the overall performance of the system. There are new tools and analysis methods that account for these differences in quality. They help to generate better overall system performance, and most importantly reduce primary energy demands and thus CO_2 emissions. Figure 3 illustrates the variety of inputs and outputs in a building system that are evaluated, optimized and combined to produce this improved overall performance.

The methods for reducing building energy demand that have been implemented up until the present have surely been successful; however, building CO_2 emissions continue to rise globally, and to make the steps necessary to combat this dangerous process we must consider new and improved ways to move toward zero emission buildings.

Solutions for Today

There are many solutions to move us toward zero emission buildings. Some are broad in scope and applicable at many levels, in the form of new techniques and analysis methods, and others apply to specific new technologies, based on those new techniques and analysis.
– Exergy: As we have already noted, the past solution set for high performance buildings lacks an appropriate perspective that includes the concept of energy quality and not just quantity of energy. This quality impacts how effectively we use primary energy. We can employ the term "exergy" in the development of new building systems to facilitate possibilities for improvement that would otherwise be imperceptible using energy analysis alone, and therefore minimize primary energy demand while avoiding common energy-based design constraints. This opens the door to improvements not only in performance, but also in architectural and design opportunities.

Exergy originates in a combination of two fundamental concepts of thermodynamics. These are the concepts of energy conservation and entropy generation. Energy conservation is the origin of the standard energy balance. It is derived from the first law of thermodynamics. Entropy generation comes from

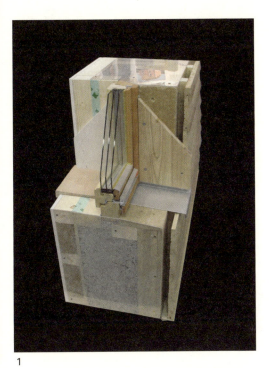

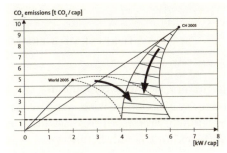

1: Illustration of the complexity and material usage in the wall construction of a *Passivhaus*. Some of this excess construction could be reduced while maintaining the same overall performance by independently reducing the primary energy demand and the CO_2 emissions with more efficient heat supply methods and technology.

2: Projected CO_2 reduction in Switzerland and the world. Through proper integration of new systems and methods it will be possible to reduce CO_2 emissions to below 1 ton CO_2/cap and year in Switzerland. The same methods can be implemented throughout the world to help bring the overall emissions to the same reduced level. This can be done without limitations on heat demand, but instead through expansion of technological advancement.

3: A house and its enormous variety of potential inputs and outputs during operation. Some energy and heat can be stored or moved in between systems from a variety of interfaces with the environment. Heat loss is just one potential flow that can be controlled. There are many others from solar inputs to ground heat storage.

4: This ceiling panel can supply heat at a low temperature using its large surface area while activating the thermal mass of the ceiling structure to increase the effective heat transfer surface area. At the same time other functions, such as exhaust air and lighting, can be integrated into the system, making the overall installation very compact and less material-intensive.

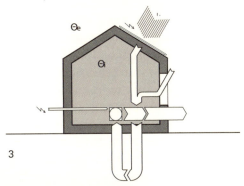

the second law of thermodynamics and defines the loss of potential in systems due to dispersion or what are known as irreversibilities. These arise due to the directional nature of processes like heat flow, which can only spontaneously occur from hot to cold. In a thermal system like a building, the amount of entropy generated in any heat exchange is directly related to the temperature difference across which the exchange takes place. The exergy in a thermal system is simply a combination of the energy that would be calculated in an energy balance with a portion subtracted that represents the loss in potential due to the change in entropy.

A common example is to compare exergy in a battery with that found in a hot pot of water. Based on the heat capacity of water, the pot of water can be heated to the point where it has the same amount of energy as the battery, but a battery can be reversibly charged and discharged. If we are going to hook up a thermal engine to the pot of water to extract work, we can only extract work from the flow of heat in one direction. We can never extract the entire potential energy equal to the energy in the battery because some is inherently part of the directional flow of heat. The irreversible nature of the process limits the thermodynamically feasible amount of energy that can be extracted. That amount of available energy, which is not solely defined by the heat capacity of the water, is exergy. The higher the temperature of the water compared to its surroundings, the higher the potential, and thus the exergy. Thus, since the heat and energy demand of buildings represents a potential that must be met by some primary energy demand, we can reduce that potential that must be met through exergy analysis in ways that might be missed by energy analysis alone.

The low exergy (LowEx) revolution for buildings comes from this additional evaluation of system potential made possible by the use of the concept of exergy. The application of exergy analysis follows the necessary shift of focus away from heating/cooling demand based analysis focused solely on reduction of quantity, and toward primary energy minimization and renewable energy maximization through the optimization of quality, thereby achieving the largest reduction in CO_2 emissions possible. This means that we don't just try to limit the heat exchanges through the buildings exterior, but we also focus on the primary flows coming into the energy system of the building. These flows represent the exergy available to the system, and they have a quantity and a quality, both of which can be evaluated using exergy analysis. This evaluation supports new design techniques and opportunities, while at the same time providing the basis for the development of new integrated technologies that can drastically reduce the primary energy demand of buildings.

These techniques and technologies are based around the principal of minimizing the unnecessary temperature differences in the supply and distribution of heat to a building. Larger temperature gradients cause larger reductions in exergy, or in other words, more exergy destruction. Exergy analysis allows us to minimize this destruction through the use of more intelligently designed systems. This also leads to better system integration because as the temperature gradient in one system is reduced, this leads to more ideal temperatures being supplied amongst the interconnected systems.

– LowEx Systems: The influence of temperature gradients in exergy analysis is the basis for a fundamental LowEx concept, which is low temperature heating and high temperature cooling. By employing thermally activated building systems (TABS) to exploit the large heating and/or cooling surfaces available in buildings, lower temperature differences between the supply of heat or cooling and room air are needed to provide adequate comfort. An example of a system that provides a variety of functions including conduction of heat into the ceiling for low temperature heating and high temperature cooling is the ceiling panel shown in Figure 4. In this case, heating is achieved with a supply temperature of just 28 °C and cooling with 18 °C.

Exergy destruction stems not only from heat transfers, but also from other losses in building systems, such as pressure drops in ventilation systems. By examining ways to minimize ducting and excessive air supply, this exergy can also be conserved. This is demonstrated in some decentralized ventilation techniques that can be provided by systems such as the Airbox technology shown in Figure 5. This system can be integrated into the façade of a building and provide fresh air directly into a room with very efficient fans. Not only can systems like this reduce, or even eliminate the necessity for duct installation, but they can also take direct advantage of the wind loading on building façades to minimize required fan power. This is a novel way to utilize renewable energy directly, while maintaining indirect control and over the system, which is not possible with natural-ventilation-only systems.

There are many other integral concepts and components that can be utilized to create a LowEx system. The key is again the minimization of temperature gradients and exergy destruction. This can be achieved in ways as simple as redesigning hot water supply to be accomplished at a lower temperature because the large majority of hot water is used at or below 40 °C, while it is almost always stored above 50 °C. It can also be the elimination of unnecessary heat exchanges in the system. Exergy destruction also includes all potential waste streams in the building that might carry usable heat, and thus valuable exergy. For example, both exhaust air and wastewater can provide significant amounts of heat if recovered properly, thereby generating significant improvements in overall system performance, and also offsetting primary energy inputs.

– Heat Pump and Geothermal Sources: The core component of a high-performance LowEx building system is the heat pump. The potential of the heat pump in the building sector is vastly underestimated. When incorporated into the LowEx design philosophy, not only is a heat pump a useful component, but the LowEx minimization of temperature gradients in the system has the potential to double the amount of heat that can be supplied per unit of primary energy input compared to typical heat pump installations. Therefore, the heat pump system that many consider to be comparable to high temperature heating systems, such as boilers and furnaces, is more than twice as good, while at the same time eliminating the large exergetic losses inherent in these other high temperature heat generation and supply systems.

The reason that there is this extraordinary potential for heat pump systems is that their performance is directly related to the heating supply temperature. The heat pump coefficient of performance (COP) is a measure of the ratio of heat supplied to the energy input to run the heat pump. The beautiful thing about the heat pump is that the heat itself is not generated, but rather supplied from natural renewable sources as shown in Figure 6. This can be the air outside, the ground below, or any source of waste heat that might otherwise be lost. These sources are not of adequate temperature to be directly used to supply heating, so the heat pump exploits a refrigeration cycle to 'pump' heat from these lower temperatures to adequate higher temperatures, sufficient for heating. The difference in temperature from a lower temperature source to a higher temperature supply, otherwise known as the heat pump temperature-lift, has a direct impact on performance independent of the amount of heat that must be supplied.

This is where the all-important LowEx temperature factors in. The heat pump COP is inversely proportional to the temperature-lift that the heat pump must overcome to bring the source heat up to an adequate supply temperature. By minimizing the supply temperature and by optimizing the renewable heat source supply, this temperature-lift is significantly reduced in a LowEx system. This is dem-

5

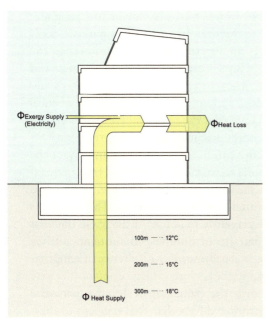

6

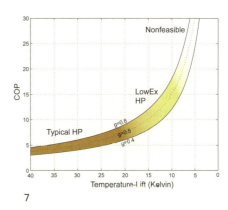

7

5: This decentralized air supply system can be installed easily into the floor or wall where it can be connected directly to supply adequately conditioned air to the space. This reduces the necessary material and space for ducting and minimizes the associated losses from these supply structures.

6: The flow of heat being pumped from a renewable source, in this case the ground, into a house by a heat pump. This can be accomplished with a small exergy input, usually in the form of electricity, when low exergy systems are employed.

7: Plot of the increase in performance (COP, ratio of heat pumped to electrical input) of a heat pump as the temperature-lift that the heat pump has to supply to pump heat from a colder source to a warmer sink decreases.

onstrated in Figure 7 where the dramatic rise in performance is illustrated as the temperature-lift that the heat pump must supply is reduced below 20 °C. This is of course easily possible with integrated LowEx systems. By utilizing the higher temperature of the earth through systems such as deep boreholes, we can acquire temperatures of at least 10 °C, even up to 15 °C or higher, depending on the geothermal gradient, which varies across regions. The combination of these source temperatures with the low temperature heating system, as described previously, results in a temperature-lift of 20 °C or less. Furthermore, there is a large potential for the harvest of higher source temperatures by recovering waste heat from sources like exhaust ventilation and wastewater, which have the potential to supply significantly higher source temperatures to the heat pump system.

By following this LowEx paradigm, there is the incredible potential to supply more than 10 units of heat to a building with only one unit of primary energy input. This drastically changes our consideration of how buildings are designed, especially relative to how heat is supplied to the building. The same goes for cooling systems, because a heat pump is simply an air conditioner run in reverse. Everything that we can do with temperature-lifts for heat pumps can also be achieved with the proper design of cooling systems. Therefore, with integrated LowEx design, the heating and cooling can be supplied with a high-performance heat pump using very little primary energy, so little in fact, that the potential for supplying the required primary energy with renewable energy becomes much more feasible.

– Renewable Systems: This renewable energy can be supplied by many novel concepts. The field of renewable energy is rapidly expanding and its potential increases, while prices continue to fall. Large-scale concepts for alternative renewable energy generation, such as the solar updraft tower, have the potential to replace the centralized power production systems currently in place. At the same time the integration of photovoltaics into a wide variety of building components will be capable of offsetting significant amounts of the demand for delivered electricity, along with the associated transport losses.

This integration concept folds back into the principal of LowEx with the extraction of low temperature heat from standard PV cells. This concept of thermal photovoltaic (PVT) has the potential to significantly increase the usefulness of the PV alone. The heat pump can utilize the warm temperatures that are a byproduct of the solar cell operation to increase its COP while at the same time actually improving the solar cell performance and longevity by keeping the panel itself cooler.

Consider an application of this LowEx PVT integrated system. The newest PV cells, which are being mass-produced at prices that achieve grid parity for the first time (First Solar/OC Oerlikon), have an efficiency of at least 10 percent. Now, if that electricity is supplied to a heat pump with a COP of 10, already we have 100 percent worth of the solar energy being supplied to the building, far exceeding the performance of any high temperature solar thermal collector. Even higher COP values can be achieved when we utilize some of the slightly higher temperature heat being captured from the PV cell using the hybrid system. A prototype is shown in Figure 8. We can potentially utilize upwards of 60 percent of the remaining radiation not converted to electricity in the form of this medium temperature heat.

Along with this considerable expansion of PV potential comes the issue of timing. Many of the potential LowEx heat sources that we could acquire are available at times when they might not be needed. For example, the higher temperature solar heat source could dramatically increase the efficiency of hot water production, but it might arrive at times when there is no hot water demand. In order to account for these overflows we have developed dual-zone borehole system shown in Figure 9. By having separate warm and cool boreholes, the excess warm and cool flows into the building system can be independently captured and stored throughout the year, providing particular benefit in the seasonal differences from summer to winter. These overflows come not only from a PV system, but also from the supplies of waste streams like hot water and exhaust air, as well as passive solar inputs of radiation through windows into the heating and cooling distribution networks in floors and or walls. These can all be exploited directly in systems that have a demand, or stored in our independent thermal reservoirs in case there is an overflow.

-- LowEx Materialization: This revolutionizes the way in which we consider the energy supplied to a building, which in turn suggests new opportunities in the design and material selection of the building itself. This is the second, and equally important aspect of the building sector as a whole: what is the impact of the material that is supplied to create the structure and systems within the building. How can we claim to minimize the primary energy demand if the materials going into the construction of the building require more primary energy than the building does over its entire operational lifespan? For many extensive buildings this is the case.

For a typical *Passivhaus* construction, the extra material input necessary to achieve the extreme insulation requirements, thereby achieving the requisite heating demand, has a significant energy demand. This grey energy and the subsequent grey emissions from its production should not be overlooked. For the typical *Passivhaus* construction, the grey energy from the material inputs is equivalent to around 25 years of building operation, which is possibly longer than the lifespan of the building.

We must find new and innovative ways of considering the concept of exergy, in both operation as well as what is embodied in the production, utilization, and disposal of buildings, as well as their components and materials. This will be the only path to actually accomplish the elimination of the unsustainable level of emissions that comes from the building sector.

But with so many components and materials involved in the creation of buildings, how do we go about addressing this significant aspect of the building sector's environmental impact? One way we can take a broad stroke at this part of the problem is to exploit the new freedoms that LowEx systems bring to the building design itself. These originate from the fact that exergy analysis and integrated high-performance heat pumps allow us to minimize the primary energy demand independently of the heat demand. Thereby we are no longer tightly constrained by high levels of insulation to achieve high-performance buildings.

In fact, if we compare the cost of installing additional insulation with that of drilling a borehole to increase the source heat temperature for a heat pump (and thus the COP), we find that the point of equal investment requires far less material input in the combined system than in a system focused on insulation alone. The designer is free to create structures that are less burdened by mass and materialization. This leads to less material demand and to new options in design that might not otherwise be possible without sacrificing performance in terms of heat demand.

– Lightweight Design and End-of-Life: With the ability to independently minimize primary energy demand, the architect can successfully implement more sustainable concepts such as those that arise from the theories of lightweight design. While the thermal performance of the building skin must of course meet some reasonable level of performance to allow the integration of low temperature heating and high temperature cooling, the potential for less encumbered designs is immense. This flexibility also leads to more freedom that facilitates the incorporation of natural inputs like wind and sun into building and therefore building system design.

Lightweight design also leads to improvements in the construction materials themselves. One of the most massive construction materials, cement, has seen drastic changes. Its enormous impact in terms of emissions can be significantly reduced by new formulations. This includes ways to reduce the CO_2 generated by its production, as well as ways to create more lightweight versions. Expanded lightweight concrete as shown in Figure 10 can maintain a high level of strength, use less material, and at the same time significantly increase the thermal performance of the concrete. The resistance to heat transfer, from exterior surfaces to interior spaces, can be more than doubled. When combined with low exergy systems, this results in the potential for lightweight walls that do not require excessive layers of insulating materials, which not only reduces the overall material requirement, but also reduces the complexity of the construction. This makes the building easier to dismantle and recycle when it is decommissioned.

Consideration for the end-of-life (EOL) situation for a building is one of the most neglected aspects of its impact on the environment. It requires farsighted consideration into the future for a wide variety of components and materials. Still, common practices can be applied. These start with the simple gathering of data on how the materials and components will be implemented and combined in specific applications. This is where lightweight design again has an advantage. Simple structures with low material requirements can be designed in simple ways, with a reduced set of mixed non-recyclable inputs. In a large component with many material inputs, the potential for deconstruction and recovery of the individual inputs is reduced or is limited because a huge amount of work is required to achieve the necessary separation. Lightweight construction can achieve intricate new designs, while at its core maintaining elegant construction techniques that already have the potential for a simple deconstruction and recycling process.

Lightweight designs also involve the consideration of methods alternative to those that depend solely on the simple physics of individual structural components alone. Innovative methods that take advantage of magnetism and the interaction between various materials can make constructions possible that would otherwise be difficult to implement when limited by a single material. Active systems that utilize pre-loading or pressure/vacuum applications can generate flexible systems that are capable of modulating their function depending on the desired state, such as Werner Sobeks Station Z (see text by Werner Sobek, page 34). This type of thinking facilitates new possibilities in lighting applications such as flexible, removable or exchangeable systems, allowing for an adaptability and sustainability of design that would not otherwise be possible. Thus, in renovation, these systems clearly lead to new options for improving existing building stock. New

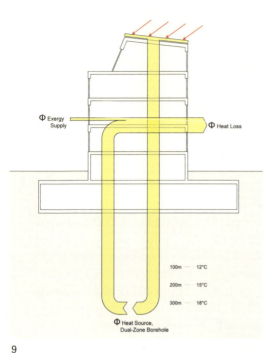

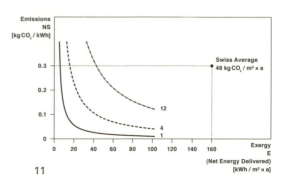

8: A prototype of an inexpensive hybrid photovoltaic system that employs a very simple heat exchange to reduce the operating temperature of the PV panel while supplying this heat to the low exergy building system.

9: This picture illustrates how the earth can be used at various temperature levels to store both excess heat captured during times of excess solar inputs as well as excess cool during winter months. This is done by exploiting the thermal gradient in the earth which increases 1-4 degrees per 100 m. Thus, the warmth is stored deeper, reinforcing or recovering that higher temperature, while the cool is stored at a shallow level maintaining cooler temperature.

10: An example of new concrete formulation with a much higher thermal resistance than standard concrete.

11: A plot of the energy usage per year and area of building versus the CO_2 intensity. This plot can serve as a graphical tool to demonstrate various paths toward reduced CO_2 emissions through different levels of efficiency and renewable energy implementation.

installations that can be implemented, as well as old systems that can be removed without major construction requirements, have a huge potential benefit in grey energy reductions and EOL considerations. The utilization of fabrics and other lightweight skin material are greatly expanding the possibilities in renovation and even new construction (see text by Sheila Kennedy, page 46).

There are many possibilities to design buildings with low grey energy materials and an EOL scenario wherein the building is completely recyclable. These range from new physical systems, like new foam materials and foldable components, to new design practices and concepts, such as designing rooms to evolve from one function to another, eliminating renovation or unnecessary demolition and new construction. Nevertheless, the main obstacle is not in finding the improved structural design possibilities themselves—they will evolve naturally—but rather to bring these considerations for grey energy/emissions and EOL into the mainstream.

Implementing low grey energy materials that are recyclable goes hand-in-hand with new low exergy building systems. The combination of these two philosophies opens us up to a fresh perspective in building design. Instead of emphasizing the construction of barriers between our buildings and the environment, creating separate spaces of artificial comfort with minimal influence from outside, we can generate an active system that maximizes the exploitation of natural forces and energy reservoirs. This system of a more active building will be in contrast to the current *Passivhaus* paradigm. It will open up the performance levels achieved by *Passivhaus* to a much wider range of design possibilities, while also increasing the sustainability of the construction itself. Sustainability will no longer form a constraint on the building design, but rather create a guide to new and greater possibilities.

The Desired Effect

There is a vast potential for these new active low exergy strategies, but along with their implementation there will need to be verification. New tools must be developed and analysis methods must be implemented and verified. The core component will be the development of new software tools. There are already many tools available that combine full three-dimensional CAD with material databases and energy analysis. These will help to provide building designers with real-time information on both the operational performance of potential designs, as well as the impacts of particular material selections and construction decisions.

There will also need to be ways to standardize the evaluation of the performance of buildings. In order to move toward a goal of zero emissions it is helpful to implement tools to illustrate that progress. One descriptive illustration is shown in Figure 11. By plotting the energy usage per year and per area building (kWh/a-m^2) on one axis, and the CO_2 intensity of the used energy (kg-CO_2/kWh) on the other, we can separately view two principle aspects of the path toward zero emissions; the first is efficiency, and the second is renewable energy.

Through efficiency measures and reductions in primary energy demand we reduce the energy used and move to the left. But these reductions can only bring us so far. There will always be some energy input required in the building. We can overcome this goal by increasing the use of renewable energy, either in the mix of the centralized electricity supply or by implementing decentralized power generation technologies like integrated photovoltaics or small scale wind. The plot illustrates the isolines of the building emissions per year and per area of building. These lines create targets that can be reached by implementing the two strategies. Tools like this can create a common platform and understanding, which can then be used to strive for zero emission buildings. They also provide a common basis for the evaluation of the success of LowEx building systems, and can include the energy and emissions due to the material inputs, and can provide a holistic view of the performance and energy inputs into the building operation and construction. Combining renewable energy with low exergy technology will facilitate CO_2 reductions, but to approach zero emissions from material life cycle and to avoid emissions from EOL influences will require more far reaching actions and more decisive decisions during the design phase.

Designs guided by the goals illustrated in the conceptual diagram above, along with the support of software tools, have the potential to instigate the required change in the building sector. They will create the framework for new practitioners and builders to implement the new technologies and concepts that have been explained in this text. Instead of focusing on the cost of individual upgrades and piecemeal changes to the way buildings are built, this new toolset will allow for a smooth shift to better conception, creation, and evaluation of building construction and renovation.

Thus, we will achieve buildings with our target of zero emissions. It will take major change, but as we've shown, there are many techniques and technologies that make that change possible. It is only a matter of bringing these new possibilities to the fore, and making them a part of standard practices. This shift will bring about the necessary reduction and elimination of the presently significant negative impacts that the building sector has on our environment and society. At the same time, the strategies provided here will lead to new and expanded possibilities for architecture and design. We do not seek to limit the way our built environment is created; rather we present new ways to let it grow freely with a set of flexible design principles. These maintain freedom of form, as demonstrated by the potentials inherent in lightweight construction, while mandating sustainable integration with the environment in material and EOL considerations, as well as in improved system operation facilitated by exergy analysis. It is with these principles and the guidance of experts from diverse fields that we can accomplish this clearly difficult, but evidently possible and realistic goal of eliminating CO_2 emissions from the building sector.

About the authors: Hansjürg Leibundgut is Professor at the Institute of Technology in Architecture at the Department of Architecture of ETH Zurich. He is partner with Amstein + Walthert AG. He has been a member of the Technical Competence Center of the Holcim Foundation for Sustainable Construction since 2006.

Forrest Meggers is a researcher in the Building Systems Group at the ETH Zurich under Prof. Dr. Hansjürg Leibundgut. Meggers has a BSE in Mechanical Engineering and a MSc In Environmental Engineering from the University of Iowa where he researched sustainable building design. He is also a LEED Accredited Professional and served on several committees for the USGBC. He is author of many papers on low exergy building systems. In fall 2011, he will take on the leadership role in a team of researchers to evaluate the potential of low exergy systems in hot and humid climates, as a part of the Future Cities collaboration at the Singapore-ETH Centre for Global Environmental Sustainability (SEC) in Singapore.

Conditioning the Desert

How to Create Usable Outdoor Public Space in Masdar City

TOBIAS WALLISSER / LAVA

During the time when the development of Dubai was at its height, our office (LAVA) was invited to participate in a competition to design the center of Masdar. Masdar is an ideal city to work on as a designer. With a masterplan by Foster + Partners, it was conceived as the first CO_2-emission-free city in the world. The competition brief asked for the design of a new iconic building to house a conference center, along with a five-star hotel, some housing, and a shopping area: the same ingredients that could be found in many masterplans under development in the UAE. The question for us was: How to make a tangible difference and push the qualities of the architecture beyond formal exuberance? Our answer was: by addressing and overcoming the distinct lack of public space. The Emirates don't have a long tradition of formal urban development and in regard to urban experience are quite disappointing for any Western traveler. Cities in the Emirates lack noteworthy public space, which, according to our Western notion of urbanism, is an essential element of a city.

Dubai is a prime example of an urban model without outdoor public spaces. Dubai began as a fishing village on a creek. It was then transformed in the 1960s by mainly English engineers according to the ideas of modernist urbanism of the time. They built highways, interchanges, and the first high-rise buildings—with late modernist façades that respond remarkably to the climate. Within 30 years, the modern city of Dubai was planned and erected. The most prominent urban elements are either inaccessibly lined up as objects along the central highway or projected out into the sea as artificial islands. The footprints of most of the high-rise buildings along the central highway, Sheik Zayed Road, are so narrow that parking garages are positioned at the back of the main street, facing the adjacent low-rise quarters. The only "public spaces" are huge multi-story shopping malls with adjacent ski slopes or integrated ice rinks. The outdoors only exists in wintertime—or on the finely manicured greens of golf courses along the creek, regulated by precise protocols.

Modern Abu Dhabi was built using a grid typology imported from US cities. The city blocks are narrow, forcing houses to protrude over the pedestrian walkways. While the typology is proven, the proportions were changed, and the streets are too wide in relation to the height of the buildings. Along the coastal road, called Corniche, a couple of pleasant green spaces can be found, which are frequented in the evenings and during the winter. While they are remote from shopping malls or other attractions, these spaces form a public promenade and offer urban quality, although without the contribution of any significant buildings or urban fabric.

The abundant supply of oil made it possible to import late modernist and postmodern Western architecture and embed it into a street network driven by infrastructural concerns and engineered efficiency without paying attention to public quality. The great leap both in pure size and speed of development made any comparison to the urban qualities found in older local developments impossible. Much has been said about the development of urban agglomerations without urban planning, but here, it truly reflects the socioeconomic reality of the place.

Abu Dhabi has started to tackle the issues and has created an urban planning council. A long-term development plan for the city until 2030 was formulated, including a framework for public transportation and guidelines and reviewing procedures for new developments. These moves toward a unified and organized approach were collected, summarized, and promoted in a publication called MASDAR CITY—*one day all cities will be built like this*, wherein it was summarized that: "Abu Dhabi's long-term goal is to create an economy which is not reliant on fossil fuels. As the economy diversifies, the city will change and to this end the government of the UAE has drafted a long-term urban vision for the emirate—the Abu Dhabi 2030 plan. The plan sets out the systematic, intelligent and organic growth of this burgeoning and diverse city."[1]

To us, the most interesting of these developments is the Masdar Initiative, an urban development project triggered by a 17-billion USD grant from the Abu Dhabi government. The vision for Masdar is described in MASDAR CITY as "a living city that will house around 1,500 clean tech companies with 40,000 residents and 50,000 commuters, and provide a research and test base for its technologies. It will be an exemplar of environmental best practice and a demonstration of what is possible. (...) Strategically located at the heart of Abu Dhabi's transport infrastructure, Masdar City will be linked to the center of Abu Dhabi and the international airport by a network of existing road, and new rail and public transport routes. The City will be car free and pedestrian friendly. With a maximum distance of 200 meters to public transport and amenities, and complemented by an innovative personal rapid transport system, the compact network of streets will encourage pedestrians and community social life."[2]

The Masdar project forms an urban exception in the Emirates as it is conceived as a fully functioning modern city that emulates the best of traditional Arab city designs and architecture, such as wind towers, narrow streets, shaded courtyards, and compact walled city design with modern amenities. Foster + Partners made reference to walled cities in Oman and Yemen in their masterplan. These cities feature a clear separation between the inside of the city and the outside, but also have a dense urban fabric with narrow streets. A dense urban development provides the potential to think about urban spaces in the way the Nolli Plan depicted and described Rome, where indoor and outdoor public spaces are seen as equal parts of an urban fabric. As urban planners, we saw the potential to apply this recognition as an organizing strategy for the development of the plaza.

Energy-efficient building design, renewable energy generation, recycled waste, and fossil-fuel free transport are all meant to ensure carbon neutrality. The environmental performance of Masdar City is one of the key design principles, but it is important to the creators that it also provides an enviable quality of life. Masdar could be described as the first attempt to create a CO_2-emission-free knowledge city whose inhabitants don't only work toward the transition of the UAE to a post-oil society, but also live it. Its inhabitants will be a mixture of Western and

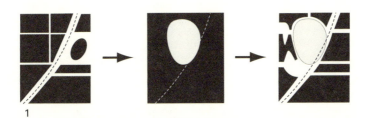

1

2

3

1: Masdar Plaza diagram, showing the switch from the original masterplan to the concept of the hollow center.
2: The Masdar City masterplan by Foster+Partners is inspired by walled cities in Oman and Yemen: It has a clear separation between the inner city and the its outskirts, as well as a dense urban fabric with narrow streets.
3: An iconic public space instead an iconic building as the new center of Masdar.

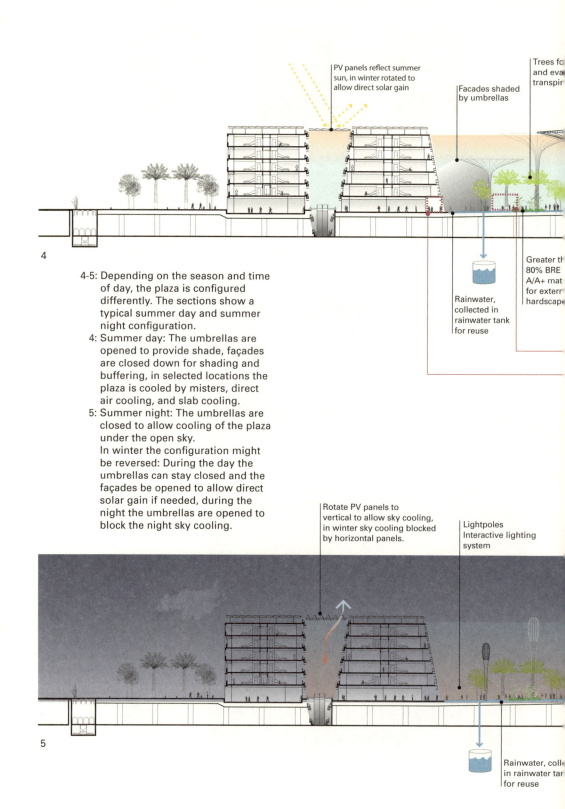

4-5: Depending on the season and time of day, the plaza is configured differently. The sections show a typical summer day and summer night configuration.

4: Summer day: The umbrellas are opened to provide shade, façades are closed down for shading and buffering, in selected locations the plaza is cooled by misters, direct air cooling, and slab cooling.

5: Summer night: The umbrellas are closed to allow cooling of the plaza under the open sky.
In winter the configuration might be reversed: During the day the umbrellas can stay closed and the façades be opened to allow direct solar gain if needed, during the night the umbrellas are opened to block the night sky cooling.

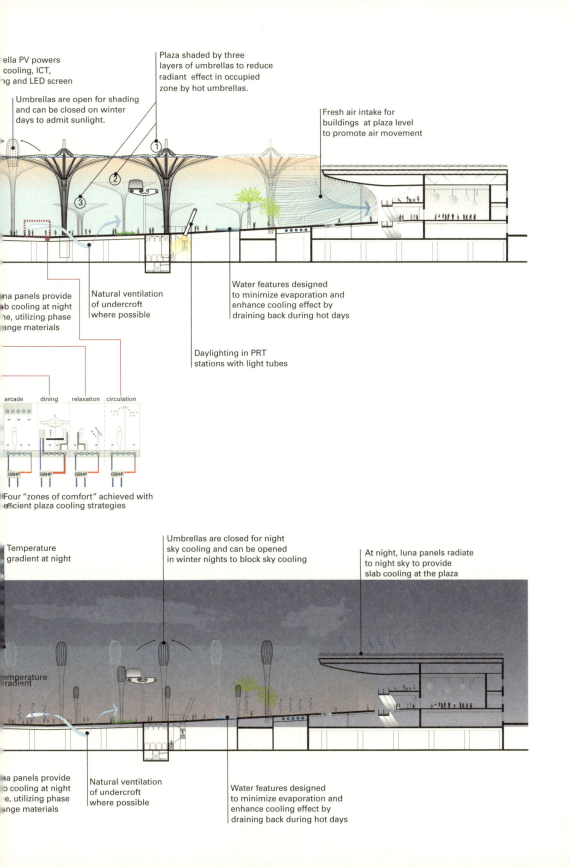

Eastern researchers and business people fusing their respective traditions into a new hybrid lifestyle centered on the vision of renewable energy.

At the end of 2008, after working on a couple of hotel projects in Abu Dhabi (all currently unbuilt), we had the chance to participate, as a young practice, in a field of 17 international architecture firms with excellent delivery records, in an invited competition for the Masdar Hotel and Conference Center (MHCC). The competition brief called for an iconic design for a hotel and a conference center facility located at the center of Masdar City. Masdar provided the possibility to actually experiment with public space, due to its dense urban environment with a clear boundary, an inside and an outside. Therefore we decided to design a public space as the heart of the city rather than just another iconic building trying to compete with numerous developments in the Emirates and the projected ADFEC (Abu Dhabi Future Energy Company) headquarters, designed by the American architecture firm Smith + Gill, located next to our site.

All great historical cities contain iconic urban spaces—Athens, Rome, Constantinople, Florence—and we recognized the desire on the part of the government to use Masdar to promote and build outstanding modern architecture throughout this city of the future. Yet, at the same time, imaginatively designed and actively utilized public open areas must complement this symbolic architecture. It is always the successful combination of those two elements that creates unforgettable urban developments.

We decided to integrate the Arab significance of the oasis with the Western notion of a civic forum. Our design is inspired by nature, with mankind at the middle of the development. The new center, which we like to call "The Plaza," is designed with the specific purpose of uniting people from different cultures and backgrounds. Our "Oasis of the Future" is a new type of civic center—generating and guiding human interaction through natural flow, by exercising control of ambient temperatures, the use of light, heat, and cooling, and the command of water, to name but a few elements.

In addition, we have incorporated the topographical features of the "wadi," the local word for a dry riverbed or valley, into the interiors of the hotel and conference facilities, and we also used fabrics to resonate with the Bedouin ancestry and history of the people and the city. Our vision for the Masdar Plaza is that it will become the "Oasis of the Future," meaning that it forms a link between bygone days and the modern era. It is a location with the explicit role as the communal epicenter of the world's most modern city, a magnet for social interaction and commerce.

Simultaneously, it must achieve global recognition and identification as a beacon promoting the dawn of a new age, one where ecology has precedence over waste.

All indoor qualities are echoed by a specific design of the adjacent outdoor spaces. Program from the building interiors bordering the square is extended to the outside, blurring the boundaries of inside and outside along the edge of the plaza as much as possible. We positioned areas for "slow" activities, characterized by their long duration, around the edges of the plaza, while leaving the central part as a transitory space. Despite the extensive size of the plaza (which is as big as St. Peter's square in Rome), the differentiation of activities and surface treatment will always relate to a human scale and to human activity. The plaza can be used for large-scale gatherings as well as for more private meetings. Being the true center of a city, this space will become the reference point for any visitor as well as the new landmark for the inhabitants. We intend for it to be a true icon, in the sense of a public achievement at the foundation of an urban society.

But even if we are able to implement a public space in the typological tradition of the European city with a central void surrounded by dense solid fabric, it is hard to create a public space that will be inhabited given the extreme local climate. Normally, in this context, Western architects have reacted by abandoning the creation of public space, and resorted to an "indoor city." However, there are alternatives, as we can see in other urban cultures from the same climate zone, which have a different urban history than the UAE. In Saudi Arabia, people have found ad-hoc solutions to tune the climate of outdoor environments used for public functions using evaporative cooling, spraying mist, or shallow water ponds to reduce the ambient temperature. The Western contemporary city also has a history of conditioning outdoor climates, mostly through heating rather than cooling, and this is usually not employed as a way to condition public urban space. For instance, outdoor conditioning is used in applications like the heating of the fields of football stadiums for extended seasonal play. For the production of public space in the contemporary Arab city, outdoor climate conditioning seems a totally appropriate strategy—given you can power it with regenerative energy and, in this case, adhere to the Masdar guidelines. Once you fulfill the Masdar requirement that all energy has to be produced locally, there should be no further limitation to the quality of life of Masdar inhabitants.

Social sustainability is measured by the activities occurring in public spaces. To make these activities possible, we need to fulfill the criteria of human comfort especially in hot climate zones. For Masdar Plaza this would only be possible between

6

7

6: During the day the umbrellas provide shade, reducing the solar heat gain at the plaza to less than 10%. In combination with active cooling powered by the energy gained from photovoltaic cells covering the upper surface of the umbrellas a comfortable temperature can be achieved.

7: At night-time all umbrellas will be closed to allow efficient cooling of the plaza from the sky.

October and April without actively climatizing the outdoor space. During the hot and humid summer months we need additional means for shading and cooling.

The climate concept developed by our engineers from Transsolar in Germany aims to limit the perceived temperature on the plaza to 32 °C—which Abu Dhabi residents consider a comfortable temperature, cool enough to spend time outside. Besides air temperature, the perceived temperature is influenced by humidity, the temperature of the surrounding surfaces, radiant heat, wind speed, and the clothing and activity of people. Thus the climate concept requires controlling the air temperature of the plaza as well as its humidity and the air exchange with other parts of the city.

The core philosophy behind our formal approach to architecture is the use, inspiration, and adaptation of natural principles in the built environment. Technology is not an end in itself. It must be made invisible and integrated into a comfortable and non-technical user experience. One example of how this has been integrated into Masdar Plaza is our "Sunflower Umbrella" concept.

The umbrellas cover a total area of 22,700 m^2, which is equivalent to 85 percent of the entire plaza's surface. There are a total of 54 umbrellas, in three sizes, that shade the plaza. The largest are 26 m tall and span 30 m in diameter. The others measure 20 m and 15 m in diameter and are 16 m and 10 m tall respectively. Their arrangement is inspired by the stratification of a rain forest, where smaller trees grow below the higher ones. Placing the smaller umbrellas along the edges of the plaza allows us to minimize the gap between building façade and umbrella and to adjust the scale in direct relation to the activities below. The umbrellas capture the sun's rays during the day, limiting the solar gain on the plaza to only ten percent of the level obtained without shading. To achieve this, they will be coated with a so-called "low-E" (low-emissivity) coating from below. At night, they fold up and release the heat retained during the day, and to complete the cycle they reopen again each day at dawn.

Probably the most unusual aspect of the concept is the active cooling of the plaza floor during the day. According to the zoning of different activities on the plaza, we identified areas with active conditioning and areas without. Cooling is done applying two different means. One is a floor cooling system using water chilled by ammoniac and the other is a soft conditioning system that releases cool air from the umbrella masts and from the arcades of the surrounding buildings. All energy necessary for the operation of both systems is produced by photovoltaic cells that cover 20 percent of the umbrellas. During the year, there is even more energy produced than what is required for cooling. This makes the plaza comparable in terms of energy generation to regular buildings of the Masdar masterplan. In other words, a comfortable outdoor climate can be achieved without borrowing energy from the adjacent buildings, limiting their efficiency. At night, Masdar Plaza will be lit by hundreds of light posts, which trace the movement of passers-by. The light posts can also be activated directly using mobile phones. It will become an interactive light installation, allowing for direct interaction between the inhabitants of Masdar and the transmission of information from Masdar to the world.

Masdar Plaza could therefore be more than merely a technological breakthrough by making the conditioning of public space a feature of Masdar urban development; it could also have an impact on society in the Emirates and the way local and Western people interact with each other and within an urban space of a modern city. More importantly, it could become a blueprint for the integration of public space and urban development in hot climates around the world.

What we do in Masdar isn't as "out of the blue" as it may seem at first. In fact, it references an old tradition in manipulating local climate that was introduced by palm house architecture in Europe during the 18th century. The palm house quickly became a generally accepted typology of an interior space heated by passive solar gain. Later this was used for the overwintering of exotic plants, but increasingly became a public space within which people could gather and socialize. In the same way, the climate-conditioned plaza of Masdar could establish a new typology for exterior space, in this case cooled with solar energy, a typology which could be sensibly implemented in climate zones where it is too hot during summer months to comfortably spend time outdoors. Masdar Plaza is like a palm house *without the house* that essentially allows people to "oversummer" in otherwise unbearable tropical heat and participate in the public realm of civic society.

1.) See MASDAR CITY—*one day all cities will be built like this*, publication by Masdar 2009.
2.) Ibid.

About the author: After studying architecture in Berlin, Stuttgart, and New York, Tobias Wallisser worked for 10 years as Associate Architect at UNStudio in Amsterdam, where he was responsible for the Mercedes-Benz Museum. In 2007, he co-founded LAVA, an architecture think-tank with offices in Stuttgart and Sydney, along with Chris Bosse and Alexander Rieck. Since 2006, Tobias Wallisser has taught Digital Design at the State Academy of Fine Arts Stuttgart.

An Illustrated Index of Re-inventing Construction

Compiled and drawn by Something Fantastic
Texts written by Jessica Bridger
with additional contributions by Mei Li, Forrest Meggers, and Udo Thönnissen

A-Frame Cabin: The A-frame cabin was a consumer product in the United States and Canada, gaining popularity in the 1960s as post-war consumer culture grew hungry for vacation homes. The A-frame structure, with two steeply angled roof sections that begin near the foundation, was part of a modular home kit developed by Lindal Cedar Homes. This modular A-frame was designed as a kit home, with all of its pieces delivered to the home site pre-cut, ready for easy assembly. S.W. Lindal developed the A-frame cabin after seeing modular housing solutions in use in WWII during his time in the Canadian Army. The choice of the A-frame style of construction is material and energy efficient. (→ *drawing 1; image 14, p. 97*)

In contrast to → *passive daylighting*, active daylighting collects and concentrates sunlight with the help of mechanical devices to increase efficiency and input. Most devices for active daylighting track the sun with mirrors and reflect sunlight into building apertures throughout the daylight hours. Active daylighting can be used for specific purposes, such as for indoor agriculture, in vertical farming, or more holistically, to reduce energy consumption by mechanical lighting in buildings. It is increasingly used in public spaces, such as underground shopping areas or railway stations, such as Berlin's Potsdamer Platz station. Complex new active daylighting systems in development use optical fibers to lead light around corners or over larger distances. Devices like the → *solar tracking skylight* are available on the consumer market for active daylighting. (→ *image 4, p. 96*)

Adobe Architecture: Adobe is one of the oldest architectural building techniques and materials. Adobe can be used in different ways and construction methods, enabling a certain flexibility and ease in building. Adobe is made from sand, clay, and water, mixed with one of many organic materials, such as straw (this specific mix is known as cob), sticks, or livestock manure. In typical adobe construction the materials are locally sourced, making the composition of the adobe regional in recipe. It can be formed into bricks and then sun-dried, known as → *mudbrick*, or it is used as a liquid mix, which is then attached to structures made from wood or mats of woven leaves, which is called → *wattle and daub*.

Common in arid and desert climates, adobe has excellent heat shielding and cooling potential for interior spaces. Due to a high → *thermal mass*, adobe is excellent at regulating interior temperatures in hot environments. Solar gain and ambient heat are absorbed into exterior surfaces, preventing any penetration of heat into interior spaces. Any heat absorbed during the day is then radiated, from the adobe exterior, back into the cooler exterior air at night.

Present in → *vernacular architecture* dating back centuries, adobe is regionally common in certain climates. In contemporary research into construction materials, adobe is of particular interest, especially in

1: Typical A-frame cabin

Active Daylighting: Active daylighting is the use of natural daylight for lighting in diverse applications.

1: **Air Purification and Oxygenation with Plants**; Mother-in-law's tongue.

2: **Adobe**; The ancient city of Bam in Iran is the biggest structure entirely built from adobe.

3: **Adobe**; House near Phuthaditjhaba. Qwa Qwa. Photographed in 1989 by David Goldblatt.

4: **Active Daylighting**; Lightpipes at Potsdamer Platz undergound train station.

5: **Adobe**; The baya bird's cob nest benefits from adobe's high thermal mass.

6: **Adobe**; Minimalist adobe building by Rael San Fratello Architects in Marfa, Texas.

7: **Adobe**; This building in Marfa is made from sundried adobe bricks.

8: **Air Forest**; This inflatable architecture by Mass Studies located in Denver, Colorado is illuminated at night.

9: **Aramid Fibers**; Characteristic honey-like color.

10: **Adobe**; High adobe tower houses can be found in the city of Sanaa in Yemen.

11: **Air Well**; Ancient water harvesting structure utilizing condensation, Trans-en-Provence, France.

14: **A-Frame**; Often used for holiday homes.

12: **Allotments**; Where everyone is his own architect.

13: **Arboform**; Composite material made from wood.

Air as Construction Material · Albedo Effect

response to the demand for sustainable building materials and environmentally neutral or positive architectures. Adobe has qualities similar to ➤ *rammed earth* in applications involving passive heating and cooling. Innovation in adobe composition, structural reinforcement to achieve higher maximum heights, and the modernization of the esthetics of vernacular practices are some areas of current interest and research. ➤ *Super Adobe*, for example, reinforces normal adobe using two humble, inexpensive, and plentiful materials: barbed wire and industrial/military grade sandbags. ➤ *Haus Westend Gruen* is a contemporary architectural project in Berlin, Germany, that modernizes the esthetics of adobe architecture.
(➤ *images 2-3, 5-7 p. 96; image 10, p. 97*)

Air as Construction Material: Air that is kept under a pressure different from that of our atmosphere can be used either as lightweight structural mass under compressive stress, like in an air mattress or an inflatable video screen (at higher pressure), or function as a glue, to keep things together, like in a vacuum pack (at a lower pressure). Pneumatic structures are easy and fast to inflate, they can be transported easily, and are generally lightweight. To achieve a specific pressure, air is usually separated from the surrounding atmosphere by flexible membranes which also define the properties and limits of the structural element that is produced. Membranes differ in flexibility and opacity, thickness and strength. ➤ *Tensairity*, a combination of an air-filled membrane under compressive stress and wires under tensile stress, can hold heavy weights and is used, for example, for bridges. An example of air used as a glue that keeps building parts together is ➤ *Station Z* in Sachsenhausen, developed by Werner Sobek Engineers.

Air Forest: The Air Forest is part of Mass Studies' experimentation with ➤ *air as construction material*. It is a temporary inflatable pavilion built on the occasion of the National Democratic Convention in Denver, Colorado in 2008. Parallel to the convention, an event entitled Dialog:City invited 10 architects and artists to create site-specific projects in Denver. Mass Studies was asked to create a structure for an open public space intended for the convention and related events. The structure they designed and erected is 56 m by 25 m long and 4 m high. The structure is hexagonal, with each column connected to a group of five others into a single module, which were then combined into a large structure. It was inflated by 14 motor-powered air pumps, which were located in the bases of the columns. The columns were lit during the evening. The construction of a temporary structure overhead of the visitors to the convention and the general public effectively created the notion of a space below, for casual public use and event staging.
(➤ *image 8, p. 97*)

Air Purification and Oxygenation with Plants: The use of indoor plants to purify air and provide oxygen is often overlooked in favor of more technologically advanced methods. NASA, the National Air and Space Association of the United States, recently studied the use of common houseplants to purify and oxygenate air in residential and commercial buildings. For a home of 2000 square feet (185 m^2) fifteen plants were recommended to achieve suitable results. The top plants recommended are: 1. *Philodendron scandens 'oxycardium'*, heartleaf philodendron; 2. *Philodendron domesticum*, elephant ear philodendron; 3. *Dracaena fragrans 'Massangeana'*, cornstalk dracaena; 4. *Hedera helix*, English ivy; 5. Chlorophytum comosum, spider plant; 6. *Dracaena deremensis* 'Janet Craig', Janet Craig dracaena; 7. *Dracaena deremensis* 'Warneckii', Warneck dracaena; 8. Ficus benjamina, weeping fig; 9. *Epipiremnum aureum*, golden pothos; 10. *Spathiphyllum 'Mauna Loa'*, peace lily; 11. *Philodendron selloum*, selloum philodendron; 12. *Aglaonema modestum*, Chinese evergreen; 13. *Chamaedorea sefritzii*, bamboo or reed palm; 14. *Sansevieria trifasciata*, snake plant; 15. *Dracaena marginata*, red-edged dracaena. Projects like Kamal Meattle's Paharpur Business Centre use this simple plant-based strategy to great effect.
(➤ *drawing 2; image 1, p. 96*)

2: Three air-purifying plants according to Kamal Meattle: Areca Palm, Mother-in-law's Tongue and Money plant.

Air Well: An air well collects water by promoting the condensation of moisture from the air. Evidence of air wells has been found in the Byzantine city of Theodosia, and there are three methods that have been used to create the condensation necessary for the production of useful quantities of water. High mass collectors are air wells that use the benefit of constructions with a ➤ *thermal mass* to create temperature variation suitable for the production of condensation. High mass wells are the oldest and simplest form of air wells. Radiative air wells use panels heated by sunlight to create condensation, and active collection air wells use ➤ *heat pumps* to remove moisture actively from air, similar to the way a dehumidifier functions. Active collection wells are energy intensive, however there is ongoing research into creating more efficient active air wells to harvest water from the air.
(➤ *image 11, p. 97*)

Albedo Effect: The albedo is the measure of how much light a surface reflects. In climatology, the albedo effect is used to express the extent to which light from the sun is reflected or absorbed from the surface of the earth. Absorption means that short-waved light radiation is turned into long-waved heat radiation, which warms the surrounding air. Reflected light can easily pass through the earth's atmosphere back into space, in contrast to reflected or radiated heat which can only pass through the atmosphere in small amounts, leaving the rest of the reflected heat inside of the earth's atmosphere. Reflected light is therefore preferable to reflected heat. White or light roofs, also known as ➔ *cool roofs*, reflect light, while dark roofs absorb light and radiate heat, making them larger contributors to atmospheric warming.

to gardening. Most prevalent in Europe, allotments date as far back as the early 18th century in Denmark and England and are growing in popularity in countries such as the Philippines. Allotments can be run by public or private entities and serve as a social and environmental benefit to city-dwellers with limited access to green space and a means of food production. (➔ *image 12, p. 97*)

Aquaponics: Aquaponics is the symbiotic process of cultivating plants and animals in a closed and recirculating environment. The integrated system combines the principles of ➔ *hydroponics*, a method of growing plants without soil in nutrient-rich water, and aquaculture, the farming of aquatic organisms such as fish, crustaceans, and mollusks. Aquaponic setups, which can range from small home units to large commercial enterprises, utilize the waste of one biological system (i.e. fish) as nutrients for another system (i.e. plants) to create a diverse polyculture. Raising fish in a closed tank will result in an accumulation of fish effluent that is full of nutrients but toxic to the actual fish. Aquaponic systems use pipes or pumps to direct the liquid fertilizer towards the roots of growing plants, which absorb the necessary nutrients, and then recirculate the cleansed water back to the fish tanks. With the benefits of water conservation, organic fertilizer, simultaneous plant and animal cultivation, and minimized spatial requirements, aquaponics has become a model for local and sustainable food production. (➔ *drawing 3*)

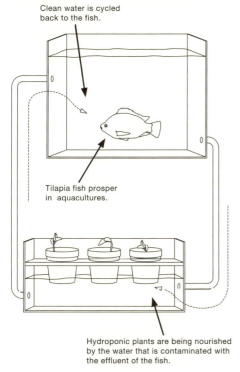

3: Aquaponics can solve the main problem of aquacultures: bad water quality.

Algae as Biofuel: Microalgae are contenders for a new biofuel-based source of energy. Although it is currently expensive in comparison to other biofuels, the energy generation potential of algae is significant. Microalgae grow much faster than land plants, can be cultivated in or even used for the cleaning of wastewater, and do not compete for land otherwise used for agricultural production. Algal biofuel is considered CO_2-neutral because any CO_2 emitted in combustion is counterbalanced by the algae's consumption of CO_2 during photosynthesis. Fuels from algae are seen as some of the most efficient second-generation biofuels.

Allotments: Allotment gardening is a specific form of ➔ *urban agriculture* where small plots of land are distributed for cultivation by individuals and families. Allotments differ from community gardens in that land parcels are divided and assigned to specific people rather than tended by a larger collective. Gardeners typically pay a small fee for the sole use of allotment land, which is usually between fifty and four hundred square meters and must be dedicated

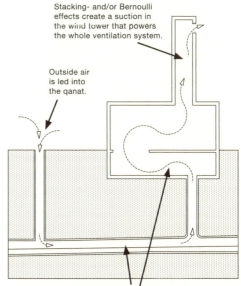

4: The Arabic cooling system consists of multiple, interconnected elements.

Arab Indoor Cooling System: The Arabic cooling system was developed more than 1000 years ago and relies on several basic physical principles like the ➤ *Bernoulli effect,* ➤ *evaporative cooling,* and ➤ *thermal updraft.* It consists of different elements that can be used singularly but work best in conjunction: a ➤ *windcatcher* tower works as a ➤ *passive ventilation* device to create a stable flow of air through the building. Air from the air catcher can also be first led through an underground channel, a ➤ *qanat,* to cool the temperature of the air, then to the ➤ *shabestan,* an underground gathering space for the use of people during hot times of the day, or the air can be channeled through a ➤ *yakchal,* which is an insulated non-mechanical refrigerator, and then through the rest of the building. This combination of elements makes passive cooling possible, even in extremely hot climates. (➤ *drawing 4*)

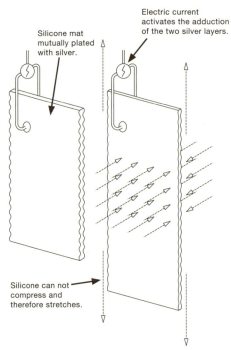

5: Diagram illustrating functional principal of an actuator.

Aramid Fibers: Aramid fibers are strong, heat-resistant fibers often used in military and aerospace applications as well as for the production of commercial products. Short for 'aromatic polyamides,' aramid fibers feature chain molecules highly oriented along the fiber axis, which allows for the formation of many interchain bonds resulting in fibers with high tensile strength. Aramid fibers were developed in the 1960s and are ideal for flame-resistant clothing and helmets due to their low flammability and lack of melting point, with degradation starting at 500°C. The excellent strength-to-weight ratio of the abrasion-resistant fibers led to their use in body armors and combat helmets. Aramids can also be used to produce items such as bicycle tires, fiber-optic cables, tennis strings, and hockey sticks. (➤ *image 9, p. 97*)

Arboform: Arboform is a biopolymer derived primarily from wood. It is made out of lignin, an abundant substance in the secondary cell walls of plant cells where it mediates mechanical strength. Lignin can be extracted and has varied material uses. Arboform, developed by the German company Tecnaro, can be injection molded just like plastic. Arboform can also be burned, making it possible to produce durable injection-molded products that are fully disposable. Arboform can also decompose passively over long periods, unlike petroleum-based plastics. Arboform is a promising new ➤ *bioplastic,* usable in a multiplicity of applications, from large-scale construction to the production of children's toys. It is nontoxic, and can be made from waste derived from paper production, wood, or plant matter. (➤ *image 13, p. 97*)

Arcology: The underlying principle of an arcology is to blend architecture and ecology to create utopian or dystopian communities, frequently housed in hyperstructures. These hyperstructures are usually designed to be self-sufficient, have a high population density and a variety of community or interest-group based organizational principles. Though the arcology is more a theoretical construct than a realizable typology, the architect Paulo Soleri has been constructing Arcosanti since 1970, an experimental community in Arizona based on the construction of an arcology as a mixture of ecology and architecture. Common in science fiction and experimental architecture, the arcology has inspired many people, from J.G. Ballard to Archigram, with their Walking City project. A contemporary example is Stéphane Malka's Auto-Defense project, a proposal for a modular megacity inhabiting larger structures parasitically as a means of guerilla city creation. (➤ *image 15, p. 102*)

Artificial Muscle from Electroactive Polymers: Artificial muscles can transform electric energy into kinetic energy using the principle of actuators. They could replace electric motors in applications from the zoom in a camera objective to landing flaps in airplanes. Artificial muscles are very efficient as they can not only create circular movement like an electric motor, but, like natural muscles, can directly carry out traction. They are very strong and are able to undergo large deformation even under considerable force. There are different modes of operation, but they all have in common the use of electroactive polymers. One system consists of a silicone skin that is covered on both sides with silver. When exposed to an electric current, the silver layers press the silicone together and make it expand. When released, the silicone shrinks back into its original shape. Artificial muscles are being investigated by researchers from all fields of engineering and architecture. (➤ *drawing 5*)

Augmented Reality: Augmented reality is a concept and range of technological strategies that allow an enhanced understanding of and interaction with one's environment. There is a growing use of technological devices with cameras and GPS systems to add additional layers of information to the world we perceive visually, even in seemingly mundane situations. Early commercial examples include programs like "Berlin Fahrinfo," which has a function which allows the i-Phone to allow visual tags to appear overlaid over a real-time image from the phone's camera function on the screen of the iPhone, identifying dynamically the user's location relative to nearby transit stops, and "Foursquare," which maps the placement of people in an open social network, in real time, in cities across the world. Keiichi Matsuda's short film *Augmented (hyper)Reality* imagines a not-so-distant future of reality both augmented and overlaid with layers of information and advertising. The Montreal project *Quartier des Spectacles* used augmented reality in the form of projected lights to create wayfinding elements in addition to decorative enhancements.

Autoprogettazione: Autoprogettazione is the name of a collection of DIY furniture designs by Enzo Mari, first published in 1974. Alongside images of 19 pieces of furniture it is a detailed manual helping amateurs and home users to construct the designs pictured. Autoprogettazione, which is Italian for "self design," is a term coined by Italian designer Enzo Mari. The wooden furniture pieces are all composed of standard lumber, cut to specific lengths and assembled with the help of minimal tools. Mari's idea was grounded in criticism of the increasing industrialization of furniture design, manufacturing, and by extension, common taste, and with Autoprogettazione Mari sought to give people a sense of craftsmanship by encouraging them to produce their own product based on the manual, customize it, and send images of their pieces back to him. Autoprogettazione furniture is still built and developed today by amateurs, and there even are ➡ *manuals* online of Autoprogettazione designs made from Ikea elements. (➡ *drawing 6, image 22, p. 102*)

AVATAR: The Advanced Virtual and Technological Architecture Research Laboratory (AVATAR) is a research group and collective located at the Bartlett School of Architecture at University College London. AVATAR's primary focus is the impact of advanced technologies such as virtuality, new media, nanotechnology, protocells and cybernetics on architecture as well as interior, graphics, and multimedia design. The Lab offers a Master's degree in architecture and also serves as an international center for collaboration in the field.

Bamboo Architecture: Architect Simón Vélez builds structures primarily made of bamboo. His architecture utilizes the unique material properties and ready availability of bamboo in most environments. Bamboo is almost as strong as steel yet is only a fraction of the weight, and is a renewable and recyclable material. Used as a building material for centuries, it has maintained a relatively ➡ *vernacular* or decorative use until recently. The work of Simón Vélez has helped bring bamboo into the realm of sustainable building materials and new processes of construction. His projects engage bamboo materially and structurally, and Vélez has developed specialized building techniques, including customized fasteners, joints, and connectors for his unique architecture. Similar to the use of bamboo for both the ➡ *bamboo bike* and ➡ *bamboo scaffolding*, bamboo architecture exploits the fastest growing plant in the world as one of the best sustainable building materials. (➡ *drawing 7; image 18, p. 102; images 26-27, p. 103*)

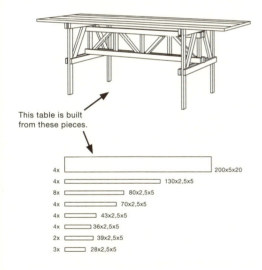

6: A table from Enzo Mari's Autoprogettazione series and the necessary pieces.

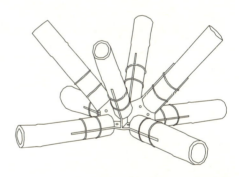

7: Custom bamboo joint system developed by Simón Vélez.

Bamboo Bike Project: The Bamboo Bike Project by the Earth Institute at Columbia University examines the feasibility of using bamboo, an inexpensive material, to build bikes as a means of transport in economically disadvantaged contexts in Africa. The use of bamboo in these situations is ideal because it is easy and fast to grow, lightweight, and cheaper than steel or carbon fiber. Bamboo bikes can be made locally, and their production is potentially a source of local employment. Transportation by bike is cheaper, more environmentally conscious, and more flexible than by motor vehicle. Bamboo bikes are not only a promising form of transportation for individuals, as they can also be built and used to move cargo and/or multiple passengers. The Bamboo Bike Project is investigating all of these propositions and is involved in designing the bike itself as well as the development systems for the growth of the raw materials, bike production and maintenance. Because of the ease of production, the bike is expected to evolve, with designs being customized for different terrains and uses and using different raw materials for the construc-

15: **Arcology**; Archigram's walking city from 1964.

16: **Bioluminescent Lighting**; Lightning bug.

17: **Bamboo Bike Project**; Making affordable bikes from local materials.

18: **Bamboo Architecture**; Simón Vélez' church without religious affiliation in Cartagena, Colombia.

19: **Bamboo Bike Project**; Development aid by engineers.

20: **Bamboo Scaffolding**; Commonly seen in Hong Kong.

21: **Baugruppe**; A meeting of a Berlin housing cooperative in 1900.

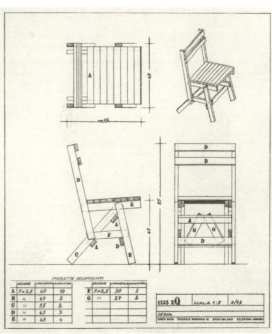
22: **Autoprogettazione**; Enzo Mari's plans explain how to build his furniture designs from common wood pieces.

23: **Beefalo**; The mind of a cow in a buffalo's body.

24: **Bamboo Rebar**; In use in Thailand.

25: **Beehaus**; A simple method of urban beekeeping.

26: **Bamboo Architecture**; A bamboo building by Simón Vélez in the making.

27: **Bamboo Architecture**; Interior of church by Simón Vélez.

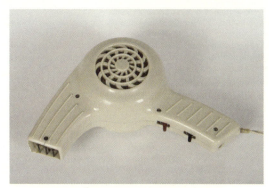
28: **Bioplastics**; Bakelite was replaced by oil-based plastics in the 60s.

tion of the bikes. (→ *images 17,19, p. 102*)

Bamboo Rebar: Bamboo rebar is a promising alternative to metal rebar. Readily available in many locations, bamboo is relatively inexpensive, and does not corrode or rust, which can cause the failure of concrete structures made with standard steel rebar. There is much current interest in the use of bamboo as rebar, although it has been a part of many → *vernacular* building traditions that predate concrete and steel construction. → *Adobe* reinforced with bamboo rods might be a viable building material strategy of the future since it has renewable and energy efficient properties. (→ *image 24, p. 103*)

Bamboo Scaffolding: Bamboo scaffolding is an alternative form of scaffolding for construction projects. Bamboo scaffold is less expensive than the common steel scaffold and can be produced locally in many contexts, therefore reducing the transportation costs typically associated with scaffolding. Bamboo scaffold is as strong as steel scaffold and much more lightweight. It is more flexible and easily customizable by virtue of its organic nature. It can be cut, bent and manipulated onsite to suit even the most complex architectural features and conditions for construction. Different varieties of bamboo have differing structural characteristics, from inherent strength and flexibility to overall length and diameter. The scaffolding can be built from a range of bamboo varieties to suit the specific needs of each scaffold project. The technique of building scaffolding from bamboo originates in China and is one of the few historic building techniques still used there today. The construction of bamboo scaffold is highly individual to workers and teams as the techniques are variable, unlike the modular construction of steel scaffold from a generic set of parts. Commonly, the technique for bamboo scaffolding is passed down through families or from worker to worker by apprenticeship. The techniques are fundamentally unchanged from those of centuries past. Bamboo, akin to regular steel scaffold, can be recycled from project to project, and additionally the bamboo can be repurposed or disposed of sustainably. (→ *image 20, p. 102*)

Barra System: The Barra system is a system for indoor climate control that uses elements of a → *passive solar building design* developed by Italian engineer Horazio Barra. The Barra system relies on → *thermal mass* and a collector wall, similar to a → *trombe wall*, which can collect and store thermal energy from the sun as heat. This stored heat can then be distributed through a building via channels incorporated into walls and floors which use passive ventilation as a result of the thermosiphon effect, wherein warm air naturally rises, and cold air naturally falls. The Barra system has more consistent indoor conditions from north to south than other passive solar houses because of the distribution of heat using → *passive ventilation*. Cold air, from nighttime temperature swings or from natural wind conditions, can also be drawn through the Barra system.

Baugruppe: A *Baugruppe* is a special kind of housing cooperative that originates in Germany. A *Baugruppe* is made up of individuals and families that pool together resources to fund a new building project, commonly for residential use. Commonly these projects are organized by the group itself, an architect or another entity as an alternative to the traditional model of developer-created building projects. A *Baugruppe* can have social aims, or simply be an organization of people looking for greater control over the construction, organization, and eventual administration of their living environment. (→ *image 21, p. 102*)

Beefalo: Beefalo are fertile hybrid cattle and buffalo crosses. The beefalo combines the best aspects of beef cattle and buffalo. Buffalo meat is lower both in fat and cholesterol than beef. Buffalo are efficient grazers but lack the placid disposition of beef cattle. The beefalo has meat much like the buffalo and the pleasant nature of cattle. Raised first in the southern USA, the beefalo has become increasingly popular worldwide as an alternative to beef cattle or buffalo farming. (→ *image 23, p. 103*)

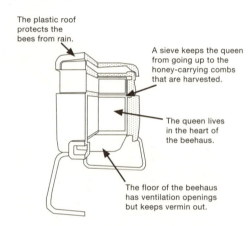

8: The Beehaus is a compact, simple way to keep bees.

Beehaus: Beehaus is a beehive especially designed for keeping bees in gardens or on rooftops. It provides bees with a safe home and makes beekeeping straightforward and fun. In this regard it opens up ways to practice agricultural techniques in urban areas and use the capacities of the city in a new way. Bees can fly up to 2 km high, so they can be kept on rooftops and can fly in and out the beehive undisturbed. Modern bees need more space than they did in the past because queens have been bred to be more prolific egg layers. The Beehaus uses deep beekeeping frames, which allow the whole colony to live in a single brood box. This simplifies the inspection of the bees and is less disruptive compared to a double brood box system, making the bees calmer and easier to work with for the beekeeper. The Beehaus has triple-pocket insulation to help keep the bees warm in the winter and cool in the summer, making beekeeping feasible in a range of climates. A bee colony held on a city rooftop can produce up to 100 kg of honey a year. Urban beekeeping is being promoted as one of the facets of the growing → *urban agriculture* movement. (→ *drawing 8, image 25, p. 103*)

Bernoulli Effect: The Bernoulli Effect, also known as Bernoulli's principle, describes the relationship between the flow speed and pressure of a fluid; most notably, an increase in speed occurs with a decrease in pressure. Published in 1738 by Dutch-Swiss mathematician Daniel Bernoulli, the principle can be applied to both hydrodynamic systems (i.e. fluids move faster through a constricted pipe) and aerodynamic systems (i.e. air pressure helps an airplane achieve lift). In architecture, the Bernoulli Effect is the basis of many ventilation systems, especially ➔ *passive ventilation* systems that utilize no mechanical energy. Designers often employ Bernoulli's principle for ➔ *passive cooling* and ➔ *passive ventilation* to generate suction or control speed of air flow with windcatchers and deliberately sized windows and openings. (➔ *drawing 9*)

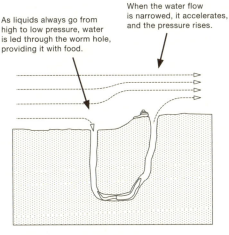

9: The Bernoulli effect is used, among others, by the rock worm to ventilate its marine dwellings.

Big Dig: The Big Dig was a project in Boston, Massachusetts, that rerouted 2.4 km of a six-lane elevated highway below grade, along with other large road and infrastructure projects. The Big Dig was intended to reconnect Boston's inner and waterside districts, by removing the Central Artery section of Interstate 93, and to alleviate significant shortcomings in the ability of the Central Artery to handle modern traffic volumes. The highway was built in 1960 to handle a daily load of 75,000 cars, a number that by the mid-1990s had swelled to 180,000. The project was conceived of in the 1970s, planning begun in the 1980s, and construction was completed in 2008. Depressing a large highway below street grade in a construction site as complex as a varied urban fabric led to multiple problems, and multiple innovative engineering solutions. Similar projects have been begun in other urban environments, as city and land use change with demographic shifts and industry changes combine with environmental and social concerns.

Bioluminescent Lighting: Rachel Armstrong, a researcher from University College London, is investigating the use of light derived from biological sources. Inspired by the symbiotic relationship between luminescent fish, like angelfish, and the bacteria that enable them to glow, research is being conducted into the potential application of similar bacteria in architectural or material contexts. Potential is seen in the investigation of altering bioluminescent bacteria to emit enough light to be useful in urban or other environments, as a possible source of energy-efficient lighting. Armstrong is also involved in research into carbon-absorbing surfaces and other projects involving nanoarchitecture. (➔ *image 16, p. 102*)

Bionic Engineering: Bionic engineering is the practice of deriving engineering concepts and principles from the biological world. These concepts and principles are extracted from their context and application in the natural world and translated for use in man-made applications. Examples include the ➔ *Bernoulli effect*, which mimics the structure of termite hills for air circulation and ventilation, and the structure of the honeycomb, which maximizes stability with minimal material, frequently borrowed for many ➔ *honeycomb-shaped structures*.

Bioplastics: Bioplastics are materials that behave similarly to petroleum-derived plastics yet are made from a variety of alternative organic polymers. Bioplastics were an area of research prior to the rise in use of petroplastics, and are a current subject of research and design due to the rising cost of petroleum and the growing awareness of the environmental consequences of oil-based products. Petroplastic is problematic in the short term because of carbon and chemical emissions issues, and over the long term due to the consequences of using materials that do not degrade or decay, and the slow leaching of toxic chemicals from some plastics. Pre-oil bioplastics include materials like vulcanized rubber, a material made from natural rubber, usually treated with sulfur to harden and stiffen it. Vulcanized rubber is still used today for example for bowling balls and other applications. An early generation of cellulose-based plastics was developed in the mid-19th century, though this was largely abandoned with the rise of oil-derived polymer plastics. Currently, research is focused on finding polymers for the production of new plastics with materials including cellulose, starch and sugars, along with microorganisms and biologically derived oils as source materials. Bioplastic is being explored as a replacement for petroplastic in both permanent and short-term applications. Bioplastics are currently used in many single use and disposable container applications, especially for food packaging. As many bioplastics can degrade through a variety of means (sunlight, decomposition by microorganisms, dissolution) they are a significant improvement on petroplastics environmentally. The biggest barriers to efficient and widespread entry into the material market for the new plastics are cost, application and production. Some bioplastics can be produced on standard petroplastic production lines with no or minimal modification, reducing the total cost of production significantly. An example of a new bioplastic with a promising future is ➔ *corn-based plastic*. (➔ *image 28, p. 103*)

Bioremediation: Bioremediation is the use of bacteria, fungi, plants or animals to remove contaminants from the air, soil or water. Bioremediation can happen *in situ*, or onsite where the contamination occurred, or *ex situ*, when the contaminated material is removed for remediation in a different location. Bioremediation with bacteria and microbes is common in situations where petrochemicals and other chemical contaminants are present, while bioremediation with plants, also known as ➤ *phytoremediation*, is used for the extraction of heavy metals, pesticides, and other contaminants. Bioremediation is used in ➤ *living machines* to remediate water.

Bloom Energy Server: The Bloom Energy Server, also known as the Bloom Box, is a device that converts liquid or gaseous hydrocarbons, such as gasoline or propane, to generate electricity in the location in which it will be used. The solid oxide fuel cell (SOFC) uses an electrochemical conversion process to produce electricity directly from oxidizing a fuel. SOFCs can operate in varying scales with differing amounts of energy output and are considered highly efficient and relatively inexpensive. They can be flexible in fuel usage, stable over the long term, and are advantageous in their silent functioning and low emissions. Bloom Boxes have the potential to shift energy production and power consumption from the conventional model in that power can be produced and consumed on the spot rather than delivered from a centralized location. Future production of home-sized units would allow for a more decentralized and flexible energy system for buildings and cities. (➤ *image 38, p. 109*)

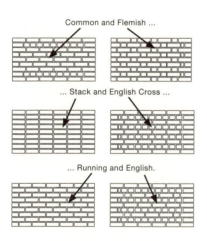

10: Different regions have their own traditional brick bond patterns.

Board House: This project by architect Elke Reichel, in Marienberg, Germany, is a contemporary reinterpretation of the log house. ➤ *Log houses* are simply built wooden structures made from relatively untreated or milled logs. The board house is made from ➤ *upcycled* and recycled boards. Similar to a log house, the wooden façade is also both structure and shell. Using trash wood, the house is a sustainable approach to architectural production and because the wood is sourced from multiple prior uses, it has a heterogenic appearance, which gives the façade a unique striated look. The boards are set in alignment on the interior of the house, and have a rippled profile on the exterior, again as a result of the dimension of each board being slightly different. The corners are joined in a method borrowed from more traditional log houses. This kind of construction is similar to ➤ *wa pan*, where materials are recycled from building to building. (➤ *image 34-35, p. 108*)

Brick: Bricks are one of the most basic construction materials. As one of the first materials produced directly for construction, bricks have been around in some form or other for centuries. The commercial red-brown brick that is common worldwide is made in an energy-intensive process, however bricks are economical and easy to build with. Bricks have been an area of interest and experimentation for many years, partly because of their ubiquity in the construction industry. Solar power production of brick is one avenue of production under exploration, while Eladio Dieste's structures inspire us with his use of brick as a graceful and light construction material. Though commonly used in specific patterns, such as herringbone or running bond, brick was also used in projects like Peter Behrens' Hoechst AG Headquarters building in Frankfurt, Germany. (➤ *drawing 10; images 31,32, p. 108; images 40-41, p. 109*)

Bricks for the Gando School: The organization Bricks for the Gando School was founded in 1998 by architect Francis Kéré to build a school in his home village in Burkina Faso. The organization built a series of school buildings from sustainable and natural materials. Building techniques were adapted to local labor and resources. The structures are made with compressed earth block load-bearing walls. Concrete beams with steel bars support the ceiling layer of compressed earth blocks. ➤ *Passive cooling* and ➤ *passive ventilation* are achieved through the use of generously sized window openings and a corrugated metal roof set onto a steel truss, which allows air to circulate between the roof and the ceiling. The roof is large enough to overhang the structure, shielding it from direct sun. The high ➤ *thermal mass* of the compressed earth blocks also supports the passive cooling of the structure. The organization subsequently built housing for teachers on the site, and has inspired other neighboring communities to launch their own school construction projects. (➤ *image 36-37, p. 109*)

Building Information Modeling (BIM): BIM is a software-based solution for the design and documentation of construction projects. Intended as a holistic approach to architecture, construction, and building, BIM software allows an architect to design a building while generating a file from which sufficient information for construction and building can be gleaned. BIM software tends to work in 3D, allowing one single object to be digitally drawn. This object, in an ideal BIM situation, contains information suitable for the production of a complete construction documentation set. Though BIM is much less glamorous than the other digital software, ones that allow the parametric and other varieties of new forms, BIM is becoming more and more popular as a new way of approaching the traditional divide between architect's design drawings and the necessity for a separate translation of these into buildable elements.

Cactus Juice to Waterproof Mortar: The juice of the very common Indian fig Opuntia Cactus or Prickly

Capillary Glass · Carbon Absorbing Surfaces

Pear Cactus has been used as an additive to mortar and ➝ *adobe* mixtures for centuries. Indigenous to the Mediterranean regions of Europe, Tunisia, Israel, Egypt, and many South American countries like Mexico, Chile, and Brazil, the plant is very popular for its sweet fruit, but its young cactus pads (nopales) are also eaten, especially in Mexico. The cactus juice is won from the plant's pads and, depending on the regional ➝ *vernacular* building techniques, is then added to mortars or adobe mixes for binding and waterproofing. The technique has just been reactivated in Ethiopia by the artist Meskerem Assegued. Mixed with salt, loam, and lime, the sticky juice is painted onto the exterior surfaces of houses to seal them against rain as done at ➝ *Dirk Hebel's SUDU project (p. 315)*. (➝ *image 33, p. 108*)

ing capillary glass suitable for similar applications. (➝ *image 30, p. 108*)

Cappadocia Cave Dwellings: Cave dwellings are a traditional building technique in the region of Cappadocia in Anatolia, Turkey. Volcanic deposits have shaped the ground in unusual ways over the centuries in the region, which is completely underlain by soft sedimentary rock, suitable for easy excavation and carving, as well as above ground natural "fairy chimneys" that are large pillars of eroded soft rock. The first cave dwellings were meant to be hideouts for the early Christians, and therefore had to function as enclosed systems. The two largest cave-based settlements are Derinkuyu and Kaymakli, and at one time housed up to 10000 people. A 9 km long tunnel connected Derinkuyu and Kaymakli. In addition to dwelling spaces, churches, houses, and monasteries were dug into the caves, and even today the older houses are half-cave, half-house in most Cappadocian settlements. This has a seasonal benefit: in wintertime, families can retreat to the cave areas of their house, which have similar properties to those of an ➝ *earth shelter*. (➝ *drawing 11; image 42, p. 109*)

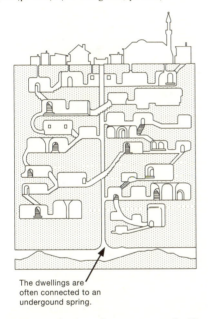

11: Section of a Cappadocian-type cave dwelling.

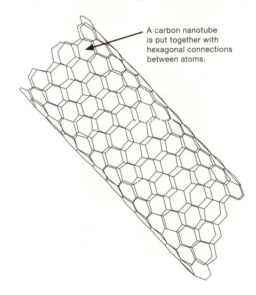

12: Structure of a carbon nanotube.

Capillary Glass: Capillary glass is a kind of glass that is constructed with small capillary tubules contained within the glass. It has excellent thermal insulation in comparison to more standard kinds of glass. The technique of capillary glass is based on the pelt of a polar bear, whose translucent hairs have been thought to help capture minimal sunlight in their cold environment. Although it has been demonstrated that polar bear hairs do not conduct light as previously thought, the theory helped inspire the use of translucent insulation materials (TIMs) as glazing in windows, air collectors, and other configurations: the capillary tubules act as small air cushions and prevent the convection of gases in the space between panes when mounted as multiple glass windows or façade surfaces. This prevents unwanted heat loss. Capillary inlays also reduce solar gain and therefore minimize unwanted interior heat. Its visual qualities are comparable to those of standard glass, mak-

Carbon-Absorbing Surfaces: Carbon-absorbing surfaces are surfaces treated with commonly available chemicals that are capable of absorbing carbon in certain chemical reactions. This is part of the work that researcher Rachel Armstrong is involved with, along with ➝ *bioluminescent lighting* in architectural contexts. One carbon-absorbing surface treatment under current experimentation is the use of oil, laced with a salt such as magnesium chloride, which is sprayed onto surfaces. The oil then sticks to the surface, and the reaction of the salt and carbon dioxide in the air begins a process of crystallization, whereby the CO_2 is absorbed. This produces a surface covered with white

29: **Carbon Nanotubes**; Close-up of an extremely dark surface coating made from carbon nanotubes.

30: **Capillary Glass**; Translucent and insulating.

31: **Brick**; Peter Behrens' Headquarters of Hoechst AG in Frankfurt recalls a gothic cathedral.

32: **Brick**; Roof of Hoechst AG building in Frankfurt.

33: **Cactus Juice to Waterproof Mortar**; The juice of Mexican nopales is used as an additive for construction materials.

34: **Board House**; The reinvention of a traditional log house.

35: **Board House**; Beautiful recycled wood façade.

36: **Bricks for the Gando School**; The buildings were designed according to passive ventilation principles.

37: **Bricks for the Gando School**; The Gando School was designed by Francis Kéré.

38: **Bloom Energy Server**; Decentralized energy production and energy storage.

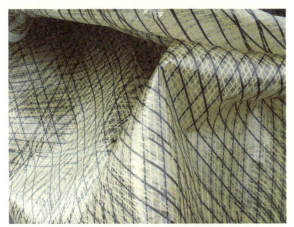

39: **Carbon Nanotubes**; Being used as reinforcement in composite materials like this woven sail.

40: **Brick**; The Monadnoc Building's southern half is a steel frame construction.

41: **Brick**; The nothern half of the structure is the tallest commercial building without steel or concrete supports.

42: **Cappadocia Cave Dwellings**; Houses could be carved out of the soft stone.

crystals, making the carbon dioxide absorption visually apparent and esthetically pleasing. Armstrong and colleagues are currently conducting experiments to determine the amount of carbon that can be bound using this method, as well as testing different salts and compounds to maximize the effect.

Carbon Nanotubes: Carbon nanotubes are tubular carbon structures with incredible strength. They are basically made from single or multiple graphite sheets and owe their strength to the strong carbon bonds present in graphite, being even stronger than those in diamond lattices. Nanotubes naturally align themselves in rope-like structures. Carbon nanotubes, mostly in the form of composite fibers in polymers, have many applications that take advantage of their strength, such as in tennis rackets, building materials, and clothing. Due to their unique conductive properties applications such as the use for paper batteries, ➡ *solar cells*, and ultracapacitors have been proposed. (➡ *drawing 12; image 29, p. 108; image 39, p. 109*)

Carrotmob: A carrotmob is a special kind of smart mob, using ➡ *crowdsourcing*, to organize groups of people for targeted consumerism. Smart mobs use computer-mediated communication to form big groups of individuals. The carrotmob is a form of consumer activism where a community buys a lot of goods from one company in a small time period to reward a business' commitment to making a socially responsible change in their operations. Often the changes are of an environmental nature, such as energy-efficient upgrades. The name carrotmob is derived from carrot and stick, an idiom that refers to a policy of offering a combination of reward (carrots) or punishment (sticks) to effect certain behavior. Carrotmobs are often explained as a reverse boycott and are thus known as "buycotts". The carrotmob was created by Brent Schulkin, and the first event took place in March 2008 in San Francisco. The carrotmob ➡*meme* has since spread internationally as a strategy of social commitment.

Cellulose Acetate: Cellulose acetate is a ➡ *bioplastic* based on cellulose. It is produced from natural cellulose and can replace oil-based plastics in many applications as it is thermoplastic and can be processed similarly to petroleum-based plastics. For example, it can be injection-molded and is easy to pigment. Like ➡ *plastics on the basis of corn (PLA)* it is made from renewable resources and most of its modifications are to a certain extend biodegradable. In fiber form it is used in textiles, where it absorbs and swells less than other cellulose-based fibers, making it lightweight and low-maintenance. Furthermore, it can be used for packaging or in other applications for commonly used objects and products.

Ceramic Engineering: Ceramic engineering describes the science and technological processes of using nonmetallic, primarily mineral compounds to create objects or structures. Ceramics includes diverse materials such as glass, pottery, and zirconium dioxide. They can be used to make products as varied as sharp but brittle knives and extremely hard ball bearings. The versatility, strength, and heat resistance of ceramics have helped the field of ceramics research grow to a multi-billion dollar industry. Recent strides have been made with bio-ceramics for use in surgical and orthodontic work due to the ease of bonds between certain types of ceramic and bone. Further exploration into different material properties has also led to the emerging field of bio-inspired ceramics, ceramics with structural composition similar to living organisms. The abalone shell, the strongest non-mechanical substance known, has inspired intensive study in the field of materials science in attempts to recreate its properties through ceramic engineering. (➡ *image 48, p. 112*)

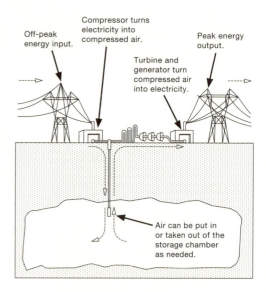

13: Compressed air storage can help to balance out peak energy needs in an electricity network.

CityCar: The CityCar is a small electric automobile designed and prototyped by the Smart Cities Group at the MIT Media Lab. Developed for short trips in congested urban spaces rather than for long distances, the CityCar accommodates two passengers with room for storage, and runs on lithium-ion batteries stored in the floor of the vehicle. It produces no tailpipe emissions and is designed to achieve the equivalent of 150-200 miles to the gallon of gasoline. The CityCar architecture differs considerably from a conventional car in its extremely small frame and its use of four electric motors rather than a central engine. The digitally controlled motors, located in each of the four wheels with their own drive motor, steering, and suspension, operate independently of each other and enable the car to spin on its own axis and move sideways between lanes without turning. Without a central engine or traditional drive train, the CityCar can fold to park and fit three or four to a single parking space. The cars can be recharged through inexpensive home units, which the Smart Cities Group hopes will one day be available at workplace parking structures and public parking spaces. Combined with larger and more conventional four-seater vehicles, the environmentally friendly and spatially efficient CityCar could eventually be an important component of thoughtfully designed urban mobility systems.

Cob: Cob is a building material similar in composition to ➤*adobe*. The cob material is composed of clay, sand, water, and organic material, frequently straw. The procession resembles that of ➤*rammed earth*: it is used in layers of material, set down in courses, then compacted, commonly with human or animal trampling. The process of compaction is known as cobbing. Each course is laid down, cobbed, and then allowed to dry. Additional layers, with selective gaps for doors and windows, are then layered successively on top. Cob is centuries old, perhaps dating back thousands of years, and originated in the Maghreb and al-Andalus areas, later spreading into Europe and beyond. With a high ➤*thermal mass*, cob structures benefit from flywheel effect cooling, whereby solar gain and outdoor temperatures are absorbed without penetration into the exterior walls during the day, and the resultant heat is released back into cooler nighttime air. Cob fell into disuse with the rise of concrete and other building materials, but is currently enjoying a small renaissance concurrent with renewed interest in earth architecture. (➤ *image 44, p. 112*)

Collaborative Consumption: Collaborative consumption refers to an economy fuelled by the collaborative actions of sharing, lending, giving, and bartering rather than personal consumer purchases. In a collaborative economy, items no longer needed by one individual are sold or given to other individuals outside of the standard industrial marketplace. The practice has increased dramatically with the rise of online networks, auction and classified ad websites, and social media platforms that allow borrowers, lenders, givers, and receivers to communicate easily and efficiently. Potential reasons for the rise in collaborative consuming are a cultural shift away from the dedicated purchasing of 'hyperconsumption' and a response to changing economic forces and resultantly reduced buying power. Assets redistributed through collaborative consumption can include consumer goods, accommodation, and workspace as well as less tangible resources such as skills and hours of work.

Composite Materials: Composite materials are materials made of two constituent components. Each component retains its material integrity yet acts in tandem with the other component. Reinforced concrete is a composite material: the concrete mix and steel bars act together for increased strength in comparison to a simple concrete by virtue of the steel bars, but they never become merged into one another. In reinforced concrete, the concrete is the matrix material into which the steel is set.

Compressed Air Energy Storage: Compressed Air Energy Storage (CAES) is a way of storing energy for future usage, primarily energy generated at off-peak (lower cost) times for use at on-peak (higher cost) times. Methods of storage include use of electrical or wind power to compress air into underground 'mines' made of solids such as concrete or stone, or fluids such as hot oil or molten salt. Once removed from storage, the air must be expanded via air engine or turbine before being used to power a generator or even a car such as the Tata ONE Car. CAES is still a subject of ongoing study to determine the most efficient practices. (➤ *drawing 13; image 49, p. 112*)

Concrete Ship: A concrete ship has a hull made from reinforced concrete, also called ferrocement. Concrete ships are also known as ferroboats. Concrete ships were built mainly during wartime when steel was in short supply, and concrete ships were used during both world wars as transportation and supply vessels. The first concrete ship to be patented was built in 1948 by Joseph-Louis Lambot. Although concrete ship construction is relatively rare today, it is sometimes used for engineering education purposes to demonstrate the potential of concrete in combination with careful and thoughtful design. (➤ *image 45-46, p. 112*)

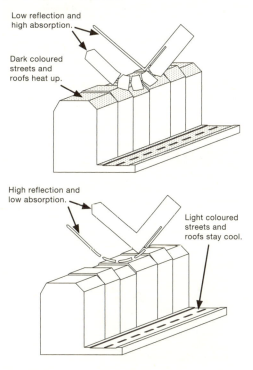

14: Hot and cool roofs – absorption versus reflection.

Convection: Convection is a kind of ➤*heat transfer* that is based on the movement of elements, usually liquids or gases. Convection is typically evident in weather phenomena where air currents of different temperatures converge. A special heating system, so-called 'gravity heating,' works without a pump to exchange warm and cold water within its heating cycle and relies on the principle of convection, increased by ➤*thermal updraft* that causes warm water to rise and cold water to sink.

Cool Roof: A cool roof is a roof that has a high ➤*albedo effect*, and therefore reflects a large part of the solar rays that hit it, preventing solar gain and the radiation of heat typical of a regular, or not cool, roof. A cool roof can be achieved through various means: the easiest and most publicized is to paint roofs white or light colors. This method was proposed by the U.S. Energy Secretary Stephen Chu, and it is estimated

43: **Dymaxion House**; Prefab monocoque structure.

44: **Cob**; Straw adds strength in adobe applications; shown here: mudbrick.

45: **Concrete Ships**; An alternative to hulls made from steel.

47: **Cool Roof**; If every roof was painted white, climate change could be decreased dramatically.

46: **Concrete Ships**; Developed and patented by Joseph-Louis Lambot in 1955.

48: **Ceramic Engineering**; Ceramic blades do not wear out.

49: **Compressed Air Energy Storage**; Compressed air fuels Tata's first air-driven car.

50: **E3**; A six-story wooden structure in Berlin.

51: **Earthship**; Most earthships are handmade.

52: **Day Labor Station**

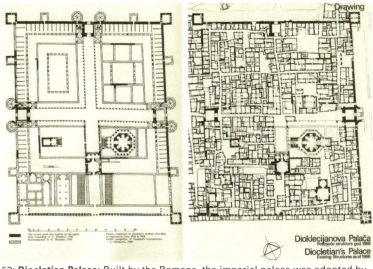
53: **Diocletian Palace**; Built by the Romans, the imperial palace was adopted by multiple dwellers over the centuries.

54: **Engawa**; Between the inside and outside of Japanese houses.

55: **Diocletian Palace**; Layers of building periods are visible today.

56: **Earthship**; A home built from a DIY instruction manual.

that if all the world was to adopt cool roofs, it would decrease atmospheric warming through increased energy efficiency and solar reflection by an amount equivalent to removing the emissions of all the cars on the road today for 11 years. 90% of the roofs in the world are currently dark in color: there are three main ways to remedy this. The first is by building roofs with pale colors, the second by painting existing roofs pale colors, and the last by building ➔ *green roofs*. (➔ *drawing 14, image 47, p. 113*)

Cordwood Construction: Cordwood construction is a traditional construction technique established around 1000 years ago and used in Greece, Siberia, and later also in Asia, Europe, and the Americas. The natural building method involves constructing walls from short pieces of debarked tree laid crosswise in combination with mortar mix and insulation fill. Cordwood houses generally have a high thermal storage capacity but only mediocre insulation properties, although ➔ *thermal mass* will vary based on factors such as type of wood, wall thickness, choice of insulation materials and mortar recipe. Cordwood homes are often chosen for their characteristic look, ease of construction, and maximization of interior space due to the common round shape. As they are mostly built from small pieces of wood, often sourced as a by-product of timber production, cordwood homes can be comparably cheaper than standard houses if the owners participate in the building process.

Cradle to Cradle Design: Cradle to Cradle Design (sometimes shortened to C2C or referred to as regenerative design) is an approach to design thinking based on biological processes and natural systems. C2C suggests that human endeavours, such as industry, society, and commerce, can be modeled on the ecological intelligence of natural metabolisms (i.e. the cycling of nutrients). C2C design aims to create systems that are efficient and virtually waste-free, whether in manufacturing, economics, urban environments or even social systems. The goal is to allow commercial and industrial activity to harmoniously coexist with the natural world. For example, manufacturing under the C2C model means only using materials that fit into two categories: 'technical' nutrients that can be recycled and re-used in other processes, and 'biological' nutrients that can decompose without negatively affecting the environment. Once C2C products are no longer usable, they can be dismantled and either distributed for re-use or left to decompose.

Crowdsourced Classrooms: Crowdsourced classrooms are open, collaborative, publicly accessible schools that utilize the web to facilitate real-world educational events and classes based on the idea of ➔ *crowdsourcing*. People can access the online platforms to offer their skills as teachers, search for specific subjects, and self-organize classes in various communities around the world. Crowdsourced classrooms offer no specific curriculum and have no single real-world location. Organizations using the crowdsourced classroom model include The Public School and The School of Everything, whose websites offer educational opportunities for students, teachers, and organizations. Classes can range from large public lectures to hands-on demonstrations to one-on-one tutoring in any subject, including technical skills, academic subjects, or creative talents. Crowdsourced classrooms help democratize learning and increase educational opportunities by connecting people with skills or knowledge to teach with people looking to learn.

Crowdsourcing: Crowdsourcing is the use of large groups of people to engage in tasks or activities through an open system. Crowdsourcing is commonly a strategy that engages a public, without discrimination or any barriers to participation, aside from the required know-how for a particular task or action and knowledge of the task or activity being crowdsourced. Crowdsourced activities are increasingly popular and are promoted on the internet regardless of their real or virtual status. Crowdsourcing can use a centralized or distributed model for inception, leadership and management.
For example, there can be a call to develop a new technology, to carry out a design task (also known as crowd-based design and distributed participatory design), refine or carry out the steps of an algorithm or software code, or help capture, systematize or analyze large amounts of data. The latter is the principle of open wikis like Wikipedia.org. Crowdsourcing can produce solutions from amateurs or volunteers who work in their spare time and produce solutions for free charity networks like, for example, ➔ *practicalanswers.com*, a website resource where problems are broadcast to an unknown group of solvers in the form of an open call for solutions. When it functions as a problem/answer finding tool, crowdsourcing can help to improve products or processes. ➔ *Kickstarter.com* is a crowdsourced way of financing independent projects, while ➔ *carrotmobs* are crowdsourced ways of rewarding businesses for socially positive actions through the leveraged buying power of the crowd.

Day Labor Station: The Day Labor Station is a project introduced by the organization and architecture firm Public Architecture. The Day Labor Station addresses the practice of day labor in the context of the United States. Day laborers are hired for jobs by the day, and are a fixture in the informal economy. Typically, day laborers can be hired from known street corners, where they congregate and await an offer of work. The work options usually involve physically demanding work, in construction, agriculture or manufacturing. Moving services, gardening companies, and private individuals also hire day laborers. Because the work available to day laborers is temporary and unstable, and requires a certain amount of taxi-style queuing for work, groups of day laborers congregated on public streets are often the source of social misinterpretation. The spaces where day laborers wait usually lack basic public amenities; they have no shelter, easy access to restrooms or other basic conveniences. The low social perception resulting from the lack of formal space belies the importance of the day laborer as a part of the informal sector of employment and work, which is essential to the success of the economy as a whole. (➔ *image 52, p. 113*)

Diocletian Palace: Located in Split, Croatia, the Diocletian Palace was built by the Roman Emperor Diocletian in the 4th century AD. Later abandoned by the Romans, the palace complex stood empty until the 7th century, when area residents, seeking refuge from increasingly dangerous bands of barbarians, occupied the protected structures. These refugees established a city within the palace complex, repurposing elements of the building into dwelling spaces, market halls, and other uses needed for urban life, as well as using courtyards and other outdoor spaces as enclosed public areas, in a very dense but protected urban environment. Today, the palace is still partially used and occupied as a city-like structure. This is an example of a ➛ *recycled city*, constructed from the remains of previous palace uses. (➛ *images 53, 55, p. 113*)

Distributed Energy Sources: Distributed energy sources are those that can function as a part of a network of multiple energy sources, as opposed to a single centralized source. Distributed energy can come from renewables like ➛ *solar cells*, ➛ *vertical axis wind turbines (VAWT)*, ➛ *horizontal axis wind turbines (HAWT)* or small hydroelectric devices. The benefit of distributed energy is that is does not necessitate centralized sources and distribution networks with energy moving only in a single direction to supply users. Instead, distributed energy, as an organizational paradigm, encourages the creation of an interconnected web of sources from multiple means of energy generation. Distributed energy is one part of what would make a ➛ *smart grid* "smarter" than the current norm of a simple grid and central sources. Distributed energy is central to Jeremy Rifkin's notion of a third industrial revolution to reorganize energy and society in a sustainable and responsible way.

Downcycling: Downcycling happens when products or materials are reused or reformulated into lower-quality materials or products. It is a frequent occurrence in many recycling processes. This inferior quality can manifest itself in weaker, more brittle, or less transparent products that have a host of other downgraded properties. A simple example of downgrading is that recycled glass frequently has a greenish cast as a result of imperfect sorting before the glass being recycled is melted, which results in some colored bottles being included in a batch that is intended to be perfectly clear. Downcycling is the opposite of ➛ *upcycling*.

Drosscape: Drosscape is a conceptual framework and term that assists in the redesign and reuse of waste landscapes. As a concept developed by landscape architect Alan Berger, drosscapes are integral to urban design practice in regions marked by deindustrialization. A drosscape is the landscape byproduct of urban sprawl, industrial shifts, and defunct infrastructure. As the logical outcome of spatial shifts resulting from changing economic and technological conditions, drosscapes are not inherently positive or negative spaces, but instead are spaces in need of special consideration and attention. By naming and codifying drosscapes, and in creating a taxonomy of drosscapes, Berger calls attention to spaces which are not glamorous or otherwise desirable for reuse from a traditional paradigm, such as abandoned malls, housing development leftovers, and infrastructure rights of way.

Dual Zone Borehole: Dual zone boreholes are an improved version of common geothermal heating systems that take advantage of different temperatures occuring at different depths. The boreholes are drilled into the earth which provides heating and cooling from the thermal reservoir of underground soil, rock or water. Pipes are inserted into the hole to act as heat exchangers and extract the valuable, free, and renewable energy from the ground. Below a depth of around 5-10m, where seasonal conditions no longer have an influence, the ground temperature is constant. It starts at the average annual temperature of the region, and as one drills deeper the temperature increases. This increase can range from 1 to 3°C per 100m of depth. The deep borehole reaches warmer temperatures that allow for ➛ *low temperature-lift, ultra-high COP heat pumps*. The shallow borehole provides cooler temperatures that are capable of cooling directly. Because the two zones are independent they can also be independently regenerated. When heat is not being extracted from the deep borehole, any excess heat acquired, such as from a ➛ *hybrid photovoltaic*, can be used to regenerate, or even augment, the temperature of the warm zone. The same is true of the shallow borehole and any excess cooling.

Dymaxion House: The Dymaxion House by R. Buckminster Fuller was designed to be the "house of the future": the strongest, lightest, and most environmentally friendly yet cost-effective housing ever built. Originally conceived in 1927 but not built until 1945, the Dymaxion House came in the form of a DIY kit, shipped in a metal tube, and it could be assembled on site in nearly any location. The Dymaxion House was heated and cooled without additional energy and constructed to be virtually maintenance-free. The design used one central stainless steel column with radiating structures similar to bike spokes, which supported the roof. Each house was assembled at ground level and then winched up the central mast. Fuller designed the Dymaxion House to address various issues like easy shipment and assembly, the efficient use of resources, waste management, and especially cost. For the price of a car, Dymaxion dwellers would enjoy features such as a waterless packaging toilet that shrink-wrapped waste for later composting. One of Fuller's innovations was a ventilation system based on the "dome" or ➛ *Bernoulli Effect*, which sucked cool air down into the dome. After World War II, he attempted to mass-produce the houses in partnership with an aircraft production company, but this failed due to his refusal to make changes to the design. A modified prototype of the Dymaxion House was built in Wichita, Kansas for investor William Graham. The structure, also known as the Wichita House, was eventually donated to the Henry Ford Museum in Dearborn, Michigan, where it is the only existing example of Fuller's visionary design. (➛ *image 43, p. 112*)

E3: E3 is a project in Berlin, Germany, initiated by a ➛ *Baugruppe*. E3 has many hallmarks of a project arranged by a *Baugruppe*, including design elements that are the result of the direct preference of the ownership group rather than a developer or architect's decision. E3 is made entirely of wood, a preference of the *Baugruppe*, with an appended concrete stair required by fire safety regulations. The code in other contexts would have value engineered a wooden construction out of the project, however E3 took the opposite track; the concrete stair became an entrance and landing for each unit, drawing added value from requirements. The wooden structure has no inner pillars or carrying elements, making it possible for each resident to completely customize the floorplan of their own unit. The E3 project uses solar panels and geothermal heating. (→ *image 50, p. 113*)

Earth Shelter: Earth sheltering is the use of earth-based strategies to increase the → *thermal mass* of a building. By increasing thermal mass, a building can be made energy efficient, with passive cooling in summer and passive heating in winter. Earth sheltering has been used throughout history, and can apply a variety of strategies. There are two main ways to create an earth-sheltered building: digging into the ground or an existing cave or hill to bury part or all of a structure, or using techniques that pile earth against and/or on top of a structure, creating a hill-like mass of earth. Buildings in Cappadocia, Anatolia, Turkey are examples of homes and other spaces built into and carved out of soft rock, and sod houses are a → *vernacular* example of buildings covered in earth to benefit from the climate. The Earth Ship is a kit house that can be partially buried as an earth shelter.

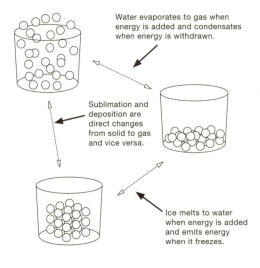

15: Evaporative cooling is based on the fact that energy is needed to actuate a state change.

Earthship: An Earthship is a type of autonomous home, made of natural and recycled materials, designed by American architect Mike Reynolds. Earthships follow most principles of sustainable construction like → *passive solar building design*, the use of → *thermal mass* to regulate indoor climate, insulation, and the use of solar energy and the site's local resources and preconditions to minimize their reliance on fossil fuels. They also have a system that collects rainwater, reuses greywater, and minimizes the amount of blackwater. A signature feature of many Earthships are walls made from a → *rammed earth* construction, commonly → *rammed earth tires* or → *tire bails*. Earthships were initially designed and built by Reynolds for his own purposes. He subsequently developed the DIY 'Packaged Earthship' kit for consumer use, complete with a construction manual and plans that can be delivered anywhere on the planet, via mail, to spread his idea, the Earthship design, and knowledge about sustainable, autonomous housing. Earthships built from the DIY kit have been erected in a variety of climates and have proven to perform well. They can be built in either an economical, spartan manner or as lavish, luxury homes. A concentration of Earthships has been erected in Taos, New Mexico, creating an ad-hoc Earthship community. (→ *image 51, 56, p. 113*)

Ecovation: An ecovation is a renovation with ecologically positive principles held as a central concern in improvements.

Engawa: An engawa is a veranda-like structure typical in some Japanese homes. The engawa acts as a liminal area between the house and the outside, most commonly a private courtyard. The façade of the home along the engawa is usually sliding doors, made from rice paper in traditional applications, or glass in more contemporary buildings. This allows the doors to be opened to the outside, making the engawa part of the interior space, and the exterior space more closely connected to the outside. This has many benefits, among them passive ventilation and cooling, and when layers of doors are used, the house can become a machine capable of careful calibration in response to the climatic conditions, such as sun angles, wind speeds and other atmospheric conditions. (→ *image 54, p. 113*)

Evaporative Cooling: Evaporative cooling is a cooling method using liquid evaporated into the surrounding air. This causes the air to cool and provides a method of cooling which is not dependent upon mechanical systems or chemicals. Evaporative cooling in architectural applications can be as simple as sprayed water in a discreet area, or as complex as a mechanically augmented evaporative cooling system. Evaporative cooling systems were used with → *wind catchers* in the Middle East to enhance the cooling capabilities of the air which circulated through the ventilation system. Some contemporary designers, in the age of energy efficiency, are experimenting with designs that integrate evaporative cooling into contemporary contexts. LAVA's → *Sunflower Umbrellas* in Masdar City use this method to cool an open space on a large scale, while Studio Gorm's → *Flow Kitchen* uses evaporative cooling for a modular kitchen design. (→ *drawing 15, image 58, p. 118*)

Fab Tree Hab: The Fab Tree Hab, designed by architects Mitchell Joachim and Javier Arbona and environmental engineer Lara Greden, is an inhabitable two-story home grown from seeds with walls of woven roots and vines packed with clay. Based on the ancient art of "pleaching" (training trees to grow and join in a certain form), the house also utilizes modern technology such as milling software to achieve exact structural effects. The architects designed the Fab Tree Hab to be extremely energy efficient, utilizing solar power for electricity and recycled rainwater in the plumbing system. Many elements of the building were conceived specifically to accommodate house growth, such as soy-based windows that can expand over time. Joachim and Arbona envision that a whole house could take five years to grow, depending on the environment. They hope to plant the first prototype by 2015. (→ *image 59, p. 118*)

Fake Estates: Fake Estates is a project by artist Gordon Matta-Clark. Matta-Clark became aware of a municipal practice in New York City whereby small plots of unusable land, or gutter spaces, were auctioned to public bidders. These spaces were the result of remappings, rezonings, and infrastructural changes. The artist purchased fifteen such gutter spaces, and from 1973 until his death, assembled an archive of documents about his useless space. He considered this an "anarchitectural" work, and the piece, even unfinished, underlines the difficulty of mapping in relationship to social space and current regimes of land ownership, as well as the value of architecture in relationship to space. This project is an important precursor to work like Atelier Bow-Wow's Pet Architecture.

Fiber Reinforced Concrete: Fiber reinforced concrete is a concrete that has increased structural integrity in comparison to a standard concrete because of the addition of fibers to the concrete mix. Glass, synthetic and organic fibers can be added for a variety of effects and purposes.

Flow Kitchen: The Flow Kitchen is a design project by Studio Gorm. The kitchen uses, as the designers say, 'terrestrial mechanics' to offer all functions necessary to prepare food. In addition to this, the kitchen gives the user a better understanding of how natural processes work: Flow Kitchen grows, stores with the help of → *evaporative cooling*, cooks, and composts food to grow more. Each part of the kitchen is based on very simple principles and techniques which can be used independently but work best in combination with others. Together, they create a flexible system that reuses resources and enables a dynamic flow between products. (→ *image 67, p. 119*)

Fog Collection: Fog collection is the process of obtaining water from atmospheric moisture using manmade devices such as fog fences. Fog fences are typically large linear surfaces made from materials such as canvas, mesh, or woven wire that can capture droplets of water through condensation. The water then runs down the fence to be collected in a trough or container located at the bottom of the fence. Fog collectors are useful in that they take advantage of existing climate conditions and require no external energy to operate. They are ideally located in mountainous areas near the ocean where fog is common and rainfall limited. (→ *image 70, p. 119*)

Foodprint: Foodprint is a project and initiative that examines the relationship between food and urban environments. Founded by Nicola Twilley and Sarah Rich, Foodprint looks at the way food and cities shape each other. Foodprint examines a range of social, political, cultural, economic, and spatial factors involved in the production of food and the development of cities. Analysis of food deserts, future agronomy, → *urban agriculture* practices, and visualizations of the complex data related to food and cities is presented and disseminated at revolving conference-style events, open to all, in various cities in the USA. Foodprint's creators use → *crowdsourcing* techniques to generate content, funding, and interest in the project.

Freecycling: Freecycling is the recycling of products from person to person without monetary exchange. Freecycle.org is an online exchange platform that encourages people to offer unwanted objects that are possibly desirable to others. Everything from leftover construction materials to unwanted books can appear on Freecycle, in addition to listings for markets, restaurants or cafés that give away excess, unsold food instead of disposing it as trash, as is common practice. Freecycle uses the power of → *crowdsourcing* to create a marketplace.

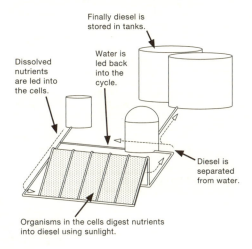

16: Fuel sweating organisms could produce an alternative to fossil fuel extraction.

Fuel-sweating Organism: Fuel-sweating organisms are genetically altered single cell plants, developed by the Massachusetts company Joule Unlimited, that can produce ('sweat') fuel from sunlight and CO_2. Compared to → *biofuel from algae*, these plants directly produce a fuel similar to diesel without an extraction step: the plant's output is practically usable to fuel cars. So far, the technique has only been tested in the laboratory. It has to undergo larger-scale testing before this potentially cost-effective, clean way of producing energy can become reality.
(→ *drawing 16, image 65, p. 119*)

Gae House: The Gae House, located in Tokyo, was designed by Atelier Bow-Wow in 2003. The house has a very unusual form and natural lighting strategy. The House has only few vertical windows because of privacy concerns due to extremely close neighbors, and a top-heavy form because of zoning laws and a narrow site. The house's footprint and first two stories are approximately 4.2 m wide, but the third story has a cantilevering roof that adds approximately 1 m to the total width. The underside of the cantilever is made from glass panels, which provide natural light and are the only "windows" in the house.
(→ *drawing 17; images 57, 60-61, p. 118*)

Galalite: Galalite is a → *bioplastic* which was developed at the end of the 19th century. It is made by immersing the naturally derived milk protein casein in formaldehyde. The name Galalite derived from the Greek words *gala* (milk) and *lithos* (stone).

57: **Gae House**; Indirect lighting.

58: **Evaporative cooling**; A misting fan works best in dry climates.

59: **Fab Tree Hab**; Could be reality in 2015.

60: **Gae House**; Interior view.

62: **Green Roof**; Chicago City Hall's roof heats up less in summer.

61: **Gae House**; Exterior view.

63: **Galalite**; A pre-oil plastic resembles ivory.

64: **Green Roof**; ACROS building in Fukuoka, Japan designed by Emilio Ambasz & Associates.

65: **Fuel-sweating Organism**; Will these little monads solve our energy problems?

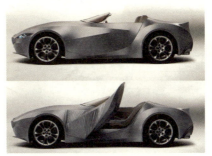

66: **GINA**; Concept for a car based on a carbon skeleton with a textile membrane skin designed by Chris Bangle.

67: **Flow Kitchen**; Studio Gorm's kitchen is an object and a sustainable statement.

68: **Gridshell Structures**; Pier Luigi Nervi's Palazzo dello Sport in Rome.

70: **Fog Collection**; The only method of gaining water in certain regions.

69: **Greenhouses**; The Eden Project in Cornwall, UK, is an enclosed climatic system.

71: **Greenhouses**; This is the best-selling greenhouse on the market.

Producing Galalite works to some extent similarly to the making of cheese. Galalite is fireproof, can be formed at about 100° Celsius and can easily be pigmented. It was mainly used for the production of jewelry and buttons. After World War II, Galalite was widely replaced by petroleum-based plastics except for the production of plectra (guitar picks), where Galalite is appreciated for its pleasant texture. (➔ *image 63, p. 118*)

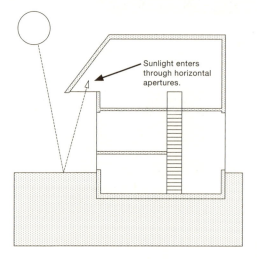

17: The Gae house has a room that is only indirectly lit by sunlight.

Geographic Information Systems (GIS): Geographic Information Systems are a digital combination of cartography, statistical analysis, and database information. GIS can be used to store, analyze, and manipulate data, which is then displayed. This data visualization takes the form of a map. Because GIS is based largely upon quantitative data sets, it can be manipulated with great ease for a variety of applications and purposes. Data sets ranging from land use, population, and ➔ *soil maps*, and infrastructure elements to economic, political, and socially defined information can then be analyzed spatially and visually. Some information and data are given a whole new traceability by the combination with maps. GIS is common in cartography, land surveying, utility, and infrastructure management, natural resource management, geography, urban planning, emergency management, navigation, and in localized search engines. It has great potential for added creative uses, as future technological development and technological literacy increase the ease of use.

GINA Concept Car: The GINA concept car, or Gina, is a prototype built by BMW. It reinterprets the relationship of the car's structure to functionality. Gina is made from a textile skin around metal and carbon wire elements. The elements and skin are flexible, hence the car can be reconfigured in multiple ways and the car's components and features appear to be "on demand." This flexibility also implies that any user can fine tune the car by customizing it to suit even quickly shifting needs and uses. This is a drastic departure from current cars, as they rely on an exterior rigid skin mounted over a fixed frame. The Gina is extremely lightweight and requires less raw material to manufacture than typical car construction. The principles demonstrated in Gina are applicable beyond car manufacturing, and the idea of the skin over a skeleton has been of enduring interest to architects and designers. (➔ *image 66, p. 119*)

Great Pacific Garbage Patch: The Great Pacific Garbage Patch is a gyre, or large system of rotating ocean currents, composed of marine litter located in the North Pacific Ocean. Also known as the Pacific Trash Vortex, the gyre is made up of discarded plastics, chemical sludge, and other small particles and debris. Various estimates of the size of the garbage patch range from areas the size of Texas to the size of the continental United States due to a lack of specific standards for determining the size of a trash gyre and which particles are included in the patch. As the patch is composed of plastics that break down to smaller and smaller particles, it is not generally visible as a continuous debris field or even discernable by satellite photography. Rather, the patch is defined by a higher concentration of debris mass than average. It is thought to have formed gradually as oceanic currents drew marine pollution from Japan and North America towards a relatively stable area of the North Pacific. Research has shown that the plastic debris affects at least 267 species worldwide, including many marine birds and animals that directly ingest toxic pollutants from the plastics. Even animals higher up the food chain such as humans can be affected by consuming fish that have fed on other marine animals like jellyfish that have absorbed the toxic chemicals. Several research projects have been initiated to study the patch, raise awareness of its existence, and investigate possibilities for cleanup or harvesting of the plastic debris.

Great Street Games: Great Street Games was a temporary urban game, by KMA, the UK-based firm of media artists Kit Monkman and Tom Wexler. It is an example of ➔ *augmented reality* used to add a previously nonexistent use to an urban environment using technology. The game utilized light-based image projection in combination with thermal imaging technology to enable participants to play light-based games in public spaces. The projections, placed in three different cities, pitted the players from each city against players from other cities in a three-day tournament.

Green Roof: A green roof is a kind of building roof that is covered in vegetation. There are two kinds of green roof, extensive and intensive, categorized by their intended use and the nature of planting. The intensive green roof is named as such because it requires intensive maintenance and care. Intensive green roofs are more similar to garden plantings, involve soil depths suitable for a wide range of vegetation, and are often intended for occupation by roof users. Extensive green roofs are usually accessible only for maintenance, and use planting strategies that require limited care and upkeep. Both kinds of roof reduce energy demand on buildings by providing insulation and absorbing heat from solar gain, and both can be used to augment ➔ *evaporative cooling* strategies. Green roofs fit into the ➔ *cool roof* concept. (➔ *images 62, 64, p. 118*)

Green Streets: Green streets are streets that reinvent the paradigmatic street section typical in most urban and suburban environments, where a road with curbs is bounded by sidewalks and intermittent storm drains. Due to the problems associated with water run-off collecting pollution from road surfaces, lawn chemicals, and other sources during storms, a green street uses alternative means to collect and store or partially remediate this runoff. This approach to storm water is under development, with communities exploring different options for storing, treating, and releasing the water collected. The intended benefits of green streets go beyond water management, and include habitat creation and esthetic improvements.

Greenaid: The Greenaid machine is a standard gumball/candy street vending machine repurposed to dispense seed bombs for ➔ *guerilla gardening*. Created by design firm Common Studio, the Greenaid machine is intended to serve an educational purpose in spreading the word about guerilla gardening practices in urban and semi-urban environments. Seed bombs are a common guerilla gardening method, whereby a homemade mixture of seeds, fertilizer and soil is made into a small pellet or ball, suitable for use as a plant projectile for future blooming.

Greenhouses: A greenhouse is a manmade structure in which plants are grown. Its roof and often walls are built with a material that allows sunlight to pass through. These transparent materials, primarily glass or plastic, allow solar energy from the sun to enter the greenhouse, where it is then absorbed by air, plants, soil, and other elements inside. The energy is prevented from leaving the greenhouse by the roof and walls through the process of convection. Unlike air outside, which mixes with cooler air to drop in temperature, air in the greenhouse maintains heat energy to warm the plants and soil. Greenhouses can be constructed in many shapes and sizes and are generally relatively inexpensive and easy to build. Due to their ability to control growing conditions year-round and also protect plants from pests and adverse weather conditions, greenhouses are of particular importance in cooler climates and can often be a major contributing source to stable food production. (➔ *image 69, 71, p. 119*)

Greenhouse Effect: The greenhouse effect is a natural phenomenon in which the earth experiences a rise in temperature due to atmospheric gases known as greenhouse gases. Solar energy in the form of visible light leaves the sun and is absorbed at the earth's surface, then re-radiated back into the atmosphere as thermal radiation. Greenhouse gases (including water vapor, carbon dioxide, nitrous oxide, and methane) absorb the solar energy leaving the planet and re-radiate the energy in all directions, including back down to the earth. The recycled heat energy sent back down to earth helps keep the planet warm enough to sustain many forms of life. Without greenhouse gases, a much higher percentage of solar energy would escape into space and the average temperature on earth would be approximately 15°Celsius cooler. The greenhouse effect plays a role in climate change because global warming is thought to be due to a strengthening of the greenhouse effect, caused by an increase in greenhouse gases released by human activity.

Greenhouse in Wedding: The Greenhouse is the house of Vera Tollmann and Christian von Borries, located on a Berlin rooftop. The ➔ *greenhouse* is based on a project by Paris architecture office Lacaton and Vassal that was displayed at Documenta X in Kassel, Germany, in 2007. Assisted by architects herberle.mayer, Tollmann and von Borries constructed the house using what are typical elements in any greenhouse construction. This unusual typology for a house and such a site have led to a set of living conditions that deviate significantly from the norm. Based upon a minimal lifestyle, the house functions as a large open-air room in summer, and is scaled back to a smaller and interiorized space in winter. Though this can be seen as a limitation, the house has spectacular views, excellent light qualities, and cost as little as 600 EUR per square meter of construction.

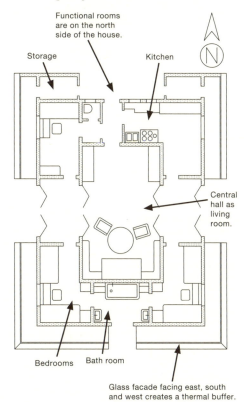

18: Plan of the growing house by Martin Wagner.

Grey Energy: Grey energy refers to the hidden energy used to produce, deliver, and dispose of a product. Grey energy can be the solar energy and nutrients required to extract an apple from nature or the commercial energy required to manufacture and assemble and decompose a car, which is also called embodied energy. Several different methodologies exist for calculating a product's grey energy total, which is rarely if ever communicated to consumers.

Gridshell Structures: Gridshell structures are structures made of grid or lattice forms, set into a double curve. Gridshell structures can be made from almost any material, as long as the material can be set into a nearly even grid, and can be bent enough to achieve a double curve. Common materials for gridshell structures are wood and steel. Gridshells are frequently made by first constructing a grid out of the given material, and then this grid is manipulated into a doubly curved form. Gridshell structures were pioneered by Vladimir Shukhov, also the inventor of the ➛ *Shukhov Tower*, a latticework ➛ *hyperboloid* structure. The ➛ *Weald and Downland Museum Workshop* in Chichester, England, is made of a Gridshell Structure, a contemporary facet of this ➛ *open air museum*. (➛ *image 68, p. 119*)

Growing House: The Growing House was designed by Martin Wagner and was built in 1931. It is a single-family house with a layered façade reminiscent of the rings visible in a crosscut tree trunk. The rooms of the house are situated around a central living room with functional rooms like the kitchen and storage spaces facing north and the bedrooms and bathrooms facing east, west and south. The arrangement around the living room allows for openings from the room through the second ring of rooms and into the outdoor space that surrounds the house. The openings allow the living room to be opened up completely, creating two wide corridor-like connections to the outside, closed partially to allow access only from the interior spaces in the second ring or completely separated from the rest of the house, functioning somewhat like a traditional room with two closable doors. The building is also partially surrounded by a glass façade so that the house benefits from direct sunlight and passive heating. The outdoor space is strictly programmed, with outdoor program in a close relationship with indoor program. Finally, a hedge is used as a last binding layer for the property. (➛ *drawing 18*)

Guerilla Gardening: Guerilla gardening is the practice of growing or tending plants on land that is not owned by the gardener. Guerilla gardening is practiced on all scales, from large-scale land adoption and adaptation, to something like ➛ *Greenaid*, which dispenses seed bombs to encourage plant growth. Guerilla gardening is practiced for a number of reasons, from land ownership reform protests to simple encouragement of greenspace, most commonly in urban and semi-urban environments, and even the growth of plants for food, in guerilla ➛ *urban agriculture* situations, or in rural areas for similar reasons.(➛ *image 78, p. 218*)

Haus Westend Grün: Haus Westend Grün in Berlin, Germany, is a villa by ZRS Architects and Engineers. The original building from the 1930s was partially destroyed during World War II and only provisionally covered with an emergency roof directly above the mostly intact ground floor. When the building was renovated in 2007, an upper floor was rebuilt, using a wooden formwork filled with and then covered by ➛ *adobe*. All partition walls were made from clay bricks. The entire outer façade of the building was insulated with 12 cm of adobe, made from reeds and a basic clay mortar. This was then covered with fine white clay for esthetic reasons. Because of the high ➛ *thermal mass* and passive cooling capabilities of the adobe, the house needs only 40% of the energy it previously required for heating. It is comfortable in summer temperatures, and energy was also saved by using natural materials for the construction. Calculated over a 50-year life cycle, the building has an energy saving potential of 50% in comparison to a similarly sized villa built according to a more typical construction method and using typical materials. (➛ *image 77, p. 218*)

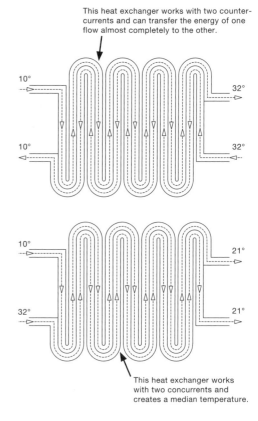

19: Two versions of a heat exchanger.

Heat Exchangers: Heat exchangers are devices that enable the passive transfer of heat from one material to another, which can be liquid or gas. The basic structure of a heat exchanger consists of two chambers separated by a wall or reservoir that operate according to the laws of thermodynamics. They may be as simple as two adjacent piping systems, one filled with heated material and another with cooled material, which allow for the passive diffusion of heat from one to the other until temperatures equalize. Heat exchangers are advantageous in that they require no additional input of coolant or power and can be used to conserve heat energy in industrial processes. (➛ *drawing 19, image 75, p. 218*)

TAKE ON COMPLEXITY

In comparison with nanotechnology and life sciences, architecture, urban planning, and construction-related engineering seem to be very simple scientific subjects: Reality proves that anyone is able to design and construct a building or to develop a formal or informal urban quarter, yet only few are qualified to crack the DNA code. But times have changed. The broad discussion about sustainable development during the last two decades has brought back an almost forgotten dimension to construction: complexity. This chapter deals with the potentials, opportunities, and risks that emerge from a practice-oriented dialogue about complexity and its re-establishment in architecture and urban planning.

Many architects and engineers dislike uncertainty and unpredictability. As a consequence they usually deal with complexity reluctantly. But complexity isn't a threat but instead it offers a broad range of opportunities.

If we want to take on complexity we must first learn from nature; our ecosystem is a perfect example of a complex system. Nature teaches us openness, nonlinear dynamics and self-organization. In the same manner, we should accept, design, and use single buildings as well as urban districts or whole cities as complex systems that are highly interrelated with their social and natural environment. And as complex systems they exhibit nonlinear dynamics, in the sense that they are uncertain, unpredictable, and unstable and also contain the potential for self-organization in bifurcation points from which new solutions have the potential to emerge. Furthermore, we should accept that the planning, design, and execution of a building are all complex processes that do not follow strict rules and sequential procedures. On the contrary, the processes are characterized by unexpected zigzags and many feed-back and feed-forward loops. To take on complexity means to manage uncertainty, ambiguity, and instability—with regard to both process and product.

In the context of the built environment this means that for a specific problem or request there is always more than one feasible solution and also that functionality must be diverse. A functionality of manifold variety relates to the different components of a building but also to its layout and use. For example, a building envelope should be like a human skin. Human skin is multifunctional in the sense that it protects from dust, water and humidity, but it also allows the intake of oxygen and helps to control body temperature through perspiration. What a smart and high-tech component: Without it, a human being could not survive! Despite our academic discourse about intelligent buildings, we are still far away from what nature was able to create through evolution.

A second example deals with the nonlinear dynamics of space and form. Usually architects design buildings in response to the visions and requirements of their client, taking into account the peculiarities of the specific site and its environment, and following the prevailing laws and building regulations. If one looks at the same building twenty years later, it is usually apparent that the owner, the use, the users have all changed, as well as the inner layout and the external appearance. The building has undergone a substantial transformation that was neither predicted nor technically foreseen when it was originally designed and constructed. In some cases this transformation can be realized easily and in others it requires a tremendous effort and a lot of money. Similar effects can be observed at the urban scale when looking at brownfields or the continual transformation of neighborhoods, for example.

If you are able to take on complexity you don't need to resort to simplification and abstraction, as many architects have, particularly during the era of modernism. The built environment, as part of our social and natural environment, is far too complex for simplified approaches and solutions. Architects and urban planners have to take into account the complexity of the issues and objects they are working on. They ought to make use, in a proactive way, of the openness, the nonlinearity and the self-organization of the buildings and districts they are shaping. By doing so, complexity will no longer be a threat but instead a source of manifold opportunities.

Against this background, I would like to stipulate some maxims regarding the fruitful management of complexity in construction. Concerning the end product of architectural design and urban planning, i.e., buildings and cities, we should:

- Consider a building as a strongly interrelated element of a preceding, extremely complex, human and natural system
- Plan and design not only for the initially defined use but also for unexpected transformations

- Foster diversity of use, layout, materials, and technologies
- Apply the principle of integration instead of deconstruction and segregation
- Achieve an economy of means and reduce metabolism by multiplicity and multifunctionality (i.e., one item fulfills more than one purpose)

If we consider the process of planning, designing, and executing a building we should be prepared to:

- Take decisions on the basis of fuzzy, i.e., incomplete and uncertain information
- Involve internal and external stakeholders at an early stage
- Manage projects through leadership, team work, and forward coupling

These maxims are just hypothetical; they still need to be proven. But if we are not brave enough to start on the basis of some hypotheses, we will never find out.

Hans-Rudolf Schalcher

About the author: Hans-Rudolf Schalcher is Professor Emeritus of Planning and Management in Construction (Institute for Construction Engineering and Management), Swiss Federal Institute of Technology (ETH Zurich). He has been a member of the Management Board and Head of the Technical Competence Center (TCC) of the Holcim Foundation since their incpetion 2004. Hans-Rudolf Schalcher represented the TCC in all regional and global juries of both the first and the second Holcim Awards competitions.

TAKE ON COMPLEXITY

In Favor of Flow

How to Naturally Ventilate a University Campus Building in Tropical Vietnam

KAZUHIRO KOJIMA / C+A

By considering the flows of people and wind, architecture can be liberated from dependence on machines and installations. Our winning scheme for a new campus for the architecture school of Vietnam National University in Ho Chi Minh City was driven by our ever evolving ideas about fluidity in architecture, and our concern for sustainability within the context of the project. The climate of Ho Chi Minh City is humid and hot, it has a rainy season and all of the challenging conditions of a tropical jungle. Despite those conditions we wanted to seek solutions other than the usual sleek glass tower with mechanical cooling and air conditioning units humming in the heat. We had three broad priorities for the development of the site: to cultivate it by minimizing the negative impact of the development, to use passive cooling and ventilation to minimize the use of mechanical cooling and ventilation, and to combine both of these in a sensible and sustainable form of architecture.

Our first concern was how to integrate the campus into the context, without "bulldozing" the vibrant and diverse ecology of the Mekong Delta. Agriculture in Southeast Asia has traditionally been based on a sustainable model, composed of traditional practices and knowledge. The exhaustion and exploitation of nature is avoided through such a model. Sensible treatment of the land and cooperation with the climate were the norm in Vietnam for hundreds of years. However, economic development in Vietnam has brought new development projects and a hunger for agricultural and vacant land. This land is often found on the outskirts of cities like Hanoi or Ho Chi Minh City. Clearing, leveling, and bulldozing are the normal treatment for plots of land like the site given to us in the competition.

The Mekong Delta is a complex mix of land and water tuned to a fine balance. A network of small waterways stretches around the site of the campus project. The fluctuation of the water level on the site between the rainy and dry seasons is about 1.5 m and the site becomes completely submerged during the rainy season as the waterways swell. To minimize land reclamation, a ring-road embankment was designed to surround the main campus, thus allowing us to build without the leveling, land reclamation, or clearing, and to integrate the campus into the context by bringing the surrounding mangrove forest and river into the campus.

Temperatures in Ho Chi Minh City are high throughout the year, but cooler winds are common, providing some relief from the heat. The prevailing winds come from three branches of the adjacent river. We also knew that shaded areas were quite comfortable in all but the most extreme heat. These are basic observations, yet they are so often overlooked. Given these conditions it was possible to design a campus that would not rely solely on mechanical air conditioning, due to the use of passive ventilation and cooling techniques in the building's structure, and by simply strategically planting more mangrove trees to enhance the existing forest and shade the campus.

Like in many other countries in Asia, mechanical air conditioning in Vietnam is proliferating rapidly with economic development. New large-scale developments and buildings, with glass façades similar to those in Singapore, Dubai, or Europe, make mechanical air conditioning a prerequisite, and evidence of this can be seen everywhere in the city. There are profound differences between the climate of Southeast Asia and that of Paris or Tokyo. Western glass towers are prone to a high degree of solar gain, and they are insulated and air-tight due to the need to combat cold temperatures. We realized it was a mistake to replicate the buildings of those fundamentally different climates and contexts in tropical southern Vietnam.

1: The new campus was designed to slip into the surrounding landscape.
2: The building façade is made of bamboo and mangrove, raw materials that allow the wind to flow through the porous surface.

3

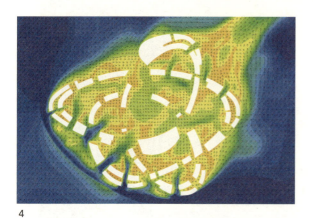

4

3: Model of section through the building, showing classroom and learning spaces in relationship to circulation corridor and exterior.
4: Computer-generated model of fluid dynamics for the site and building. Models like these were used to finely tune the building's performance and functionality.

We can reduce the building's contribution to global warming by reducing the use of mechanical air conditioning, which minimizes the release of hydrofluorocarbons (HFCs) and other refrigerant gases into the atmosphere, as well as associated environmental loads from production of air conditioner units. Southeast Asia needs solar shading and cross ventilation to create comfortable buildings, almost the complete opposite of Western requirements.

We also propose building with the material resources, human resources, and techniques present in the context. Bamboo and mangrove are easy to acquire locally, though they are rarely used in construction. We are interested in collaborating with the local workers to develop new ways of utilizing these materials. Construction processes will be adapted to local conditions, and simple, conventional methods will be used when possible. The Japanese concept of *Mottainai*—a term to express regret when the value of a resource is squandered—was important. We want to avoid everything superflous, considering only the necessary inputs before designing, so as to avoid too much waste.

The building is generally designed as a post-and-beam reinforced concrete structure. This is a conventional construction method in Vietnam, one that builders are familiar with. We chose mostly porous façade materials that could aid in passive ventilation. In addition we designed the building to prevent solar gain, with double roof construction, and jalousie windows with louvers. The building is ventilated through a very simple and centuries-old method of using the chimney effect, wherein warm air inside of the building naturally rises, and is released outside through openings in the structure of the roof. Roof sections and the exterior walls are clad in materials that reflect solar rays. In some cases, solar panels will be installed to absorb the power of the sun for use in the building. No energy from the electrical grid is required to power air conditioning, ventilation, dehumidification or illumination. Instead, all of these things are powered from local sources, controlled by simple mechanisms, and easily operated by the occupants of the building.

Through the meetings with the teaching staff and students of the university, we established the exact programmatic requirements for the project. Because natural and sustainable resources were prioritized—and their use maximized—a new spatial configuration was derived. The floor area required for specific program elements was converted into strips and color-coded by program. We then defined "black" areas and "white" areas to differentiate uses. "Black Spaces" are those that have a one-to-one correspondence between space and usage. For example

7

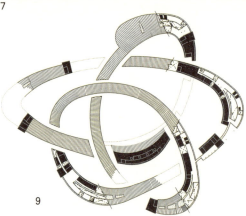

9

7: The campus is designed to have a rich and layered environment, conducive to learning and interacting, both formally and informally.
8: The main corridor serves as circulatory spine and continuous loop throughout the campus.
9: "Black Space" and "White Space" concepts were used to help define and separate defined and fluid uses of space.

8

laboratories, toilets, and utility spaces are all "Black Space." "White Spaces" are those that are not restricted to a single usage, but are instead fluid spaces where different usages are possible on different occasions. For example, studios, meeting rooms, and large stairs are all "White Space."

These considerations led us to create loop-like structures from the strips of program, arranged around a central dividing wall; like a spine this wall gave backbone to the form of the entire project. We also developed a sided scheme: the inner side of the spine-wall was designed to have most of the "Black Space," while the outer side housed most of the "White Space," including a continuous open space, generous enough to allow fluid circulation. Junction spaces were created throughout the campus, to allow for easy circulation between loops, enhancing the overall fluidity while minimizing spatial interruption or dead ends. The junction spaces are also shielded from both direct sun and from rain, expanding the advantages offered by the climate while minimizing the shortcomings. People, architecture, and climate all meet in the junction spaces, smoothly and with great benefit.

Through the spatial organization of loops, and the porous qualities throughout the structure, the lives of those on the campus and the wind and weather come together. By employing the idea of *Mottonai*, we enable all of the forces on the site to intertwine and combine for mutual benefit. Instead of closing out the elements and fighting them by mechanical force, we steady the flow of wind on the site and harness control through elegant means. Even daily squalls become integrated into the building, by the design of rain catchers to provide grey water for building use. The daily flows and patterns of people and weather run uninterrupted, and the flexible use of space and sustainable principles enhance the fluid design of the new campus in the Mekong Delta.

About the author: Kazuhiro Kojima is Partner at C+A (Coelacanth and Associates Tokyo) and Professor at Tokyo University of Science. His projects cover a range of scales in various countries and climates and deal with space and activity. These projects have resulted in concepts such as "Black and White," "Space Block" and "Fluid Direction." Monographs and books about his work include *Kazuhiro Kojima* (2G .43, Editorial Gustave Gili, 2007) and *CULTIVATE* (TOTO Shuppan, 2007). The project "Low-impact greenfield university campus, Ho Chi Minh City, Vietnam" was awarded the Global Holcim Award Silver in 2009.

TAKE ON COMPLEXITY

Building on Speed

Realizing the Nestlé Chocolate Museum in Ten Weeks Without Construction Documents

MICHEL ROJKIND / ROJKIND ARQUITECTOS

I am part of a generation of Mexican architects who complained about living in Mexico. We complained about living in a third world country, and that progressive architecture was impossible in Mexico. We thought our lack of a sophisticated construction industry would prevent us from achieving the proper construction of our designs. However, over time I realized that it was wrong to complain, and what we have here in Mexico is something to brag about. We have good labor work, high quality labor work, and it is inexpensive in comparison to digital fabrication. Our concern is how to make complex architecture happen with the regular budget for a simple building, and in our context. That is the give and take: the place where our office has expertise.

I'm an architect who began by doing construction and I'm grateful I started that way. If I design a building I should also understand how it is going to be built. It has to go hand in hand, the architecture and the construction. I know a lot of architects who design and have no idea how to build what they design. If you're an architect and you don't like construction or understand construction, it is really difficult. Plenty of designers don't want to get their shoes dirty going to a construction site. I can't make architecture that way, I am always thinking consciously about how to build in a cost-efficient way, and in a way that translates well for the local workers. This makes it easier for us to design, and usually it is inexpensive in comparison to what it would cost to do the same thing in many other countries.

The attention to the context of the architecture is equally important when we work abroad. As an architect you have to understand where you will build, which companies will oversee the project. Only then can you can figure out what's possible. You study architecture to practice architecture anywhere, not just in your own country. You're supposed to have the ability to be a good architect in any part of the world. It would be absurd to do really acrobatic architecture in places where there's no way you can achieve it, or where it would cost a fortune to construct.

A good example of how necessary it is to understand local construction capabilities is the phased competition for the Ordos housing project, led by Herzog & de Meuron in Mongolia. The entries in the first phase were all back-twists and somersaults ... all the projects were so complicated. It is absurd to see these big firms going into other countries, doing the same thing they were doing in their country. When the teams went to the site after the first phase, they realized that the workers only knew basic, local construction techniques. In the second phase, the projects were more down to earth. Most of them were made of brick and most were really simple.

Of course, the easiest way to construct now would be to send digital files to a fabrication company, have them produce everything offsite, then come onsite and assemble the building. A lot of companies brag about doing it, but when you see the projects firsthand, you notice things like seams being mismatched. But, we're getting there. What I like in contrast about my working method is that it remains a very human-centered design-build process. We're stuck in a digital mode with the computer, and in that perfect digital world. Nobody is getting in your way there. But then, no matter what, it has to come down to people for the fabrication and construction. In Mexico, we can't send out a 3D file, and then have workers assemble everything like a puzzle. Here, we have to sit down with everyone involved in the construction process and explain the project. We bring many different scales of models: site models, detail models, so everyone can come to understand what we're doing, and can see what we're trying to build in a tangible, three-dimensional way. It is similar to how architects behaved in the past, going onsite and making changes and adjustments and supervising the construction actively.

We usually get the project 80 percent complete in our office, in drawings. There's always something that can be improved onsite. When you're onsite during construction, you will always notice things you missed in the model or in the renderings. Even if you make hundreds of models, there are things you will miss. In theory, you're supposed to hand over a set of drawings for construction and it is supposed to go perfectly well. In Mexico, my experience is that it doesn't. If you don't have very intense site supervision, you might not recognize your project when you finally see it completed.

The Nestlé project in Mexico was one of our projects where we were forced to work almost completely onsite. It was the result of a competition brief where we'd been asked to do an inner pathway, like a bridge, for people to observe chocolate production at the Nestlé factory. Normally, when we work on a project we try to push things forward, to challenge the client and their perceived needs. We did some research and found that there was not a chocolate museum in Mexico, which was absurd because of the cultural history of chocolate in Mexico: the Aztecs basically invented chocolate. Based on that research, we made the argument that it would be nice to have the observation area, but it would also be nice to have a chocolate museum alongside the highway. We proposed also to create an iconic landmark, by constructing this bridge and museum with a 300-meter façade facing the highway. This could enable Nestlé to crossover from merely selling their products to giving something back to the city and community. Sustainability isn't only about ecology or energy; it is also about what a project gives to the city and the community.

After our proposal was presented to Nestlé at their headquarters in Switzerland, our client from Nestlé in Mexico came back to us with good news and a bit of bad news. The good news was that they'd use our design, do the entrance, and save the museum idea for later construction. The bad news was that we had two and a half months to do the entire project. Two and a half months to design the project and to get it built.

We panicked a little. We basically moved our office to the site. We had seven people there. I was there three to four days a week. I stopped all the other projects in the office. We worked closely with the contractor, who was the only one who could be convinced to do the project that quickly. We jumped from a

1

2

3

4

1-4: Due to the short construction time of two and a half months, the building was erected with almost no construction documents under intense site supervisions by the architects. Diagrams, sketches, and models used on the construction site served to communicate the project to the workers.

5: Layers of paneling were affixed to the underlying steel structure, through a continual process of small adjustments.
6: Red pieces visible on the lower right are a test section with the Hunter Douglas corrugated paneling, which would be used as both façade and integrated drainage system.
7: The two and a half months construction process photographed over time. One of the only elements to remain constant throughout the process was the glazed section of the façade, due to the fabrication lead-time for the glass.

small-scale model, to a bigger scale model, to the 1:1 scale model onsite. Most of the drawings for the project were done after it was built.

We used workshops to communicate with all of the workers on the project. We worked in three eight-hour shifts on the site, briefing each shift of workers for each shift. Diagrams and models were used to help explain where the structure had bends, twists, and how those elements were supposed to work structurally. When you bring it down to simple terms, work goes more smoothly, and this transparency keeps it from descending into this mechanistic role for the workers. They become actively engaged in the project, excited about interesting work, and really come to understand the architecture you've designed.

The project was explained in terms of a primary structure as a skeleton, a secondary structure supporting the internal panels, with sheet rock, acoustic, and insulation panels inside of it, and then a third structure holding the exterior panels. We drew this out in chalk on the sidewalk or the floor of the project. We moved so quickly that these chalk sessions served as the design documents.

By the end of the first week we had already poured the foundation with quickset concrete and were able to take the wood formwork out and start working on the structural elements. We did the foundation and supporting columns in concrete while we created and built the steel structure at the same time. When we poured the concrete for the floor slab, we were ready to assemble the 8-12-inch I-beam steel structure as the main structural support. Then the second layer gave shape to the rest of the body, and a 4-inch HSS steel section was welded on top of the first structure. The workers used rebar and string to mark building elements out, and blocked the folding elements out in rebar. They would then place the I-beam, and cut it there on the site, on the floor, and then weld it together. The structural engineer slightly exceeded the dimensions of the intended structure because he didn't have the time to calculate it out fully. This was okay, as we could make it work with the increment of the dimensions, and our working method onsite.

You design intentionally, and then mistakes and accidents just happen. You have to design in a way that allows mistakes to happen, to know that maybe something doesn't join exactly like you'd planned. You can figure out onsite how to make it work. We were working in a fluid way, based on problem-solving. For instance, the outer panel skin was designed to fit precisely, so we had to work with that constraint. It became a strategy game. We also had to lift the building because factory processes were going on underneath that couldn't stop.

The factory was still working the entire time, and people had to be able to pass underneath the structure.

The limited timeframe meant we had to work with the materials available at the time. I called Hunter Douglas to find out what materials they had in stock for the outer panels in red, to match the color of the Nestlé logo. Given how many square meters we needed, they only had corrugated panels in stock. Originally we'd wanted flat panels. With only that corrugated material, we started thinking about how to design with the corrugated panels, how we could turn them to our advantage. We tried shifting the lines of the corrugated metal, and realized we could use the corrugations to channel rainfall, and created an integrated drainage system, where originally there was none. That led us to work with the folds in the structure, to further direct the water off the structure. We used the steel beams, underneath the corrugated metal, as the main drainage pipe. In that way the limited choice of material available to us because of the time constraint improved our design.

We understood there were design decisions that had to be made immediately. We used tempered safety glass for the 300-meter façade. It takes eight weeks to produce panels in that dimension and type of glass. Even before all the folded elements had been completely worked out, we had to set the dimensions of the glass. As a result, we had to work with the glass always in mind. Two and a half months is not long enough to have things fabricated multiple times, so we had to plan properly from the start to bring everything together in a fluid way.

The tight timeframe was something that we took for granted and accepted when we were constructing and designing. We didn't question it. After we were done with the project, Enrique Peña Nieto, the governor of Mexico, gave a speech in the building, a big event. I found out later that he'd needed a site from which to give the speech, and he'd spoken with Nestlé, telling them that they didn't have to go through the regular permitting process if he could deliver the speech from the new building. That was the reason for the deadline. It is funny, that as the architect, I didn't understand that this was the reason for the extreme pacing until that day, the day of the speech. It was ridiculous; if they had told you that before, you might have said no. But I think I'd still have done it. But that makes you understand that the pressure didn't come only from the client, from Nestlé itself, it came from the Mexican government as well.

Other parts of the project forced us to think and act at lightning speed. Some of the light fixtures weren't there on time for the opening of the building. We had

to go to a particular area in Mexico City where all kinds of interior fixtures and construction materials are sold, and we chose something from there. We adjusted the project to the limitations. When people from abroad see the images from the construction site, they often say it is awful and that it looks like a war zone. But I am proud of the way we work; this is Mexico. Obviously there are really nice construction sites, like in Europe or Japan where everything is spick and span, but most of the time, in the real world, construction sites aren't in perfect order.

The way of working on your feet, and understanding your context is something integral to our work as an office. The labor here, the skilled labor, is very specific to the context and we take advantage of it as much as we can. On another project, the PR 34 house, we had complex metal work, and the original ironworkers on the project, coming from a traditional building background, couldn't do the work correctly. There were complex curves that normally wouldn't be in a building. We needed workers who were used to curved forms, not ones used to regular rectilinear buildings.

There's a place in Mexico City called Colonia del Torres, where, if you crash your car when you are a teenager, you go to have it fixed. In maybe half an hour, while you're eating tacos in the corner, the workers in the garages there will fix your car. They can do mechanics, but more importantly they do excellent bodywork with raw sheet metal. They're amazing; they get the dents out, paint it, and it looks like nothing happened. You come back home and your family never knows you crashed the car.

I went to Colonia del Torres and hired the bodyshop guys to work on the metal of the PR 34 house. I knew they would be able to execute the complex curvatures in metal because they did similar work for cars. Why not also for architecture? It was really fun to be on the site when we brought them onto the project. At first there was a lot of confusion about why guys from a bodyshop were working on an architectural project.

We design digitally first, and then take advantage of the local labor work. The people who work on the project are extremely important with every project. It isn't always the contractor; they always sell themselves as capable of doing anything and as understanding how to construct your design, but this isn't the case. All too often you see their guys on the site with your drawings, their faces clueless: they don't know what they're building. You have to hire the right people, and understand what each person can do, how to communicate with everyone on the project, and how to make the context an advantage, not a hindrance.

That way of thinking is present within our everyday architectural practice; how we deal with the urban qualities of a project, the infrastructure, the public, the building, the construction capabilities, the materials, and everything in general. I see design and architecture as a range of processes. I've seen many firms get stuck with their way of designing. They know it so well it becomes boring even to them, always doing things the same way, using the same process every time. I think it is crucial to understand why you do the things you do. And as far as my office is concerned, we like to exercise our brains in new ways and have a good time.

Text documentation: Jessica Bridger

About the author: Michel Rojkind is a Mexian Architect. After studying Architecture and Urban Planning at the Universidad Iberoamericana in Mexico City, he opened his office Rojkind Arquitectos in Mexico City in 2002. While thriving in this creative, chaotic environment and rethinking possible interventions of architecture at a worldwide level, Rojkind has also lectured internationally and has been a Guest Professor at various universities.

TAKE ON COMPLEXITY

Challenge the Standard

Reinventing Typologies and Programs for Housing and a Fire Station in Mexico City

FRANCISCO PARDO / AT 103

Most people would say that mixes are good. I think that for our office (at 103) it has been the best part of the design process. My partner Julio Amezcua and I were both educated in Mexico City, at an architecture school with a technical background. After studying at Columbia University's more theory-based and software-heavy program during the late 1990s, our way of thinking had become a big burrito, between a taco and a sandwich — Tex-Mex food gone digital. After moving back to Mexico and starting our practice, this model was not helping us at all and we became frustrated by the lack of understanding on the part of our clients and contractors. Formal complexity with its own vocabulary and way of thinking was not going to be easily integrated in Mexico's culture of construction. We realized that it was almost impossible to explain our ideas. Once we designed a project of folding planes with very complicated angles and folds. It was impossible to draw the project in the traditional way using plans, sections, and elevations. Therefore we tried different ways of representation that for our contractor, however, were impossible to understand. Hence the project was never built. Later we understood that this project could probably have been built if only we had been able to solve it differently and more simply. We realized that when you make a piece of architecture it has to make sense to everyone involved in its making: the client, the architect, the contractor, and the actual workers. Today, we believe that the best projects are the ones that address the problem in a beautiful design solution, bringing to equilibrium all of the inputs, without compromising the architecture.

Two examples of the work of our office will explain this in two different ways: the first project, the Lisboa7 houses, is a project where we took typical housing typologies and manipulated them to address the specific site, the specific market, the local materials, and our client. The second, the Fire Station project, is the manipulation of political desire, cultural memory, and social factors, through an atypical combination of programs.

Lisboa7 Housing

We were hired by a developer to build a housing project in the Juarez neighborhood, between the center of Mexico City and the new financial corridor located along Reforma Avenue. The area around Reforma Avenue is currently undergoing major changes in density and program, including the addition of luxury apartments, retail, and office spaces. The adjacent blocks in the different neighborhoods will be affected by these new developments, and will naturally act as service areas for this new financial corridor. In order to avoid gentrification and its homogenizing consequences, we thought it was important to develop intelligently designed low- and middle-income housing. Empty building lots in the hinterland of Reforma Avenue, which have existed since the earthquakes of the 1950s and 1980s, provided a perfect opportunity for such a project. We were particularly interested in this hinterland because it seemed to offer the possibility to counter-balance the high-income-focused development along Reforma Avenue and to avoid the seemingly inevitable long commute for lower income workers employed in the area. We felt that the area should be made to function as a symbiotic system, wherein all of the socioeconomic conditions could feed each other without competing.

The market for low- and middle-income housing was little explored in the area, and the few new buildings were examples of what we did not want to do with the Lisboa7 project. But luckily our client was a developer with an open mind, and this was part of what allowed us to achieve the project.

We were able to identify a series of design variables, and manipulating these variables helped us to arrange our scheme differently from the traditional way of organizing housing blocks. We wanted to make a project that could change the perception of the space, by playing with the same parameters that every architect has to deal with, namely height, density, and use. The site given was 14 m wide with a 50 m depth, running east to west, with a tall building near the southern edge. This area of Mexico City is built on top of a drained lake, and this means that the water table is only a few meters below. This results in unstable ground conditions, which makes foundation systems expensive and complicated, and it also makes comparatively large structural elements necessary. With the possibility of earthquakes added to this, conditions for building a project are very difficult.

At first we analyzed the typical developer-style scheme that places one housing block at the front of the site and one at the back. In such an arrangement only a few units face the street. Inside the block apartments face each other, which affords them little privacy, which in the traditional residential culture of Mexico is actually a very important element. We thought this typical developer scheme did not work well in general, and would not work at all for our project. It is based on purely formal city rules that are too simplistic and do not take into account the value of space. They only seem to interpret space in a plan view, from the top down. The city allows only a certain number of stories and requires a minimum of 30 percent open area on the plot, and this means that developers go for the maximum density possible. As a result, simple straight blocks are created, but we knew there had to be an alternative.

We decided that it did not make sense to base the project on creating street views, as due to the geometry of the lot it was impossible to have all units benefit from those views. It seemed much more likely to us that we could generate the project by working with the 30 percent open space that the city code obliged us to leave unbuilt on the plot. We realized that we could manipulate this space—most of the time only treated as an empty and unutilized leftover—to become the genuine spatial asset of this project. This then became our game plan: to design the 30 percent void, instead of the 70 percent mass.

We divided the maximum mass allowed into six volumes. Each volume was 3.8 m wide, and each of the six volumes had views to the west, forming a series of structures like domino pieces, all facing in one direction for privacy. The east

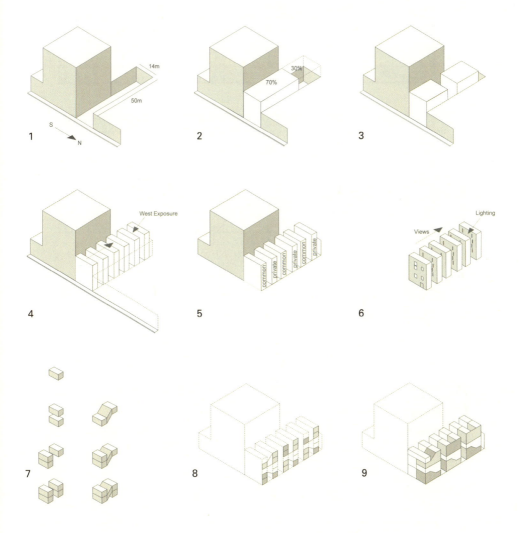

1 - 10 Site organization diagrams.

1: Existing site
2: Building envelope as implied by code
3: Standard developer solution with one unit at the front and one at the rear
4: Our solution with dispersed volumes
5: Programmatic distribution
6: Views and gardens
7: Units
8: Unit arrangement
9: Final apartment arrangement
10: Internal circulation corridors

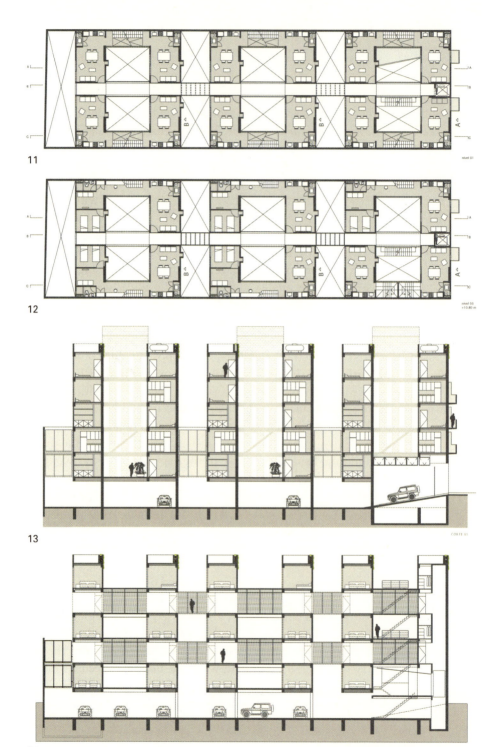

11: Ground plan level 1
12: Ground plan level 3
13: Section AA
14: Section BB

elevations were designed to have small openings with translucent glass, to allow morning light into each unit, while maintaining privacy between units.

We were really excited about the result: We had managed to create a nicer quality of space, natural light, and good ventilation for all the units. However the area of the façade had increased by 300 percent—the developer would hate this! Of course such a solution is more expensive than building a single block with a smaller amount of exterior walls and façade, and developers work with cold hard numbers: their margin is usually very narrow, especially in a non-luxury housing project. We felt like we were back at the start, but then we realized that skipping the exterior finishes would save a significant amount of money. After all, do we ever really need them? We convinced the developer that by increasing the façade area one would have better light quality and cross ventilation as well as privacy in all units; also spaces would look bigger than they actually are, bringing inside the patios as an extension of the space. In order to pay for the extra cost we proposed to him to remove all exterior finishes and leave the envelope with just two materials: exposed concrete for structural elements, and exposed cinder blocks for the infill. By working with these simple materials and construction techniques, we would actually expose the way in which almost all of Mexico is built, and in that sense it would be a kind of homage to the country and its builders.

The solution we presented aimed at providing a better quality of space and thus a better quality of living for the tenants, instead of focusing on the decorative aspects of the building, usually reflective of the aspirations of the occupants, who commonly buy apartments merely based on the superficial aspects that don't necessarily improve the qualities of the space.

To test that solution we had to make it work as a system. We broke the volumes into 60 modules of 36 m^2 each, that could be combined into housing units of up to 144 m^2 (4 modules). This module size had the benefit of giving the developer the opportunity to include buyers who would use bank loans for low-income housing which are limited to spaces that do not exceed 36 m^2. This way we were able to attract a mix of occupants with a range of incomes.

The building has five floors and the units are accessed via 50-m-long corridors on the second and fourth floors. These corridors are covered with translucent fiberglass panels. Thus, they are naturally lit through the patios but at the same time maintain privacy for the units. At night, when the building's security lighting is on, the corridors become giant akari lamps, which glow through the translucent paneling to softly light the patios and the inside of the apartments.

15

16

17

18

19

15: Street façade with exposed concrete and cinder blocks.
16: Lisboa 7 built, showing context near Reforma Avenue. The building blends into the context yet is fundamentally different.
17: Due to the vertical penetration of the building with six courtyards, all rooms receive light from two sides and appear larger than they are.
18: Apartments sharing one courtyard maintain privacy by differential use of glass. While the larger windows of one apartment use clear glass, the small windows of the facing apartment are done in translucent glass.
19: The exterior walls of the access corridors consist of corrugated panels of translucent polycarbonate, which allow daylight into the corridors without violating the privacy of the apartments arranged around the courtyards.

Each unit has one to three floors, all of which face a central patio and are configured as a U-shape or as an L-shape. Rather than an apartment, each unit is conceived as a house. Arranging the spaces around the central patio creates a sense of privacy, and is a reference to colonial architecture, where the central patio typology uses the void space as the core of the house, and as a lighting and ventilation element.

In order to provide enough spatial flexibility to allow occupants to adjust the arrangement of the internal spaces, and to allow for modular flexibility, we designated a wet wall, which could serve either a kitchen or a bathroom. As a result, the scheme works progressively, from a one-module configuration up to a four-module configuration, and it can be reprogrammed based on the budget and needs of the occupants. One module could be a bedroom and a bathroom, but the same module could also be a living space and a kitchen, or a studio and a bathroom, or a dining room and a kitchen. The wet wall is the only place in the units where fixtures are installed, and this lowered the construction cost and minimized the need for complicated interior renovations.

With Lisboa7, we took risks by stepping away from the established ideas of the typical housing typology in Mexico, by deviating from the use of superficial ornamentation to impart status-based "value," and by not deferring solely to a high-tech, environmentally sustainable discourse. We understand that in our context, for our social and economic conditions, it is important to focus on socially sustainable ideas instead of trying to mimic the architecture of other countries that are dissimilar to us in climate, in economic conditions, and in construction techniques. For instance, we did not insulate the walls. But that is not dramatic as we also dispensed with heating. Both conditions are quite common in Mexican homes and people know how to live with this. For us the priority in this project was to provide meaningful and satisfactory spatial configurations for people to live in. We think that in order to actually improve living conditions across all socioeconomic levels, and to prepare for the fast and unpredictable changes in urban environments, we have to work with the local problems and the local conditions.

In the case of Lisboa7, the priority was to manipulate the housing typology typical to Mexico City, by breaking the building volumes into components and reorganizing them to fit the structure of the complex, with the understanding that the large empty voids were not lost square meters, but instead an element that could increase the value of the constructed square meters over time. These considerations were very important as the margin for design, both spatially and financially, was very limited in this project. This was much to the contrary in our fire station project, which I want to discuss below, where we had a much larger margin for design moves.

Fire Station

On the night of October 20th, 2000 the biggest nightclub in Latin America, named "Lobohombo," located on Avenue Insurgentes, a busy avenue in the center of Mexico City, caught fire, leaving 22 people dead and more than 30 people injured. An electrical short started the fire and people were trapped inside of the club because the emergency exits were locked, the building had no windows, and the few doors that were unlocked were not sufficient to evacuate all of the people. The fire spread quickly due to cheap interior materials, poor quality installation, and most of all because of the loose fire regulations and corrupt fire inspectors and owners.

After the tragedy, the city government, in an effort to clean up the fallout and mess after the fire, appropriated the nightclub's site and hired us to design a fire station. This decision was a highly symbolic one. Fire stations in Mexico, like many places, are a typology emblematic of closed and mysterious buildings associated with strong morals and unselfish principles. To make a public building of this nature at the site of the tragic fire was clearly a deliberate act of remembrance, with the symbolic intention of something akin to social justice. More than that, the decision displayed downright exorcistic logic: as if to make sure that there would never again be a fire at this site, a fire station had to be built on its very ashes. And indeed, the government official who approached us to design a fire station on the site of the club spoke about the government's wish to give the people "a phoenix to rise from the ashes." His main concern, however, was that the project could not be just any fire station; it had to be the *biggest* and *most modern* fire station in Latin America. This somewhat awkward fixation on bigness resonated only too well with the way that the fire catastrophe had been discussed in the media. While there had been rampant speculation about the fire, with varied numbers of casualties and causes, the one thing that was mentioned by every reporter was that Lobohombo was the biggest nightclub in Latin America. But why was it an important fact that it was the biggest nightclub in Latin America? It could be seen as part of the Mexican love of collecting banal world records—the biggest taco (of course we have that, if not us, who

20

21

20-21: The aluminum façade of the building appears closed and is interrupted only by lines of light, indicating which of the three fire brigades are currently out working. At the ground floor, however, the building is completely open and accessible to the public.

else?), the biggest publicly performed Michael Jackson dance, the biggest cheese cake, the most people kissing at once, the biggest piñata, the biggest Christmas tree, and, of course, the biggest nightclub in Latin America. But on the other hand, this issue of bigness actually played a crucial, and very favorable, role for our project: because the fire station had to be big, it actually became too big for the program it was to fulfill; but it was precisely this excess space that was to become the genuine potential of the project as we soon found out when we started designing it.

As the first step we had simply designed a big box as a generic container for the program with the maximum density allowed on the site. After looking at the size of this maximized box, however, we realized that it was too big for a simple fire station. We made the decision to raise the container six meters above street level to bring the city into the site. The city extends under the building as a public space for visitors or pedestrians, and so we gave the site back to the city as a public building and as an element of infrastructure.

The second design move came as a result of our examination of the turning radius and mobility specifications for the various firefighting vehicles, from the ladder truck to motorcycles. We made a comprehensive movement diagram tracing these circulation patterns, and let it inform our design; all of the vehicular traffic can enter the site front first and then turn around completely to face the street again while inside the site. This is important for the speed and efficiency of the firefighters leaving on a call, and this 360-degree turning can be done without blocking the complicated traffic on the avenue itself. The diagram of these movement patterns on the ground level also helped us to organize the circulation and openings into the building above.

For us, the generous volume of the box was the perfect excuse to reprogram the contents of the symbolic container of the fire station. With the client busy worrying about the size, the form, and the political discourse, we felt that we had the chance to design the program as we wanted. We came up with the idea to incorporate two other programs, a civic center for the community and an elevated public plaza for visitors and events. The inspiration for these additions was born out of the conditions of the project itself; the civic center and public space were the phoenix rising from the ashes. We wanted to provide space where the public could be informed about basic safety issues and measures, as clearly there was no standard of inspections from the government, and little public education about things like fire safety or disaster measures.

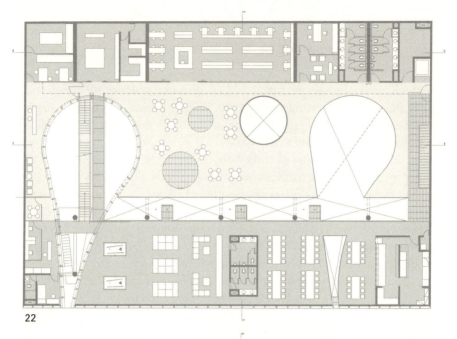

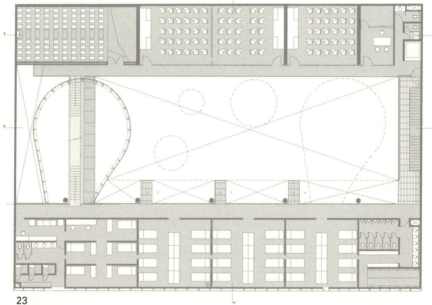

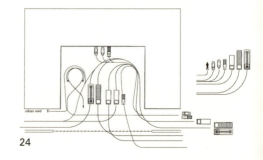

22: Ground plan level 1.
23: Ground plan level 2.
24: Movement diagram of different vehicles. All vehicles can turn 360 degrees on the site to allow fluent traffic on the street.
25: Ground plan level 3.
26: Cross section through courtyard.

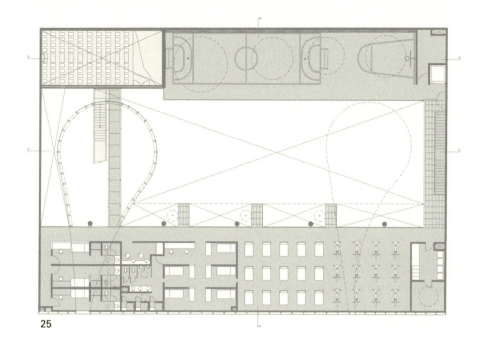
25

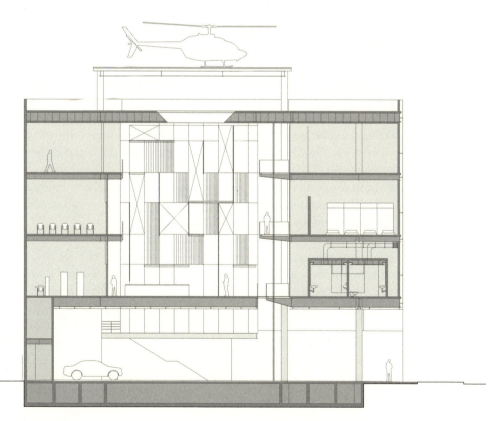
26

The civic plaza was the link between the community and the fire station; it is the street and the public space that wrap both programs together, and both of these new programs became an important element in the political discourse surrounding the project. The new social program is a chance for the public to see the interior world of the fire station, as a spectacle and as a learning experience for kids and families. The civic center program included classrooms and an auditorium as instructional space in which to teach the community about fires, earthquakes, and floods. We also provided space for a bookstore dedicated to history and prevention of fires and natural disasters, a coffee shop, and a souvenir shop. People are welcome in the building and people are part of the building.

The center void of the building is the civic plaza. It is always connected visually to the sky and to the city. This 20-m-tall space is the buffer between the program of the fire station and the public program, and interacts with both. Round openings allow a vertical visual connection, ventilation, and natural light for the interior spaces. It is a central court, with a similar function to a central court in colonial Mexican architecture: all the spaces are arranged around it, and it closes itself to the city, for the benefit of intimacy for the spaces surrounding it. The building is thus both, open and closed. The part of the building used by the firemen is closed, very much in tune with the traditional fire station typology. But the rest of the building that is programmed with public functions is very much open and connected to the city.

The vertical circulation element is the pivot of the building, allowing circulation of two systems. On one side firemen circulate freely throughout the building and on the other visitors can circulate without interfering with the firemen's work. In this way both programs can use the same building despite their completely different functional properties. They complement each other by creating equilibrium between the institution and the community.

The program for the firemen was divided over three floors. The first floor contains the office spaces, the cafeteria, and rest areas; on the second floor are the dormitories, which are further divided between men's, women's, and highly ranked firemen's sleeping quarters; and finally, the third floor is the gym, training area, and the sleeping quarters for the station chief. All the floors have access to multiple fire poles, via platforms or drop areas that will bring the fireman to their trucks, ready to go. These platforms and poles are placed next to the translucent façade of the fire station, and also run down through a gap between the civic

27: The raised level of the courtyard can be used for public venues without disrupting the operation of the fire station

plaza and the fire station. When the firemen go out on a call a big spectacle is created as they spring into action.

The fire station is divided in thirds, housing three troops of firemen. All troops can perform the same activities simultaneously, so it is really three fire stations together in one building. In fact, there was a lack of sufficient firefighting capacity in the area which necessitated a bigger fire station.

The main façade is a solid aluminum wall, mostly closed to the exterior, with only two slit-like windows, like long, linear peepholes, to make it possible to see inside of the building. The façade is divided into three sections, each with neon lights, one section for each troop. The neon lights are lit for each troop that is out working. The "light code" enables a visual dialog between the building and the city, and it subtly reveals the activity inside the building without exposing everything at once.

In the end, everyone got what they wanted: the government managed to calm the community by giving them a space as a deliberate act of remembrance, and they got what they asked us for: the biggest fire station in Mexico as a civic monument. The community was happy to gain a building that helps everyone to learn about safety and security, and that encourages people to come together. Lastly, we also achieved what we wanted to achieve because we were able to place extra program into the container of the building to give the community more than just a monument, and give the government more than just a big fire station. After all, mixes are good.

About the author: Francisco Pardo is an architect from Mexico City, educated at Columbia University. He is principal of the firm at 103, based in Mexico City, in partnership with Julio Amezcua. His projects have been published worldwide and he has lectured at various institutions. His firm was selected as part of the series "Emerging Voices" at the Architectural League of New York in 2009. He has taught at a range of institutions in Mexico and the United States; currently he is a Visiting Professor at the University of California, Berkeley.

TAKE ON COMPLEXITY

The Cook, the Prospector, the Nomad and their Architect

Three Approaches to Building with Local Resources

JEANNE GANG / STUDIO GANG ARCHITECTS

Issues of form in contemporary practice have a tendency to take priority over issues of construction. Today, illustration and rendering techniques—even more remote from construction—are becoming prioritized over form. This reality of our time reflects the ease with which we now employ digital media to convey ideas. However, in many projects the construction of the building itself presents an opportunity for the architect to design and create beyond the two-dimensional image. Construction materials have unique physical characteristics that are underexplored or have yet to be discovered, making it possible and exciting to work with them as generative forces for a project, rather than relying on form or imagery as a starting point. A building has the potential to be "about concrete," for example, in much the same way as a painting can be "about paint."

To create a building "about material" is not the same as to refine material and construction techniques in buildings. There are many architects who aspire to perfect their craft and whose work represents a lifetime of continual refinement.

These architects patiently improve details with subtle changes: an endeavor that spans decades and dozens of buildings. The details are often highly expensive and require elite museums or private mansions with large project budgets to absorb their cost. This trajectory of fine tuning (which some would call fetishizing) lacks curiosity, the willingness to be surprised, the thrill of bold experimentation, and the chance to make a discovery. The accomplished master is in many ways no longer allowed to explore because his clients expect him to repeat and refine specific forms and details—years of polishing a single groove create a furrow so deep that escaping it is often impossible.

How then, to create a building with an idea that begins with construction material and technique, but which is liberated from this obsession with refinement? To do so, architects must be unafraid of radical experimentation and commit to investigations that can be deployed on relatively conventional construction sites. Within the manifold constraints of ordinary construction, the search for something new requires a focus on the materials at hand, combined with the use of tactics found outside the traditional architectural office. Looking to numerous other modes of working offers alternative ways of seeing, thinking, and making.

The Cook

Before the mass industrialization of agriculture and the construction of modern infrastructure made nearly any food available anywhere, at any time of year, cooks had to both shrewdly plan and improvise each day to create delicious dishes from what was actually available. Today, with the growing popularity of the local and slow food movements, cooks are choosing to return to this way of working—challenging themselves to prepare delectable meals using only those ingredients that are naturally available in their specific location and growing season. This necessitates a certain kind of experimental approach, different from the exotic-combination zeal of those who have every food imaginable at their disposal. It also requires cooks to work with more intention, anticipating what will become available and how it can be incorporated with the staple goods already in supply. It is essential for these cooks to remain flexible and open to every sort of culinary possibility, and to making adjustments to their original menu, if they are to please palates and pocketbooks.

THE COOK, THE PROSPECTOR, THE NOMAD AND THEIR ARCHITECT

The creation of our SOS Children's Village Community Center project in Chicago, Illinois, demonstrates that the exploratory architect who seeks an architecture about material works in much the same way as the locally and seasonally focused cook. Given the project's limited funding (SOS is an international non-profit organization dedicated to child welfare), the building was largely shaped by the process of securing the materials for its construction—many of which were donated by manufacturers and builders. This condition precluded honing the architect's favored details, and instead led to defining a new design process, whereby materials and details were conceived of as a flexible set of placeholder elements. Each design element, from the exterior cladding to the stair design, was treated as a variable; as each new donation was secured, it was studied in relation to all of its immediately adjacent parts. By means of that conception of the design, each donation could affect other elements, re-shuffling or re-integrating them, or even suggest new donations to be sought.

Unlike the practice of "value engineering," which eliminates or substitutes materials in favor of less expensive alternatives, here specific windows, finishes, skylights, and plumbing fixtures were all variables with equal potential. When the original donation of masonry for the exterior was withdrawn by its donor, we began to explore what the building would be like in its most raw, stripped-down condition, with its primary façade created by poured-in-place, exposed concrete donated from another source.

The choice to showcase this normally concealed material was not without issues; one of the first addressed was the problem of the cold joint—the lineation that forms when concrete pouring is interrupted and later resumed—in an exposed concrete wall. The height of the exterior wall at SOS required two separate pours, making a visible cold joint along its surface unavoidable. Rather than trying to hide, straighten or control this line, our consideration of the potential of concrete as a poured fluid led us to investigate the visual effect of the cold joint. By multiplying the number of cold joint lines and making the line of each joint more dynamic, we elevated the significance of the "casting" action in construction. Simultaneously, we varied the concrete mix design, which—because different strengths are different colors—visually intensified the differentiation between the horizontal layers. The final architecture preserves and reveals the physics of a once-fluid material in the building's "strata-wall." The building benefits structurally from the use of multiple combined concrete mixes, as the different characteristics of each mix work together to make the cantilevered entrance walls possible.

1: SOS Children's Village Community Center in Chicago: The visible striation of the joints between concrete pours was accentuated by the use of different colored concrete. Throughout the process donated building materials were used to their full potential.

THE COOK, THE PROSPECTOR, THE NOMAD AND THEIR ARCHITECT

By exploiting the readily available, leftover products in the building industry and construction process, we, like the cook, innovated with what we could get our hands on. Our role in the project departed radically from that of the traditional architect: we became organizers of a set of chance circumstances, remaining flexible and open to an array of possibilities that only achieved their distinctive flavor when the building was finalized.

The Prospector

Since prehistoric times, we, as humans, have looked to (or below) the earth for the materials we cannot grow or cultivate ourselves. Though mining has evolved immensely over the intervening 45,000 years, today the same basic steps still comprise the mining process. Prospecting is the initial exploratory phase in which a material deposit is sought through physical means. Once discovered, its feasibility for mining is analyzed, by measuring the deposit's estimated value against the cost of its removal, or excavation. Excavation methods have varied widely, based on the material resource type and its location, but the vast majority of removal techniques have all been extremely destructive to their natural environments.

This could be different if mining was refocused on the man-made world — if architects took the same evaluation framework and used it to locate and exploit a new resource: the built environment. The prospecting architect could mitigate the environmental degradation typically concurrent with new construction by locating materials that have already been used, evaluating their potential, and giving them new life in architecture. From leftover steel to pulverized rubber, bulk quantities of useful things pass through metropolitan areas on a daily basis. In many contexts there are salvage industries whose sole purpose is to sort, store, and re-sell materials from this plethora of resources. The only real issue preventing their reuse in construction is that these materials are not always in a finished condition, ready to be transferred into architecture — they currently require the curiosity and persistence of a prospector to locate and utilize.

The Ford Calumet Environmental Center project mines the city to find locally available and salvaged materials from its site and surrounding context: a historic industrial region south of Chicago, once the largest steel producing region in the United States, which is also an important resting stop for migratory birds. The Environmental Center will be a place where people come to learn about these

2

3

4

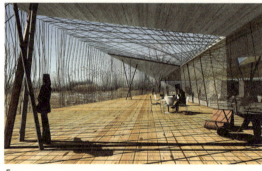

5

2-3: The Ford Calumet Environmental Center was built in an area of Chicago formerly known nation-wide for steel production. Materials were sourced from local producers as well as from local scrap and salvage yards.

4-5: The design incorporated a nest-like appearance, partially to protect migrating birds from collisions with the transparent elements of the façade. The space between the exterior and interior of the building creates a deck for observation of the marsh and surroundings.

interesting and seemingly divergent identities that will be reconciled in the building's "nest-like" design.

Natural prospectors themselves, birds have an eye for the abundant and available materials that can be used for their nests. Our project team worked in much the same way: we began design by surveying nearby industry and its products, as well as the stocks of local material in salvage yards adjacent to the site, to determine what was available and potentially valuable for the project. Armed with this knowledge, we designed a building which employs reclaimed materials in new ways, profoundly redefining construction's typical method of specifying and sourcing materials. Differing types of salvaged steel sections are bundled together like twigs—in lieu of melting and reshaping them in a more energy-intensive process—to form the building's column structure. Slag and glass from broken bottles find a new purpose as aggregate in the terrazzo floors. Reclaimed bar-stock and re-bar form a basket-like mesh that wraps an expansive outdoor porch, protecting the site's migrating birds from collisions with transparent glass, which they cannot see.

Perhaps perfect salvage will one day be available on order, with a point-and-click from a desktop, but until then making architecture from nearby scrap still seems both elementary and urgent in a world that is overflowing with waste. As demonstrated by the Ford Calumet project, architectural practices can meet this challenge by cunningly prospecting available materials, mining the city for its undervalued and discarded resources.

The Nomad

Most of the industrial world measures success by mass. The more tons of concrete a plant produces, for example, the more successful it is perceived to be. A powerful alternative model is provided by the concept of "lightness", as it is inherently understood by nomadic peoples. Working as a collective, nomads transport themselves and their provisions from place to place. Their transient way of life is characterized by few material possessions and a deep connection to nature. Their portable habitations are designed to be as light as possible, without sacrificing strength and protection, and adaptable to varying climate and site conditions.

Learning from the nomad, architectural practice can expand beyond the obvious lightweight fabric tensile structures, to pursue a more holistic notion of "lightness": one which seeks adaptability and a deeper connection to the environment through considering the structure's relationship to its climate and ecology. Interesting new possibilities for design and construction arise as we begin to consider reducing weight, materials, and their environmental burden in more complex ways.

The search for this sort of lightness helped drive the Lincoln Park Zoo South Pond project, in which we revitalized an urban pond in the center of Chicago. Originally designed in the early 20th century as a shallow reflecting pool, it was wastefully replenished by city drinking water. In its new iteration, the redesigned pond is substantially deeper and filled by rainwater runoff that is filtered by plants around its perimeter. As the water level fluctuates with the seasons and the weather (including drought), a visit to the pond becomes an experience connecting visitors to these natural cycles.

Two structures enhance visitors' experience of the pond habitat. The boardwalk invites people to meander along a path, exploring both the water side and land side of the riparian edge. The boardwalk leads to the education pavilion, at the eastern edge of the boardwalk. Constructed of prefabricated wooden elements and fiberglass pods, it forms a sheltering arch for educational classes. Each member of its lattice-like structure is curved in two directions. The bending action used to make the wooden elements, similar to that of bent wood furniture or boats, provides additional strength and allows the pieces to be smaller and lighter. In the case of the pavilion, the pieces were light enough to eliminate the need for large construction machinery; instead, only two persons were needed to assemble the structure using steel connection plates and simple tools. Cladding the structure's outer surface are pod-like, lightweight fiberglass domes that were also able to be assembled by hand, each of them lifted into place by a single person.

Mimicking nomads, architects who design for lightness achieve inventive solutions as they explore using less material with greater strength. This recognition of the dynamic natural cycles of a project's site and context, and the design of spaces that offer people, as users of the architecture, a direct connection to those cycles is an equally important strategy toward reinventing construction with a deeper ecological purpose.

As we worked on the three projects, acting as the cook, the prospector, and the nomad, we found that each project grew richer—in a way that a simple formal gesture never can. Being as attentive to the working process as to the building form injected a whole new range of possibilities for each project. It allowed us

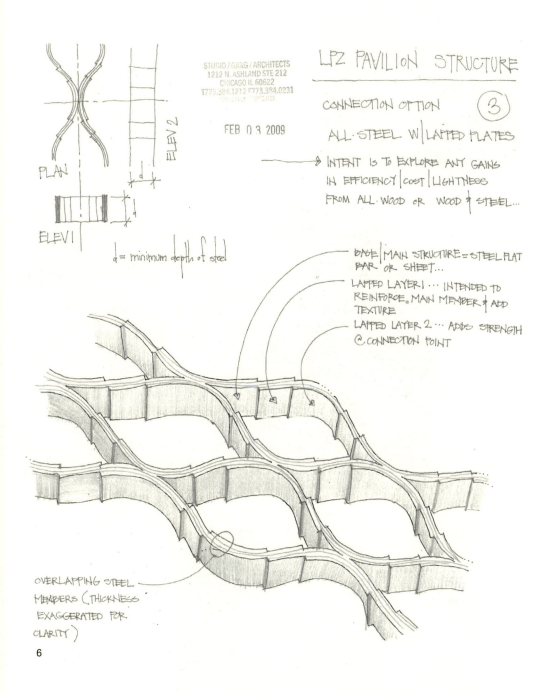

6: Lincoln Park Zoo South Pond project. One of the options analyzed for the pavilion's structure.

7

7-8: The pavilion could be assembled in one day with a minimum of two people, and no heavy machinery.
9: Fiberglass domes used to clad the openings that provide shelter from the elements.
10-11: The pavilion is both a site for program, such as public Yoga classes, and an icon for the park. In the evening the pavilion is lit, and creates a focal point along the pond.

8

9

10

11

greater freedom with the design, and a stronger connection to the essence of each site and all of its constituents. Like the cook, we assembled with what we had, like the prospector, we found and extracted what was of use, and like the nomad, we sought lightness and simplicity.

The discoveries made during the design of the SOS, Ford Calumet, and Lincoln Park Zoo projects could never have been achieved through the use of drawing alone. Instead, we developed unexpected and radical design solutions by implementing a variety of tools and methods, including innovative physical models, prototypes, material testing, and—of particular importance—collaborations. These intense working sessions with builders, engineers, and craftsmen challenged all involved to try new methods outside their traditional boundaries of expertise, and resulted in increased knowledge and additional tools for each team member to use, both on the project and into the future.

This collaborative and multi-faceted way of working, contingent on an architect's willingness to leave behind the confines of software programs and expand traditional modes of practice, is critical if we are to reinvent construction. Great possibilities for innovation arise when we take cues from innovators outside architecture and attempt to see the world anew through their eyes. Architecture is a fluid profession, one that is not only evolving but radically changing. New architects hoping to reinvent construction might find more inspiration in learning from the cook, the prospector, or the nomad, than in serving as apprentices to the masters of refinement.

About the author: Jeanne Gang leads Studio Gang Architects, a practice generating some of today's most innovative and creative works of architecture. Her projects confront pressing contemporary issues, including climate, urbanization, and technology. Published and exhibited widely, her work has been shown at the International Venice Biennale, the Smithsonian Institution's National Building Museum, and the Art Institute of Chicago. She is an Adjunct Associate Professor at the Illinois Institute of Technology where her studios have focused on megacities and material technologies.

Buy One, Get One Free

Doubling the Space for the New Architecture School in Nantes

ANNE LACATON AND JEAN-PHILIPPE VASSAL
LACATON & VASSAL ARCHITECTS

When we built the Architecture School in Nantes we applied a principle we had developed for housing projects like House Latapie, the House in Coutras, or the social housing complex in Mulhouse, which was designed to provide as much space as possible within the given budget. By using inexpensive construction materials or entire prefabricated building systems like a standard greenhouse, we had managed to double the living area of these houses. All three houses consist of a consolidated unit with proper insulation, that contains all the rooms requested by the client and a second unit of the same size constructed as a light winter garden structure without heating or insulation.

In our first house, House Latapie, we conceptualized the winter garden as an extension of the garden. However, the way the family used the space made us realize that it was much more than that, the family actually used it as an extension of their living and dining rooms on the ground level. Suddenly, they had twice as much living space. This unexpected proliferation of space radically questions the very design methodology that modernism had invented for the construction of affordable housing—the concept of an *existenzminimum*. This approach was based on the reduction of building costs through the minimization of both the number of elements in the program (which reduces the potential variety of events occurring in a home) and the size of total space. Doubling the available space allowed us to escape the limitations of the *existenzminimum* in favor of an *existenzmaximum*, that includes and openly invites domestic activities which neither the architect nor the inhabitant can anticipate.

We think it is of utmost importance to a student of architecture to experience that the production of space is not simply equivalent with building anew, but already takes place when you appropriate a given space. We therefore decided from the very beginning of our design process for the new Architecture School of Nantes to create considerably more space than what the brief had requested. The site for the project measures about $5,000\,m^2$. Divided by a street and directly adjacent to the Loire River the site benefits from a lot of open space in its vicinity. Hence, we saw no reason to leave a part of the site unbuilt or to create an interior courtyard. And since the site is also located in the city center, where land is very valuable, we wanted to take maximum advantage of the site.

The brief of the client not only determined the program of the school and the construction schedule. It also explained the school's approach to teaching and the kind of spaces needed for that. It offered the possibility of making levels every seven meters, which allowed for the addition of intermediary levels. The concept reminded us of the *Eco Houses* which Frei Otto and Hermann Kendel had realized for the IBA Berlin in Berlin-Tiergarten between 1987 and 1991. They proposed three houses to be built as open "Garden Shelves" with two concrete platforms at 6 m and 12 m height, supported by massive beams and girders. Interesting to us in this project was that instead of adding floors, Frei Otto actually multiplied floors by treating each floor as a ground floor. This concept had fascinated us immensely and inspired the design concept for the Architecture School in Nantes. The essence of the concept is a building with several superimposed ground floors rather than a succession of floors which are connected by a staircase. Stacking concrete floor slabs and inserting the school between them, we created residual spaces on every level, which were completely unexpected and loaded with potential.

Conceptually, the project comprises two separate design steps. As a first step, we conceived a large-capacity industrial-type building—like something that could have preexisted in this very industrial part of Nantes—and in a second step we in-

1: Building the Architecture School in 2 steps: First a large-capacity concrete structure is built, then the spaces of the Architecture School are put in it.
2: The school emulates an existing industrial-type building, that was reused as an architecture school.

serted an architectural school into it. The building site was a completely empty lot on which one could imagine a warehouse might have once stood, because the island of Nantes was once an industrial port. After constructing a very robust concrete structure, we filled it with a light steel structure. Considering the long-term use of a building, we think the idea of developing it in two phases is a sustainable concept. For who knows if the architecture school will still be there in 20 years? And if it is not, the light steel structure can be transformed or easily dismantled. And the concrete structure is generous and generic enough to accommodate other utilizations. We are inspired by the concept of the loft and we emulate the way we inhabit old industrial buildings today with programs that sometimes did not even exist when these buildings were first built.

Our design started by stacking concrete floors every seven meters. The space in between would then be furnished with intermediary levels where necessary. Determining the position of the parking lots within this structure was a crucial decision for the layout of the entire building; it was in fact the most difficult element to place. The easiest option would have been to bury the parking lots halfway or completely. But that would have meant that we would have had to create a complex and costly structure in order to protect them from flooding and groundwater; this was contradicting our intention to build a structure capable of absorbing anything. Putting the parking lots on the ground floor would have destroyed the site's continuity with the city, and this continuity was essential to us. It was also impossible to put them on the roof, because we had already decided to turn it into a large terrace. Thus, the best solution was to put them on the first intermediary level. In order to provide the requested 130 parking lots we decided to add a second intermediary level. For each parking level we needed a ceiling height of three meters, plus three meters between parking and ground floor. We therefore expanded the first main level from seven to nine meters. This resulted in main levels at the height of +9 m, +16 m, and +23 m, which would be connected by a ramp.

Because a ramp takes up a lot of space, we tested different positions for it. At first we tried to accommodate the ramp inside the building, but that did not work. Finally we decided to place the ramp outside. That move had an immense impact on the whole project, because placing the ramp outside changed its status completely. It turned more into a street similar to those that feed villages or cities on hills. This solution allowed us to create large exterior spaces to accommodate the necessary space for the turns of the ramp. At the west and south façade the ramp is approximately 120 m long and has an inclination of five to six percent, which

3

4

5

3-5: Like an inclined street, a ramp connects the city with all the levels up to the roof terrace. Ramp and terraces provide an additional 6,000 m² of outdoor space for the Architecture School.

6: (Next pages) A polycarbonate façade with large sliding doors envelopes the unprogrammed spaces, a floor to ceiling glass façade the programmed spaces.

enables a vertical rise of ten meters. In the end this unusual circulation concept produced an additional usable surface of 6,000 m² for ramps and terraces which represent more than the area of the site. The ramp proves to be one of the most important elements of the building, also because it serves various functions. Running along the west and southwest façades it not only provides welcome shade, but also lets you discover the entire building. By generating a system of connected balconies, and linking them to the large roof terrace, it reveals that the main floors are not simply stacked building levels, but an extension of the ground.

The ground level is conceptualized as a completely public space. Therefore it contains all the spaces that were to be shared by other parties than the school: the lobby, the large 250-seat auditorium, the big hall for manufacturing prototypes, and the exhibition gallery. It was absolutely crucial that the ground floor of the building was literally the continuation of the ground of the city; the floor of the ground level was to be on the exact same level as the street and covered with the same material—asphalt. At first everybody accepted our idea of the continuation of the ground floor, but later there arose misunderstandings resulting from an incorrect ground study, which alleged that the ground was not stable enough. Therefore the project manager wanted to pour concrete instead. We really had to fight very hard for our idea that people should be able to experience the ground floor having a different nature than the upper levels. We imagined the ground floor as an urban texture, with a suppleness that would almost allow you to "sink" into it. A concrete slab is inert and has much less potential than a floor that can accept 6, 7 or even 10 tons per m². It was this potential that we wanted to preserve. After almost two years of endless debates, we eventually arrived at a compromise: we partially placed metal floors in the area of the workspaces, which cover roughly 30 percent of the ground floor. These floors rest directly on the foundations and can be modified or removed at any time.

The architecture school proper starts on the first main level. That is where research facilities, classrooms, administrative offices, and the library are located. Further up are the students' design studios and the professors' workspaces.

The main levels of the building positioned at +9 m, +16 m, and +23 m had to be able to support the intermediary floors. The main floors were designed for a capacity of 1 ton per square meter, which required concrete floors of 90 cm, including trusses. For the primary structure we cooperated with a medium-size concrete contractor who specializes in prefabricated systems. This firm's solutions always proved to be very efficient. The posts for the lobby, for example, were produced hollow for transport and filled with concrete on location. The very thick concrete floors required the secondary structure for the intermediate floors to be very light and thin in order to provide sufficient ceiling heights on each floor, important also because the secondary structure, designed to be adaptable and changeable over time, must be able to be taken down easily.

The school comprises presently two types of space: The first type are the programmed areas with standard ceiling heights between 2.70 m and 3.50 m and floor to ceiling glass sliding doors with aluminum frames. This façade allows you to open 50 percent of its elements; it provides access to a balcony and is equipped with sunscreens.

The second type of space consists of the un-programmed open areas. These spaces of double height are enveloped by a simple transparent polycarbonate skin only, which creates an intermediary climate. Large parts of this polycarbonate façade can be slid away and will actually be open for long periods during the year. Long polycarbonate panels between the sliding parts and the ceiling can be pivoted horizontally, allowing hot air to escape. They are opened and closed by a rack-and-rail mechanism used in horticultural green houses, which effectively regulates the school's climate during the summer. In the winter these spaces function as winter gardens; due to passive solar gain they reach a temperature of approximately 10-12 °C naturally, which is warmer than outside and comfortable enough as a room climate if you keep your street clothes on. Upon entering the classrooms from these intermediate spaces one moves from an intermediary temperature into heated rooms with a temperature of approximately 21 °C. Since the temperature difference between heated rooms and winter garden is only ca. 10 °C, less energy is needed for heating which allowed us to implement smaller heating systems and led to considerable savings in the construction budget. All spaces, except the auditorium, use natural ventilation. The volume of the classrooms was adjusted according to the number of users, so that the necessary air circulation can occur naturally.

To fulfill the goal of maximizing space without increasing the given construction budget we had to be extremely cost-conscious in regard to the construction materials, technical equipment, and operating costs. Rather than limiting, it was stimulating the design process. The challenge lies in finding appropriate systems and using one's intelligence to adapt them optimally to one's needs. Of course one has to adapt one's solutions to what a company can realize, but this is not difficult. It gets difficult when one has to deal with standards and regulations. The

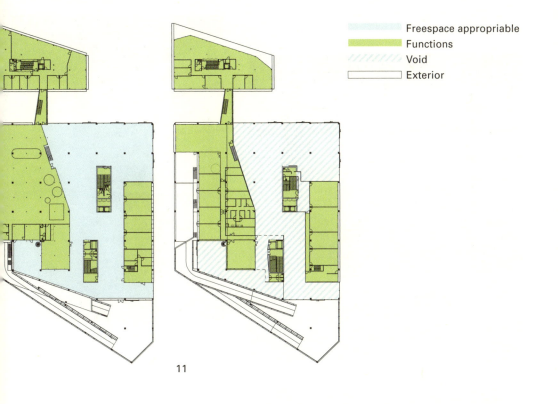

11

15

16

7: Level 0.
8: Level 0, Mezzanine A.
9: Level 0, Mezzanine B.
10: Level 1.
11: Level 1, Mezzanine.
12: Level 2.
13: Level 2, Mezzanine.
14: Roof terrace.
15-16: Sections.

18

17

17-18: The unprogrammed spaces function like a big wintergarden: In winter the space is heated by passive solar gain. In summer large sliding doors allow hot air to escape.
19: A light steel structure provides intermediary levels, which accommodate the programmed spaces of the Architecture School. These spaces are accessed via the free double-height spaces.
20: The ground floor of the school is the continuation of the city, containing all the public programs plus ample free space that can be appropriated depending on the needs of the school.

19

20

only solution to this is to develop a positive attitude and find a way to turn them upside down and make them work for you. In fact some regulations, such as the accessibility for the handicapped, actually require larger spaces, which in the end create more comfort for everybody. The smaller a space, the more complicated and tedious it is to build. When spaces are larger constraints can be worked out a lot easier, such as changes that need to be incorporated into the design during the construction process. In the case of the new Architecture School in Nantes there were many such changes: the cafeteria was transformed from a snack bar without a kitchen into a canteen able to serve 300 meals; the local city plan was changed, allowing the addition of another floor to the smaller building facing the Loire; the parking policy of Nantes was changed, which allowed us to dispense with the second parking level and use the space instead for additional project studios which the school had asked for. All these changes could easily be accommodated. And this will also be the case for future adaptations due to the robust basic structure that can be utilized according to various needs and that is spacious and flexible enough to absorb these changes without compromising the basic concept.

In their specifications the architecture school had asked for 12,500 m² of space. We added 2,500 m² producing 15,000 m² of programmed space. It has proved that the additional space was actually necessary and easily occupied. Moreover, we added another 5,000 m² of double-height free space, plus another 6,000 m² of terraces which means that the school now has 26,000 m² of usable space with an unexpected freedom of use which is in part also unprecedented for an architecture school. For us it is a manifesto of how to work with space. Don't tailor your design to the brief, because it inevitably represents only a limited understanding of the situation's potential. Make room for the unexpected side effects of life which often turn out to be desirable. In other words: Don't reduce, but potentiate.

About the authors: Anne Lacaton is principal of Lacaton & Vassal Architects, based in Paris. She holds a Diploma from the School of Architecture, Bordeaux, and a Diploma in Town Planning from the University of Bordeaux. She was a Visiting Professor at the Ecole Polytechnique Fédérale de Lausanne in 2003-2004 and 2005-2006.

Jean-Philippe Vassal is principal of Lacaton & Vassal Architects, based in Paris. He graduated from the School of Architecture, Bordeaux, and spent the following five years in Niger as an architect and town planner. He has lectured at the School of Architecture Versailles in 2002-2005, was Guest Professor at Düsseldorf Peter Behrens School of Architecture in 2005 and at the TU Berlin in 2007-2009. He is currently Guest Professor at Ecole Polytechnique Fédérale de Lausanne.

TAKE ON COMPLEXITY

Squaring the Circle

Building a Tower the Tirana Way

PETER SWINNEN AND JOHAN ANRYS / 51N4E

In 2004, we won an international competition to build a multi-purpose high-rise tower in Tirana, the capital of Albania. If all goes well, the tower will be completed in 2011, seven years later. That it took so long to realize this project has to do with many factors, most importantly, however, with the brutally idiosyncratic reality of Tirana which does not compare to any other urban condition we had worked in before. It was a challenge to which we came fully unprepared.

Tirana is a very upfront capital without subtlety or escape, and so are its people. Tirana's history is diverse, it has suffered a number of unresolved wars, riots, dictatorships, and pyramid economics. The country is based on the *Kanun*, a set of traditional Albanian social laws often related to blood revenge. Although Albanians know that the 21st century has arrived, they don't really deal with it. Daily life radiates an almost insulting roughness, which, after a while, becomes endearing and truly sincere. All logic that we had up until established had to be abandoned. Tirana weighs on your (West European) stamina.

SQUARING THE CIRCLE

If you want to develop a high-rise project in Tirana, you have to forget any preconceived ideas about how to approach this task elsewhere and embrace the place wholeheartedly, internalizing its logic before you even begin to think how you can contribute to, or transform, this reality. Tirana offered us the opportunity to conceive and build in an environment that is not found elsewhere in Europe today: West Europe learning from Tirana, rather than the other way round, was our mission.

The first thing that struck us was the quality of the light, which is absolutely superb and slightly surreal. The climate is Mediterranean. The presence of the dramatic Daijti Mountains, a mountain range surrounding the entire city center, became the main backdrop.

In 2003, the city of Tirana, headed by its larger-than-life mayor Edi Rama, had commissioned a masterplan for the redevelopment of the city center. The laureate architects of the French Architecture Studio proposed a Hausmanian doctrine that would uneasily rewrite the heart of Tirana into a car-free zone bordered by ten towers. Since 2003, different parts of the masterplan have been offered as individual competitions, hardly any succeeded to go beyond the proverbial drawing table. Today, the city cannot confirm that either the towers, or the city center development will be completed, because of Tirana's intricate real estate situation, a leftover from Communist times. Due to its client, the Tirana International Development Company, the TID project, however, turned out to be one of the few exceptions. TID managed to acquire over 70 small lots, some not bigger than $2\,m^2$. The competition could start.

After two months of concentrated work in our Brussels office, we went back to Tirana, ready to present our proposal. The jury was composed of unrivaled international architects (Elia Zenghelis, Josep Luis Mateo, and Valerio Olgiati, to name just a few). Representatives of the public were carefully chosen, ranging from Miss Albania to West European deputies. The entire event was broadcast live on national television. Architectural CNN... The future of Tirana was now! Whether you believed it or not!

Our competition proposal revolved around the question: "How can we catch Tirana's light in a tower?" The solution was a super-ellipse, a volume starting from an ellipse and ending in a rectangle. The subtle transition between the two basic shapes created a tower, which captured the light fully and changed the profile when viewed diagonally. From the top corners the façade sloped 6 m inwards, forming a gentle cantilever. Viewed from the Kavajes Boulevard, the main axis leading from the airport into the city, the tower's silhouette gracefully but strongly complements the historical line-up of the Skanderbeg Square, the Mosque, and the Clock Tower. Because of potentially seismic action, we were convinced that a diagonally interwoven net of columns would be the most effective solution. It would also emphasize the rather smooth three-dimensional development of the skin with which we tried to capture the light. The specific central location of the tower called for a façade that would work on both an urban and a private scale and would comprise of various elements that would correspond to the Mediterranean conditions, both on interior and exterior: loggia / shaded loggia / shaded window / textured surface with view through / textured surface cladded with light. We decided to enter the competition on the basis of a terracotta *Moucharabieh* principle, made out of small and basic components following a geometric yet flexible pattern that connected to the tower's structural column net. The Moucharabieh was to provide maximum sun protection, which is mandatory in Tirana, where temperatures can rise up to 40 °C. Moreover, unlike a glass façade the Moucharabieh could deal in a more graceful way with Tirana's high air pollution which is resulting from a number of still unpaved streets and the utilization of old leaded gasoline by virtually every car. Tirana requires strong lungs.

Programmatically, the tower was conceived in a way that can be re-programmed in a rather flexible manner, even during construction. It comprises of two basic parts: the fixed program and the flexible program. The fixed parts are ground floor shopping and a rooftop restaurant. The main body of the tower consists of an office and housing program, depending on the market. But it was actually one small detail that awarded us the competition. On the site, next to the street, we found a rather dilapidated structure, a seemingly lost item, engulfed by the unstructured daily Tirana frenzy. Little did we know that this monument, a tomb, had been dedicated to Suleman Pasha, a general in the Ottoman Empire, who had founded Tirana in 1614. Apparently, the French masterplanners had not been fully aware of or had simply overlooked this historical relic. However, here it was on our competition site, and a tower, a true monument, was to be built right next to it. We decided to design the base in a way that it would cantilever over the Suleman Pasha Tomb, restoring its true scale and grandeur. The quarter dome that resulted from this intent created an instantly ethereal aura for the city's founder and proved to provide a pretty good urban hangout as well. The day after the competition, the newspapers were wild about this revolutionary idea, hardly

1

1: On the competition site, right next to the proposed tower, there already existed a monument dedicated to Suleman Pasha, founder of Tirana, that had been completely ignored in the masterplan.
2: Morphing from an ellipse into a rectangle, the tower captures Tirana's exceptional light and changes the profile when viewed diagonally.
3: The first design was composed of a diagonally interwoven net of columns that the architects considered the most effective solution for potential seismic action.

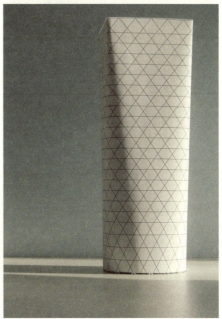

3

2

4: 1:1 mock-up of the first design.
5: After a year of struggling with inadequate communication a 'collaborative drawing method' was established; plans were projected on a whiteboard, so that all team members could freely sketch on the plans, over and over again.
6: 1:1 mock-up of the revised design with different panel versions.

mentioning the tower. Suleman Pasha's dignity was restored! So was Tirana's founding history—perhaps their only certainty.

On the day of the newspapers' laudation, the client, who had been part of the jury, congratulated us wholeheartedly, however, stating in the same sentence that they really disliked the project. Especially the façade, which in their eyes was too Muslim, too closed, too cheap! Our allusion to the Islamic past had not been fully unintentional, considering that up to 70 percent of the inhabitants are in fact Muslims. During the rule of dictator Enver Hoxha, religious practice and symbolism had been suppressed as a principle, depriving Tiranians of any kind of overtly cultural markers until to day. The client's final argument was that the tower's façade did not sufficiently reflect the future image of Tirana. We decided to call an immediate stop, a reflection period for all team members, allowing everyone time to critically re-evaluate the program. After a couple of weeks the client was very surprised when he understood that we were even more critical about our initial project than he was. We believed in the light, we believed in the powerful directness of the super-ellipse, the historical line-up, the way it constructed public space, and last but not least, the redemption of Suleman Pasha. But the budget, which had been communicated to us only after the competition, seemed entirely insufficient. It was clear to us that the original Moucharabieh façade principle had to be dispensed with, because it was impossible to work with standardized elements. The diagonal structure had to be rethought. Each column needed different angles and even required different lengths so that all columns would have been unique. This design was out of the question in face of the budget and under the local building technology. The client gladly accepted our suggestion to rethink the façade, which he had judged being too Communist anyway. But the alteration of the diagonal structure, which they considered the true exponent of Western flair and technology, took a piece of work to convince them differently. Not only did he refuse to change the structural concept, he even surprised us with the promise to have a 1:1 concrete mock-up of the diagonal structure finished by the time we came back to Tirana. We congratulated him and withdrew into silence for a couple of months. Eventually he came up with an argument why it's better not to go on with the diagonal structure, actually repeating the same reasons we had brought up before. We could finally focus on the actual goal of our project: How to capture Tirana's light.

We found a simple but effective solution in using standardized façade elements to cover the 3D volume. Albania is a country without a tradition of pre-cast

7

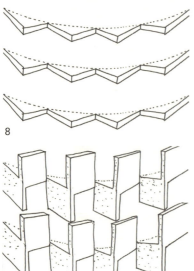

8

9

7: The base of the tower comprises of a quarter dome that cantilevers over the Suleman Pasha Tomb and restores its true scale and grandeur. The people of Tirana acclaimed this gesture more than the tower itself.

8: Each floor slab has different triangular protrusions: they are the most angular at the base and gradually dissolve into a straight line towards the top. Thus the circumferences of all floors are equal in length, allowing for a single panel dimension to complete the entire façade.

9: The façade panels are roughly half a floor high and are connected to the floors, not to each other, creating standing and hanging 'balconies.'

technology, but Albanians are magicians of cast-on-site concrete. You can ask for whatever you want, they deliver it. Trying to cash in on this wonderful—and in Western countries rather forgotten—craftsmanship, we developed a design concept for the façade whereby the shifting circumference of the envelope would be complemented by constantly changing triangular protrusions. The triangles at the base are the most angular, softly opening up towards the top floor. Like teeth of a saw they gradually dissolve into a straight line. The circumferences of all floors are equal in length, making it possible to conceive a single panel dimension to complete the entire façade. The panels have a height of roughly half a floor and are connected to the floors, not to each other, creating standing and hanging 'balconies.' When seen from inside one can perceive the disconnecting panels creating an artificial horizon, the thinnest panoramic cutout conceivable. The gap between panels offers sufficient building tolerance, yet smoothly unifies the reading of the façade, and most of all provides a surface onto which the Tirana light can project itself in abundance. To be affirmative about these assumptions we proposed to have a 1:1 mock-up built. This mini-construction site taught us to decipher the Albanian way of working, but even more strikingly, the Albanian way of thinking. Everything is theoretically possible, but you need to explain it in a way that they can really understand the final intention. Although the contractor could read our drawings, he could not extrapolate from them, which often resulted in wrongly executed construction parts that subsequently had to be taken down. It made us realize that execution drawings had little meaning in this context, other than preparing legal documents for the sake of the local municipal authorities. On the other hand, the contractors had an unseen 1:1 relationship with the actual building material, which opened up new possibilities. After a year of struggling with inadequate communication we managed to establish a specific way of working which could be described as 'collaborative drawing.' Since not everything could be tested with to scale or full size models, we decided to bring a video projector into the design meetings. The plans were projected on a whiteboard, so that all team members could freely sketch on the plans, over and over again. This extremely physical way of adapting plans became the true motor of the process, bypassing the failures of verbal communication. We are using it now all the time.

The first test panels were mounted on the mock-up; plasterboard dummies enabled us to check whether the open-closed ratio made sense. A couple of weeks later, the first concrete panels arrived, fully polished concrete slabs consisting of local black granite set in white cement with white silicon quartz. The latter radiates a transparent quality when viewed from close by, the former offers a beautiful deep glow. Seen from afar, the panels become an abstract sky-colored cladding from which the constituting parts are rendered non-decipherable—an urban garment whose concept of the triangular protrusions fools the (lazy) eye into thinking that it is a continuous field. Conjointly, the concept of the triangles allows for a low-tech construction method that fits Tirana's building culture which is accustomed to erecting projects at 300 EUR/m². To evaluate the feasibility of our new façade proposal the client ordered a 1:1 mock-up with plasterboard panels hung from a concrete structure to be built. He came with a team of more than ten people, all in suits and sunglasses, accompanied by wives, friends and friends' friends. Seeing the construction principle in a nutshell in real dimensions allowed them to imagine that the tower could be built this way.

Once the design was approved the search for a manufacturer could start. We went to Italy, Belgium, and Turkey. In the end, the client settled for an Albanian solution, setting up a local production plant, providing a long-term investment in Albania's manufacturing sector and enabling us to be directly involved in the fabrication process. Each panel is made by hand, resulting in a crafty 12-cm-thick plate, which is then polished to expose the aggregate. The finished panel is 10 cm thick. The final decision for an Albanian production facility was triggered by the need to establish a low-cost production environment. In Albania each panel costs about 500 EUR, in Belgium it would cost 1,500 EUR.

But the construction detailing was not the ultimate bridge to be taken. We had to adjust to working without clear standards and building norms, which in the end resulted in a field rife with possibilities. We felt that things could be shaped, regulations could be written, standards be defined, tests be made. It was truly exhilarating to operate as a free agent within a vacuum of regulations. The TID tower is actually the country's very first project that complies with legal fire regulations and it is the first project for which construction site meetings were held. In Albania, an architect normally stops working when he hands in the building permit. There is no such thing as site supervision, nor is there any form of liability. So parallel to the development of truly contextual building details and ditto methods, we equally had to venture into negotiations guaranteeing professional rights that we—as West European architects—had taken for granted. In the end, the contractor took a fond liking to the construction site meetings, as did the client. It became their weekly moment! In turn, we decided to set up a local office,

10

11

12

10: Mounting of the panels starting from the top. The concept of triangular protrusions conforms to Tirana's low-tech construction method of casting concrete on site.
11-12: Seen from inside, the gap between the panels creates an artificial horizon and offers sufficient building tolerance.
13: (Next pages) The tower's silhouette complements the historical line-up of the Skanderbeg Square, the Mosque, and the Clock Tower.

headed by a German ex-pat architect who leads a group of local draftsmen/architects, who were desperately needed to strategically avoid the 'lost in translation' effect. From our Tirana office, located on the top floor of a nearby building, we could see that our initial gut feeling to rethink both the structure and the façade was the right decision. We avoided West European import and created something new: not local, not foreign, but something new, yet to be appropriated.

Three years after winning the TID competition we applied for the Skanderbeg Competition, a major competition aiming at redeveloping Tirana's main central square, a pantheon of Albania's history, which is located just off the TID Tower construction site. Competing with offices like Daniel Libeskind and MVRDV, we banked on our Tirana gut feeling experience. We proposed a straightforward non-romanticized ambitious project and got the commission. All of a sudden the Tower regained its square, it's last missing link to perform on the Tirana stage.

About the authors: Peter Swinnen is Master Flemish Government Architect and unit master in architecture design at ISACF La Cambre Brussels. Johan Anrys is an architect and assistant for architecture design at University of Leuven ASRO. In 1998 they founded together with Freek Persyn the architecture office 51N4E in Brussels. In 2004 51N4E received the prestigious Rotterdam Maaskant Award for Young Architects. Since 2007 51N4E has doubled its impact through the establishment of a Balkan office in Tirana.

TAKE ON COMPLEXITY

Best Used Before

The Asian City and the Quest for a Time-specific Architecture

MINSUK CHO / MASS STUDIES

In a fast-developing country such as Korea, where the average life expectancy of a building is considered to be 30 years, the construction process over the last few decades has been dominated by the logic of "bigger, faster, cheaper." But speed in itself is not a virtue and often unnecessary, even in Asia. In Korea the speed of growth has often been used as a legitimization for control and oppression, for any kind of artificially created urgency easily leads to social streamlining. This phenomenon has produced the stalk homogeneity of our physical environment, which has been the outcome of ambitious housing projects that aimed at the construction of one million apartment units within five years in the early 1990s.

This problem, however, does not concern Korea alone, it applies to the broader context of Asia. Unlike the European City and its traditional refinement and gradual transformation of existing urban fabrics, the Asian City is based on a logic of replacement that shows little empathy with the past. Whenever and wherever change is needed, buildings are simply demolished and replaced by new ones.

Martine Sitbon Shop: Designed to Stay, Gone After Two Years

In our practice we have experienced this 'forced temporality' in architecture already in our first project that we built in Korea. The "Martine Sitbon Shop" (2002), a collaboration with Slade Architecture and Ga A Architects, was an attempt to transform a 100 m² garage into a state-of-the-art fashion boutique. This task involved the transformation of the raw concrete interior of the garage through re-skinning, as well as the transformation of the garage door into a sophisticated boutique storefront with special glass cladding that required skillful craftsmanship and the use of custom-made hardware for the glass walls. The entire process took two months — half a month to produce a design concept and a model, and one and a half month construction time — and required intense, nonstop supervision on site. We were designing and building at the same time while trying to stay within a tight budget. Considering the short time frame and the limited resources allotted for this project, we felt very accomplished when we had finished, for the realization of a project like this would have taken at least a year in New York City where I had previously practiced. This sense of accomplishment, however, was abruptly disappointed two years later, when the client sold the building to a developer who wanted to "maximize the site's potential." The store was replaced by a larger building, because in the meantime the neighborhood had developed into a very thriving commercial area. The explanation for why the store had to be built at such speed had finally revealed itself two years after its completion: It had quite literally been a pop-up building within a pop-up city, a characteristic of the current hyper-dynamic urban conditions in Asia, generated by a thriving economy.

Puzzled by this experience of 'forced temporality' in architecture, we have tried to stay away from such commissions. At the beginning of our practice, one out of two commissions were of this kind. Accepting these commissions would have easily characterized our firm as specialists for pop-up architecture. But our goal was to create buildings that would last for a longer period of time, if not forever. We therefore focused our efforts on creating 'permanent' buildings. Unconsciously though, architecture's uncanny complicity with temporality has never stopped to fascinate us — maybe because the urban reality in Korea is very temporary, for a variety of reasons. On the one hand, a substantial part of the country's building stock is younger than 60 years because of the devastating bombardments during the Korean War; on the other hand, the Korean Way of Life and the country's

1-2: Martine Sitbon Shop, Seoul, an example of an Asian pop-up building, designed and built in two months, dismantled only two years later.

attitude towards space resulting from it, are very temporary in nature as well. The fabric of the city changes quite quickly over time, and this 'transience of being' has its charms as well. We wondered whether one could define 'temporary architecture' in such a way that the material strength and durability of the construction are a direct function of the anticipated duration of the activity it is supposed to host. This interdependence of space and duration could potentially provide a model for a 'time-specific' architecture that deals with time as sensibly as 'site-specific' architecture deals with place. Foregrounded particularly in the development of public sculpture during the 1970s and 1980s by artists like Richard Serra, Claes Oldenburg and others as a response against the "drop-sculpture" of the 1960s, site-specificity had been welcomed by architects under the influence of postmodern contextualism and its critique of the modernist idea of the tabula rasa. The architectural notion of site-specificity contained the idea of a building that was perfectly tailored to its specific spatial context; it was a building that could only work in the very *here and now* of that particular site, and nowhere else. The project was generated by its site. In time-specific architecture in turn, the entire logic of a project—its structure, materials, and construction process— would have to be defined relative to the building's anticipated duration.

We had the good fortune to test this hypothesis on a series of commissions for 'temporary pavilions' we received. The three pavilions had very precise specifications both in terms of program, size, and budget as well as in terms of time, namely the time available for design and construction as well as for the expected period of existence. Processing these different parameters in the design of the pavilions, we wanted to see how these particular conditions would register in the specific architectural outcome of the projects

Ring Dome: Designed to Stay for 26 Days

The Ring Dome was the first pavilion we built. It had a small budget and was supposed to host the celebrations for the Storefront for Art and Architecture Gallery's 25th anniversary in New York. Joseph Grima, then the gallery's director, created a diverse program of events that took place outside the gallery space in an underused park and spilled out their artistic practice into the larger public. This 26-day marathon of events included an art exhibition, a symposium, a block party, a performance, film screenings, a block party, a taco stand, a book launch, and more.

3

4

3-4: Ring Dome pavilion, New York, commissioned by Storefront for Art and Architecture Gallery director Joseph Grima. Built in two days from hula-hoops, it hosted a number of events for the gallery's 25th anniversary.

The project was located in Petrosino Park, which is a traffic island at the intersection of Lafayette Street and Kenmare Street in the Soho district. The small triangular site, surrounded by a steel fence with an entrance on the southern end, which was not really utilized but had a high visibility, lay in a dense urban context. Approximately 1,000 plastic hula-hoops with a diameter of 80 cm each, tied together with about 10,000 zip ties to form the dome structure, were used to create the Ring Dome. We used hula-hoops made of translucent white PVC to draw more attention to the empty unused site. Seen from afar in daylight, the ring dome appears to be a soft white blob, resembling soap bubbles; but its openness becomes more apparent as one draws nearer. One part of Petrosino Park is boldly defined by the pure geometric form and at the same time provides an open, ambiguous space. The dome served diverse purposes: as a display wall for photography, a prop, a projection screen, a banner, and a support for decorations for various events. At night, electro-luminescent wires, fitted inside about 200 of the hula-hoops, glowed gently and created a completely new environment.

The structure of the Ring Dome was designed in such a way that it could be easily assembled and disassembled by non-professionals, such as students, artists, and other volunteers. Instead of a design that requires every component to fit perfectly, the random method of adding hula-hoops to stiffen the surface of the dome allowed many unskilled people to participate. A second Ring Dome, a smaller version called Ring Dome Junior, was built in the atrium of a shopping mall in Kitakyushu, Japan, conducted by Joseph Grima with a few elementary school kids over a weekend workshop. The structure had been completed in the phenomenal time span of two mornings and one afternoon, with almost all of the work done by the kids alone.

Designed for experimentation, adjustment, and with an almost primitive assembly method, the main objective of the Ring Dome project was not the final result, but the celebratory, shared experience of constructing the piece, an event in the vein of the annual Burning Man Festival—the act of construction as a festive collective event. The Burning Man Festival ends by burning the final product of the collective effort, and likewise, the Ring Dome was simply dismantled by severing the zip ties. Unlike the Burning Man structure, the main material (hula-hoops) of the Ring Dome was subsequently distributed as toys, returning them to their original purpose in a more environmentally friendly conclusion. By distributing the construction material to the public, we tried to share the collective memory of the temporary construction and the events within.

This structure became quite popular, and perhaps because of its effectiveness, it was constructed two more times in the following year: for the Milano Furniture Fair in 2008, hosting the event of the Italian design magazine *Abitare* at the Galleria Vittorio Emmanuele, and at the Yokohama Art Triennial.

Air Forest: Designed to Stay for Seven Days

Some time after the Ring Dome, we received a commission from the Denver Office of Cultural Affairs to build a temporary pavilion to host Dialog:City, an arts and cultural event for the public inspired by the occasion of the National Democratic Convention which Denver had hosted in 2008 and where the future President of the United States, Barak Obama, was declared the Democratic Candidate for the Presidential Elections, later that year. Ten artists and architects had been invited to design or exhibit site-specific projects at various locations in the city, for the public to converge and to spark a dialogue across the city through innovative cultural initiatives, during the period of 24th to 30th August. Our task had been to create a temporary public space for a series of small cultural events such as a Yoga Health Festival, a cocktail party for the convention, a high school play, and the Dialog:City closing party, as well as an outdoor space for the general public to enjoy.

The project Air Forest had a larger budget compared to the Ring Dome, but only three days for its construction. Our site was located in east-central Denver in the City Park, the largest and most notable of all the Denver parks. This historic 1.3 km² park has large open grass fields, with Ferril Lake at its center, and trees around the lake and the park's perimeter. The given site was vast, and the temporary construction had to fill this large empty open space. We asked ourselves: How can we build a big and cheap structure in three days, without creating any waste?

Situated 1,609 m above sea level, Denver's climatic condition is very sunny and hot during the day, yet characterized by strong winds from the Rocky Mountains at night. We realized that we could exploit this unique climatic condition for our pavilion by building a temporary structure that provided shade for events taking place during the day, but protected against the strong wind at night. As a result, the Air Forest was a 56 m long and 25 m wide pneumatic structure, composed of nine hexagonal canopy units, of 4 m height. These units were interconnected with one large piece of fabric, which was then inflated by 14 air-blowers, located

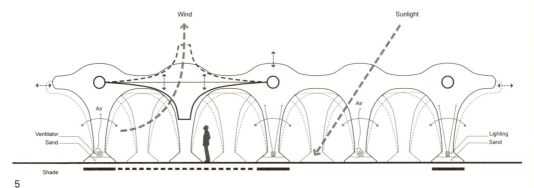

5

6

5-7: Air Forest, Denver: The pavilion, a 56 m long and 25 m wide pneumatic structure, was inflated by 14 air-blowers, located inside the base of the columns. Held down by sandbags footings, no other foundation work was necessary.

7

inside the base of the columns. These columns were 5 m apart and held down by sandbags as footings. No other foundation work was done, thereby preserving the original ground condition throughout the event.

Six of the pneumatic columns were hexagonally connected to a unit, creating a circular opening on their inside perimeter. Out of the nine total hexagonal units formed, three of them were left open-air, while the remaining six had vortex-shaped meshes that hung from them, providing shade from the harsh sunlight for the public. The nylon fabric was coated with a gradient of silver dots, whose reflective surface mimicked the colors of the surrounding environment; at the same time creating playful dotted shadows on the people under the structure.

The structure acted as a giant device to measure the site's conditions. Not only did it sway gently with the wind, but it also acted as a barometer to detect the changes in the air pressure. The installation became structurally weaker as the air pressure dropped due to cooler weather (or) after sunset. However, the pneumatic structure did not the users, quite the contrary causing a sensual interplay with the audiences. After the event, the large structure was packed neatly into a box of one cubic meter to be reused in the future.

Korean Pavilion for the Expo 2010: Designed to Stay for Six Months

For our most recent pavilion, the Korean Pavilion for the Expo 2010 in Shanghai, we again had to work with the requirement of faster, bigger, and cheaper, but on a much more extensive scale. The design competition for the selection of the Korean Pavilion took place after most of other countries' pavilion designs had been selected, with the possible exception of the pavilion of the United States. We therefore were confronted with yet another intensive battle against time. However, we felt that in this particular situation, it was to our advantage knowing most of our surrounding context (which happened to be composed of mostly round objects) while working on our proposal for the competition. Although we knew it would only be a temporal city of a six months duration, we were able to respond to the context as a somewhat real, serious "urban" condition due to this delayed schedule, instead of creating a singular object in a blank condition, which was the case for most other pavilions.

Korea took one of the 10 largest sites, which was around 6000 m². The brief required us to maximize the buildable area in proportion to the size of the site.

Among the almost 190 pavilions of the Expo 2010, 49 countries, including Korea, had built their own pavilion. They can be categorized as "ducks" (in the Venturian sense), typically built by developed countries, while the rest are "decorated shed" pavilions, rented readymade warehouse-like structures, clad on the exterior and in the interior in a specific way to express each country's identity, in a more limited way than the duck types. Despite the desire to build a large structure with an iconic presence within a relatively short time period, the extremely low budget for the Korean Pavilion (it was three to eight times less per square meter than that for the other "ducks"), we had to deliver a "duck" with a "decorated shed" budget. However, we accepted it as an important, relevant challenge for Expo 2010, which had a strong emphasis on sustainability—quite a contradiction considering the amount of capital required for this temporary city.

For this challenging condition, we imagined that Han-geul, the Korean alphabet, was a unique Korean invention that would be accepted by the 50 million Koreans both as an icon and as a very practical solution due to its composition of simple abstract geometries of horizontal, vertical, diagonal lines and a circle. We called our design a "duck shed" typology in the sense that the duck (icon) we pursued consisted of simple geometries instead of a specific form; the overall volume was designed to be perceived as an amalgamation of various Han-geul letters. The primary geometries of Han-geul letters are universal to different cultures, similar to those used in Roman letters or Arabic numbers. The letters can therefore act as 'open' signs, which could be engaging for a larger audience than just Koreans. These letters could then be translated into different architectural elements at various scales; the flexibility of organizing different letters, allowed us to rigorously respond to the site. Unlike most pavilions that had a strong singular iconic form, this systematic "formal" strategy created multiple presences that responded to the various conditions surrounding the site. Almost every "formal" and iconic element in our building can be explained in a purely functional manner. For instance, the forms of the letters translated directly into circulation, including elevators, escalators, stairs, and vestibule elements. Some letters were applied as the cantilevered entrance or the necessary openings.

On a smaller scale, the Han-geul letters were applied to create a variegated surface pattern. The exterior surfaces of the Korea Pavilion were clad in two types of what we call "pixels," both made of 6 mm-thick aluminum composite panels: "Han-geul Pixels" and "Art Pixels." The Han-geul Pixels are glossy white panels with a relief of letters in four different sizes, the combination of which forms

8

9

10

8-9: The Korean Pavilion at the Expo 2010 in Shanghai was clad in two types of "pixels"—glossy white "Han-geul Pixels" and colored "Art Pixels."
10: The Korean alphabet, Hangeul, inspired the shape of the building.

the majority of the exterior, mainly the peripheral surfaces. Most of the non-peripheral exterior surfaces are composed of Art Pixels, made of the same material, but matt white, which are color-printed with artworks composed of poems written and hand-drawn by the Korean artist, Ik-Joong Kang. About 40,000 of these panels texture the façade, contributing a bright palette of colors, and unity throughout the Korean Pavilion. The Art Pixels, individually autographed by the artist, will be sold after the Expo and all sales proceeds will be donated to an international charity organization. Not only will it raise funds for a good cause, but this social and artistic process, the recycling of façade units as artworks, will also enhance the sustainability of the Korea Pavilion in a unique way, by directly and critically addressing the sustainability of this temporary structure that is only six months in use. 90 percent of the remaining construction materials, such as its steel elements, are recyclable as well and reduce the construction cost by 10 percent.

The effects of these two types of panels had also been our exercise in mass customization by means of digital construction, i.e. CNC cutting and the folding technique for the Hangeul pixels, as well as the color printing technique for the Art Pixels. Without these technological advances, having more repetitive elements would have been the only way to build cost-effectively. These two construction techniques allowed us to create a cladding system that comprised of 40,000 panels which are hardly repetitive, but cost-efficient. However, we had to create a lot more computer drawings for the CNC cutting and the digital images for the color printing than for a typical building. The two strongly textured and colored panels turned out to be an excellent strategy for the fast and cheap Chinese construction situation we were confronted with, because they camouflage small construction flaws (such as uneven joint distances, etc.) well.

The function of temporary structures ranges typologically somewhere between architecture and performance events. Their intended temporality favors an architectural approach that is not limited to the design of an object, but takes into account the entire life cycle of its materials. It is through these temporary constructions that we gain wisdom in building "bigger, faster, and cheaper," a notion that has been over-quoted during the rapid urbanization process. It is true that this kind of approach, which guided the architectural practice and the construction reality in Korea, has been condemned and blamed to be responsible for the current cityscape, which is composed of monotonous apartment blocks. In general, however, temporary structures by nature are built for the public at large (bigger), to exist for a short period only (faster), and to use as little resources possible (cheaper). It can therefore be asserted that the concept of building bigger, faster, and cheaper reaches its full potential especially in temporary constructions.

	Ring Dome	Air Forest	Expo Pavilion
Design Duration:	2 months	5 months	7 months
Const. Duration:	2 days	3 days	10 months
Bldg. Duration:	26 days	7 days	6 months
Size:	61 m²	673 m²	7683 m²
Material Reuse:	Hula hoops	The entire PVC/nylon pneumatic structure, Lighting/Air-blower	Art Panels, plus 90% of the construction materials are recyclable.

Xi Gallery: Designed to Stay for 20 Years

There is, however, also an abuse of temporary architecture and its corresponding typologies, in Korea. The pavilion as such enjoys a high popularity in the guise of the sales pavilion for apartments, called "Model House." Yet it is anything but a pavilion, if the etymology of the word, which goes back to the French "papillon" meaning "butterfly" is taken seriously. Growing up in a cocoon and hatching from it to fly away and stop in places of interested, the butterfly represents a perfect example of a pavilion's ideal performance. At home in transit, a pavilion engages only temporarily with a specific site; like a parking trailer it always refers to the 'there and then,' not the 'here and now.' Defying stasis, it is a monument to process.

The Model House, on the other hand, blind to the smart transformative powers of the butterfly. By discarding materials when no longer needed instead of transforming them into something else, it renders a distorted image of the temporary. The Model House is a by-product of the massive housing developments that have sprung up in Korea over the last few decades that showcases representative apartment units in order to market them. A Model House is typically a large, overly decorated shed, built on a rented empty lot near the construction site of the future apartment complex that showcases three to four full-scaled apartment units, extravagantly furnished, along with their respective sales offices. It usually takes two to three months to build and usually has a lifespan of no more than

11

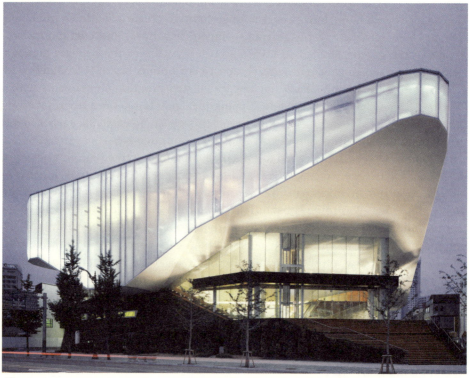

12

11: Xi Gallery in Busan City, is a new type of a Korean Model House. On the top floor it contains showflats of apartments on sale, while the levels below are dedicated to cultural programs.

12: Instead of only 2 years, this Model House has a life time of at least 20 years.

one to two years. This ubiquitous typology that appears and vanishes like a mirage, epitomizes the Korean developers' "hit (the jack pot) and run" mentality, in which the model of the Model House suffers temporary schizophrenia: while its program is planned to expire after one to two years, its architecture is built as if it was to stay around substantially longer. The butterfly has turned dinosaur, no longer knowing how to fly. To overcome the schizophrenia you need to decide to either adapt the material durability of the architecture to the temporary nature of the program (and make it lighter and recyclable), or to adapt the nature of the program to the longer lifespan of the architecture.

Following the big success of the Model House condition during the 1990s — and perhaps significantly strong guilt resulting from an awareness of its unsustainable condition — the Korean apartment building industry has changed course and engages with home buyers over a longer term to create a healthier and longer lasting client relationship by starting to integrate cultural and community programs in the Model Houses to create an added value to the primary function of marketing apartments. The leading apartment brands began to compete with their own type of brand space that integrated two program components within a semi-permanent structure. While keeping the same functions normally accommodated by the Model House (exhibition of mock-up apartments, sales rooms), it began adding cultural components and community services.

When we were initially asked to take on a commission to design this new type of Model House, we were skeptical and asked for the program brief in order to decide upon our involvement. We were quite stunned by the fact that the cultural component was to be substantially bigger than the sales component of the entire building. Because of it we trusted their promise that this would not just be another ploy of a cultural element playing a frivolous and decorative role, masking commercial activity. We also liked the location, within an underdeveloped, under-privileged area of Busan City, where any form of cultural input will be beneficial, especially since we knew that there would be no support towards the establishment of cultural activities from the public sector in this area in the near future.

With respect to time and temporariness, the Xi Gallery project still bore the usual signs of a hideously rushed construction schedule: it took five months from the conceptualization of the building to the construction documents, and another five months — which, given that the construction site operated in three shifts a day, is equivalent to a typical construction schedule of 15 months — to construct a roughly 10,000 m² building that was expected to stand indefinitely, but at least 20 years. The client had guaranteed this minimum duration of the building, this had been our important prerequisite. Only an extended lifecycle for such a structure justifies the enormous efforts put into fabricating such an environment. The longer the lifespan of the building, the more it makes sense to invest in the architectural quality of its interior space instead of only in the façade as in the "Model House" typology, where the excessive decor of the shed is supposed to compensate for the poor quality of the interior space.

It has been almost four years since the Xi Gallery opened in 2007 and it has since developed into a dynamic place filled with activities, including cooking classes, yoga classes, musical performances, and other spontaneous events, such as arty and design exhibitions (it has become a popular place for the end-of-the-year exhibitions of Busan's architecture students), indoor flee markets, weddings, etc. The sale of apartments still takes place on the top floor, but it is no longer the main program as before.

Working on temporary projects like the three pavilions and a semi-temporary project like the Xi Gallery had a lasting impact on the way we think about our "normal" buildings. The dichotomy between temporary and permanent architecture appears more and more artificial to us. In fact we question whether there is such a thing as permanent architecture at all. Sooner or later all buildings will be temporary, whether they are transformed, demolished, or recycled. But the temporary includes a wide spectrum of radically different time scales, spanning from days, decades, centuries, and beyond. And the construction of a building always entails a statement about its expected lifespan. Instead of longing for an impossible permanence in architecture we should start to enjoy the innumerable gradations of its temporality.

About the author: Minsuk Cho is a Korean architect. He graduated from the Architectural Engineering department of Yonsei University (Seoul, Korea) and the Graduate School of Architecture at Columbia University (New York). In 2003 he founded his own firm, Mass Studies, in Seoul. Since then has realized a number of internationally recognized and award-winning residential houses and high-rise buildings in Korea.

Heat Pump: Heat pumps are devices that facilitate the movement of heat energy from one environment to another. Heat pumps can work in either direction, meaning they can heat by bringing heat energy into a space, and cool by removing it. Similar to air conditioners, they use indoor and outdoor coils to act as condensers and evaporators. However, heat pumps differ from air conditioners in their use of a reversing valve to change the flow of refrigerant, allowing the coils to switch roles as needed. Heat pumps use relatively little electrical energy because they also extract energy from the surrounding environment. They can generally be divided into air source heat pumps, which utilize heat from outside air, and ground source heat pumps, which extract heat from soil or groundwater. Ground source pumps, also known as geothermal heat pumps, can be used year-round as the ground and groundwater stay at a relatively constant temperature throughout the year. This leads to more effective performance and energy efficiency than air-source pumps as well as many other forms of heating. (→ *drawing 20*)

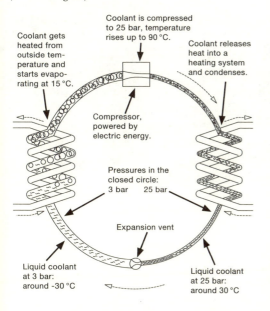

20: Working principle of a heat pump with example temperatures and pressures.

Heat Transfer: Heat transfer is the movement of energy as heat from one place to another. Heat transfer always occurs in one direction, from warm to cool, to establish thermal equilibrium, following the second law of thermodynamics. The basic methods of heat transfer are convection, conduction and radiation. → *Heat exchangers* are used to passively transfer heat from one place to another through heat transfer. Heat transfer is also the catalyst for → *phase change materials*. As the heat transfer moves in one direction to equilibrium, the total amount of energy available during this transfer is expressed by exergy. Conduction is the transfer of energy (heat), usually between objects in direct physical contact, by atoms and molecules, between one and another. When the molecules and atoms of a hot object touch those of a cooler object, the warmer molecules vibrate and transfer electrons to the molecules and atoms of the cooler object. Conduction is most common with solids. Materials that are highly conductive, such as copper, can carry heat and electricity.
Convection is the transfer of energy (heat), usually between an object and its environment, by the movement of fluids. For example, a warm radiator in a cold room releases convective currents as the room and radiator move toward thermal equilibrium. These convective currents are sometimes significant enough to move lightweight objects like paper.
Radiation is the transfer of energy (heat) through electromagnetic waves. Radiation occurs between all objects and environments that are above absolute zero. No medium is necessary for thermal radiation. For example, the earth is heated by means of the solar radiation of extremely hot gases on the surface of the sun. Because no medium is necessary for radiation to occur, the energy from the sun can be transferred through the vacuum of space. Objects with a high → *thermal mass* can absorb and store a lot of this solar radiation. A → *solar cooker* can use solar radiation in concentration to cook food without fuel.
Heinrich Böll Foundation Building, Berlin: The headquarters of the Heinrich Böll Foundation in Berlin, built by E2A architects, uses the waste heat of its internet servers as a heat source. Heat is harvested from the server farm in the building from the cool racks. This harvested heat is used to heat water from 23 °C to 28 °C as it passes through a centralized heating system, and this hot water is then distributed to radiators by a building-wide pipe system. During warmer months, this same system of water pipes draws cool water from the cellar, where → *evaporative cooling* reduces the water temperature to 20 °C. The building also has a smart ventilation system: the central atrium of the buildings functions like a lung, exchanging air through the roof during summer. During colder months, the air is led through a heat exchanger, which is a simple method of → *passive ventilation* that avoids significant heat loss in winter.
Heliotrop: Heliotrop is architect Rolf Disch's private residence in Freiburg, Germany. Heliotrop is constructed according to → *active solar* principles, and uses a large photovoltaic shield to produce five times as much energy as Disch and his family require for heating, lighting, and other household energy uses. The house can rotate completely around its vertical axis, and can turn either its closed back or open front to the sun, depending on the season and the activities taking place inside the house. The 200 m² of the interior are laid out economically, avoiding corridors by attaching all rooms to a spiral staircase that winds itself up and around the exterior of the house. Structural parts of the house were built from wood as often as was feasible. The form of Heliotrop minimizes exterior surface area, helping to keep unwanted heat input from solar gain and heat loss in wintertime low. The energy needed to turn the house and the independently rotating solar shield on its roof equals that

72: **Heliotrop**; A house that can follow the sun.

73: **Heliotrop**; Turning the house consumes less energy than a fridge.

74: **House in Cap Ferret**; House and forest interweave in L+V's house at the Atlantic Ocean.

75: **Heat Exchanger**; Low-tech – high impact.

76: **House in Cap Ferret**; Trees can move naturally within the house, photograph taken during construction.

77: **Haus Westend Grün**; Atypical esthetics for adobe.

78: **Guerilla Gardening**; An abandoned flyer box in Toronto is turned into a flower box.

79: **Hesco Bastion**; This construction element uses local gravel and soil, and is commonly used by the military.

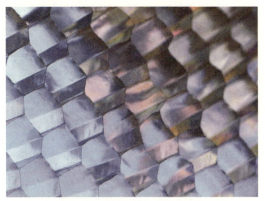

80: **Honeycomb Structures**; This aluminum component material profits from the efficiency and strength of the bionic structure.

81: **Holland Pavilion**; MVRDV dedicated each floor to a Dutch landscape.

82: **House in Coutras**; Taking advantage of the commercial greenhouse.

83: **House Inside a House**; Layering principle.

84: **Hopkins House**;

85: **Hopkins House**; Industrial elements become esthetically desirable.

86: **Hopkins House**; Standardized façade.

of a third of an energy-saving fridge. The house was finished in 1994. (→ *image 72-73, p. 218*)

Hempcrete: Hempcrete is an alternative to cement. It is made from a mixture of hemp and lime, and possibly includes other aggregates. Hempcrete is less brittle than traditional concrete, and as a result does not require the expansion joints typical in concrete constructions. Hempcrete has less compressive strength than low-grade concrete, which means that it needs structural reinforcement in many applications. This limitation is balanced out by good insulating properties, as well as a low density and carbon-neutral production. Hempcrete is carbon negative as the hemp plants and the material itself both remove CO_2 from the air.

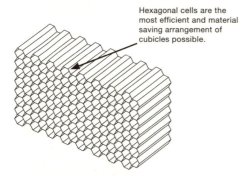

21: Isometric illustration of honeycomb cells.

Hesco Bastion: A Hesco bastion is a combination of mesh gabion and heavy-duty fabric liner. It was initially developed by the British firm Hesco under the name "Concertainer(R)" as a barrier against floods and to protect against marsh and beach erosion. Similar to a standard gabion, the stiff mesh can be filled with almost any material, even particulate materials when a fabric liner is added. The Hestco bastions can be easily transported and filled on location. They are quick and easy to erect, and can be combined and stacked to form walls. Today, Hesco barriers are used in nearly all United States military bases in Iraq, as a temporary or semi-temporary barrier against blasts from explosives or small-arms fire, but they are also used for their original, more peaceful purposes. (→ *image 79, p. 218*)

Holland Pavilion at the Hanover Expo: The Holland Pavilion at the Hanover Expo in 2000 was designed by MVRDV. The pavilion was designed to be a stacked tower of landscape conditions emblematic of those in Holland. The five stories of the pavilion contained representations of everything from forests to flower production fields to polders, and were united by water elements. The pavilion was meant to express the fact that most of the land in Holland was created through human intervention, yet it does not seem overtly artificial. Visitors moved through the pavilion from the top, accessed by elevator, and the most immediately expressive example of a natural condition, at the bottom, where man-made intervention in the landscape condition was most apparent. The complexity of creating a variety of landscapes and conditions in a stacked structure involved a high degree of innovative structural and landscape architectural know-how. Somewhat like an inverted → *green roof*, the Holland Pavilion can also be seen as a precedent for the idea of the → *vertical farm*. (→ *image 81, p. 219*)

Honeycomb Structures: Honeycomb structures are natural or engineered objects with an internal structure that resembles a honeycomb, a series of hollow columnar cells usually hexagonal in shape. Honeycomb structures occurring in nature include beehives and bone, while man-made honeycomb structures can be used to engineer products such as helicopters and jet aircraft. Depending on their density, size, and material used, honeycomb structures can vary widely in strength and stiffness. Their high stiffness to weight ratio and use of composite materials make honeycomb structures a valuable tool in high-performance industries such as aerospace and automotive engineering. (→ *drawing 21; image 80, p. 219*)

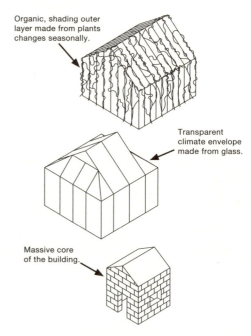

22: The three layers of Ungers' House Inside a House.

Hopkins House: The Hopkins House is the residence of Hopkins Architects' founding partners. Built in 1976 in a London conservation area, the house was built using construction techniques developed for larger commercial buildings, which Hopkins Architects were working on at the time the house was designed and constructed. The house is constructed on a small structural steel grid of 2 m by 4 m with perimeter columns to support the cladding and glazing without sub-frames. Metal decking for the floor and roof surfaces is supported on a two-way grid of lattice trusses. Side walls are made from a metal decking sandwich, and the remarkable front and back walls are made from floor to roof sliding glass doors without vertical frames. The interior is open plan, with

Venetian blinds as spatial dividers and melamine partitions to separate bath and sleeping rooms. (→ *images 84-86, p. 219*)

Horizontal Axis Wind Turbine (HAWT): Horizontal axis wind turbines have a horizontally oriented rotor. They are the most common kind of wind turbine. The horizontal axis turbine is capable of generating over seven megawatts of electricity, and turbines generating up to ten megawatts are currently in development. HAWT can be placed on- or offshore, and must be oriented toward the wind, either by fixed placement or flexible adjustments during operation. The HAWT can generate more total power than the → *VAWT*, or vertical access wind turbine, and is limited only by the length of the turbine blades and height to access maximal wind speeds. Projects like the → *Makani Power* seek to push wind power generation beyond what HAWT and VAWT are capable of by placing turbines, kite-like, high in the air.

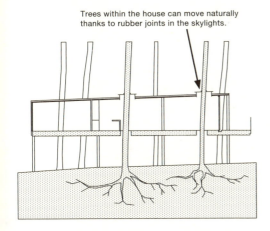

23: Section of Lacaton Vassal's House in Cap Ferret.

House Inside a House: House Inside a House is a principle promoted and repeatedly proposed by Oswald Matthias Ungers. The principle is figured in a design that consists of a relatively small, massive stone house that has sufficient → *thermal mass* to create a comfortable, stable indoor climate. A second shell around the core of the house is a thermal barrier made from insulating glass. The space between the core of the house and this layer functions as a buffer zone between exterior and interior space. This liminal space benefits from solar gain during cold times of the year, and from wind protection. A third shell, covered by deciduous plants, allows sunlight into the other layers during the winter while the plants do not have leaves, and shades the other layers during warmer months when the plants have leaves. This is an alternative way of organizing a house that takes advantage of → *passive heating* and → *passive cooling*. (→ *drawing 22; image 83, p. 219*)

House in Cap Ferret: House in Cap Ferret is a private home designed by French architecture firm Lacaton + Vassal. The house is located on a dune on the shoreline of Arcachon Bay, and is within a pine forest. Due to concerns about the vegetation and the delicate sand dune, the house is supported by 12 micro-piles, set 8-12 m deep into the ground. This creates minimal disturbance in the dune and forest ecology, while still enabling the plot to be built upon. In an additional, unprecedented measure, the house was built around some of the trees, which are enclosed in special structures to allow for growth and the natural swaying motion of these living and thriving, partially indoor trees. (→ *drawing 23; images 74, 76, p. 218*)

House in Coutras: The House in Coutras was designed by Lacaton+Vassal architects and built in Coutras, France, in 2000. The house consists of two, partly altered, standard greenhouse sections, manufactured by Filclair. This choice of design was inspired by the prefabricated possibilities of → *greenhouses* adapted to be a residential structure. The context of the House in Coutras is rural and characterized by the wide-open vista afforded by the limited structure, sparse vegetation, and flat landscape. This made the perfect setting for a transparent house. Up to 50% of the sides of the house can be opened by means of large sliding doors, and in combination with the integrated standard greenhouse roof openings, the House in Coutras benefits from passive ventilation and passive cooling. The space measures 290 m² and is split into two parts with different climatic attributes: whereas one was left uninsulated, the other was supplemented with a secondary insulating glass layer that allows year-round use as a habitat containing the kitchen, bathrooms, and the bedrooms. The uninsulated, conservatory-like part can be used as a generous living room especially during spring and autumn, but it is not heated apart from through passive solar heat gain. (→ *image 82, p. 219*)

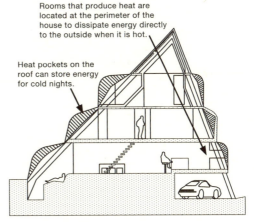

24: Section of FAR's House in Heat.

House in Heat: House in Heat is an unrealized project for a house by FAR Architects. It uses a traditional A-Frame building structure that mindfully arranges

Hybrid Photovoltaic · Hydroponics

space according to temperature. Because the specialized and thick ➙ *A-frame* roof traps warm air, space is arranged so that the occupants of the house can achieve maximum comfort with minimal mechanical help during colder times of the year, partially a ➙ *passive heating* approach. Heat pockets within the roof store heat for use in the house. The straight sides of the house can be fully opened to the outside, allowing cross ventilation during warmer months. This ➙ *passive cooling* and ventilation is augmented by heating and cooling pipes that run through the floor, which can be temperature controlled for both seasonal conditions and different programmatic demands. The façade of the House in Heat is heat-sensitive, and registers temperature conditions by means of subtle color changes.(➙ *drawing 24; image 93, p. 224*)

Hybrid Photovoltaic: Hybrid photovoltaic panels incorporate a system that captures heat and converts solar energy into electricity. This allows for a higher overall performance when the heat provides a useful function within the building. A large proportion of the incoming solar energy can be put to use.
In the case of integrated ➙ *LowEx* systems, the heat can be captured and utilized at a much lower temperature compared to typical systems. This allows for a more simple and inexpensive design. In such a case, the electrical input can be used to operate a ➙ *heat pump* while the heat can be used as a source from which the heat pump can supply heat. The slightly higher temperature heat can allow for a ➙ *low-temperature-lift, ultra-high COP heat pump*, even when meeting higher temperature demands, such as for hot water. The system also allows for the passive capture of warmer ambient conditions that can be used to regenerate the deep borehole in a dual zone borehole system.

interlock with one another, which makes construction without any additional mortar possible. Mortar or additional structural reinforcement can be used as an optional measure dependent upon individual applications. The blocks can be produced in diverse environments because the soil or earth used is usually sourced locally, and therefore there is easy and inexpensive or free access to most of the raw materials needed for blocks made with the Hydraform press. (➙ *image 88, p. 224*)

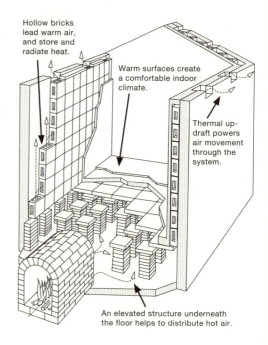

26: Principle of a Roman hypocaust heating system.

Hydroponics: Hydroponics are a range of methods for growing plants without soil. Commonly understood as a water-based method, hydroponic cultivation can occur in liquids or in perlite, vermiculite, gravel, sand or a range of other materials, though the investigation of aeroponic methods is a specific branch of exploration into plant propagation without soil or other matter. The hydroponic process specifically involves the application of specialized liquid fertilizers to supply plants with nutrients. These solutions are specifically engineered to deliver nutrients directly to plants with maximum efficiency. Hydroponic fertilizers are different from regular fertilizers in the directness of application and in the presence of micronutrients in addition to the classic triad of phosphorous, nitrogen, and potassium. Micronutrients are calcium, magnesium, sulfur, boron, cobalt, copper, iron, manganese, molybdenum, and zinc, and are usually sought out by plant roots in soil, and supplied to the plant in trace amounts. In hydroponic methods, the plant is fed the proper micronutrients directly.

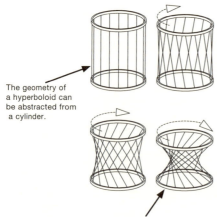

25: Double-curved, hyperboloid shapes can be very strong.

Hydraform Press: The Hydraform press is a machine designed to produce interlocking bricks for building purposes. The bricks are made from compressed soil mixed with a small amount of cement. The blocks

Hydroponics are one method of agricultural production well suited to vertical farming. Because they do not have the normal requirements of soil-based agriculture, hydroponics can be used to generate food environments that would otherwise prove to be challenging for any meaningful crop yields.

Hyperboloid Structure: A hyperboloid structure is a double curved structure built from straight members. This is an ideal construction for tall and thin structures. It is also used for purpose-driven structures like cooling towers and water towers because the double-ruled surface of the hyperboloid structure results in a large amount of unusable volume compared to the total volume of the structure. The first hyperboloid lattice structure was a 37 m water tower by Vladimir Shukov, who later became known as the designer of the ➤ *Shukhov Tower*. (➤ *drawing 25; image 87, p. 224*)

Hypocaust: A hypocaust is an ancient Roman heating system using ➤ *thermal-activated building components*. In hypocaust heating systems, a flow of hot air was channeled through walls and floors with a high ➤ *thermal mass*. The source of heat for the system was an oven, connected to a heating room situated under the floors of the occupied space of the building, and from this room, warm exhaust was released into the channels in the walls of the building. The system was first invented for thermal baths, but was subsequently used in many typical Roman villas. Hypocausts required a lot of energy from combustion to heat the oven, though the system of channels could be adapted for a different energy source, one that is potentially more sustainable. (➤ *drawing 26, image 90, p. 224*)

the interior of the igloo, which can be heated by an open fire, is terraced and uses ➤ *thermal updraft* to create a warm sleeping zone on the highest level and a working zone on a middle terrace, while the lowest terrace and entrance are dug into the ground and form a sort of 'cold sump' that collects all the cold air from inside the igloo, allowing the upper sections to stay warmer. (➤ *drawing 27; images 89, 91, p. 224*)

Infra-Lightweight Concrete: Infra-lightweight concrete is a ➤ *lightweight concrete* with an extremely low density and respectively good insulation qualities. Whereas lightweight concrete is defined by a weight of less than 2000 kilos per cubic meter, infra-lightweight concrete is setting a new standard at a weight of less than 800 kilos per cubic meter. Infra-lightweight concrete is still being tested and improved by a team of developers around Mike Schlaich, who also built his house in Berlin-Pankow from the new material to experiment on site. Doses of additives and agents have to be fine-tuned. For instance, the wet concrete has to be viscous enough to flow into the mold easily but it must not segregate. There is also the danger of overheating, causing cracks when cooling down. The setting concrete cannot dispense the heat that is developed during the process because of its great insulating capacity. Naturally, concrete cannot simply be replaced by infra-lightweight concrete. The new material behaves differently in terms of creeping and contraction. Also, strength under pressure and torsion is different from normal concrete. As it is less watertight, reinforcement cannot be carried out with steel, which could corrode, but with glass-fiber sticks. So far, it has not been possible to build large concrete ceilings without additional support, but on the other hand, pictures can be hung up easily, simply by driving nails into the concrete wall. (➤ *image 92, p. 224*)

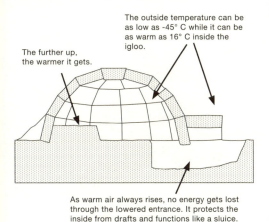

27: Section showing the igloo's different climate zones.

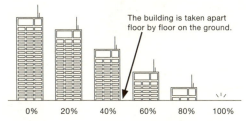

28: Principle of Kajima Cut and Take Down Technique.

Igloo: Igloos are ➤ *vernacular*, often temporary Inuit buildings made of compressed snow that can be found in extremely cold climates. The igloo uses several tricks to achieve and maintain a comfortable indoor climate. Firstly, compressed snow is wind-proof and has insulating qualities that can maintain a temperature difference between inside and outside. Secondly,

Jua Kali: Jua Kali crafts are made by entrepreneurs and craftsmen in Kenya. The term "jua kali" is Swahili and can be loosely translated as "under the hot sun," in reference to the location of these entrepreneurs place of work and sales. Jua Kali craftspeople are upcyclers who make use of materials from a multitude of sources in their products. These materials are frequently extracted from other items or uses and modified. Because the patterns of use and availability in Kenya are quite different from those in wealthy westernized countries, Jua Kali has evolved into a sophisticated network of reuse patterns, techniques and trading. Jua Kali craftspeople, as a prime example of

87: **Hyperboloid**; Water tower in Poland by Jan Boguslawski.

88: **Hydraform Press**; Mechanized mudbick production.

89: **Igloo**; Undergound entrance blocks cold air from entering.

90: **Hypocaust**; Short pillars on the ground are part of this ancient heating system.

91: **Igloo**; Upper, warm levels are covered with pelts and serve as beds.

92: **Infra-Lightweight Concrete**; In Mike Schlaich's house in Pankow the material was used for the exterior walls, but not for the floor slabs.

93: **House in Heat**; FAR architects' re-invention of an A-frame house.

94: **Kotatsu**; Similar under-table heating is used in Spain.

95: **Kajima Cut and Take Down Technique**; Step-by-step-demolition enabes 99% recycling.

96: **Le Cabanon**; Le Corbusier's minimal house is situated in Cap Martin.

98: **Lime Mortar**; Proof of the durability of lime as mortar is the Pont du Gard in France.

97: **Le Cabanon**; Interior mock-up built by the furniture manufacturer Cassina in 2006.

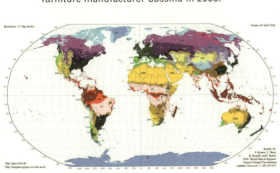

99: **Koeppen-Geiger**; Mapping climatic characteristics around the world.

100: **Lost in Paris**; Living surrounded by ferns and bacteria; A project by R&Sie(n).

the benefits of ➛ *upcycling*, were featured in the recent book, ➛ *Making Do*, by Steve Daniels.

Kajima Cut and Take Down Technique: This is a technique of deconstruction developed by the Japanese company Kajima. Instead of starting the process from the top, which is the common way in deconstruction, the Kajima take down demolishes the building floor-by-floor from the ground. A set of jacks, a load transferring frame, and a core wall system are installed, to make it possible to lower the building slowly floor by floor as it is demolished safely at the ground level. This unique process of demolition results in decreased demolition noise, decreased dust dispersion, and most importantly the ability to reclaim, reuse and recycle materials. Waste can be sorted into 30+ different kinds of materials at a recycling rate of 99% for an average building. The specific materials removed from the building being deconstructed can be scheduled with precision in the demolition process, because the Kajima take down works in a more linear way, floor by floor, unlike other techniques. This makes it easier for recycling firms to work hand-in-hand with the deconstruction process, enabling them to efficiently harvest materials. ➛ *Keller Easterling's essay in this book (p. 265)* takes techniques like the Kajima take down and applies them in a new market model for the subtraction of buildings. (➛ *drawing 28; image 95, p. 225*)

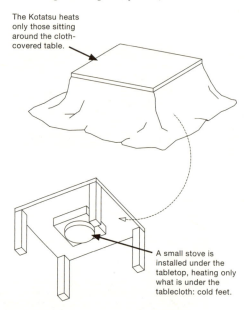

29: How Kotatsu heating works.

Kickstarter: Kickstarter is a new way to fund creative ideas and ambitious endeavors. It leverages ➛ *crowdsourcing* to find and fund creative projects. It assists artists, filmmakers, musicians, designers, writers, athletes, adventurers, illustrators, explorers, curators, promoters, performers, and others, to bring their projects, events, and dreams to life. Kickstarter is based on the premise that a good idea, communicated well, can generate interest quickly, and be of benefit to a large and diverse pool of people using the internet, and that this critical mass can be leveraged to provide funding for the idea. Essentially a method of fund-raising, Kickstarter is powered by a unique all-or-nothing funding method where projects must be fully funded or they will be rejected. To fund a project with Kickstarter, the project's creator/initiator explains the goal, the approach, and the basic idea of the project on the Kickstarter website, trying to convince visitors to the site to support the project. Every project has a funding goal (a pre-set dollar amount) and a time limit (from one to ninety days) set by the project creator. When the deadline is reached, one of two things happens: "Funding Unsuccessful": If a project has NOT met its funding goal, all pledges are canceled, and no money changes hands, or, "Funding Successful": If a project has met or surpassed its funding goal, all backers are debited for their promised contribution, and funds go directly to the project creator. Project creators are then responsible for completing the project and any deliverables promised to backers.

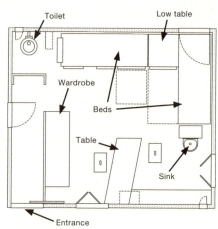

30: Plan of Le Corbusier's cabin *Le Cabanon*.

Köppen-Geiger: The Köppen-Geiger climate classification system is the most commonly used climate classification system in the world. The Köppen-Geiger system works on the principal that natural vegetation is the most accurate expression of climate. Vegetation groups are used to organize climate zones, which are classified first into six main groups: Tropical/megathermal climates; Dry (arid and semiarid) climates; Temperate/mesothermal climates; Continental/microthermal climate; Polar climates; Alpine climates. These groups are then split into multiple subtypes. These classes are mapped using data about average annual and monthly temperatures and precipitation, and seasonal precipitation in relationship to the vegetation groups, by zone. This method of climate classification was first published in 1884 by Wladimir Köppen, with subsequent changes and improvements made by Köppen and a later collaborator, Rudolf Geiger. (➔ *image 99, p. 225*)

Kotatsu: The kotatsu is an item of furniture from Japan that combines a table, futon, and heat source for use as an alternative to expensive and energy-consuming central heating. It consists of a futon draped between a table frame and table top with a heat source underneath, designed so that a person can sit at the table and cover their lower body with the blanket. Modern kotatsu primarily use electric heat as opposed to the traditional charcoal heaters. The encapsulated space of the kotatsu allows the user to minimize the area required for heating, thus consuming less energy by volume. Similar concepts from other countries include the Kang bed stove from China, the Ondol underfloor heating system from Korea, and the Roman Hypocaust, although the latter two are spread out over a larger surface area rather than a single item of furniture. (➔ *drawing 29; image 94, p. 225*)

Le Cabanon: Le Cabanon is a small house built by Le Corbusier in 1952 in Cap Martin. Originally planned as a holiday house for his wife, Le Corbusier used the little cabin himself, living and working there. The wooden cabin measures only 3.66 m by 3.66 m but includes a bed, toilet, sink, desk and a chair. There is no kitchen as Le Corbusier was supplied with meals by a nearby restaurant. Le Corbusier developed the room and its furniture in detail during his search for the ideal minimum number of elements needed for a functional and pleasant living space. The cabin's interior resembles that of a sophisticated yacht or mobile home. (➔ *drawing 30, images 96, 97, p. 225*)

smooth surface. Lightweight concretes with expanded glass pearls reach densities comparable to those of beech wood (U=0.32 W/mK), which imports a very good insulation quality regarding its resistance. An extremely light version of lightweight concrete, ➔ *infra-lightweight concrete*, has just been developed. (➔ *drawing 31*)

Lime Mortar: Lime mortar is a type of mortar made from lime and an aggregate material mixed with water. Common until the introduction and subsequent popularity of ➔ *Portland cement*, lime mortar is one of the oldest types of mortar: it can be traced back to the 4th century BC and was used in ancient Greece and Rome. Although Portland cement is faster setting and has greater compressive strength, lime mortar is both porous and incredibly durable, and structures made using it have endured over thousands of years. (➔ *image 98, p. 225*)

Living Machines: Living machines, wetland machines, and eco-machines are constructed wetlands or other water-based vegetation purification machines, commonly used as water treatment systems. Living machines can be used extensively in large-scale outdoor settings, and are capable of treating high volumes of water without achieving potability, or they can be smaller-scale indoor systems, capable of rendering potable the wastewater from a building or complex. The principles that underlie a living machine rely primarily on an understanding of the purifying and filtering capabilities of various plants, and the proper application of low-tech and plant-based treatment in combination with high-tech systems, such as UV sterilization for water intended to be potable. Israel is one of the world leaders in the use of living machines to treat water, some 70 % of which is then reused to irrigate crops. (➔ *image 103, p. 231*)

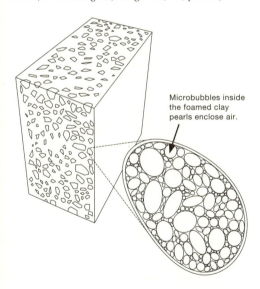

31: Lightweight concrete with expanded clay pearls.

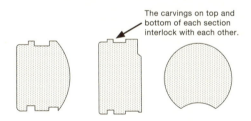

32: Possible sections for log house components.

Lightweight Concrete: Lightweight concrete generally consists of a mixture of ➔ *Portland cement* and light aggregates. Common aggregates in lightweight concretes are expanded clay pearls or expanded glass pearls that have little inclusions of air and a closed,

Log House: Made from stacked and joined wood, log houses are one of the oldest building types, common in areas with an abundant supply of wood. Logs are a simple way of building houses as they can be used raw or milled, air-dried or kiln-dried to stack into the house structure. The wood serves the dual functions of providing the structural support necessary for the house to stand as well as forming the complete shell of the house, all from one simple construction and material. A variety of log profiles are used, depending on climate, the need for adjustments due to the dynamic nature of wood as a changing natural material, and building technique. The style of the corner joining of a log house also varies. Log houses can be sold as modular kits, shipped to a site, or they are offered as custom or DIY projects with locally sourced materials where available. Interest in simple wood construction has increased in contemporary projects, one example being architect Elke Reichel's modern interpretation of a log house in her ➤ *board house* project. (➤ *drawing 32, image 101, p. 231*)

Lost in Paris: Lost in Paris is a residential building by R&Sie(n), located in Paris. The house is clad in a green layer of some 1,200 **Dryopteris filix-mas** or common male fern. The ferns live in 300 specialized glass beakers and are fed ➤ *hydroponically* a special mix of bacteria, which provide the nutrients necessary for healthy fern growth without the weight of soil. Rainwater is collected from the roof for the fern wall. The plants are tended by the owners of the house, and the bacteria mix is adjusted according to season and plant health. The green wall is set a small distance away from the concrete structure of the house to prevent root infiltration from damaging the structure. (➤ *image 100, p. 225*)

LowEx: LowEx is a short form of 'Low Exergy' and describes a new way of creating high-performance buildings and community systems. LowEx systems use the concept of exergy to minimize excessive temperature gradients in heating and cooling systems. These temperature gradients occur where heat is transferred or generated in building systems. A simple energy analysis will overlook the losses in quality of heat as the temperature decreases, as long as the amount of energy stays the same. But when the temperature in a supply system decreases, the quality of that supply also decreases. This is accounted for by an exergy analysis. LowEx systems are designed on the basis of this awareness of both the quantity and quality of energy. These include low-temperature heating and high-temperature cooling systems where larger surface areas for room conditioning are employed in a way that the same power can be supplied without necessitating large temperature gradients. Also, the use of ➤ *heat pumps* plays an important role in LowEx systems design because the operation of heat pumps is directly dependent on temperature gradients in building systems. The lower the temperature gradient, the lower the temperature-lift the heat pump must supply. This results in ➤ *low temperature-lift, ultra-high COP heat pumps* and a lower primary energy demand of the system.

Low Temperature-Lift Ultra-high COP Heat Pump: The coefficient of performance, or COP, of a ➤ *heat pump* is a measure of the amount ratio of heat supplied by the system to the input to run it. This performance is directly dependent on the temperature-lift that it must supply. As the temperature-lift is reduced the performance of the heat pump is increased. This relationship is also non-linear. For reductions from a 100 degree steam heater to a roughly 60 degree radiator, the performance increase may be around 20%-50%, but by reducing the temperature further such that the lift is reduced to below 20 degrees, the performance can be more than doubled. In this case, upwards of eight units of heat can be supplied with each unit of energy, usually in the form or electricity. This reduced electricity demand can be more easily met with a set of hybrid photovoltaic panels. The low temperature-lift ultra-high COP heat pump utilizes standard technologies that are readily available. Attention must only be paid to proper sizing of the heat pump components so that the low temperature-lift can be seen in operation of the unit at the desired temperature points. When properly designed and integrated into a building system, this heat pump provides the heart of an integrated ➤ *LowEx* building system.

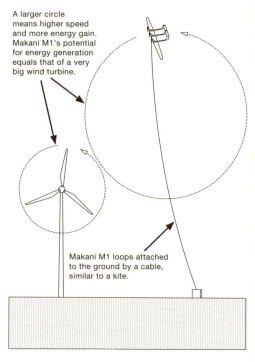

33: Comparison of Makani Power principle and common HAWT.

Makani Power: The Makani Power project is a wind turbine project from Squid Labs, a technology and engineering innovation collective. The brainchild of inventor Saul Griffith, power is generated using a kite-like turbine. The turbine is a wing, which resembles a small glider plane. These are suspended high in the air, where the wind speed is significantly faster than the wind speeds at the height of vertical or ➤ *horizontal axis wind turbines*. The Makani wing mimics the movement of the tip of a vertical turbine blade, as it is this part of the blade that generates up to 75% of the total power generated by a ➤ *vertical axis wind turbine*. Multiple Makani wings can be deployed, arrayed in a circular pattern. (➤ *drawing 33, image 102, p. 231*)

Making Do: *Making Do* is a book by Steven Daniels about innovation in Kenya's informal sector. This informal sector is marked by the sophisticated reuse of materials, creative problem-solving and the use of techniques vastly different from those of more traditional economies and building systems. ➤ *Upcycling*, or the use of old materials in higher

quality end products, is featured. The book focuses on the ➤ *Jua Kali*, entrepreneurs and craftspeople who take part in the complex socioeconomic system in the informal sector of Kenyan commerce and construction.
Manual: A manual is a handbook or printed set of instructions which enables people to accomplish a specific task, like building, fixing, or operating something, without requiring the knowledge of an expert. In many cases, it only offers simple instructions and does not explain how or why things are done. Manuals can be a way of communicating practical knowledge or ideas, frequently in a hands-on way, e.g. an application manual enables us to use a computer without understanding why and how it works. Examples of manuals are the construction manuals for DIY patternbook furniture by Enzo Mari, entitled ➤ *Autoprogettatione*, and Gerrit Rietveld's 'How to Build Tables and Chairs', the simple construction briefs from the website ➤ *practicalanswers.com* and the manual for the ➤ *Earthship*, a self-constructed house.

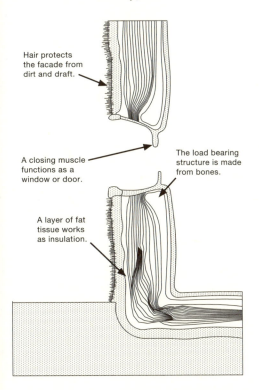

Hair protects the facade from dirt and draft.

A closing muscle functions as a window or door.

The load bearing structure is made from bones.

A layer of fat tissue works as insulation.

34: Section of Michael Joachim's Meat Habitat.

Mapungubwe Visitor Centre: The Mapungubwe Visitor Centre by Peter Rich Architects is situated at the confluence of the Limpopo and Shashe rivers. The Centre is part of a so-called poverty relief project using ecological methods and materials. The complex landscape was both the inspiration for the design and the source of most of the materials for its construction. This resulted in a composition of structures that are authentically rooted in their location. ➤ *Timbrel vaulting* is used to construct the billowing forms that expose the arched edges of their thin shells. This simple but smart technique involved not only local workers but also local materials. (➤ *images 105-107, p. 231*)

Matrix Material: Matrix material is the term for a material, used in a ➤ *composite material* mix, which the other material can be set into. Common matrix materials are ➤ *Portland cement*, plastics, and resins.

Meat Habitat: The In Vitro Meat Habitat is a concept for an organic dwelling made from meat cells proposed by architect Michael Joachim, designer of the ➤ *Fab Tree Hab*. Described as a 'victimless shelter', the meat habitat would involve no harm to animals and instead consist of pig cells cultivated in a laboratory. The 3D printed extruded pig cells are treated with preservative to kill bacteria and fungi, and combined with a recycled plastic scaffold as well as several other powders and chemical substances. Tissue, bones, and skin would represent insulation, siding, and studs in walls that include sphincter muscles that open and close for doors and windows. The current prototype of the non-perishable concept home is basically cured pork or pig leather measuring approximately 21 m^2. (➤ *drawing 34; image 104, p. 231*)

Meme (Internet): An internet meme is a piece or unit of cultural knowledge that is created on, disseminated through, or otherwise made directly possible through the internet. A meme, as introduced by Richard Dawkins in 1978's *The Selfish Gene*, is a specific piece of cultural information passed from one person to another. It is partially analogous to a gene in that it is assumed that a meme is transmitted from person to person, and that the meme has a life of its own, evolving and subject to remission, exclusion or evolutionary obsolescence. Memes transmitted or created via the internet are subject to the evolution of the internet itself. Internet memes range from the meaningful and important, such as the video of Neda Agha-Soltan's death during protests of the Iranian elections in 2009, to the amusing and functionally useless trick of leading people to specific obscure 1980s music videos, by artist Rick Astley, a practice known as rickrolling.

Microgeneration: Microgeneration refers to the practice of individuals or small groups generating zero- or low-carbon forms of energy to satisfy their own demand. Examples of microgeneration technology include small-scale versions of wind turbines and hydroelectric power installations (known as micro hydro), photovoltaic solar arrays, and ground source ➤ *heat pumps*. Beyond the form of energy production, the producer will also require a small amount of infrastructure to store and convert the energy for practical use. Microgeneration is a new application for homes that enables them to be energy self-sufficient and no longer reliant on a grid. However, some microgenerators may choose to connect to the regular electricity grid, primarily for financial recompensation schemes.

Military Reserves as Nature Preserves: Military reserves, bases, and training areas are commonly large swaths of land, where access by humans is limited and highly controlled. Exempt from the pressures of development and human encroachment, these areas of land are little disturbed habitats. For this reason, the land of a preserve frequently functions as a formal or informal nature preserve, and allows for endangered species to benefit from indirect military protection. Although these are usually accidental and informal nature preserves, formal funding is provided in both the United States and the United Kingdom to support some of these nature preserves. Some of them also benefit from the direct involvement of military personnel in the maintenance, management, and upkeep of the preserve. The preserves can also function as valuable in-situ research sites for scientists to study the flora and fauna of a particular place. For example, in Fort Stewart in Liberty County, Georgia, USA, scientists are working on the preservation and reforestation of *Pinus palustris* (the long-leaf pine), an important component of many endangered habitats in the American South.

Mini Cows: Mini cows are tiny livestock that can be kept in urban spaces. In an era of increasing interest in suburban and ➝*urban agriculture*, most of the focus has been on fruit and vegetable production. Possible and fruitful even on a small balcony, crops have been the DIY food darlings. Producing milk by keeping miniature breeds of cow and goat, i.e. tiny livestock, makes the production of protein possible in many homes. Breeds like the Dexter, Mini-Hereford and Lowline Angus stand about 1 m tall, require little pasture space and can produce enough milk for a small family. Front yards, garden plots and courtyards could soon become homes for these mini milk makers.

clay, sand, and water. Fibers added to the mix, such as straw, can give the bricks special attributes. The mixture is shaped and dried in the sun for about 25 days. One constraint of the mudbrick is its limited lifespan: Buildings made from mudbrick last no longer than about 30 years and then have to be replaced. (➝ *image 113, p.232*)

Mudhif: A mudhif is a ➝*vernacular* architecture form made entirely of reeds. It originates in the swamplands in the southern part of Iraq. The mudhif is a communal building, and is built collectively by members of the community. Typically used for religious and ceremonial purposes, the mudhif is usually paid for and maintained by a local sheik. (➝ *drawing 36, image 108, 110, p.232*)

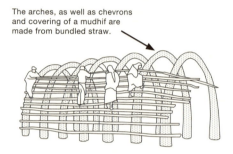

The arches, as well as chevrons and covering of a mudhif are made from bundled straw.

36: A mudhif under constrcuction.

35: Mobile homes are typically monocoque structues.

Monocoque: Monocoque is a construction technique that uses an object's exterior to support its structural load, as opposed to using and internal frame or truss covered with a non-load bearing skin. Monocoque construction was pioneered in aircraft, and is today the predominant automobile construction technique. Monocoque construction in architecture makes it possible to create interior spaces without either columns or load-bearing walls, allowing larger open spaces and therefore greater creative diversity in program possibilities. Examples of Monocoque construction are concrete shell structures or geodesic domes. The Media Centre at Lord's Cricket Grounds is a semi-monocoque aluminum structure designed by Future Systems and built by the Pendennis Shipyard in Falmouth, utilizing the company's boatbuilding experience. (➝ *drawing 35, image 109, p.232*)

Mudbrick: Mudbrick is one of the most common construction techniques for ➝*adobe* buildings. A mudbrick is a firefree brick made of a mixture of

Nanoarchitecture: Nanoarchitecture is a branch of architectural practice that uses ➝*nanotechnology* and nanomaterials to solve architectural, environmental or other problems. ➝*carbon-absorbing surfaces* are an example of a nanomaterial used in nanoarchitecture.

Nanotechnology: Nanotechnology is a field of study and source of innovative research that deals with things on an atomic or molecular scale that are measured in nanometers, or billionths of a meter, hence the name. Nanotechnology is being used in the ongoing development of new materials, making them more complex, smaller, lighter, and stronger in a way more finely tuned than was possible prior to the rise of nanotechnology. Nanotechnology is the manipulation of materials at the molecular level, chemically assembling new structures by means of molecular recognition or nanomaterials. Nanotechnology is also the reduction of existing things to the scale of nanometer measurements, which changes the quantum mechanics of the materials and their physical properties. Gold becomes soluble, aluminum combustible; the insoluble becomes soluble, the stable becomes reactive. Nanomaterials have been used in things as common as zinc sunscreen, and are being researched as components for new kinds of solar panels and printable batteries.

Natural Fiber Insulation: Natural fiber insulation refers to a method of insulating buildings with natural, renewable, or agricultural waste materials such as straw, hemp, cotton, wool, or linseed. The varying properties of natural fibers can sometimes cause problems for use as insulating materials such as low

101: **Log House;** Structure and insulation at the same time.

102: **Makani Power;** A new way of power generation using circling gliders.

103: **Living Machines;** Organic sewage plant.

104: **Meat Habitat;** The future of building?

105: **Mapungubwe Visitor Centre;** Timbrel vaulting enabled wide, thin spans.

106: **Mapungubwe Visitor Centre;** Local craftsmen at work.

107: **Mapungubwe Visitor Centre;** The building in Limpopo, South Africa by Peter Rich Architects won a Holcim Award in 2008.

108: **Mudhif**; Most Iraqi swamplands, where mudhifs were traditionally built, today are endangered or dried out.

109: **Monocoque Structures**; The Media Centre at Lord's Cricket Ground built by Future Systems in 1999.

110: **Mudhif**; A building made entirely from straw.

112: **The Oakland Museum**; A roof turned into a park.

111: **Natural Fiber Insulation**: House in Eschenz by architect Felix Jerusalem.

113: **Mudbrick**; The great Mosque of Djenne.

114: **Ningbo Muesum**; This museum by Amateur Architects in China is made from recycled bricks.

115: **Paper Log Houses**; Detail of Shigeru Ban's design for Cobe.

116: **Pack Chair**; Open, shake, wait, sit.

117: **Open-Air Museum**; Traditional buildings from all over Switzerland were relocated to Ballenberg Open-Air Museum, close to Interlaken.

118: **Open-Air Museum**; This 17th-century mixed-use house was originally situated in Villnachern, in central Switzerland.

119: **Paper Log Houses**; In use in Bhuj, India, in 2001.

inflammation temperatures and high flammability. To address these issues, materials can be treated with flame-retardant chemicals. A notable example of straw insulation is a house in Eschenz, built by architect Felix Jerusalem. The outer façade was constructed from plastic sheets made from polycarbonate reinforced with glass fibers. Underneath was a layer of pressed straw that not only insulates but serves as the structural element of the house. The prefabricated straw elements, which can be seen through the sheets of polycarbonate, allowed the building to be finished within only four months. (➤ *image 111, p.232*)

New Food Movement: The New Food Movement describes a cultural shift from the highly industrialized production of artificial and processed foods towards the more local and sustainable production of natural and organic foods. Stemming from issues such as rising obesity rates, animal welfare, food safety, and environmental awareness, the New Food Movement prioritizes food made by people over food products from factories. Through efforts such as supporting small farmers and producers, educating on urban agriculture, and emphasizing home cooking and preserving, supporters of the movement hope to achieve varied goals such as reforming school lunch programs, minimizing farmland degradation, improving standards of animal husbandry, and encouraging healthy eating. The global movement is driven by the diverse efforts of citizens, teachers, organizers, farmers, and activists. Notable advocates include the international Slow Food organization, journalist Michael Pollan (author of *The Omnivore's Dilemma* and *In Defense of Food*) and American First Lady Michelle Obama, whose 'Let's Move' campaign promotes healthful food with the goal of ending childhood obesity.

Ningbo Historic Museum: The Ningbo Historic Museum in Ningbo China by Amateur Architecture Studio is built entirely of ➤ *wa pan*. Essentially a whole-building approach to recycling, the Ningbo Historic Museum is made of reclaimed materials from old buildings. The appearance of the building clearly reflects this genesis with the façade composed of an intricate yet hodgepodge collection of roofing tiles, stones from other walls, and a range of other materials. Inspired by older architecture projects using wa pan, the head architect, Wang Shu, designed the façade to a certain point, and let the remainder be dictated by material availabilities and the choice of the workers. Though the building is in a relatively contemporary style, intentionally echoing the mountains typical of Ningbo and the surrounding area, use of a centuries-old building technique, modernized for the project, provides continuity from past to present. (➤ *image 114, p.232*)

Oakland Museum of California: The Oakland Museum of California is located in downtown Oakland, California, and was opened to the public in 1969. It is a museum and a large public space at the same time; a hybridized condition of planting on structure. Designed by architect Kevin Roche and landscape architect Dan Kiley, the museum has three levels of open space and galleries, organized around a central yard space. Almost 2500 m² of green space are punctuated by broad stairs. Innovative solutions were needed to support the unprecedented and extensive planting on structure and to provide adequate drainage. The museum was designed to function as a public space and is unusually innovative in its combination of public and private space and architecture and landscape spaces. (➤ *image 112, p.232*)

On the Bri-n-ck: The On the Bri-n-ck project was a wall constructed under the direction of architect Ingeborg Rocker at the Harvard Graduate School of Design. The wall was designed by Rocker and her students, and built by a 6-axis ABB robot. The robot arm constructed a 1:1 scale model of the project, which was designed in 3D, and then translated into commands for the ABB robot to follow. The wall undulates and re-curves onto itself, for structural stability, similar to a ➤ *thin-shell structure*. The wall was 3.5 m tall, and 8 m long, and was constructed from wooden pieces, purposefully sized to be similar to standard, industrially produced ➤ *bricks*. This was done to demonstrate the possibility of using an everyday material in combination with an innovative technology.

Open-Air Museum: Open-air museums are used as models of real-world conditions. They are frequently used as reproductions and concentrations of knowledge from specific regions or historical periods. They are reconstructions of actual conditions, and in this way they spread knowledge that might otherwise be lost. In reviving this knowledge it can be made current again and inspire further development. The open-air museum originated in Scandinavia in the 19th century. There is potential for the open-air museum to be used as a didactic tool in new contexts and for new purposes.(➤ *images 117-118, p. 233*)

Open Architecture Network: The Open Architecture Network, online at openarchitecturenetwork.org, is a platform for sharing architectural ideas in an open source community. The idea behind the network is that by sharing architectural and design ideas and strategies in an open environment, it is possible to improve people's lives through architecture and design. The network serves as a collaborative resource, a project ➤ *wiki*, and a forum for ideas. The network is an offshoot of Architecture for Humanity, a non-profit organization, and was born out of a frustration with the difficulties in sharing and exchanging ideas, especially in difficult contexts, for example, in disaster relief situations or informal settlements.

Pack Chair: The Pack Chair is designed by François Azambourg, and it is sold partially formed. The chair is made from a sealed polyester fabric form, with a double layer lining containing two liquids that make polyurethane foam when combined. This phase change of the materials is initiated by the owner of the chair, and results in a quickly solidifying form. This allows the chair to be fairly compact before it is essentially activated and finished by the end user. (➤ *image 116, p. 233*)

Paharpur Business Centre: The Paharpur Business Centre, located in New Delhi, India, was created by Kamal Meattle as an office building with an innovative and effective air purification system in a city where air pollution is a significant concern. Meattle was familiar with a NASA study that examined ➤ *air purification and oxygenation with plants*, in particular, common house plants. Taking inspiration from the study, Meattle integrated some of the plants recommended by NASA in a rooftop greenhouse that serves as a finishing step in the process of air purification and oxygenation for the building. According to a study conducted by the Indian Central Pollution Control Board, eye irritation was down by 52%, respiratory symptoms by 34%, headaches by 24%, lung impairment by 12%, and asthma by 9% in the Paharpur Business Centre. The building was rated by the Indian Government as one of the "healthiest" buildings in Delhi, and this is in part due to the use of plants as an integral part of the building's infrastructure.

varies according to context, although easily accessible, recycled or repurposed inexpensive materials are used consistently. In the first paper log houses in Kobe, Japan, beer crates were used as a foundation, and plastic tarps as a waterproofing element on top of a pitched roof. Subsequent paper log houses have been modified; for example, insulation has been added to the paper tubes, and roofing techniques have been adapted to specific regional conditions. (➤ *drawing 38; images 115, 119, p. 233*)

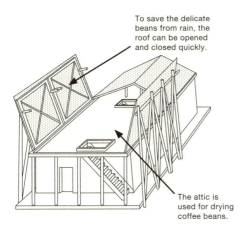

37: Principle of a typical Paisa house.

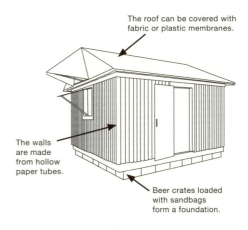

38: A paper log house designed by Shigeru Ban.

Paisa House: Paisa houses are a traditional type of housing in some parts of Columbia. There are different kinds of Paisa houses, but all are constructed from bamboo, which provides excellent structural stability during earthquakes. Earthquakes occur frequently in some regions of Columbia and regularly destroy the simple concrete buildings which are common in the country. The flexibility of bamboo gives Paisa houses their structural stability and is attracting considerable interest in the building industry. A special version of the Paisa house includes context-specific programmatic elements, including a device to dry coffee beans, a source of income for many Columbian farmers. Coffee beans have to be sun-dried before they are roasted, however, the beans spoil if they come into contact with rain. The Paisa house accommodates a platform on the roof where coffee can be dried and easily and quickly covered by shutter-like roof panels when rain is imminent. The roof can be opened and closed according to the weather and needs of the inhabitants. (➤ *drawing 37*)

Paper Log Houses: The paper log houses by architect Shigeru Ban are assembled from paper tubes. Ban has been exploring the use of paper tubes as "logs" since 1989, and he constructed the first paper log house in 1995, in Kobe, Japan, as a post-earthquake shelter. The paper log house has been used in multiple post-disaster contexts. The basic construction depends on material surpluses, and

Papercrete: Papercrete, a fibrous cement, is a building material made from mostly organic components. Consisting of a mixture of paper, clay, sand, and Portland cement, it can be easily mixed from commonly available materials. The paper component of papercrete can be almost any kind of paper product, and can be a possibility to ➤ *upcycle* paper collected for standard recycling. Producible either industrially or on a small scale, papercrete has many positive qualities. Weighing between 15 and 20 lbs per square foot, Papercrete is a lightweight material compared with concrete, which weighs 137 lbs. It has an insulation value of R-2.8 per inch, similar to polyethylene foam and fiberglass. Potential applications are numerous, with organizations like ➤ *Rural Studio* undertaking building projects with papercrete.
(➤ *images 128-129, p. 239*)

Parabolic Trough: A parabolic trough can turn solar thermal energy into electric energy with the help of a turbine. Similar to the principle of the ➤ *solar cooker*, sunlight is reflected by a long, mirrored parabolic trough onto a tube that is situated at its focal point, where it heats a circulating, liquid coolant. The heated coolant, with the help of a ➤ *heat pump*, warms water to 300 degrees, so that it can power a steam turbine to generate electricity. Because of its shape, the parabolic trough does not have to be readjusted towards the sun and can therefore be a simple, low-tech structure. The fact that it stores a certain amount of energy in its coolant makes it operable at night, which is its great advantage over other solar-driven power plants. One dis-

Passive Cooling · Passive ventilation

advantage of parabolic troughs, however, is that they can only be operated effectively in regions around the equator. These regions often have problems providing the water needed to power the steam turbine. (➡ *drawing 39; image 126, p. 238*)

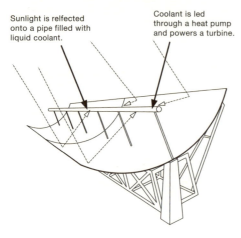

39: Parabolic troughs use solar thermal energy to generate electricity.

Passive Cooling: Passive cooling is a means of preventing heat from entering the interior spaces of a building and/or removing heat after it has entered such spaces. Passive cooling uses solar energy or other natural cooling sources, like ➡ *evaporative cooling*, ➡ *passive ventilation*, etc., to control indoor climates. The exact application of these strategies and specific design of the system depends on the prevailing climatic conditions. Passive cooling techniques help to maximize building envelope efficiency by minimizing heat gain from the external environment and to efficiently release heat gain back into the exterior from building surfaces. Passive cooling engages structures like the ➡ *wind catcher*, and is sometimes used in combination with ➡ *evaporative cooling* to further maximize cooling potential.

Passive Daylighting: Passive daylighting is the use of natural daylight for lighting in diverse applications. In contrast to ➡ *active daylighting*, where mechanical or other active systems track daylight by following the sun, passive systems are non-mechanical, and rely upon building orientation and organization to optimize the use of natural daylight. A south-facing orientation, for example, provides optimal daylight in the northern hemisphere, while a northern orientation is best for the southern hemisphere. Calculations of seasonal sun angles for optimal window and skylight positioning and other similar simple analyses can be undertaken to make passive daylighting as effective as possible. A building complex in Germany increased the amount of natural daylight present in the buildings and decreased the need for electric lighting by adding 5500 m² of skylights, utilizing four bands of 4 m wide skylights with a running length of 170 m. Openings for ➡ *passive ventilation* were

also included into the structure to release excess heat energy. The Fraba building, a factory in Germany, used passive daylighting as a guiding design principle. (➡ *image 122, p. 238*)

Passive Solar Building Design: Passive solar building design reduces or eliminates the need for mechanical heating and cooling by designing with solar heat gain in mind. This is a completely passive approach to heating and cooling that has to be considered in the planning phase of a building. Similar to passive ventilation strategies, passive solar design manipulates the building and its apertures both to control solar heat gain for direct heating and to control unwanted heat. Passive solar building design uses direct and indirect solar gain for heating in combination with the use of building elements like the ➡ *Trombe wall*, heat absorbing materials like ➡ *adobe* and phase-change materials for slowing indoor air temperature swings. ➡ *Windcatchers* are also used for the enhancement of passive ventilation, in relationship to passive solar building design and design strategies like ➡ *earth sheltering*, special orientation and shape of buildings, as well as the use of wide roofs or vegetation. Passive solar building is dependent on a specific knowledge of the sun's cycles throughout the day and the year for the exact site of a building. It can be combined with other indoor climate control techniques and minimize their energy consumption and maximize their capacity.

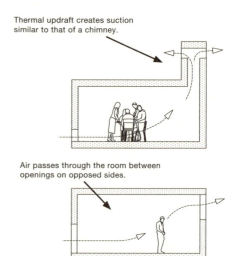

40: Thermal ventilation and cross ventilation: two basic principles of passive ventilation.

Passive Ventilation: Passive ventilation typically relies on using physical principles like the ➡ *thermal updraft* that naturally results from the tendency of warm air to rise and cool air to sink, and by the effect of cross ventilation, by creating unimpeded airflow through a building. Many passive ventilation systems rely on the building users to control windows and vents as dictated by site conditions and conditions within the building. The building's situation and relation to land forms or, for example, adjacent woods, determines the capacity for passive ventilation to be effective in cooling and ventilating a building. Passive ventilation can occur intentionally through the control of air movement through openings such as windows or doors from wind pressure and/or indoor-outdoor temperature differences or through the unintentional or uncontrollable air flow through unintentional openings in the building envelope (infiltration) resulting from wind and temperature generated pressure differences across the building envelope. (→ *drawing 40*)

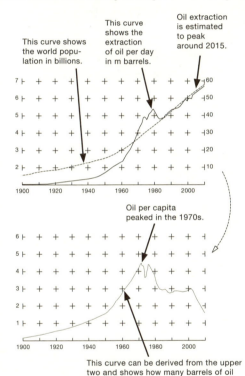

41: Peak oil in comparison to peak oil per capita.

Peak Oil Per Capita: Peak oil per capita is the point in time when the maximum amount of oil is available per person globally, after which peak oil per capita enters a terminal decline because of population growth and the eventual (or possibly already occurred) point when → *peak oil* production happens. Peak oil per capita, according to many sources, occurred in the 1970s. (→ *drawing 41*)

Peak Oil: Peak oil is the time when the maximum rate of petroleum extraction is reached globally. After this point, oil extraction enters into a terminal decline. There is much debate about whether peak oil has already occurred, and if it has not already occurred, when it will occur in future. Because a complex method of calculation is used to predict peak oil based upon known oil resources, this debate has been going on since geoscientist M. King Hubbert developed models in 1956 to accurately predict peak oil production in the USA to occur between 1965 and 1970. Currently, some believe that global peak oil production has already occurred, while some believe this will occur in 2020. → *Peak oil per capita* is another important measure of global petroleum supply. (→ *drawing 41*)

Permaculture: Permaculture is an ecological approach to designing human systems, broadly consisting of sustainable and efficient practices based on natural processes and biological principles. A portmanteau of permanent agriculture and permanent culture, permaculture aims for a harmonious and productive relationship between humans and their environment that can be sustained indefinitely. In permaculture design thinking, waste from one system becomes the resources of another system to minimize energy loss and natural degradation while increasing productivity and respecting patterns of existing ecosystems. An example of such efficient and recycled design is a chicken greenhouse, where the warmth from chickens' bodies helps to heat the greenhouse. Permaculture values can be applied to agriculture, housing, animal husbandry, energy usage and many other systems in all climates and environments.

Pervious Paving: Pervious paving materials produce smooth and durable mobility surfaces without creating an impermeable barrier. Impermeable surfaces are widespread in most settled areas, leading to large areas of sealed ground. This lack of permeability can result in washouts, location-specific erosion, standing water, runoff and a host of other environmental problems. A new generation of porous paving materials made from both concrete and asphalt is being developed. Pervious asphalt is capable of functioning exactly like regular asphalt but is permeable enough to withstand even heavy rainfall. Because it is similar in composition and functionality to regular asphalt, it can be used in more or less the same way as a standard asphalt mix. The asphalt is porous because it lacks some of the fine grain aggregates present in a typical asphalt mix; this results in small, irregularly spaced gaps in the poured asphalt. These irregular gaps allow for water percolation and drainage while maintaining the structural integrity necessary for asphalt use even in high-traffic situations. The pervious asphalt paving has the added benefit of faster water drainage from road surfaces in addition to environmental advantages. (→ *image 134, p. 239*)

Pet Architecture: Pet architecture is a term for architecture that exists in small and unusual spaces. Introduced by Japanese architecture firm Atelier Bow Wow through a book of the same name, pet architecture redefines the architectural site by occupying spaces commonly thought to be unusable for architecture. These buildings inhabit interstitial spaces in the urban environment. As explored by Atelier Bow Wow, the pet architectures are built from ad-hoc techniques, inexpensive materials and in ways that do not intentionally participate in any formalized architectural discourse. In dense urban environments pet architecture is one of many ways to deviate from standard practice and reinvent typical architectural forms and strategies. Pet architecture is the logical and pragmatic

120: **Pig City**; A highly densified yet animal-friendly method of meat production.

121: **Pig City**; Pigs are raised by a system that provides them with food, water, and clean bedding.

122: **Passive Daylighting**; Fraba Building by Bel Architects.

123: **Plant-Based Furniture**; Plants interweave during the growing process and create a strong structure.

124: **Plant-Based Furniture**; This chair is made from freeze-dried plants.

125: **Pet Architecture**; Tiny lots beget ingenuity.

126: **Parabolic Trough**; Huge solar thermal power plants could produce energy in latitudes around the equator.

127: **Playpump**; Using the excess energy of kids for water catchment.

128: **Papercrete**; Cardboard boxes serve as moulds.

129: **Papercrete**; A study project by Rural Studio in Auburn Country, Alabama.

130: **PLUS Principle**; Before.

131: **Phase Change Material**;

132: **Plywood Pavilion**; A project in Stuttgart developed by ICD & ITKE of Stuttgart University in 2010.

133: **PLUS Principle**; After.

134: **Pervious Paving**; Hard surfaces that can drain.

135: **Qanat**; The alluvial fan of a qanat creates a fertile area within the desert.

136: **Qanat**; Watersupply and air conditioning simultaneously.

137: **Recycled Buildings**; The Porta Nigra in Trier had multiple uses.

138: **Polar Bear Pelt**; White, warm, water repellent.

139: **Portland Cement**; Lina Bo Bardi's beautiful concrete architecture.

140: **Rammed Earth**; Peter Zumthor's Chapel in Mechernich.

141: **Rammed Earth**; Construction with rammed earth.

142: **POLLI-Brick**; Bottle and construction material simultaneously.

result of acting on the same themes and conditions explored in Gordon Matta Clark's → *Fake Estates*. (→ *image 125, p. 238*)

Phase Change Material: A phase change material is a material that melts and solidifies at certain temperatures that make it interesting for energy storage in architecture and other applications. As the material changes from a solid to a liquid state and back again, heat is absorbed or released. The energy present in liquid water is latent heat, and it can be released when the water turns into ice. Phase change materials can be used in passive heating systems for buildings. Phase change materials can exploit the thermal flywheel effect, working as a → *thermal mass* which is capable of a higher amount of energy storage in relation to its mass than a simple material like → *adobe* and a greater energy release as a result of the material's phase change. Grüntuch Ernst has constructed a building with paraffin wax embedded as micro-encapsulated bubbles in the material of the façade. This wax heats up during the day but does not increase its temperature as it turns from solid to liquid because all of the heat energy goes into the phase change project. The wall itself does not heat up that much during the day as a result. However, in the evening, as the wax cools down and solidifies again, it releases a small amount of heat slowly over a long period. → *Evaporative cooling* also utilizes the phase change abilities of water for cooling. (→ *image 131, p. 239*)

Phytoremediation: Phytoremediation is a specific kind of → *bioremediation* that uses plants to remove contaminants from the air, water, or soil. The plants used in phytoremediation can be harvested and the absorbed toxins can therefore be completely disposed of in a responsible manner. This method of remediation is suitable for applications where other kinds of remediation strategies would be impossible, for example where the particles or materials are too fine or unstable to be removed mechanically. Other kinds of phytoremediation practices include those that use plants to absorb toxins from soil or water, which are then released into the air via evapotranspiration, and rhizofiltration where bacteria on plant rhizomes assist in the disposal of toxins. The plants used in phytoremediation vary according to the substance of particle for removal, and the unique abilities of particular plants to take up particular contaminants. The plants are all hyperaccumulators, and can bioaccumulate, degrade or render harmless the contaminants that they take up. Common plants used in phytoremediation are members of the *Brassica* (mustard) family, *Helianthus* Sp. (sunflowers) and members of the *Populus* (poplar) family. Phytoremediative tactics are the subject of ongoing research and experimentation.

Pig City: The Pig City project by architecture and urban design firm MVRDV is a direct response to the Dutch people's love of pork. Pig City is a proposal to build a skyscraper for → *vertical farming* – for pig farming. With a population of 15.5 million people and 15.2 million pigs in 2000, the Netherlands has a pig problem. Pig farming requires a lot of space and material. Concentrated into an 80-meter high tower, vertical farming solves some of these problems in a sensible and sustainable way. Using the principles of → *permaculture*, the pig manure and methane would be recycled within the building, which would also provide space for → *aquaculture* to produce fish for pig feed and human consumption, and for additional agricultural production for the pig inhabitants. This densification of the space required for pig farming and the centralization of waste from what is normally a pollution-intensive industry help to relieve the pressure on the environment and provide the pigs with spacious, free-range, protected living conditions. (→ *images 120-121, p. 238*)

Plant-Based Furniture by Asif Khan: The furniture series 'Harvest' by Asif Khan consists of furniture made from freeze-dried plants and flowers. The London designer used local flowers in his installation on display as part of the Designers in Residence program at the Design Museum London. Khan used the extraordinary structure of plants that interweave during their growing process and therefore form a strong 'space framework'. Khan let the plants grow in the shape of his furniture pieces using molds, then freeze-dried the items over several weeks. The last step was to give the chairs and tables a preservative coating using a linseed oil-based resin. His context-specific installation took place in early spring 2010. (→ *images 123-124, p. 238*)

Plaster of Paris: Plaster of Paris is a kind of gypsum-based plaster. It hardens very quickly and is easily malleable. It can be used in diverse applications, and is frequently used in decorative projects as it is not very strong. However, plaster of Paris was frequently used in → *timbrel vaulting*, as it dries fast enough to be effective in this application where the self-supporting vault needs to be bonded together during construction as quickly as possible.

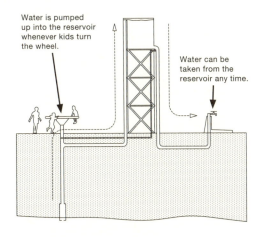

42: A PlayPump is the combination of a pump, a roundabout and a water storage.

PlayPumpWater System: The PlayPump is a water pump powered by children at play. The PlayPump looks much like a standard circular platform merry-go-round, however it is connected to a pump and pipe measuring up to 100 m below ground. As the children spin the merry-go-round, water can be pumped to the surface and into a tank suspended above ground and dispensed from a tap. The PlayPump is manufactured by a South African company, Roundabout, and costs approximately 14,000 USD. The installation of 4000 PlayPumps in sub-Saharan Africa, funded by the US and charitable organizations, is underway. Although the pump has received criticism for using playing children as a source of energy, it is still one of the best options for nonelectric water pumping. (→ *drawing 42; image 127, p. 239*)

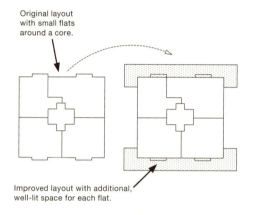

43: The PLUS Principle by Lacaton Vassal gives extra space to dwellers.

PLUS Principle: The PLUS principle is a socio-architectural strategy developed by French architecture firm Lacaton and Vassal. The architects alter existing buildings in high-density "problem" areas and suburbs, giving residents more free and private space by adding structures to their façades that provide an additional living area as well as conservatories that can be opened and closed according to season and occasion. According to Lacaton and Vassal some of the problems in the "banlieues" can be solved by simply giving inhabitants extra space which they can use individually according to their needs. A PLUS project in La Chesnaie, France, is currently under construction. (→ *drawing 43; images 130, 133, p. 239*)

Plywood Pavilion: The Plywood pavilion was developed in 2010 as a cooperation between the ICD and ITKE at Stuttgart University. It is made from 10-meter long – but only 6.5mm thick – plywood strips, which are joined to create an extremely thin and elegant building. From an engineering point of view, this is extremely thin and this thinness was made possible by pre-bending the flexible members. By doing so they were integrated as statically stiff members into a torus-shaped structure. The exact shape of the structure was developed with a combination of computer- and model-aided design processes that was based on a static model supplemented by specific data about the static properties of the plywood. The actual building components were then produced in the university's own robot-driven workshop. (→ *image 132, p. 239*)

Polar Bear Pelt: The polar bear's pelt keeps the polar bear warm in its cold habitat, creating an insulating layer of air around its body. The insulating effect is increased by the pelt's curliness and a constantly renewed grease film that makes the pelt water-repellent. The bear's skin underneath the pelt is black, absorbing sunlight that goes through the white pelt and turning it into thermal energy. It is commonly believed that the hair of the polar bear's pelt is hollow and fiber-active, which means that it can reflect sunlight internally onto the bear's skin. Although this theory was proven to be false, scientists successfully developed a → *translucent insulation material* based on the idea of fiber-active hair. (→ *image 138, p. 240*)

POLLI-Brick: The POLLI-Brick is a modular construction "brick" made from recycled PET plastic. It has a hollow form, can be filled with almost anything, and is incredibly strong for its weight. As part of an interlocking system, the POLLI-Brick can be used to construct curtain walls, interior non-load-bearing walls, and it is also suitable for applications in furniture and other smaller, non-structural functions. The POLLI-Brick was used in the Far Eastern Group's EcoARK pavilion in 2010 in Taiwan. Measuring 130 m x 26 m, the stand was constructed entirely with POLLI-Bricks made from local PET sources. (→ *drawing 44; image 142, p. 240*)

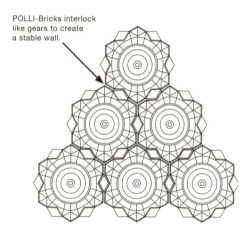

44: POLLI-Bricks are plastic bottles that can be used as building material.

Polyactide (PLA): Polyactide is a plastic based on an industrial resin called polylactic acid that is produced from corn starch. To produce PLA, dextrose is extracted from corn starch and converted in fermenters to lactic acids, which are then converted to lactides and linked into PLA chains. The PLA chains are formed into small pellets, which can be fabricated into packaging containers and other plastic consumer goods in a process that uses less energy and emits fewer greenhouse gases than conventional plastic production. PLA production is also attractive for its use of the renewable resource of corn, as opposed to conventional production that uses an estimated 200,000 barrels of oil per day in the United States. Corn-based plastics are considered by some to be the

MINE THE CITY

For a long period of time architecture's physical production was safely suspended between two material milieus: the natural resources out of which it received its construction materials, and the final building in which these resources were reapplied in a new and refined material configuration. These two milieus were clearly differentiated from one another, both geographically and ontologically. While the resources were considered part of the natural realm, the building was located in the cultural domain. Today, this dialectical relationship is undergoing a dramatic change, which becomes manifest in two major shifts:

1) The material resources of construction are becoming increasingly exhausted at the place of their natural origins, while inversely accumulating within buildings. For example, today there is more copper to be found in buildings than in the earth. As mines become increasingly empty, our buildings become mines themselves.
2) At the same time, the life expectancy of buildings shrinks. Sometimes the life span of a building seems to be equated with its depreciation period, as if the material value of architecture would extinguish once its financial value is written

off. But with frequent changes of program or ownership, it is difficult to plan buildings for generations ahead, and a short life span for buildings becomes an expression of common sense.

If we combine these two developments, we can no longer consider our built environment as a final storage site for the materials it contains. Rather we should learn to see buildings as interim storage, a transitory organization of matter that could also be redeployed elsewhere, in different ways, and for other uses. The city thus becomes an integrated mine for its own reproduction.

This metabolic understanding of the built environment, which had been foregrounded in the early 1990s by the studies of Peter Baccini and others,[1] is today increasingly incorporated by a number of architects and engineers in their practice. For now we can distinguish between three different approaches that have emerged since then:

Firstly, there is a call for a reversibility of construction, most prominently voiced by German engineer Werner Sobek. He claims that all new construction has to anticipate and enable the possibility of its future disassembly, in order to allow the building to disappear if the reason for its existence has ceased to exist. In order to remain reversible, a building must fulfill certain conditions: as such it has to use structures that can be disjointed and use materials in such a way that they can be separated from one another to be either reused, recycled or nontoxically disposed of. A substantial part of today's buildings obviously does not fulfill this precondition due to their static, irreversible structural systems and the use of complex composite materials.

A second approach that we can discern is adaptive reuse, as practiced and propagated by the New York-based architecture practice LOT-EK. Contrary to Sobek, LOT-EK claims that we can reuse existing structures, or parts thereof, by displacing them from their original context and reapplying them elsewhere and for different uses with only minor physical modifications. They have been illustrating the potential of this approach by reusing out-of-use industrial objects ranging from shipping containers to airplane fuselages as essential components for new buildings. An airplane fuselage, even if no longer used in its integral way, still embodies a highly functional apparatus that can be taken as such and deployed to a different use.

A third approach would be that of an architecture dedicated to perennial self-transformation. This is the preferred theme of French architects Lacaton & Vassal who reject demolition of buildings on principle. Inspired by endless examples from the history of architecture, they claim that one can always transform buildings whenever change is needed, by reprogramming, adding to, and subtracting from existing structures. For Lacaton & Vassal transforming an existing building is not only economically more sound (even if this is not always the case), but also socially more sustainable because one does not need to replace historically developed identities overnight by manufacturing new ones.

Common to all three approaches is the understanding that the nature of all construction is fundamentally transitory. No building is ever a completed project; the construction of a building is not complete on the day of its inauguration, it simply takes on a different modus operandi which we generally refer to as maintenance. In fact some buildings, such as the Cologne Cathedral, are permanent construction sites; somewhere on its black gothic masonry walls you can always spot some construction scaffolding with the workers of the *Bauhütte* doing repair work (they usually tour around the building, and once back at the beginning, they start all over again). But this kind of ongoing transformation is not only proper to the perennial monuments of our culture: it also applies to virtually all construction, from large institutional buildings to small residential houses, as we know from Steward Brand's brilliant historical study *How Buildings Learn*.[2] Brand showed in detailed case studies how buildings adapt to the often rapid, sometimes surreptitious, change of their programs. Brand's material history of architecture depicts the life of buildings akin to the time-lapse motion picture of the slowly metamorphosing shapes of clouds. Considering that in the developed countries of the western world architects are more and more busy with transforming existing buildings rather than erecting new ones, the profession is currently mutating from a producer of monuments to a curator of their transformation. Every act of building is only a momentary contribution to a larger whole that in itself is constantly evolving, for every transformation of the extant can, and very likely will, become the subject of yet another transformation at a later point in time.

This continuous process of transformation must radically challenge the self-proclaimed identity of a discipline that loves to see itself, despite all evidence to the contrary, as an agent of eternity. To resolve this dialectical gridlock we may find inspiration in Michael Thompson's *Rubbish Theory,* a book significantly subtitled *The Creation and Destruction of Value*.[3] Social economy, Thompson argues, had come to divide the world of possessable objects into two categories, *transient* and *durable*, which perform very differently in terms of value. While the value of the transient sinks towards zero, that of the durable seems to rise infinitely. For Thompson there is yet a third category: *rubbish*. While it cannot be accounted for in traditional socioeconomic theory rubbish has a vital function for civilization as it allows transient objects to become durable ones. Once a transient object has lost its value, it is usually discarded and put into some sort of storage—ranging from the garage to a trash dump—without ceasing to exist. This life in storage allows the object to hibernate until it is rediscovered and considered valuable again. It's the principle of the yard sale: after years of looking you suddenly discover a most exquisite piece of furniture that for its owner is just a nuisance. And isn't the city, after all, nothing but a giant yard sale? We only have to scan it in search of its discarded assets, excavating them and putting them to good use in new ways and places. Maybe we don't have to worry so much about running out of resources after all. Maybe all we have to do is learn how to mine the city.

Ilka & Andreas Ruby

1.) Peter Baccini and Paul H. Brunner, *Metabolism of the Anthroposphere*. Berlin, New York: 1991.
2.) Stewart Brand, *How Buildings Learn: What Happens After They're Built*. New York: Viking Press 1994.
3.) Michael Thompson, *Rubbish Theory: The Creation and Destruction of Value*. Oxford: 1979.

About the authors: Trained as architects and architecture historians respectively, Ilka Ruby and Andreas Ruby are the founding partners of textbild, an office for architectural communication, which operates in the fields of publishing, curating, teaching, and consulting (www.textbild.com). Among their many publications are titles such as *Images: A Picture Book of Architecture* (Prestel, 2004); *Groundscapes* (Gustavo Gili, 2005); *Urban Transformation* (Ruby Press, 2008); *Of People and Houses* (HDA Publishers, 2009); and *EM2N: Both-And* (GTA Publishers, 2009). In 2008 they founded their own publishing house, Ruby Press (www.ruby-press.com).

Re: Going Around in Circles

Regimes of Waste

MARC ANGÉLIL AND CARY SIRESS

Waste is society's dirty secret.
Mira Engler[1]

The madness of it all: round and round in circles we go, where it stops, nobody knows. That we are trapped in a vicious circle should come as no surprise. Contemporary civilization is driven by the desire to attain ever-higher standards of living, and the consequences leave much to be desired. The more intractable the challenges, the more entrenched our resistance to confront them. We dream of an endless supply of goods, while neglecting the aftermath of consumption-generated waste. Prosperity seems to ripen the principle of decay. Recalling Goethe's ballad *The Sorcerer's Apprentice*, efforts to keep means in check often spiral out of control. A self-reinforcing dynamic is fueled by the open-ended drive for material wealth.[2] And so the circle continues.

While some believe that technology is *the* answer, others are more skeptical, arguing that reductive technical idealism will only exacerbate the mess and accelerate the proverbial end. So, where are we heading? The responses range from the ecstatically positive to the emphatically negative. Optimism is played against pessimism, as is utopia against dystopia.[3] But before the doomsayers are dismissed outright in favor of a more upbeat future vision, clues may be taken from the downside of this stalemate, where crisis rules in an apocalyptic setting.

Anyone familiar with *Mad Max*, the low-budget film trilogy set "just a few years from now," might gain insight from such an adverse prophecy, one in which the world has come full circle and descended into chaos.[4] What remains of the past are scraps of civilization, scattered across a wasteland stripped of resources and roamed by marauding gangs. One human outpost in particular is given the telling name Bartertown. Here, used goods are the only material resource available, and waste, whether animal excrement or technological debris, is the currency of trade in closed-loop material and energy flows. The bottom line is that everything is re-circulated for auction in the 'house of good deals,' a marketplace of second-hand commodities. In this desolate world, Bartertown boasts its role in "helping build a better tomorrow." Yet, this pledge is remote from those championed by similar calls, for the same, in our time. There is nothing pristine in this *Mad Max* environment. With excess but a distant memory, whatever is at hand is mined for other possible purposes, yielding to a haphazard, impromptu mode of tinkering for survival. Denizens of this makeshift settlement form a rudimentary community, loosely held together by tacit rule. It is not quite clear who runs this patchwork of top-down and bottom-up governance—with Aunty Entity's apparent authority from above curbed from below by the underworld power-duo Master Blaster.

Notwithstanding the pervading scenario of gloom, a series of key diagrams are enacted in this regime of waste. When the popular notion of abundance is removed from the equation, you get a self-sustaining, albeit crude, colony of mutually reliant players, whose coexistence is strictly dependent on the cooperative re-processing of a reduced palette of resources. While utopian visions tend to frame the world from the vantage of a new beginning, one that holds out the promise of a corrective and homogenizing ideal, they seldom account for the messy reality of things as depicted in *Mad Max* to an extreme. Whether utopia or dystopia, this reality will not conveniently go away in a flight of fancy, where what is here today is gone tomorrow. Looking back at the madness played out in the trilogy, it would seem that our future is not only "just a few years from now," but can no longer be what it used to be.[5]

1

2

3

1-3: Film stills from the *Mad Max* trilogy, featuring Mel Gibson as a 'road warrior' attempting to survive in a world devoid of law and order, directed by George Miller and released respectively in 1979, 1981, and 1985.

Re: Reduce, Reuse, Recycle

But let us backtrack for a moment. Are we not already players in modern-day Bartertowns, would-be recyclers in a deteriorating landscape that has become our own profane junkyard? Supporting evidence can be found everywhere. Take, for example, the weekly classified advertisements of large metropolitan regions, such as the Los Angeles edition of *Recycler*, a free-for-the-taking circular found in every gas station, car wash, or diner. As with so many other cut-rate gazettes, *Recycler* is poorly printed on cheap, second- or third-generation paper. *Recycler* was founded in 1973, on the heels of the first Earth Day as a local advertizing platform for used goods. *Recycler* has since grown into a network with thousands of distribution points throughout Southern California and has been updated with internet-based classified listings. Anything under the sun can be found in this smorgasbord of rejects, "cars, pets, jobs, real estate, it's all here." Imagine a garage sale extended to the scale of an urban territory with more than 20 million inhabitants, where commodities are kept in circulation by a last-gasp offer prior to being deemed useless and thrown away. The operation has been so successful that it has expanded to include castoffs from the construction industry, from copper, aluminum and plywood, to appliances, doors, windows, pools, fences, and gates. Perks include therapy for overweight pets, penis enlargement treatments, and girls of all sizes offering their services.

For this hodgepodge assortment, aside and despite all good intentions, the term *recycling* might not be quite appropriate for what is actually taking place. This economy of hand-me-down merchandise functions as a delay in the linear chain that links resource extraction, production, accumulation, and consumption to waste. As a means to providing a detour in this process *en route* to landfills, *Recycler* absorbs the overflow of goods at least provisionally, while clearing space for consumers to purchase more stuff. What's more, this proxy form of recycling further brokers the proliferation of capital, which in turn results in an escalation of junk.

Modern economics is founded on waste, produced at ever more frenzied rates. As is well known, the expenditure of resources is intrinsic to consumption. It can even be argued that waste constitutes the suppressed *other* of capitalism, a dirty secret kept hidden under the mantra 'out of sight, out of mind,' though subsidized by externalized social and environmental costs. The equation seems to hold that the more profitable the markets, the more garbage produced. Con-

4

5

4: Title pages and back cover of *Recycler,* June 11-17, 2009. Free weekly newspaper with classified ads circulated in the Los Angeles metropolitan region.

5: Sketch for the recycling symbol by Gary Anderson, selected as the winning entry in a design competition sponsored by the Container Corporation of America (CCA) in 1970.

sumption begets refuse, which in turn increases the stocks and flows of scrapped material. Based on what has been termed a linear metabolism, the input of resources within the system correlate with its output in the form of detritus. Sustained accumulations of trash, amplified by the built-in obsolescence of one-way commodities, are visibly leaving their mark on ecosystems. Unsurprisingly, there is a lot of clamor about keeping waste streams in check. Calls are made to shift from linear to circular processes in order to mitigate environmental pressure from trash run amok.[6]

Such pleas are evident in the ubiquitous symbol for recycling that, as fate would have it, is printed on so many discarded products. The logo was the winning entry in a competition sponsored in 1970 by the paperboard-packaging manufacturer Container Corporation of America, designed by Gary Anderson, a University of Southern California architecture student at the time. A rallying icon for green awareness, the design could not be more simple. Comprised of three chasing arrows, the diagram circumscribes a closed-loop system, where one segment feeds into the next interminably. Though usually presented as a flat, two-dimensional image, the figure recalls the seamless continuity of a Möbius strip unfolding in space. Referencing the impossible realities of M. C. Escher's 'Strange Loop' motifs, the diagram implies the phenomenon of continuous return, a veritable perpetual motion machine fueling its own cyclical revolutions. The message is clear: waste must be tapped for all its worth.

Clearly, efforts to promote the virtues of eco-friendly practices were at the forefront of the day, for minding the environment had become a moral imperative. Yet, this is not the full story of the recycling symbol. As options for getting rid of waste narrowed quickly due to increasingly stringent legislation, companies in the US were forced to go on the defensive. Rather than mining natural sources, as was commonplace, mining discarded material took on a new value. What can ostensibly be viewed simply as a benevolent turn by industry, was actually allied with a shrewd business tactic to adhere to policy pressures and growing environmentalist demands. Reprocessing was born of necessity rather than choice. To stretch natural resources, *recoverable* material became the newly honored *raw* material. Corporate endorsement of recycling killed two birds with one stone: while providing industry with a badge of environmental correctness, endless material supply could meet endless market demand, and all of this without reducing consumption. In time, the three little arrows—without ever being credited to their author—were printed on virtually everything.[7]

The tripartite symbol was aligned with the three R's—reuse, reduce, recycle—to become a clarion call for all, for they seemed to offer a panacea for the situation. Similarly, an array of initiatives, including William McDonough's 'cradle to cradle' and Paul Palmer's 'zero waste' approaches to material life-cycle management, have recently claimed to provide equally viable solutions.[8] Though commendable, such efforts are limited in their effectiveness as long as prevalent economic mechanisms remain intact, particularly those that factor out the impact on the environment and displace the cost to the public domain.

Notwithstanding the pretense of cleanliness associated with Anderson's logo, recycling is hardly a clean-cut affair. As demonstrated in the near-future world of *Mad Max*, Bartertown is dirty and far from ideal. Material and energy shortages coupled with power struggles dictate the very political economy of waste. And, our cities are no different. The messy reality of material stocks and flows and their relevance for urban production must be acknowledged. Though commonly perceived as being in stasis, material things are in a state of flux. Matter is not just stored in the environment but incessantly circulates through it, all the while being transformed. Cities are processing machines for enormous amounts of physical substances, with the building sector alone absorbing up to 50 percent of all material resources globally used, while generating a similar proportion of construction and demolition waste.[9] To make things more complicated, cities are formed by highly heterogeneous material composites made from a range of partially incompatible parts, all transforming at different rates of velocity in mutually dependent flows. Darling of green lobbies of all stripes, the perfect circle model is broken up into a profusion of interlocking loops that are enmeshed in further cycles. With current urban development primarily relying on linear input-output processes, more and more matter is being accrued in cities, constituting a vast reservoir that has yet to be fully quarried. A case in point: there is now more copper in urban environments than in nature, suggesting only one of many material reserves that need to be recovered.[10] Were such re-sourcing to happen, our own Bartertown would become a city that is itself a closed-circuit, where—as Lavoisier's first law concerning the conservation of mass stipulates—"nothing is lost, nothing is created, everything is transformed."[11] Framing urbanity in view of a sustainable handling of material resources requires a paradigm shift premised on circular urban metabolisms, a reorientation undoubtedly requiring changes in political and economic structures.

Cities are constituted by an accumulation of matter generally in step with the accumulation of capital. With the recent increase in the mobility of capital,

6

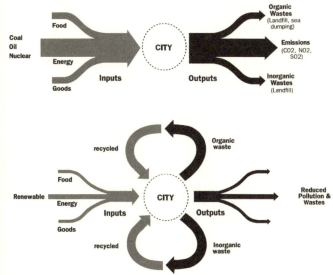

7

6: Birds scavenging mounds of refuse at the Fresh Kills Garbage Dump prior to its closure early 2001. The image appears on the cover of Heather Rogers' book *Gone Tomorrow. The Hidden Life of Garbage,* published in 2005.

7: Diagrams comparing linear and circular metabolisms in cities, from the 1995 Reith Lecture by Richard Rogers, *Cities for a Small Planet.*

material flows have accelerated and become more complex. Capitalism has always taken advantage of the simple fact that raw material can easily be converted into processed artifacts, which can be sold as consumable goods. The intertwined development of the economic system and the material requirements of society are the very stuff of 'historical materialism', a concept concerning the production and reproduction of material and social relations, introduced within political economy and its attendant discourses.[12] So, with the advent of the green revolution and the maxim of the three R's, a new chapter opens offering the opportunity to potentially rewrite economic practices as we know them. But, capitalism—in its current form—has proven adverse to both reduction and reuse, for they stand in contradiction to unbridled growth and forewarn of imminent scarcity. The remaining R, however, while at first met with resistance, has proven to be a blessing. As a socio-technological fix, recycling requires its own industry, therefore mandating more production and ensuring more consumption. By the same token, recycling has kept capitalism alive by satisfying its insatiable appetite and taking the guilt out of waste. Consuming means never having to say you're sorry.

Re: Regulate

Tracing another loop in the story, it is apparent that the knot of circles must be disciplined. The lesson from Bartertown shows the extent to which power-clashes pervade the scene and disparate interests collide, reflecting all too closely our own predicament. To enforce compliance with principles of sustainable development, an additional R, regulation, was introduced quite early on in the game, for it became alarmingly clear that waste requires regulation. If capital ran its course unrestrained, it would more than likely leave the public behind. The private sector had to be curtailed. A barrage of legislation aimed at reducing pollution and ensuring more diligent waste management was unleashed, including environmental policies, taxes, levies, and restrictions in an effort to control the entire life cycle of commodities, with similar austerity measures taken in the building industry. The bottom line was that cities would have to become cleaner.

As might be expected, a tug-of-war ensued between commerce and government, setting the tone on the playing field thereafter. While some companies complied, others looked for loopholes to evade restrictions, outwitting the system where possible. Still others sought refuge in offshore havens, where laws were either lax or non-existent. Meanwhile at home, waste evolved into a lucrative enterprise in its own right. The possibility to make money from the end-cycle of consumption turned attention away from the purely environmental to the financially alluring prospects of new markets. Recognizing in the interim that garbage means business, the political and legislative response has been to reconsider draconian policies and make it easier for companies to benefit from refuse. What one encounters here is a constant give and take in the hard-edged gamble of drawing the line, being side-lined and then brought back into play, all the while negotiating where the next line will be drawn, with bartering the name of the game.

Insofar as waste is a repressed matter, it has from time immemorial lurked in the nether world of social life. And, with waste made invisible, covert regimes below the radar have enjoyed free reign ever since. While the formal sector is engrossed in administering the logistics of refuse, other players silently operate in the margins. It is here that clandestine industries flourish. Manhole covers, copper pipes, and aluminum panels, for instance, are stolen and sold on the black market for considerable profit, thus revealing the hidden worth of the city as a veritable gold mine. Off the books and under the table, the informal sector can easily sink its talons into anything associated with value, including garbage. The recent trash crisis in Naples, yet another Bartertown of our time, is a poignant example of the skirmishes between municipal authorities and local syndicates that operate beyond legal jurisdiction. Mountains of uncollected rubbish lined the streets in Naples, producing a sickening stench that was "a cross between rotten eggs, burned skin and dead animals."[13] The results were appalling: the air was poisoned, Italy embarrassed, and, as feared, the local Mafia empowered.

Organized crime in this region, as in other parts of the world, has a strong foothold in both the construction and waste industries. Strangely enough, it is these sectors of the economy in particular that bring various strains of the underworld into a volatile alliance where different clans compete for a share of the business. Building, excavation, and demolition not only produce a tremendous amount of waste, but also spawn illicit channels for handling it. But here again, legitimate business and its illegitimate twin are mutually dependent. As is common practice, companies throughout Italy contract the Mafia to do the dirty work of disposal, including illegal dumping, waste exports, the remixing of toxic substances with other material, as well as the falsification of customs documents and merchandise certificates. Such services comprise what Roberto Saviano refers to as the business of phantom refuse.[14] Outsourcing of this breed relies on an unexpected reversal of economic principles, where money changes hands not to acquire things, but rather to get rid of things. But it doesn't end here. As common sense would have it, one fundamental rule of business is to diversify. Ergo, covert operations of Neapolitan families have turned to other dubious sources of revenue such as counterfeit fashion, money laundering, drug dealing, weapons smuggling, and prostitution. Ventures of this sort demanded a larger arena, thus turning what had begun as a local business into a global enterprise, with partners of like kind in countries as diverse as Spain, Great Britain, Bulgaria, China, Russia, and Nigeria to mention just a few. Such growth has given crime syndicates amazing lethal power to paralyze entire cities and muscle them into submission, with Naples being the most recent home turf casualty.

The trail of garbage leads next to New York, Gotham City cum Bartertown. As funny as it may seem, we know the Mafia primarily from popular movies, *The Godfather, Scarface, GoodFellas*, and so on, with television following suit in the hit drama series *The Sopranos*. Here, the main protagonist is officially involved in waste management, a vocational cover for his underworld activities as Capo of a New Jersey gangster family. The irony of the script is that waste, socially repressed as a rule, serves as the foil of choice for the protagonist's own suppressed psychological woes, which—in keeping with good Freudian practice—require therapy. His analyst is surely "accustomed to concealed things from despised or unnoticed features, from the rubbish-heap of our observations."[15]

Taking clues from real life, the plot of *The Sopranos* mirrors actual events taking place in New York in the early 1990s, when mob-controlled garbage cartels were brought to justice. The story unfolds from the mid-20th century onward. Organized crime had moved into the consumer age, with waste becoming the best thing since Prohibition. Their power stemmed from a simple precept: "Control the flow of garbage, and just as surely as if you owned the supply of fresh water or electricity, you had an entire sprawling metropolis by the jugular."[16] This fit neatly with an organization already commanding the construction industry in many parts of the country. The waste monopoly in New York was anchored territorially by an illegal geographic area rights system, granting Mob-controlled trash collectors ownership of specific customers and locations. Anyone doing business in the city had to pay what amounts to a modern-day feudal tax to have trash removed. When volumes of pure refuse diminished due to environmental laws, the Mob expanded their enterprise to capitalize on the collection of recyclables. Fortunes were made, albeit in dirty money. All this ended rather abruptly when the cartel

8

9

10

8: Article entitled "Italians raising a stink over trash" reporting on the community outcry over the mounds of waste accumulating in the streets of Pianura, a town near Naples.
Los Angeles Times, January 8, 2008.
9: Still from the premier TV-episode of the *Sopranos* showing Tony Soprano offering flight tickets for a forced vacation to a syndicate member, HBO, January 10, 1999.
10: Greenpeace activists painting "l'Europe intoxique l'Afrique" on the hull of the cargo vessel Probo Koala, involved with the illegal toxic waste dumping incident in the Ivory Coast region of Africa on August 19, 2008.

was taken down by government agencies seeking order and to formalize the previously informal waste management practices. As a consequence, waste streams needed to be redirected and new organizational structures devised. The business was handed over to the private sector and garbage disposal was effectively made a corporate enterprise.[17]

In the space opened up by the crackdown, companies moved in to clean up after organized crime, ultimately rivaling the prices of the previous cartel extortion. Two early players that spearheaded the consolidation of the garbage trade in the US were Waste Management Inc. and Browning-Ferris Industries. They began by swallowing up small local firms all over the country to form regional and then national monopolies, before spreading into international markets. They successfully seized control of waste, setting an example thereafter for multinational conglomerates to emulate. Not only was the big business of mega-trash born, but also—as in so many other sectors of the economy—corporations overtook public works functions of municipalities, making the entire affair a private matter. As such operations expanded, waste traffic crossed borders to circulate as yet another global currency and followed the path of least resistance. Waste wound up where labor is cheap, environmental legislation weak, and ethics not an issue. The irony is that while the bulk of consumer goods are increasingly produced in the developing world, the majority of consumption-generated detritus is now also deposited there.[18] Affluent nations turn out to be nothing more than a middle-world, an intermediate circuit in material flows constantly crisscrossing the planet.

And, it is these flows that are rewriting the political economy of waste. Whereas the surge in new business opportunities might stimulate ailing economies in poorer parts of the world, these same ventures can take advantage of not only being out of sight, but also out of mind. As the line dividing the legal from the illegal in this industry is so thin that it is negligible, garbage offers a good foil to hide behind. To operate in the dirty business of rejectamenta, whether domestic or elsewhere, is to enter the troubled waters of less-than-legal grey zones. An extreme case is the import and export of toxic substances. Nations predominantly in the Southern hemisphere serve as the world's dumping ground. What amounts to widespread environmental discrimination stands in direct defiance of the Basel Convention, which was ratified to regulate "trans-boundary movement of hazardous waste" particularly from developed to less developed countries.[19] Insofar as the not-in-my-backyard mentality prevails in more prosperous regions, illegal dumping continues. It encounters little opposition from those who stand to gain at either end, those too disadvantaged to mount resistance, and those all too eager to wash their hands of dirty deeds.

Re: Reframe

Rumors have it that a fourth installment of *Mad Max* is currently being discussed. That future yet again "just a few years from now", is in pre-production. With the script still open, we might consider possible scenarios. At the end of the trilogy, surviving nomads set off from their deprived world to seek a better life, with utopia once again promising to prevail over dystopia. But, as the proposed title for the final sequel, *Fury Road*, suggests, the journey to paradise will be turbulent. In our time, sustainable development holds out a similar promise of delivery from dire circumstances, for its premises and objectives are perhaps the best last options at our disposal. However, calls for sustainability have been cloaked in a moral robe fashioned on austerity, scarcity, and restraint. We are warned that a period of deprivation is imminent and encouraged to accept sacrifice and renunciation as ideals, over and above indulgence and excess. A value system centered on constraint is put forth as the road map for the way forward. Slowing down is the hymn of the day.

It is exactly such a mindset that needs reframing, without losing sight of what is at stake in this vision. While calls for a sustainable future acknowledge to the central role of capitalism in getting us there, stopping has never been a part of its enterprise. As a matter fact, no one can turn off the growth machine of capital. Thus, a possible take could be to capitalize on this internal momentum, taking advantage of the collective drive for prosperity, but to the n-th degree. This means discarding the moral robe of guilt in favor of redirected forms of expenditure. As Georges Bataille argues, the resolution of the problem cannot be formulated relative to scarcity and the shortage of resources *per se*, but rather in terms of how to deal with the abundance of energy and matter that we are wasting, if only by not using them.[20] He points out acutely that every living organism receives more energy than is necessary for sustaining life. Supplied primarily by the sun, this excess energy, which he equates with wealth, can either be absorbed for growth or expended. Basically, we are in the midst of a vast surplus of renewable energy sources that for the most part remain untapped. This argument holds for matter as an equally renewable resource, and specifically for waste. Bataille, as a matter of fact, was somehow "in favor of waste," which he reframed by jettisoning its pejorative stigma and recasting it instead as a 'gift'.[21] Lest this seem anti-ecologically minded, it is actually a call for understanding refuse in all its heterogeneity as wealth to be mined, as a material endowment to be recycled, reprocessed, and re-circulated. Framed as an economic principle, waste is expenditure with return. It must be granted new functions rather than being simply relegated to formless and useless matter. Bataille's deconstruction of a restrictive economy — preoccupied with deficiency and the fulfillment of momentary needs — opens up to a general economy predicated on how the wealth of resources available can be squandered. Re, re, re is the refrain for the future, a ritornello, so to speak, premised on recurring movements played in the different keys of energy and matter in continuous variation.[22]

Such a refrain unfortunately failed to inspire one of Italo Calvino's invisible cities. As we are told, "the city of Leonia refashions itself everyday." Here, the new is exalted in a hyper-linear metabolism where everything is used only once and then discarded. Heaps of refuse surround the city on all sides like a chain of man-made mountains. Commodities and waste are ratcheted closely together in an ever-accelerating one-way sequence of use and disposal. "This is the result: the more Leonia expels goods, the more it accumulates them; the scales of its pasts are soldered into a cuirass that cannot be removed."[23] This doomsday aftermath is well known, for as it is in the tale, so it is in our story: cities become buried by the rubbish they try in vain to reject. Although classified under the heading of "Continuous Cities," Calvino's fable falls short of portraying a closed-loop system running *ad infinitum*. He does, however, hint that the true passion of Leonians is not really the accumulation of new things, but is actually driven by the pleasure of getting rid of them. "Street cleaners are welcomed like angels, and their task of removing the residue of yesterday's existence is surrounded by a respectful silence, like a ritual that inspires devotion."[24] Waste and its meticulous handling are valued as gifts, offered by society to itself. Were we to turn the parable's missed opportunity to our advantage, a modified economy would be set into motion. Perhaps then we would come full circle in being sustained by the constant transformation of matter and energy at hand, without beginning and without end.

The authors would like to express their gratitude to Tanja Herdt, Denise Bratton, Sheldon Nodelman, and John Brockway for their valuable comments and constructive criticism during the preparation of this essay.

RE: GOING AROUND IN CIRCLES

1.) Mira Engler, *Designing America's Waste Landscapes* (Baltimore: The Johns Hopkins University Press 2004), p. 14.
2.) John E. Fernàndez, "Beyond Zero," published in *Volume: After Zero*, Vol. 18 (New York: Archis, AMO, and C-LAB 2009), p. 8.
3.) See Kevin Lynch's juxtaposition between 'Waste Cacotopia' and 'Wasteless Cacotopia' as two extreme models of worst case scenarios, in Kevin Lynch, *Wasting Away. An Exploration of Waste: What it is, How it Happens, Why we Fear it, How to do it Well* (San Francisco: Sierra Club Books 1990), pp. 3-10.
4.) *Mad Max*, directed by George Miller and featuring the then little-known actor Mel Gibson, was released in 1979. The film's sequels, *The Road Warrior* and *Mad Max Beyond Thunderdome*, appeared in 1981 and 1985 respectively. The first installment of the trilogy opens with the narrator framing the plot in a not too distant future.
5.) Author's modification playing on Paul Valéry's aphorism "The future is not what it used to be." The original in French is "L'avenir n'est plus ce qu'il était." *Oeuvres* (Paris: Gallimard 1957).
6.) See Peter Baccini and Paul Brunner, *Metabolism of the Anthroposphere* (Berlin: Springer Verlag 1991). Herbert Girardet, *The Gaia Atlas of Cities. New directions for sustainable urban living* (London: Gaia Books Limited 1992 and 1996). Richard Rogers, *Cities for a Small Planet*, 1995 Reith Lectures, edited by Philip Gumuchdjian (London: Faber and Faber 1997).
7.) See Heather Rogers, *Gone Tomorrow. The Hidden Life of Garbage* (New York: The New Press 2005), pp. 168-173.
8.) William McDonough and Michael Braungart, *Cradle to Cradle: Remaking the Way We Make Things* (New York: Durabook 2002) and Paul Palmer, *Getting To Zero Waste* (Sebastopol, CA: Purple Sky Press 2004).
9.) John Storey, "An International Overview of Construction Materials Stewardship," in *Construction Materials Stewardship* (Wellington, New Zealand: Center for Building Performance Research, Victoria University of Wellington 2008), p. 8.
10.) Peter Baccini, "Cultural Evolution and the Concept of Sustainable Development: From Global to Local Scale and Back," keynote address delivered at the International Geographical Union (IGU) in Lucerne, Switzerland 2007.
11.) See Antoine Lavoisier, *Traité élémentaire de chimie* (Paris: Cuchet 1793), Vol. 1
12.) Karl Marx used the expression "materialist conception of history" in the preface to *A Contribution to the Critique of Political Economy*, first published in 1859.
13.) Tracy Wilkinson, "Italians raise a stink over trash," Los Angeles Times, January 8, 2008, p. A5.
14.) Roberto Saviano, *Gomorrah. A Personal Journey into the Violent International Empire of Naples' Organized Crime System* (New York: Picador 2007), p. 286.
15.) Sigmund Freud, *The Moses of Michelangelo* (1914), in *The Standard Edition of the Complete Psychological Works of Sigmund Freud*, edited and translated from the German by James Strachey, et. al. (London: The Hogarth Press 1953-1974), Vol. 13, p. 222.

16.) Rick Cowan and Douglas Century, *Takedown. The Fall of the Last Mafia Empire* (New York: Berkley Books 2002), p. 14.
17.) Op. cit., Heather Rogers, pp. 183-186.
18.) Ibid., Heather Rogers, pp. 184-188.
19.) The "Basel Convention on the Control of Transboundary Movements and their Disposal" is an international treaty signed by 172 parties on March 22, 1989 in Basel, Switzerland and effective as of May 5, 1992.
20.) See Georges Bataille *La part maudite* (1967), translated into English by Robert Hurley as *The Accursed Share. An Essay on General Economy* (New York: Urzone, Inc. 1988), "The Meaning of General Economy" and "Laws of General Economy," pp. 19-41.
21.) See Allan Stoekl, *Bataille's Peak* (Minneapolis: University of Minnesota Press 2007), Chapter 5, "Orgiastic Recycling," pp. 115-149.
22.) Gilles Deleuze and Félix Guattari, *Mille Plateaux* (1980), translated into English by Brian Massumi as *A Thousand Plateaus. Capitalism and Schizophrenia* (Minneapolis: University of Minnesota Press 1987), Chapter 11, "1837: Of the Refrain," pp. 310-350.
23.) Italo Calvino, *Le città invisibili* (1972), translated into English by William Weaver as *Invisible Cities* (San Diego: Harcourt Brace Jovanovich, Publishers 1974), p. 115.
24.) Ibid., p. 114.

About the authors: Marc Angélil is Professor and Dean at the Department of Architecture of the ETH Zurich. His research at the Institute of Urban Design of the Network City and Landscape (NSL) addresses developments of large metropolitan regions. He is the author of several books, including *Deviations* on methods of teaching and *Indizien* on the political economy of contemporary urban territories. Marc Angélil has been a member of the Management Board and of the Technical Competence Center (TCC) of the Holcim Foundation since their inception 2004.

Cary Siress is an architect and a tenured faculty member in Architecture and Theory at the School of Arts, Culture, and Environment of The University of Edinburgh and Visiting Professor at the School of Architecture at the University of Nanjing in China. He is the founding editor of the new journal *Architecture &*. Following graduate studies at Columbia University in New York, he was involved in teaching and research at the ETH Zurich, where he completed his PhD.

Architecture to Take Away

The Subtraction of Buildings as a New Construction Economy

KELLER EASTERLING

Much of the discussion about environmentally conscious construction deals with only one half of the building game—building. But why don't we also examine the other half of the game—subtraction? The subtraction of buildings is a field of play rife with potential gain, from the recycling of demolished structures, to newly empty building lots rendered redundant by densification. Just consider the artistic pleasures associated with building destruction. Historically, the construction industry has been the impetus for capital expansion, stock markets, infrastructure and labor migrations as well as a proxy of the state infrastructure building, war and reconstruction. It is an infrastructure that makes infrastructure—a self-sustaining building machine that joins forces with many different kinds of economic multipliers in the form of contagious details, financial instruments or populations of spatial products, for example. Throwing this machine in reverse, building subtraction, as a heavy industry and a design protocol, is an emergent and aggressive enterprise, within which negative development is a lucrative means of mining the city.

Subtraction

Unlike agriculture, where planting and harvesting come in quick succession, construction and subtraction are rarely regarded as cyclical, even within cyclical building markets. Construction is typically treated as the establishment of a permanent fixture; the subtraction of which may even be seen as a tragic or wasteful loss of value, property or monument. Building subtraction, treated as the unskilled labor of demolition, is associated with waste that must be quickly carted off and furtively dumped somewhere in the margins. It should give way to the real objective of this heavy industry—a newer and fitter design. Meanwhile, financing and marketing industries make of this seemingly static and durable envelope a volatile balloon of inflating and deflating value, be it a small house, a massive sports stadium or a 4000-room casino. Yet in the recent implosion of building assets, as well as their association with toxic waste and negative value, is the germ of an emergent economy.

In a subtraction economy, physical building envelopes approach the flexibility of their attendant financial envelopes such that negative development is profitable. In this context, "mining the city" is much more than a poetic or hopeful suggestion. It is an apt term to describe an extraction process comparable to those of the late 19th and early 20th century, in which heavy industry went in search of things perceived to have lasting and even accrued value through use and reuse (e.g. precious metals or diamonds). The subtraction industry similarly manipulates heavy tangibles of material reuse and urban form, as well as the ephemeral intangibles of financial structures.

Political Disposition

The subtraction economy, in many ways, already exists. The creative trick lies not in naming it, but rather in designing a political disposition for this almost obvious idea—the spin or 'English' that gives the idea some play and traction. Buildings have long been mined or harvested for their materials, and development schemes have long made a casino of physical space. It is nearly visible with the naked eye in familiar developments, from dense skyscraper cities to suburban developments to proliferating palm islands in Dubai. Buildings are harvested every day and replaced with newer formulas for profit. In the art of inverting central and marginal positions, economies of scale must be powerful enough to interrupt free market doom loops or other political stalemates that resist intelligence. (For this, the US context provides an enticing puzzle.) The subtraction industry might be compared to the nascent containerized shipping industry, wherein several watershed events accelerated growth in the industry. While a confusing proliferation of locking mechanisms initially stalled growth, the ISO standardization of the container and locking mechanism, together with the discovery of new economies in double stacking containers on train cars, catalyzed the shipping and materials handing industry. The industry then rapidly developed tools to obsessively micromanage every possible parameter to optimize profit. Similarly, there are a number of emergent episodes that begin to galvanize subtraction economies.

For instance, as has already been noted, the invisible force field of financial markets is already deleting building as evidenced by dead malls, empty big boxes stories and abandoned suburbs. While the wealthiest markets have well-rehearsed techniques for deleting the constructions of the disenfranchised to make way for more building, here the tables are turned. It is an interesting moment to consider a stabilizing spatio-financial protocol that might in turn be applied to situations where poverty rather than financial markets are the reason for deletions. Yet, even before the financial crisis, from the blunt instrument of slum clearance to selective demolition and replatting, cities have long manipulated violent ecologies of subtraction to change urban land values. In Detroit, the Bronx and Philadelphia, or Youngstown, Ohio, shockwaves of value attrition, and disenfranchisement have passed through the city and reduced it to rubble without need of bulldozing municipal programs. Other force fields of subtraction, like, for instance, a highway network or power utility clear not only the land they physically occupy but also a quotient of territory that radiates from them.

In other episodes that manifest a subtraction economy, the business of demolition has itself become a site of technical innovations. Implosion techniques have become popular for building types, like casinos or stadiums, which are frequently destroyed and rebuilt in response to seemingly ephemeral parameters related to new program wrinkles or desires. They accelerate the time-lapse of building and rebuilding to reveal that, while buildings are frequently associated with permanence, they are attached to unstable, changeable marketing formulas. Countering expectations, implosion works well on buildings that are relatively young and structurally coherent. Moreover, the implosions themselves have been sources of spectacular entertainment, like the familiar New Year's Eve implosions in Las

Vegas. The Japanese construction giant, Kajima, is developing not only new construction heroics but also new technologies for building deconstruction. Given the value of land in urban Japan, there is a premium on a surgical style of subtraction. There is a method of demolition that lowers successive floors in a multi-story building on jacks, so that all demolition work can be performed on the ground floor with greater safety, economy, and a 99.4 percent rate of recycling.

Moreover, most of the tonnage of construction materials in the world goes to making roads, and most successful reuse scenarios also involve roads. Consequently, road construction and removal also attract equipment innovations and economies of scale that make material mining a successful enterprise. The trade journals like Construction and Demolition Recycling Magazine are filled with "advertorials" for material mining equipment that uses magnets, screens, blasts of air or bouncing and waving conveyors to separate and sort materials. Some of the vehicles are essentially mobile recycling plants, not unlike a harvester or combine, that tune subtraction economies by eliminating transportation costs. A vehicle like the "Eco-Crusher," or the "Quarry Trax," can demolish a roadway and distribute the crushed material all along its length, ready for use later as soil stabilizer.

Germany's material mining industry is an existing model, one crucial component of the subtraction economy. Regulated since 1972, this now mature industry recycles over 85 percent of construction materials. Architects and engineers train to address an obligatory *Kreislaufwirtschaft*, or the life-cycle infrastructure of material streams. Germany has developed material classifications, and assisted in crafting ISO's quality assurance standards for construction and demolition waste. The German automobile industry tracks and barcodes its material streams. *Kreislaufwirtschaft* principles are also working to elevate reuse values for concrete and brick rubble.

A number of new development protocols have also demonstrated the profitability of subtraction. For instance, marshalling the abstract financial and environmental valences of physical territory, the REDD (Reduced Emissions from Deforestation and Degradation) program or the Yasuni protocol in the Amazon, demonstrate the potential profitability of negative development. REDD trades intact forest for emissions credits. The Yasuni protocol trades in certificates that pay to keep oil in the ground beneath an especially rich and sensitive forest preserve. Both programs yield a net value to undeveloped land.

Any number of amplifications or combinations of these practices already provides the underpinnings of a profitable subtraction economy—one that allows the building, as the physical outcropping of the real estate market, to approach the flexibility and volatility of the throbbing financial envelope that surrounds it. To give velocity to this economy and spread further rumors about its existence, two pilot projects are presented here as smart phone apps: STREAM, a marketplace for material recovery and TAKEAWAY, a new playbook for gaming space.

STREAM: A Materials Marketplace

While in some parts of the world waste is managed in intelligent material streams, in many places, like the US, efforts to manage the material of a subtraction economy are more frequently associated with pious volunteerism and the quixotic virtues of saving or recycling, as attended by glacial processes of reform and regulation. Artistically, these efforts are largely marginal or tedious. An industry to extract or harvest construction materials juggles a complex cocktail of parameters including regulatory incentives, equipment, volume, reuse scenarios and transportation costs. A material alchemy of these factors can psychologically and economically alter the value of material. One emergent phenomenon within material management systems is special software that crunches numbers between these variables to discover opportune relationships within a market.

For instance, in the UK, WRAP (Waste and Resources Action Program), is a non-profit group that works with the construction and demolition industry to develop markets for recycled products. They have developed and provide a powerful online tool for calculating profitable recycling. Similarly, in the US, the Environmental Protection Agency (EPA) has sponsored "decision support tools" to help waste managers test scenarios and determine new environmental economies. These tools are aimed at the broad spectrum of solid waste, and there is not currently a specific tool for construction and demolition waste. Amidst anecdotal state regulations, the EPA establishes no national waste regulation but rather offers encouragements or "challenges" to business to recycle a relatively low 35 percent of materials. The three largest waste managers in the US have multi-billion dollar businesses and already have their own techniques for calculating waste generated revenue. The emerging trade industry, comprised of groups like the National Demolition Association (NDA) or the Construction Material Recycling Association (CMRA), struggles to create salience and volume.

Rather than waiting on the possible successes of a web-based calculator or the glacial reforms typical of recycling regulation, a web-based marketplace like STREAM has ramifying and potentially more powerful consequences in the US scene. Assuming that some of the best ideas often inflect and reposition extant situations, a materials market place is not dissimilar to any of the other online markets like Amazon, Ebay, or Yoink that have entirely changed the audience and venue for trading new and used goods. During the current financial crisis, many of the components of homes and workplaces have been traded in these markets. Portable fixtures, appliances, equipment, interior finishes, remaindered tools and materials—from floor boards to roof shingles, and even portable recycling plants like the Eco-Crusher itself—have been sold on Ebay. A materials market could extend to not only small lots of used surplus material but also to tonnage or volume of material removed in a building subtraction.

If the greatest obstacle to productive volumes in the construction and demolition material stream is the sense that speedy disposal is the only option, a web-based market place on a GPS-enabled smart phone, would allow quick reference to an alternative harvest. A used bookseller on Amazon determines price by referencing a database of ISBN values, calculating shipping costs in relation to the weight of the book, and making a bid in relation to those of other sellers. Similarly, a very simple building material calculator/converter that could reference selected market values (e.g. dollars/tons of copper, local transportation costs/ton) would be the equivalent of a quick ISBN reference. The user would list tonnage and location, but as with the online marketplace in general, the prices and bids themselves provide the live feed or the market database of values. Just as the seller's and buyer's reputation grows on Amazon or Ebay, so the material supplier will earn a reputation for the condition and presorting of the expended material. While large amounts of waste might continue to be handled by large facilities, such a market would encourage entrepreneurialism among the small and midsize operators. Operators would be able to increase their own volume and inventory by harvesting the materials from numerous construction projects. The seller, who used to pay a disposal fee for material previously known as waste, can either sell the material or trade its determined value for removal. Already the largest disposal companies have replaced metal containers with more flexible 3-yard nylon bags that can be purchased at home improvement stores.

With a sly and resourceful political disposition, material mining in this marketplace quickly becomes a game, within which compounding volumes and opportunities gain a momentum that inoculates against bureaucratic delays and powerful lobbies. Allied industries related to the various recovered materials such as concrete, gypsum, wood, steel, asphalt, aluminum and copper can build their industries around viable volumes and myriad reuse scenarios. The more valuable metals have long had a market, as the 'gold teeth' of building. Concrete production is a matrix that has come to accept many different kinds of recycled material from glass to asphalt shingles. Reused wood is now part of a biofuel market that must outwit the coal lobby. In the US, the gypsum reuse industry needs substantial renovation to be able to cycle the material from sheetrock back to sheetrock. Like the transshipment industry, the material mining industry will likely sponsor unforeseen territories of obsessive managing and chiseling, within which buildings, composed of a bar-coded index of materials, become 'inventory'.

Again, the US is an excellent training ground, a place to plead for the briar patch and to rehearse a political ruse that may even come cloaked in the costumes of opposition politics. Material mining can invoke the patriotism of a WWII population that saved cooking oil for munitions production. It is also capable of appropriating the label of those extraction industries that typically oppose environmental sentiments. While there is a great deal of automation in the material management industry, employment opportunities range from simple unskilled jobs, to environmental scientists, to entrepreneurs of all kinds.

A live marketplace begins to overcome obstacles to profitability in the subtraction industry. Yet, surpassing the goals of material recovery alone, subtraction entrepreneurs need further techniques for extracting profitability from negative development.

TAKEAWAY: A Playbook for Gaming Space

While there are elaborate schemes for manipulating the virtual values of buildings within the thickening layers of finance, there are fewer spatio-financial formulas for distributing risk and rewards in physical formations. The owner of a stadium, casino, office building, or home, hardly has any incentive to dismantle it for the value of material alone. The value of the intact building and lot is, under the current paradigm, frequently worth more than the lot and the building split into its component materials. The demolition of casinos or stadiums is frequent and routine because the physical envelope approaches the flexibility of market and financial instruments and because there is something more lucrative to replace it. The classic formula for profitability involves replacement with a larger or denser building, through which the developer not only recoups the building material, but also mines the space of the city for all of the profits that can be extracted from it. The elementary assumption is that densification adds value, except in locations where lack of demand creates diminishing returns.

By spatializing risk and property interdependence, a formula for subtraction would need to make building deletion profitable, even in (perhaps especially in) remote areas. Protocols or active forms designed to give physical form the flexibility of financial formulas would facilitate this negative development while, ironically, stabilizing a market. For example, the deceptively simple formula for an 18th century settlement like Oglethorphe's Savannah created dependencies between components—active forms with time-released powers designed to curb rampant speculation. The individual lot was not an independent absolute value but was often abstractly linked to other values and physical spaces in other portions of the settlement. Parcels were placed in formations composed of interdependent ratios. A ward was made up of ratios of public and private lots, abstractly linked to their central square. While this is similar to any allotment garden or common used throughout history, the lots and central space were also collectively linked to remote reserves of land outside of the town of Savannah.

Consider the Savannah formula in reverse. In the suburban landscape of US McMansions, further densification of building, at some point, results in diminishing returns. A building lot tied to derivatives on the global market through a mortgage or similar financial instrument and also to another piece of land becomes part of a complex game of lot futures and lot hedge spaces. Beginning simply with the standard gamble on densification, the value of two lots and two houses or commercial buildings on one piece of land is usually more than one lot and one house or commercial building on that same piece of land. In some cases, the value of two lots and the material remains of one building may be worth more than one lot and one building. Densification increases the municipal tax revenues, and municipalities may use these revenues to purchase remote lots that are ripe to be emptied, repurposed and revalued.

Suburbia needs open space for a number of enterprises just as New World settlements needed agricultural space. As a reserve of value, the remote lots help overcome the normal obstacles to land acquisition. They ease the city's start-up costs for innovations like solar, wind or rail than can be located on peripheral or even polluted sites. The municipality's willingness to buy the remote lots relieves the owners of failed or exhausted sites where, for instance, environmental remediation is needed or the amount owed on the property exceeds its value. The owners of the densified lots that produce the increased tax revenues become automatic shareholders in the new enterprises located on the remote sites. They have an offset or a hedge against further real estate perils since they own not only interests in their own lot but also in a diversified portfolio of lots with complementary but different programs. For banks, the protocol generates business and stabilizes loans previously in default.

Not only in the overbuilt suburbs of the affluent but also in areas that are the target of slum clearance, a subtraction economy, offers developers and landowners somewhat less violent tools of acquisition, and more distributed entrepreneurial ecology with safeguards against disenfranchisement. The protocol might be used in any location where development would be wise to retreat from exhausted land, flood plains, special land preserves or vast pastures of sprawl. The game of densification, although related to existing values, rewrites the shape of the city with new nodes of concentrated activity linked to networks of interdependent sites.

Like a reverse game of GO where clearing is valued over obstruction, a subtraction playbook is a means to game space and stabilize development investment by deleting development. When banks create profit structures that do not originate as spatial formulas, they are likely to have haphazard rather than directed spatial consequences. If cities and entrepreneurs create the active forms of profitability for banks, not the other way around, they create remote lot futures and hedge spaces, not futures trading and hedge fund opportunities. Densified sites attached to remote sites offer one elementary formula for negative development. Yet the emergent player in the game of subtraction, perhaps some combination of a flipper and a quant, would no doubt devise an ever more elaborate playbook, a show on the House and Garden TV network and a DIY contingent whose home improvement projects include demolishing the house. And while any of these might become dangerous, they would be harder to hide.

Whether in the bloated and failed real estate development of the US, in the environmentally sensitive areas of the Amazon, in fault lines or flood plains, urbanism needs lucrative techniques for throwing the development engine in reverse and transforming subtraction into a form of growth.

Selected papers:

Corrie Clark, Jenna Jambeck, Timothy Townsend, "A Review of Construction and Demolition Debris Regulations in the United States," *Critical Reviews in Environmental Science and Technology* 36, 2006, pp. 141-186.
Construction and Demolition Waste Management in Germany, COWAM Study by ZEBAU GmbH in partnership with TuTech Innovation, 2006, pp. 3, 5, 14, 17-18, 56-57.
EPA Fact Sheet, "Cutting Edge Software Tools to Cut Emissions," EPA 530-F-02-024, July 2002.
Susan A. Thorneloe, Keith Weitz and Jenna Jambeck, "Application of the US decision support tool for materials and waste management" *Waste Management* 27, 2007, pp. 1006-1020.
Waste Reduction Initiatives: Striving for Zero Reductions. Available from: http://www.kajima.co.jp/csr/report/2008/pdf_e/csr-e-38.pdf [Accessed January 31, 2010].

Selected industry websites:

Construction and Demolition Recycling, July/August, 2008, pp. 36-42, 54. Available from: http://cdrecycler.texterity.com/cdrecycler/20080708/ [Accessed January 31, 2010].
http://www.wastecycle.co.uk/wastecalculator.html [Accessed January 31, 2010].
http://www.epa.gov/epawaste/conserve/rrr/rmd/econres.htm [Accessed January 31, 2010].
http://www.demolitionassociation.com/PUBLICRELATIONS/GovernmentRepresentation/tabid/109/Default.aspx [Accessed January 31, 2010].

Interviews:

Telephone interview, Carl Rush, Vice President Organic Growth Management, Waste Management, Houston, Texas, January 22, 2010.

About the author: Keller Easterling is an architect, writer and Professor at Yale's School of Architecture. She is the author of *Enduring Innocence: Global Architecture and its Political Masquerades* (MIT, 2005) and *Organization Space: Landscapes, Highways and Houses in America* (MIT, 1999). A forthcoming book, *Extrastatecraft*, examines global infrastructure networks as a medium of polity.

Big Apple, Homegrown

Feeding New York in New York

MICHAEL SORKIN

Feeding New York in New York is an investigation into the possibility for New York City to provide all of its food supply within the boundaries of the five boroughs. At first blush, this seems improbable. How can nutrition be supplied to eight million people on a site which is substantially built and in which virtually all open space is already devoted to other uses? And, how can this be done in a responsible, sustainable fashion that respects the earth, addresses the toxic cruelties of the factory farm system, and provides both sound nutrition and ample choice to eaters?

Big changes in our thinking and habits will be required. Current standards and practices are problematic on several counts. The industrialized, fast-food regime is dangerous in both production and consumption. The questionably organic basis of the system—with its heavy dependence on mono-cultural industrialized agriculture, fertilizer inputs, pesticides, fossil fuels, standardization, corn and soy hegemony, drastic packaging, long-distance transport, labor exploitation, and other much-criticized elements—must be revised. The logic of "organic" agriculture is that its farms be small, diverse, and near. However, bringing food production home to New York will demand solutions other than the return of the small, well-managed, organically-driven, family farm. This is not to say that much farming cannot remain both organic and small-scale, conducted in back-yards, balconies, stairways, and elsewhere. New methods, however, will be essential as will great diversity.

We are habituated to a cornucopia of "fresh" foods in all seasons—kiwis from New Zealand, asparagus from Argentina, strawberries from Mexico, tomatoes from the Netherlands—all of which are incredibly energy intensive, and are bred to exclude many qualities of nutrition and flavor that a more organic process would provide. This is, in its own way, as unsustainable as the vile product of the fast-food empire; itself corrupt at every link of the chain, from farm to consumer. It's nonetheless also true that the reduction of our agricultural insanity to a matter of "food miles" is—like most reductive analyses—not as shiningly obvious as it appears at first glance. The economic rationale requires extensive attention to such externalities as labor-exploitation and the loss of the kind of autonomy that a proposal predicated on the idea of self-sufficiency is devoted to. From the standpoint of energy inputs, a cargo ship transporting apples from the Antipodes to Manhattan can be far more efficient than bringing a few dozen bushels in the back of a pick-up from an orchard in upstate New York. Even more fundamentally, a check-list mentality (like the LEED system) which simply inventories individual inputs—energy, water, fertilizer, resource depletion, climate change—has a tendency to abstract and de-individualize responsibility and de-politicize the problem.

This proposition offers its possibilities by degrees. The idea that the New York City food-shed could be completely co-terminus with its political boundaries is at the most radical end of a larger set of possibilities. Indeed, the practicalities of a regional approach have been argued by many and the dramatic rise of the local and slow food movements, the growth of many sites of urban agriculture, the proliferation of farmer's markets, and so on represent a burgeoning "new food movement." Even an extreme approach to self-provisioning might allow for the barter of local foods with more distant markets, able to produce foodstuffs that are particularly unsusceptible to regional or local growth. Coffee, a narcotic few New Yorkers can survive without, is something that will be far more difficult to produce than chicken or apples; only under a regime of the most fantastical completeness is it possible to imagine the architectural and agricultural technologies necessary to enable its local production.

It is clear, in any case, that a locally self-sufficient diet will demand substantial changes in our daily habits and styles of consumption—most of which are of very recent origin. Any plan for this will require not simply attention to the content of the New York diet but to the question of balancing nutrition and coercion. In a polyglot metropolis like New York the cuisines of many cultures are supported by and depend on the networks of globalization. A self-sufficient process will result in a certain localization of dietary components and potentially a limitation in choices. However, this dependency on the seasons and on local capacities was characteristic of human dietary habits for millennia and although the goal should be to design the most variegated system possible, it should also be in sympathy with a more general impetus to think locally. Indeed, this inquiry is an extreme instance of such thinking: the wish to bring every New Yorker closer to what is on their plate.

This approach can be enormously stimulating to creativity: New York is a global hub of imaginative and multicultural thinking and has the potential to reinvent food culture and the meanings of diversity at many levels. This problem cannot be considered "solved" if the outcome fails to provide the equivalent of the satisfactions of variety and choice New Yorkers currently enjoy. The fact that spatial specialization—thousands of square miles isolated for beef, thousands for corn, thousands for wheat—could disappear, suggests not simply the logical synergies of rotation but also the introduction of new culinary synergies and complexities as well. This new system must engage a range of technologies and media that are disengaged from the surface of the earth. Proximity and engagement with the sources of food are essential to cultivating progressive environmental consciousness.

However, in providing a system of self-sufficiency for eight million people we beg the question of a novel means of production. Even if entirely devoted to traditional agriculture, New York City would only support an order of magnitude of a million people, as modern agriculture supports around 1000 people per square kilometer of arable land. Whether in the verticalization of farming via stacked growing areas and the use of walls for farming, the use of hydroponic and green-house techniques, or even the use of "test-tube" technologies for growing "meat" without animals, providing enough food for New York's population will oblige the utilization of techniques that bear little resemblance to the arcadian image of the family farm.

SOLUTIONS
INDIVIDUAL

 **BREAKFAST**   **BRUNCH**   **LUNCH**

COFFEE	37 gal	TEA	9 gal
OMELET	36 gal	CEREAL	22 gal
TOAST	22 gal	ORANGE	13 gal

APPLE	18 gal	TOMATO	2.16 gal

HAMBURGER	634 gal
SODA	33 gal

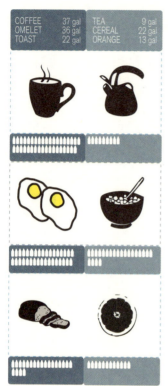

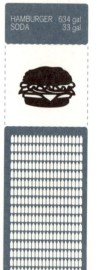

LEGEND
 = 1 GALLON EMBEDDED WATER

AMOUNT SAVED: 51 GAL — AMOUNT SAVED: 15.84 GAL — AMOUNT SAVED: 635.8 GAL

1

1: Different water consumption quantities for different diets.

☀ DINNER

SOLUTIONS
INDIVIDUAL

| SALAD | 31 gal |
| WATER | 0.125 gal |

| BEEF 1LB | 12000 gal | CHICKEN 1lb | 3500 gal |

| BREAD | 22 gal | POTATO | 7 gal |
| WINE | 31 gal | BEER | 1 pint 20 gal |

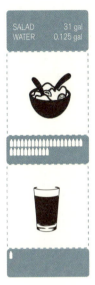
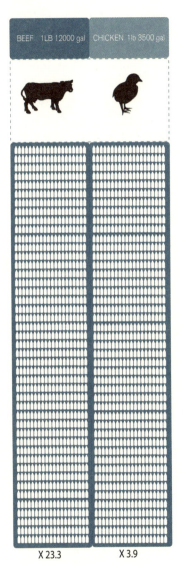

X 23.3   X 3.9

AMOUNT SAVED: 8500 GAL

TOTAL AMOUNT SAVED: 9202.64 GAL

The need for such demanding ingenuities need not necessarily conduce the complete industrialization of our agriculture. The panoply of small-scale techniques of the urban farmer will be indispensable. Every available space must be engaged, ranging from reclaiming the surfaces beneath the streets, to the use of roof-tops and the grafting of window-scaled greenhouses to existing buildings, to the conversion of yards to gardens and the use of cellars and basements, even to the dedication of a portion of every apartment for aeroponic cultivation. Our parks must support agricultural productivity, as must our waterways. Dramatic morphological shifts are possible in the figuration of the city as a whole. There is ample precedent for this, ranging from the small-scale intensification of urban agriculture in war-time to the recent—and similarly shortage-driven—proliferation of agricultural production in Havana. In all of these cases, dramatic increases in output have been achieved within the context of fixed basic urban morphologies.

One more transformational prospect for New York is the possible consolidation of the least dense areas of the city into more compact forms of settlement, which will free-up large portions of the outer boroughs for farming. It can be imagined that in a self-contained system, the nature of the figure-ground—the area of buildings in relationship to the area of streets and open spaces—can be dramatically transformed. If the city disengages from the automotive system in favor of walking, biking, and public transport, the area of street space required for mobility will contract substantially. This proposal for a new agricultural operating system for New York imagines that in many parts of the city, this space can be occupied by building and that buildings themselves will grow narrower to better conduce cross ventilation and solar access. The area at the interior of our blocks—with the assumption that the block organization that is native to our urban culture is retained—will be substantially greater, yielding a much increased area for agrarian activity. There is the possibility for a complete "figure-ground switch" in some parts of the city, wherein buildings will occupy the area now given over to roadways, freeing the entirety of the blocks the buildings currently occupy to be available for green uses.

Any serious attempt to build agricultural self-sufficiency within New York City will seriously compromise—for both good and ill—the traditional relationship of city and country, with its commingled suspicion, reverence, dependency, and symbiosis. Raymond Williams has been one of the most lucid in investigating the cultural polarities of country and city that have developed over time. "On the country has gathered the idea of a natural way of life: of peace, innocence, and simple virtue. On the city has gathered the idea of an achieved centre: of learning, communication, light. Powerful hostile associations have also developed: on the city as a place of noise, worldliness and ambition; on the country as a place of backwardness, ignorance, limitation." Marx, of course, wrote famously not simply about the alienation of the city but about the "idiocy of rural life." A transformation of New York City into a newly "rurban" condition will clearly raise not only simply technical and organizational questions but consequential social and ethical issues as well.

The ethical vector in this investigation is not in questions of cultural difference, nor in questions of cruelty (not to slight their importance) but in the ethics of distribution. This is predicated on the practices of acting locally on behalf of global thinking: seeking to show the pathways of responsibility, to set a radical precedent, to raise expectations, and to goad dramatic invention. Scarcity is not an absolute; it is defined in the relationship between available resources and the demand for them. But this relationship is not entirely straightforward. Availability is very different for a millionaire in Manhattan and a subsistence farmer in Botswana. Demand is itself a cultural construct, something very different than the idea of need. Thinking globally encourages a more egalitarian ethic, a recognition that, as far as food supply is concerned, the game really has a zero sum. In the larger scheme of things, gluttony—and our access to the concept and the possibility of achieving it—diminishes the prospects of others.

This study approaches the question of distributive justice and inequality via the idea of bearing capacity. Part of the reason that our agriculture is so widely distributed springs from the uneven global distribution of soils, water, climate, and species. The soils of New England support a population of grazers. The Midwest is suited to its role as granary. The slopes of Tanzania are superb for coffee. But cultivation is not "natural" in the sense that it is the automatic result of the convergence of climate, culture, and necessity. Cultivation always involves formalization, management, and distortion. In the end, it is more important to shorten the chain and reduce the inputs than to preserve some fantasy of the "natural", one that can only be sustained with air-freight and petro-chemistry.

As any move to a more autarkic economy, self-sufficiency in food requires substantial transformations on both the demand and the supply sides of the food equation. To begin, the average American simply wastes close to a third of a pound of food per day. Not all of this is recoverable but even were one to hypothesize a rate of recovery of five percent—a tiny number—close to 150,000 New Yorkers might be fed on what is currently abandoned.

Food waste is also water waste (and land waste, and energy waste, and...) and this occurs at virtually every stage of the process, from growing to processing to transporting, all of which are profligate users of water. Embodied water is a crucial measure of the efficiency of any food system. For example, the amount of water embedded in the daily consumption of a typical American meat-eater is approximately 4,000 gallons. A vegetarian requires about 300 gallons. Making the footprint more literal, an acre of land is required to produce 165 pounds of beef. The same area can be used to grow 20,000 pounds of potatoes. As scarcity becomes more and more of an issue, these divergences become more and more ethically charged.

At current rates of consumption and with contemporary eating habits, the food footprint of New York City is around 7.1 million acres, about 36.4 times the area of the city as a whole. We consume (or waste) around 38.2 million pounds of food every day and only a near negligible quantity of this is produced in the city. Of course, not all imports are created equal. A kiwi from New Zealand travels 14,000 miles by air, has a water footprint of five gallons per fruit, and accounts for approximately 0.85 pounds of CO_2, something like seven times the weight of the fruit itself. It takes about 295 joules of ecological energy to produce one joule of edible energy in shrimp. A demand side consideration of the problem of feeding of New York is obliged to make distinctions among foodstuffs, based on embodied energy and water, on carbon and other emissions, on up and downstream contaminants, on embodied injustice in production, on nutritive value, on public health considerations, and on suitability for local production.

As an initial benchmark for measuring the city's nutritional requirements, we assume the U.S. Department of Health and Human Services standard of 2000 daily calories of food per person, distributed according to the currently accepted food pyramid. New Yorkers currently eat an *average* diet of 2681 calories per day (that extra 681 is the equivalent of 4.3 cans of soda) and, due to wastage, this requires an actual per capita input of about 3900 calories. A quick look at these numbers suggests that if we were to eliminate waste and reduce our caloric intake to the national standard, approximately half of New York's aggregated demand for food could be eliminated. The food footprint of 36 New Yorkers could be immediately reduced to 20! This does not assume any transformation in agricultural methods, nor any gains that might be made from the extreme localization of production. Indeed, this assumes the continued consumption of dairy, meat, and other "inefficient" sources for the supply of protein and other nutrition.

Our first investigation of a self-sufficient food system proposes precisely this, a 2000 calorie diet based on current styles of consumption but with necessarily reduced quantities and 10 percent wastage, a fairly dramatic, but plausible, reduction. We have examined a number of ways to skin this cat. One possibility for the agricultural production of food sufficient to supply New York is the widespread utilization of vertical farming. According to widely-publicized research done by Dickson Despommier at Columbia Univeristy, a vertical farm of approximately thirty stories, with an area of approximately one city block and utilizing intensive hydroponics, aquaponics, and animal husbandry, would have the ability to produce food for around 50,000 people. Such installations would have additional benefits in the production of energy, the recycling of water, the capture of CO_2, the recovery of wastes, the elimination of run-off, and other value added benefits.

A solution using only vertical agriculture would require 183 farms, based upon the above figures, distributed through the city, with a total footprint area equivalent to that of Manhattan north of the George Washington Bridge. Alternatively, the number of vertical farms might be cut in half with the systematic conversion of currently vacant land and buildings, the utilization of green roofs, the elimination of parking lots, the recovery of 50 percent of existing street space (essentially the area currently given over to parking), and the utilization of a very large number of standard barges for agricultural use. This adds up to about something on the order of 150,000 acres of space at grade. This does not include private yards and gardens nor does it take any currently occupied built space out of its current use.

Successive dietary transformations would progressively reduce the demand for space, technology, and radical morphological transformation. If a 2200 calorie vegetarian diet, including eggs and dairy but eliminating meat, was followed by all New Yorkers, it could be supplied by 115 vertical farms or 58 vertical farms plus approximately 100,000 acres of other spaces for cultivation, including vertical growing surfaces, fixed to existing structures. A fully vegan regimen, excluding all animal derived nutrition, would offer a marginal improvement on this, and either diet yields a food footprint from New York City of less than one third its current size and scale.

While vertical farming represents a macro-technology for facilitating urban agriculture, a wide variety of other technical means—deployed at every scale—

might be engaged to transform the productive character of the city. Vertical agriculture is, in fact, an elaborate refinement on greenhouse agriculture and the surface area available to enclosure throughout the city—on roof-tops, streets, abandoned rail rights-of-way, barges, park spaces, etc.—is enormous. The multiplier necessary to increase the cultivated area of the city is also subject to increase via low-energy artificial lighting, via the use of wall systems and window boxes, via low-input hydroponics, aeroponics, and intensive aquaculture which can be located in spaces from basements (Japan is the world leader here) to a variety of pens in the city's waterways, and via the even more efficient emergent technology of aquaponics which unites hydroponics and aquaculture to make a more sophisticated and self-sustaining loop. Technical—and scalar—diversity is absolutely crucial to provide resilience and to protect against the variety of failures that any system is susceptible to.

A self-sufficient food system would potentially ramify morphologically at every scale with an influence that could dramatically modify the character of city space in a variety of ways, beyond its reconfiguration for intensive agricultural production. There are, for example, approximately three million households with kitchens in New York City. In aggregate, that amounts to several hundred million square feet of space of residential food prep-space. When restaurant and other collective kitchens are added to this, as well as spaces devoted to the processing of raw foodstuffs, the aggregate easily surpasses half a billion square feet of space. Additionally, we can speculate about a logical multiplier to account for the current logistical needs of food distribution both within the city—the wholesale markets, supermarkets, and bodegas; the roadway and other transport infrastructure; the waste recovery and removal systems; etc.—that would surely bring the area required for food preparation, distribution, and management to an order of magnitude of a billion square feet.

Given the likely demographic shifts that will occur in the next decades—nuclear family living arrangements are already a minority component in household hierarchy in the United States—the potential of reconfiguration, not simply of residential structures but of a variety of single-use buildings—from offices to factories—harbingers a distinctive new set of formal possibilities for both physical and social architecture. This new urban architecture is likely to be radically mixed in use—at building, block, and neighborhood scales—as well as far more autonomous in its incorporation of the various aspects of urban respiration at the local scale. Our expectation is that these new architectures will not simply embody the production and preparation of food in increasingly collectivized ways but that questions of waste, water, energy, manufacture, building, climate, and movement will increasingly become crucial components of urbanism at every scale, always with an eye to closing loops as locally as logical.

Such a system will engender a fundamental alteration to the fundamentals of our individual relationships to food and its production. Currently, we are spectators, whether to the pristine and invisibly prepared product on supermarket shelves or at restaurants where we get clean, prepared meals, which betray nothing of their origin in toil and soil. Part of the mission of this "steady-state" research is precisely to build a stronger relationship to food, to enhance responsibility, self-control, and the power of the collectivity. By moving production and consumption closer together, we hope that many new forms of food-focused conviviality and process can grow.

At the largest scale, the impact of a self-sufficient food regime will dramatically re-configure the distribution of hardscape and landscape in the city. Every apartment will bristle with green. Streets will disappear and be replaced by farms and greenhouses. Rooftops will offer agricultural, recreational, and other respiratory spaces. Green bridges will link buildings. The waterfront will reawaken as a zone of food and other production. Vast areas of private yards and gardens will be remade as small-scale agrarian plots. Parks will become productive. Rail rights-of-way will be utilized as linear farms. Low-density areas of the city will be consolidated to free up surplus territory for agriculture. The newly needless infrastructure of highways will disappear, offering hundreds of square miles for new uses. A great green grid will dominate the form of New York and nobody in the city will be out of sight of the place where the next meal is coming from.

This essay is linked with a larger research project entitled *New York City (Steady) State*, a comprehensive proposal by *Terreform Inc.* for creating a completely self-sufficient New York City.

About the author: Michael Sorkin is Distinguished Professor of Architecture and Director of the Graduate Program in Urban Design at The City College of New York (CCNY). He is Founder of Terreform Inc., a non-profit organization devoted to urban and environmental research and intervention. He is also principal of Michael Sorkin Studio. He is author or editor of over a dozen books including *Variations on a Theme Park, Exquisite Corpse, Wiggle, The Next Jerusalem, Back to Zero, Some Assembly Required, After the Trade Center* (edited with Sharon Zukin) and *Twenty Minutes In Manhattan*.

The Hanging Gardens of the 21st Century

Agriculture Going Urban with Vertical Farms

DICKSON DESPOMMIER

Imagine a building located within a large metropolitan center that has a negative carbon footprint, produces food crops in commercial quantities, and stands out as one of the most beautiful, transparent multi-story iconic structures in the entire city. That is what is envisioned for the vertical farm of the near future. This radical new approach to food production offers many potential advantages, including year-round crop production, no weather-related crop failures, and no use of herbicides, pesticides or traditional fertilizers. Bringing such a building into reality will require no new technologies, since we already know how to construct ones that favor the growth of a wide variety of plants, including most crops that the world at large consumes (grains, vegetables, herbs, fruits). These structures are high-tech, energy-efficient greenhouses, that practice "closed loop" controlled environment agriculture (CEA), and examples of them can be found throughout the developed world. Greenhouses will undoubtedly continue to expand their influence on global agriculture as climate change issues force growers to consider adopting them as an alternative to traditional soil-based methods of food production.

In order to quite literally take CEA to the next level, though, will require solving issues related to integrating the systems. Temperature controls, water management, nutrient delivery systems, monitoring growth of plants, waste-to-energy strategies, seed to harvest systems, security from plant pests and pathogens, and other issues still need to be engineered into a seamless multi-story building; a "stacked" iteration of today's greenhouse.

The vertical farm will be designed with the plants in mind, so no matter where they are built, they will be as transparent as possible so as to capture the maximum amount of sunlight. This requirement will also dictate what forms the buildings will assume. For example, long and narrow structures will in most cases be more advantageous than tall and cubical structures. The transparent façade of the vertical farm will be skinned with a wide variety of glazes to choose from (e.g., glass, plexi, ethylene tetrafluoroethlyene). The advantages and disadvantages of each will be discussed below. Utilizing diverse sources of passive energy, in addition to solar energy, will also be considered whenever availability allows (e.g., wind, geothermal), and will in most cases depend upon geographic location. Scaffolding and support components made from less dense, high-strength materials, such as carbon composites or aluminum-titanium alloys, will undoubtedly prove to be ideal building materials. That is because the vertical farm skeleton need not carry the kind of loads usually associated with typical office buildings. All plant growth will be done using lightweight hydroponic and aeroponic grow systems, rather than conventional soil-based methods.

What is currently lacking is a specific example of a working vertical farm prototype. I would like to focus on delineating fundamental functional and structural characteristics of a hypothetical small-scale version of a vertical farm, and how that integrated multi-story building might operate using hydroponic and aeroponic growing systems.

The functional characteristics of the vertical farm begin with its primary mission, which is to produce commercial levels and quantities of plant-based produce, as well as freshwater and saltwater varieties of fish, crustaceans and mollusks. Poultry could also be considered for inclusion into the menu of food items raised within the vertical farm complex. Four-legged animals such as sheep, pigs, or cattle are well outside the paradigm of the vertical farm and therefore will not be included in the discussion that follows. Despite this absence, the species richness of the vertical farm line of products is, by necessity, designed for robustness, and can therefore fulfill many of the requirements for most world cuisines. With all of this activity, the vertical farm is not planned as a single building. Rather, it will consist of a series of interconnected structures, all of which have well-defined functions in the production scheme.

An overarching principal in constructing the vertical farm is food safety and security. With respect to plant crops, a nursery is essential and should be constructed to be as secure as possible from outside influences. Its construction could be based on that of P2 facilities, commonly found at many of the world's leading microbiological research institutions. P2 facilities are air-tight rooms that have, as their single purpose, the isolation of anything residing inside them from the outside world. Hospitals commonly use P2 facilities to protect patients that are immuno-compromised from coming into contact with common microbes that, under ordinary circumstances, cause no disease, but for these individuals might prove fatal if encountered. In the vertical farm, similar precautions must be taken and prevail as a means of further securing agricultural safety. Air must be filtered and a positive pressure must be maintained in order to minimize the chances of introducing plant pathogens that are of microbial origin (e.g., rice blast, wheat rust). This strategy would also serve to keep out most, if not all, species of insect pests. Workers in the nursery and the farm itself should be required to adhere to "clean room" behavior of the kind currently associated with the electronics industries. All growing media used in the nursery, such as rock wool and other inert materials, should be sterilized before entering the production line. Since the vertical farm growing strategy is based on hydroponics and aeroponics, maintaining a clean environment should be reasonably straightforward, since soil is not involved. Monitoring for uninvited guests—insects and microbial pathogens, for example—is essential for quality control (QC). For this purpose, a QC building must be situated close to or directly connected with the nursery. It would also house a diagnostic laboratory, as well as a chemical analysis lab, and a central monitoring hub. The latter would become the heart of the vertical farm, from which workers could oversee the planting, growth, and harvest of all crops and animal products. Automated monitoring devices would measure a wide variety of parameters, such as water flow rates, nutrient levels in growth media, pH and temperature of hydroponic and aeroponic solutions, plant growth rates, and so on, and this would all be controlled from the central monitoring hub's control room. The diagnostic laboratory would, in addition to disease detection and control, evaluate incoming batches of seeds for overall quality and germination viability, and do similar kinds of testing for incoming poultry, fish, crustaceans, and mollusks.

One of the main functions of the laboratory would be to assay the composition of the produce and look for breeches of security with respect to contaminants, including heavy metals, pesticides, and other unwanted toxic substances. The lab would issue a daily chemical analysis of randomly selected crops. This is to assure consumers as to the high quality of products sold at market. It is anticipated that this would give a decided advantage to the produce of the VF in the competitive open marketplace, since no purveyor of fresh produce currently lists the chemical composition of its crops. For the first time in the history of commercial farming, the consumer would be able to know exactly what is in the food that they eat, since advanced hydroponic plant diets are composed of a known set of elements. The initial cost of a laboratory dedicated to these functions would undoubtedly be high, but as the farm concept "matures" and public confidence in, and acceptance of, vertical farm-produced food items grows, the volume of products would increase to meet consumer demand and cost would most likely go down. Eventually, as more and more vertical farms come online, further reductions in the cost of operation would make them highly competitive.

Integrating animal husbandry (aquaculture, poultry farming) with plant crops would be accomplished, in part, by producing some crops specifically for consumption by animals. This includes grains for tilapia and chickens, and algae for mollusks and shrimp. The buildings housing animals would be isolated from the plant crop building to greatly reduce the chances of the cross-contamination of each operation with waste products or would-be pathogens. Buildings housing poultry must allow for so-called "free-range" activity. This is crucial for consumer acceptance and must be strictly adhered to in the overall design of the vertical farm complex. Aquaculture is less demanding in that respect, and could be carried out in subterranean enclosures situated in the basements of buildings, such as the one housing the laboratories and monitoring stations. In both of these situations, waste management is crucial to the maintenance of a sustainable line of products.

Once a product is harvested, it is then prepared for sale. For most vegetables, no further processing is needed. Vine-ripened tomatoes, peppers, green beans, melons and the like could be sold at a local green market within the hour after leaving the vertical farm. For herbs and grains, more post-harvest processing would be necessary. This activity should take place offsite in another clean build-

1: An aquaponic system that involves tilapia or perch (up to 10,000 fish in the 5 ft deep tank), watercress and tomatoes. The water is drawn up through one pump and gravity fed through the potted plants (which remove the nitrogen from the fish waste) and back into the tank where it re-oxygenizes the tank water.

2: Vertical crop technology that only requires 5% of the average water used in conventional growing conditions. It can be installed in virtually any location, therefore adjacent to local communities and markets, which reduces both food miles and distribution costs and ensures a fresh food supply that is close to consumer markets.

ing adjacent to the main vertical farm. The isolated herb or grain could either be sold without further processing, or converted into a so-called "value-added product," for example, wheat seed into flour or corn kernels into meal.

The inedible plant material must be recycled for energy production using a variety of waste-to-energy strategies, such as those that involve some kind of incineration. Vine crops (tomatoes, beans, peppers, grapes) grow continuously, and thus the production of plant waste is minimized until the life cycle of a particular crop is completed. Again, incineration to retrieve as much energy as possible from the leftovers is essential for helping to offset energy costs of running grow lights and other indispensable electrical equipment (computers, HVAC, etc). Configuring the vertical farm to enable the harvesting and post-harvest processing of salable items requires additional secure space to be included in the design of the building. Processing animals (chickens, fish, shrimp, clams and mussels) requires a dedicated building, probably located outside the inner circle of the nursery and vertical farm for plant crops. Handling the leftovers from this operation should be similar to that mentioned above.

One efficient but initially expensive waste-to-energy option is to include a plasma arc gasifier (PAG) into each building where the processing of food items occurs. A PAG generates an extremely high temperature, inducing complete pyrolysis of any solid material, reducing the item back into its elemental components. A PAG would serve to eliminate solid wastes and generate energy. This method of incineration has become popular in Japan and in other countries like Canada and the United States.

A green market complete with gift shop would be an ideal add-on component to the vertical farm, especially if the farm were centrally located in an urban center. Consumer convenience and produce availability (24 hours a day, 7 days a week) would then converge into a continuous flow of goods to local populations within walking distance of the farm.

Other buildings could also be included in the VF complex. One might be a dedicated education center, the purpose of which would be to inform consumers about the ecological and social advantages of vertical farms. Schools could take guided tours and attend outreach seminars, designed to initiate an ongoing dialogue between the food producers and food consumers. A business center would attract new value-added businesses that could take advantage of a varied and sustainable food supply, adding much needed capital to further the cause of the vertical farm ethic and helping to create a true eco-city.

It is necessary to examine the functional, structural and material considerations for the prototypical vertical farm. In particular, I would like to examine the building housing the nursery and the plant crops, from the perspective of available building materials and their relative advantages and disadvantages. It is important to keep in mind the fact that there is not a vertical farm in current existence, so what follows is a suggestion of what might be useful to a team of designers, planners, and architects in thinking through the process of creating a multi-story building in which our food crops can be grown.

Getting the correct amount and kind of light to the plants is the central concern of any vertical farm design. All green plants depend upon the sun for their source of energy. The wavelengths that are necessary for photosynthesis are restricted to just two regions of the visible spectrum, 400 (blue) and 700 (red) nanometers. These two spectral zones of light can be radiated efficiently by employing LED (light emitting diode) lighting specifically designed for that purpose. LED lighting has been in use in an increasing number of commercial greenhouses over the last 10 years, with improving efficiency as the technology advances, driven by a newly emerging CEA industry. Today's LED grow-lights are energy-efficient and cost-effective to operate.

Organo-LED (OLED) lighting, a new iteration of LED lighting, is on the near horizon and promises to bring even greater control of the desired wavelengths of light to the vertical farm toolbox. In addition, OLEDs are flexible and are manufactured as thin sheets of specially engineered plastic. This would allow OLED lights to bend around individual plants, giving them a lighting scheme that could never be considered, let alone achieved, with natural sunlight. However, the current OLEDs are prohibitively expensive, preventing their immediate application.

In contrast to LED technology, the typical incandescent or white fluorescent light bulbs are very inefficient, because both emit more irrelevant than usable quantities of energy. With the advent of LEDs, the older and previously more typical lighting options have gone by the wayside in most commercial CEA establishments.

It is obvious that sunlight is the gold standard of plant lighting. Therefore, the ideal situation for the design of a vertical farm would be to take advantage of available sunlight and to construct the building so as to capture the maximum amount of energy possible during daylight hours. The amount of sunlight available varies widely throughout the world, so location is key in this regard. The entire Middle East, the American southwest, many parts of South Asia, and the majority of Australia all have over 300 days of sunlight, which could easily support vertical farms if they were properly configured to take advantage of this abundant supply of solar energy. Getting light into the back of a building whose front windows are oriented towards the sun has proven easier than once thought possible. Specially designed plastic-composite parabolic mirrors are now in use in some buildings to accomplish this. They are positioned in the rear of the building and direct sunlight into the building with high efficiency. The use of fiber optics remains another option to get "direct" sunlight into the vertical farm; ambient light is concentrated using a prismatic solar collector, then distributed throughout the building by way of bundles of thin glass fibers. In this case, a small but adequate quantity of sunlight could find its way to each and every plant, regardless of the plant's location inside the farm.

An orientation of the building towards the sun would be highly desirable. A slightly curved, multi-story building whose windows are made from ethylene tetrafluoroethylene (ETFE) would be my first choice for the vertical farm's transparent façade and general overall shape. ETFE is strong, pliable, lightweight, and self-cleaning. It has been used extensively around the world in some very high-end projects; for example the 2008 Beijing Olympics Swimming Cube and the Eden Project in Cornwall, England. ETFE is still a "boutique" building material and is still expensive; its continued climb in popularity with highly sought-after celebrity architects will undoubtedly drive down the price, eventually making it competitive with other transparent materials, including glass.

Glass has significant issues that make it a less than desirable material for the construction of vertical farms. Glass is used extensively in most modern buildings as the first choice for glazing, but it has several disadvantages, not the least of which is its weight. It is also fragile compared to ETFE and other transparent plastic polymers. Cleaning glass façades is time-consuming and expensive. Making several layers of glass to create insulation for the building would add even more weight. ETFE, on the other hand, could easily be made in several layers, remain relatively lightweight, and could make cooling and heating the vertical farm energy-efficient.

Some ecologically-minded designers have suggested a plastic made from the recycling of clear plastic bottles as a façade material; this is a novel solution for their reuse. Unfortunately, the kinds of plastic used to make the majority of these persistent source objects, like bottles or other packaging, obviates their use in this particular application, since over a very short time, the plastic begins to yellow due to continued exposure to UV-B solar radiation, greatly reducing the penetration of the precise wavelengths of light needed for plant growth into the vertical farm.

Many materials currently exist that can be used for the structural support of a vertical farm building, and new ones are continually coming on the market. Solid steel beam construction will probably not play a role in the main vertical farm building, but tubular steel could be effectively employed. The Eden Project made extensive use of it, to support eight large transparent domes, inside of which grow an amazing array of tropical plants. Alternative structural materials include aluminum-titanium alloys. This combination is superior in strength to steel and lighter in weight, as well. Al-Ti alloys do not corrode when exposed over long periods of time to high levels of moisture. Ultimately, however, cost and availability will determine which materials get the nod from the developer.

Included in the fundamental design of the vertical farm prototype is the requirement to incorporate an extensive array of electronic equipment. Compatible support structures must be figured into the overall design package, allowing cables, detector systems, and other essential equipment easy access to the plants without interfering with the transmission of light from the outside—if sunlight is to be the main source of energy. Grow lights employing LED or OLED technologies might offset this need if cleverly integrated into the hydroponic plastic piping.

Corrosion of electronic equipment due to high humidity from trans-evaporative plant activity inside the building must be addressed if the growth of unwanted molds is to be avoided. Positive pressured rooms would be advantageous in this regard, lessening the chances for a breech of plant pathogen security. Keeping the humidity down is another option for reducing, or even eliminating, these unwanted invaders. This can be best accomplished by de-humidification devices strategically placed throughout the facility to capture excess moisture and to recycle it for reuse. By combining these two approaches designed to limit unwanted invading species, I think there would be very few, if any, breeches of security over the long-term operation of a vertical farm that incorporated these features into its basic construction plan. Expense of operation is a real concern here, and the cost benefits of such a high-tech approach must be balanced against the eventual failure of systems due to corrosive mold accumulation. That is why beginning with a prototype is essential, serving as the test track for multi-story indoor farming. Each system to be tested will be purposely run to exceed the anticipated limits of its performance capabilities. Only then can it be determined what is possible and what is not. Yields of crops, the type of crops to be grown, the integration of aquaculture with plant-based produce, and the automation and computer-assisted monitoring operations all need to be taken out on their "shake-down cruise" as a test of suitability and process.

In conclusion, the vertical farm concept has grown into a full-fledged project over the last 10 years, from its humble beginnings in a classroom, to one that has garnered the attention of the world. Just eight years ago, Google had but one entry for the term. Today, in 2010, there are over 1,700,000 entries for the same two words, with over 500,000 sites for images of what a vertical farm might look like. All that is needed at this moment is capital and a passionate team of world experts to carry it to the next level. I fully anticipate that by the end of 2011, a vertical farm project will have come into being, and possibly multiple projects in many places throughout the world. Green construction will never be the same once the vertical farm rises up and into the cityscape. Bon appetite everyone!

This essay is part of ongoing research into vertical farming, some of which is published in *The Vertical Farm*, Thomas Dunne Books/St. Martin's Press, 2010.

About the author: Dickson Despommier is Emeritus Professor of Public Health and Microbiology at Columbia University in New York City. For the last 12 years, he and his students have been developing the concept of vertical farming as an urban agricultural solution to the global food crisis. He is the author of numerous peer-reviewed scientific articles and three books, including *The Vertical Farm: Feeding the World in the 21st Century*.

Pimp my World

How to Construct New Environments by Re-using Old Ones

ADA TOLLA AND GIUSEPPE LIGNANO / LOT-EK

For almost two decades, many architects have spent their time on complex formal expression, achieved through the remarkable processing power of modern computing, with an increasingly fashionable 'green' requirement added as a kind of ornament late in the design process. While we appreciate some of the shiny and shapely results, we see them, like so many expensive products of the recent past, as suddenly obsolete. We at LOT-EK have spent much of those same two decades investing our energy in a different way: our research and design work has tried thoughtfully to address the way that architecture deploys resources, both natural and financial, to create meaningful places.

In construction, generic material objects are customized and combined into specific architectural objects. In order to build something, you must take something else apart—whether it's merely cutting a length of rebar, or steel beam, or insulation, or a more complex construction operation of adaptively reusing an existing industrial or technological artifact. Our practice is very interested in the latter, in adaptive reuse. Instead of defaulting to the smallest, and theoretically most adaptable manufactured material, we look for large-scale objects that already have a particular integrity and complexity, and locate the operations that realize the object's architectural potential. Our research focuses on man-made objects and systems — not originally intended for architectural use — and the way they proliferate, accumulate, overlap and interfere with the built as well as the natural environment around the globe. The manufactured objects that interest us include: air-conditioners, airplanes, antennas, containers, highways, jetways, booths, boxes, cranes, ducts, lifts, lights, scraps, sheds, trucks, parking, plumbing, scaffolding and tanks. Like a skillful butcher, who respects the precious complexity and subtlety of the animal he is dissecting, we try to find an economy and a sustainability in how we cut and combine, to find a way to facilitate eating 'the whole pig'; from nose to tail, with no waste and with surprisingly recombinant recipes.

We select objects and systems for their availability and their physical 'architectural' qualities — volume, space, form, structure, functionality, material, size, transportability, assemble-ability, modularity, etc. In order to exploit such qualities, a series of operations are implemented to modify the objects and/or systems, to create complex architecture configurations, and to fulfill programmatic needs. We observe how the objects exist and behave within their 'natural habitat': the way they are stored, stocked, transported, placed, used or occupied. Operations transform objects through forceful actions that are as physical as they are conceptual, pushing the limits of basic assemblies into more complex, fantastic, challenging and compelling architectures. LOT-EK's methodology and research seeks to establish a new tectonic by challenging and embracing the entire ecology of stuff produced in our product-centered civilization.

What do we do with this stuff? First, we love it. Some of these marginal artifacts, as artists from Duchamp to Warhol have shown us, have a profound ready-made beauty and integrity. These objects require us only to look at them twice or sideways to understand that we are surrounded by anonymous perfection, and that the familiar is indeed strange. But we try to go deeper into understanding these objects' systems of production, from the economies of repetition and reproduction in industrial manufacturing, to the upstream/downstream life-cycles of raw materials, byproducts, and waste. We try to develop an understanding of objects as interdependent components in an ecology of technology: a complex local and global system of finding, moving, sorting, making, changing, and using resources, in which the physical object is an expression of otherwise invisible systems that make up our social, financial, and natural world.

What does this mean for the architecture we make? Ours is a transformative architecture, and in this way it has its origins in deliberately unoriginal sources. Instead of the inefficiency of generating a singular expressive form and adapting material systems to its requirements, we search for ways to radically customize, combine, and co-opt existing forms, assemblies, and structures. In this way, we are both luxurious and cheap. We do this with two intentions. First, we believe that some objects of human industry have reached such perfect equilibrium of form, manufacturing efficiency, and material structure that it is the task of architecture not merely to imitate them, but to defer to them: to engage in the radical efficiency of using them directly. Our second intention is to explore a new equilibrium between the built environment, and the natural and industrial systems from which that environment is sourced. We exploit the existing economies of scale, inhabit the existing carbon footprints, and creatively divert the delivery point of existing manufacturing, shipping, and operating systems. A small intervention far downstream in the cycles of those systems, such as shipping a hundred ISO shipping containers to a dense downtown block in order to build a school, both utilizes the power, and criticizes the limits of those systems. We divert, convert, invert, and pervert, in order to perfect. Beyond mere recycling or adaptive re-use, we try to catalyze new cycles of use. We choose not to choose between architecture that develops new ecologies and economies, and architecture that calms, protects, provides, inspires, and rewards the body and spirit. We don't merely seek to do more with less, we think deeply about what we measure with those words. The operations that we apply have a humanistic, as well as a tectonic intent. Like all modern architects, we like machines. But we like people more. In fifteen years of making buildings, we've developed strategies that begin with the ever-evolving lived-in experience of those buildings, and have found detailed and subtle ways of re-engineering a high-tech legacy to achieve, and therefore reinvent, humane environments.

The potential of such a transformation from object to environment become very transparent if we take the example of a standard 40-foot ISO shipping container. It has been a longstanding subject of our research, going back to an unbuilt 1995 project that deployed hundreds of them into the structure of a museum of the history of the slave trade—a poignant part of the history of shipping and of the sea in general. In terms of our approach to construction, we're particularly interested in our ongoing PUMA CITY project, because it is a building that is continually built and unbuilt. Twenty-four standard shipping containers were retrofitted and can be transformed into PUMA CITY, an 11,000 square-foot transportable retail and event building designed to travel around the world. When deployed, it is comprised of two *Puma* brand retail spaces on the lower levels. Both stores were designed to have atria at the height of two containers as well as 4-container-wide open spaces, to challenge the modular yet fixed and rigid quality of the containers' inner space. The building is fully demountable, travels by cargo ship, train or truck and it is assembled and disassembled onsite at its various destinations.

The building uses the existing container connectors to join and secure the containers both horizontally and vertically. A 20 foot cantilever pushes the usual container stack to an almost uncomfortable extreme, creating a large roof terrace and a public covered patio. Each module is designed to ship as a conventional cargo container, through a system of structural panels that fully seal all large openings, which can be removed onsite to reconstitute the large, open interior spaces. We understand this assembly as the complex consequence of a sequence of seemingly simple operations: assemble, combine, stack, shift, cut, move, and repeat.

These operations force us to understand the constructive and constituent components of buildings, like PUMA CITY, in newly intricate and networked ways. Buckminster Fuller used to ask: How much does your building weigh? In our case we know, and it weighs 39,000 kg: 42 container cargo doors, 96 wall cover plates, 25 roof cover plates, 10 floor cover plates, 3754 bolts, 72 semi-auto lock container attachment fittings, 84 bridge-clamp attachment fittings, 110 twist lock connectors, 70 bolting attachments, 15,000 screws, 300 sheets of plywood, 1 km of rubber gasket seal, and it takes 6000 man-hours for set-up. Each of these numbers represent variables that effect every other number and associated variable. We believe that all buildings should be quantitatively calibrated in this way. Its not just a question of knowing the numbers, however: it's also about constructing in such a way that the building continues to function and perform within the operational parameters of its original components.

For example, the cut and transformed containers still had to perform in a manner structurally identical to an unchanged container: possible to slip into a stack of a thousand on an ocean-going cargo ship, the PUMA CITY containers are operationally unique, but structurally generic: they had to be incredibly different and yet exactly the same as all the containers. How do you radicalize the form and normalize the function? How do you normalize the form and radical-

1

2

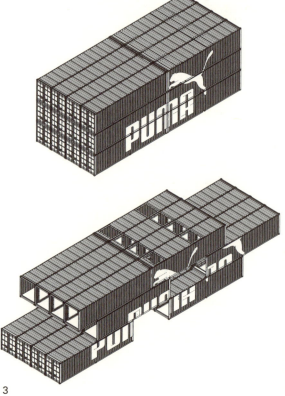

3

1: In PUMA CITY regular shipping containers are reconfigured into a retail building.
2: The electricity circuits of the various containers can be connected into one circuit by external coupling.
3: While usually stacked as a compact block, containers in PUMA CITY are pulled out to create open spaces for natural lighting and access.
4-5: On the interior, various walls of the containers are eliminated to create larger spaces, extending both horizontally and vertically.

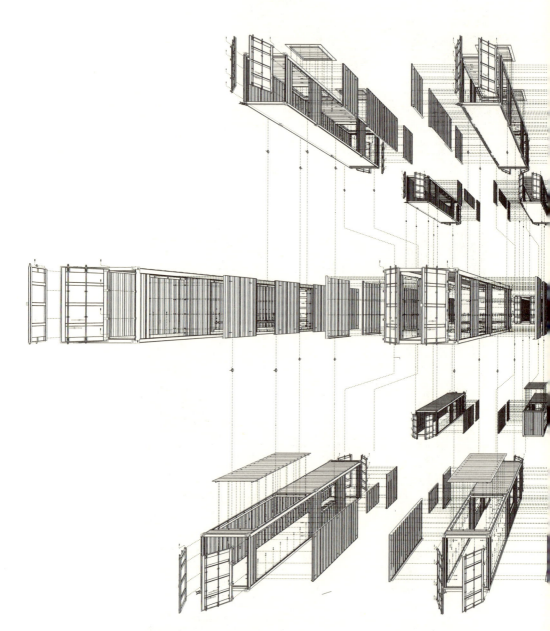

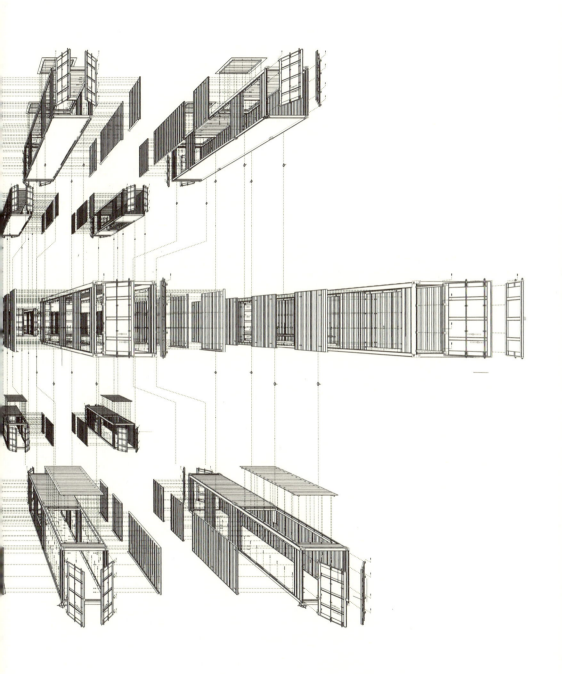

6: Exploded axonometric drawing, showing the various modular elements of the customized container construction.

ize the function? For one thing, this takes testing; the expense of testing, in turn, encourages a repetition of transformation strategies, as well as a repetition of objects. So, although this is not immediately apparent, several of the transformed containers in PUMA CITY are identical in the way their surfaces are opened, cut and shifted, even though they are not deployed identically or symmetrically within the general structure.

In a practical and specific way the cuts and manipulations of the container require, for example, adding structure along the new open edge, wherever surface material is removed. And yet this can be done in a way that respects the inherent virtues of the existing structure: instead of welding on a new column, like the columns that reinforce the corner conditions of the container, a steel plate is added, spanning adjacent corrugations in the wall-panel, thus turning the corrugations into a structurally performative element without changing their form or location. Often the more you expect to change an object, the more you end up learning from and following its existing systems. With the extreme cantilevers and shifts of PUMA CITY, we needed to keep in mind that every container is effectively a bridge; it rests only on four corner casting blocks, that extend an inch or so below the length of the container itself—establishing a standard maximum envelope somewhat beyond the physical limit of the box. So how do you shift this stack without losing the casting footer? We learned that to accommodate legacy non-standardized-length containers, sizes that had been tried at various points in the history of container shipping, there was a technology of inline castings that could support the structure far back from a corner. Sometimes, when we think we are distorting a system, we are actually going deeper into its inherent patterns and its history of development.

The same principle applies to our unbuilt competition entry for the New Jalisco Library in Guadalajara, Mexico—a project that still continues to inform our thinking and research. Instead of the shipping container, we proposed the use of over 200 Boeing 727 and 737 airplane fuselages, stacked in a north-south slant in relation to sun exposure for energy efficiency. Two shifts in the direction of the axis of the fuselages generate two large open spaces within the stack. The building utilizes the space inside the fuselages to contain and organize functions that require enclosed spaces—such as book collections, meeting rooms and administration offices—while the two large glazed open spaces house a large atrium with reading areas and two auditoriums. The library program is arranged around the large glazed atrium, which develops vertically through the entire cross-section of

7

8

7: The interior of the fuselages are modified to house the library specific program elements, such as book stacks, display shelving, as well as reading and meeting areas.
8: The dense accumulation of airplane fuselages creates in-between spaces, which proliferate throughout the building.

9

9: Arranged around two large glazed atriums, the fuselages are cut on the ends, allowing for views from each component space into the atriums.
10: The lower sections of the reused fuselages are filled with HVAC.

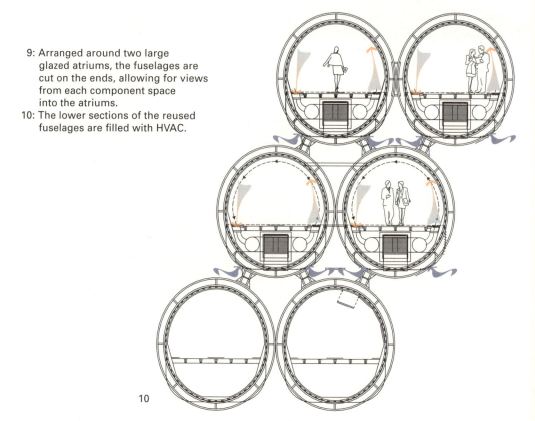

10

the building. The lower part of the atrium, located on the second level, and accessible directly from the new plaza through escalators and elevators, functions as a lobby and information center. At each upper level, reading areas bridge between the two opposite interior façades generated by the newly exposed cross sections of the fuselages, cut at the ends to look onto the atrium.

The airplane fuselages adjacent to the atrium are occupied by book collections, meeting rooms and technology centers. These cylindrical volumes envelope different activities, insulating them from the main atrium, while maintaining a visual connection through their glazed ends. The fuselages that house the book collections offer a more generous space than the standard sizes generally assigned to this function. Inside the fuselage, bookshelves run along either side and, in the middle, lower units combine shelving with seating and computers to enable a direct and local search of books. Grating catwalks and stairs span over the open spaces to connect to the other functions in the building: the offices/press-area at the second level and a bar, lounge and event space with a large open terrace at the third level. The fuselage becomes the basic module of this building, insulated and furnished according to the program. The internal subdivision generated by the existing floor joists is used to retain the upper cabin section for inhabitation, while the lower section houses independent and interconnected mechanical systems: HVAC, electrical wiring, and a conveyor belt system for the mechanical distribution of the books. These moves extend the fuselage's original served and service program configuration in a new context.

So, as with PUMA CITY, we have the same construction operations of assembling, combining, stacking, shifting, cutting, moving, repeating. We have the same principle of adaptively reusing or upcycling a remarkable but generic mechanical or technological artifact. Indeed, the passenger-cabin component of a commercial aviation jet, commonly called the "can," is traditionally the hardest element to reuse or salvage, because it doesn't contain all the desirable components, machinery, and metals of the wings, cockpit nosecone, or engines. The complexity and cost of cutting down the fuselage to retrieve the material value of the embodied aluminum can easily exceed the value of the material in its raw state: so the fuselages enter a limbo of functional and economic uselessness. In this case we prefer up-cycling to recycling: the whole object is better than the sum of its parts, if we figure out how to apply it, and transform it operationally, even if we preserve it as an object.

How do we make the most useless thing the most useful thing? As with the necessity of understanding that an ISO shipping container operates as a bridge between its corner castings, a breakthrough with the tectonic development of this project came with understanding that a jet fuselage is a remarkable bridge as well: think of it balanced on only three points of landing gear as it taxies or stands on the tarmac. Without adding any additional structural steel, we were able to understand the three landing-gear mounting points as locations from which the fuselages could be attached to a mediating steel ring structural system, with the inherent bridging performance doing the rest of the structural work. Sometimes the more you change the function, the more you benefit from the existing form, by conceptually, but not materially, reinforcing its structure.

Sometimes the better you understand an existing structure or construction, the less you change it, even as you radicalize its program. Objects and operations are mutually complicit. For an early project, TV TANK, we introduced cuts and displacements across the length of a standard quasi-cylindrical truck gasoline-transport tank. Before we broke one open, we had never been inside this seemingly familiar object: so we were very interested in the quasi-cylindrical geometry, and not so much in the interior structures, composed of flat doughnut-like rib panels called baffle walls, which modulate the fluid movement of the gasoline and provide additional structure. We removed the baffle walls and substituted other components to produce a kind of media lounge installation. However, for a later project, the Morton Loft, we used another gasoline truck tank, and became interested in the baffle walls. The tank was cut in two, with one half deployed horizontally as a multi-part sleeping loft, in which the baffle walls determined the size of the sleeping areas and served to keep them private, and the other half was deployed vertically, with a toilet on the bottom, and an elaborate shower area above. The baffle wall became the floor between the two bathroom zones, with a translucent glass insert suggesting both continuity and discontinuity between the spaces.

The more you do, the less you do. Yet even as you accept and adopt existing conditions, you're required to attend to and control other conditions that are otherwise unforeseen. For example, with the vertical bathroom tank half, all of the plumbing risers would be visible when viewed from the living space, because there's very little thickness to the bathroom enclosure into which to insert these and other systems. So we did 3D renderings and diagrams to determine the positioning of these standard, and even ugly, pipes and components; the consequence of trying to make the invisible visible is being responsible for its effects. We reconfigured our thinking about which side is the front, which side is the back, which side is the display, which side is the archive, which side is the guts, which side is the skin.

There is a logic of respectful attention to existing infrastructure that extends even to the inherent properties of the construction site itself. The gasoline tank components were installed into an existing industrial-residential loft conversion building in downtown Manhattan; they were brought to the upper-floor location as one would expect, with a large crane, on a temporarily closed street. The final rotating and tilting of the tanks into position was done by a subcontractor, who chose to construct a temporary steel cable-mounting plate, anchored in the ferroconcrete ceiling of the existing building. We were very skeptical at first, but we came to understand this as a sympathetic kind of operation: a temporary collaboration with the properties of the existing building, rather than the introduction of still another structure, scaffold, or supplemental object. We were scared for a moment, but it worked perfectly. It was done with an incredible economy of means. It was a lesson for what we do, a lesson about working economically and within natural and technological ecologies. We don't promise some utopian future technology that will make everything effortless. We don't look for a false cleanliness, or hide the effort behind constructing, maintaining, and inhabiting the built environment. Instead, we begin by looking for the hidden strength of what's already there: we look at the wrong sides of things and the insides of things, under tables and inside ceilings, for the backstage objects, products, artifacts, and systems that enable architecture to exist.

Text documentation: Thomas de Monchaux

About the authors: Ada Tolla and Giuseppe Lignano founded LOT-EK, a design studio based in New York that achieved high visibility in the architecture/art world for its sustainable and innovative approach to construction, materials, and space through the adaptive reuse of existing industrial objects not originally intended for architecture. The partners also teach at Columbia University, Graduate School of Architecture Preservation and Planning (GSAPP) and lecture in major universities and cultural institutions throughout the U.S. and abroad.

The Vernacular Rediscovered

Applying Local Construction Technologies and Materials in Ethiopia

DIRK HEBEL

African cities are the fastest growing cities in the world today. Extrapolations show that the urban population in Africa currently doubles every 10 to 15 years. The reason for this urban population growth is high migration rates into African cities. This migration occurs on a broad scale because of two main factors. Aggravated conditions for agricultural production in the global market combined with local mismanagement result in food shortages and difficult conditions for even subsistence farming. Repeated local and regional conflicts deprive a continuously growing part of the rural population of their means of existence and jeopardize their security. In the hope of better living conditions, many people move into urban environments.

Ethiopia will be confronted with a population increase of 45 million people over the next 15 years, along with increased demand for basics like food, water, safety, and shelter in not yet existing or already overburdened urban settlements. The decades to come will certainly be formative in the further long-term development of the country. Given this challenge, Ethiopia has to invent its own modes of 21st century urbanization, rather than relying on outdated models from the so-called 'developed world.' It must re-invent its indigenous building methods, construction technologies, and material use and reduce its dependency on imported materials, if there is to be any hope to escape from its satellite status as a part of the global economy.

The capital of Ethiopia, Addis Ababa, represents an ideal situation where the urban phenomena of growth, expansion, and densification can be experienced and investigated. This can be accomplished firsthand through its geographic location, demographic development, and, most importantly, its unbelievable potential in people, ideas, and interactions.

With a population of approximately 2.8 million people[1], composed of 78 ethnic groups, Addis Ababa is the undisputed metropolis of the country, and is also the location of the headquarters of the African Union (AU). Experts predict the population will reach 6 to 8 million people by 2025. Addis Ababa has the potential to function as an experimental urban laboratory for the country as a whole, through its position as the political and social center of Ethiopia. Issues of density, health care, safety, social coherence, psychology, economy, and, above all, ecology must be answered. The question of which building materials and techniques are appropriate for the primarily urban development of a whole country needs to be considered, and Addis Ababa is an ideal location for this. Newer developments in Addis Ababa show a contrary position: it has been infected with the so-called Dubai Fever—the desire to copy or import an image of economic growth and link it with political power. Glass and steel towers are misunderstood as a manifestation of positive economic development as well as the singular esthetic outcome of a modern looking city.

The Dubai Fever, manifested and virally transmitted in seductive, flashy high-gloss magazines, has reached all African cities, among them Addis Ababa. In reality, though, the city is anything but prepared for a speculative boomtown urbanism, considering that more than 60 percent of Addis Ababa's population live below the poverty line. The copy/paste of architectural strategies brings a myriad of serious problems. Instead of using locally available material, more than 80 percent of construction material in Ethiopia, including steel and glass, is imported, mostly from Eastern Asia. Investment capital, both foreign and domestic, know-how, entrepreneurship, and the possibility of the sustainable growth of local markets, all leave the country without becoming links in a value chain process. In addition, big construction sites are commonly managed by foreign know-how and leadership. The Ethiopians are mostly seen in lower day-laborer ranks. The glass towers symptomatic of Dubai Fever have a big impact on the energy consumption of the city and resultantly on the ecological footprint of the whole country. Instead of taking advantage of, and designing for, the ideal climatic conditions of Ethiopia, which fall between 10 °C minimum and rise to 30 °C maximum, the glass façades necessitate technical cooling systems, using one of the goods Ethiopia doesn't have: energy. Hence, interruptions in the electricity supply are the norm, rather than an exception in Addis Ababa.

The Grand Housing Project

In the interest of a sustainable urban development, Ethiopia needs to develop regulations for, and visions of, how to use its rich culture and its reliable resources. These are, first and foremost, locally available construction materials and know-how, such as natural stone, loam brick technology and rammed earth construction techniques. The population increase of 20 percent in the last decade in Addis Ababa has dramatically illustrated the limitations of the innovative thinking and urban planning thus far. It has neither been able to develop infrastructures and homes for a fast growing population, nor establish a sustainable means of existence for the newcomers to the city. As a 'solution' for this desperate situation, the Low Cost Housing Technology (LCH) was developed with German support. Since its introduction into the local construction sector in 2002, it has achieved visible results. Over 40,000 housing units for approximately 200,000 people have been built. At the same time, almost 40,000 jobs were created in the local construction sector, arranged mostly in the form of small business enterprises. Based on the LCH-principle, the government is trying to promote this kind of development with the recently launched "Addis Ababa Grand Housing Program"—an ambitious project aimed at constructing 50,000 accommodation units per year until 2014. However, the construction technologies used in the program are based on a concrete pillar and slab system. This kind of construction system uses principles developed in the re-construction period of post-war Germany. It's a system requiring enormous amounts of cement, gravel, and hollow concrete blocks—exactly the kind of building materials that are not readily available in Ethiopia.

1

2

3

1: Concrete constructions need formwork, in Ethiopia mostly eucalyptus wood, which promotes deforestation in the country.
2: The Grand Housing Project introduced a so-called "low cost" construction method, based on models from post-war Germany. Concrete became the absolute dominant construction material in Ethiopia, despite the fact that neither material nor know-how is present.
3: Most construction sites use 100% cement products, most of the raw material is imported from India and China.

Measures like the Grand Housing Project must be looked at with a critical eye. This widely praised strategy of generating housing, infrastructures, and jobs for the poorest, all within a single program and construction methodology proves to be an economic pseudo-cycle. When any local economy becomes almost completely dependent on an over-committed construction sector, the question arises: who can afford to build these structures in the future, moving from a government-owned program to a private one? It would be considerably more promising and sustainable to develop diverse economic and construction models, which would allow poverty and infrastructure problems to be dealt with individually and specifically. It is also preferable to apply techniques and knowledge, originating from local traditions, materials, and cultures, instead of adopting those from the global market. The use of prefabricated and imported cement components has been widely implemented in the production of housing in the Grand Housing Project, in order to facilitate building and shorten construction time. However, the construction period of projects has as a rule been longer than it projected. There are multiple reasons for this: shortages of materials, improper use of both material and technology, and unskilled manpower are among the primary setbacks to the timely completion of projects.

The use of eucalyptus trees as both a support for the concrete casting formwork for the pre-cast beams that hold the ribbed slab blocks and scaffolding material, needs to be minimized and alternatives need to be developed. An average of 800 eucalyptus tree logs were used in building each block of the Grand Housing Project. It can easily be argued that this contributes to the deforestation of the nation as a whole. For 60,000 housing units with an average of 30 units per block, 1.6 million eucalyptus trees have been utilized so far. For a country like Ethiopia, which struggles against poverty and unpredictable climate changes, it would be a tragedy to lose its already endangered and decreasing forests. Here, alternative techniques and methods have to be applied in order to achieve a more sustainable kind of construction.

Sustainability requires an integrative approach in various disciplines and is to be applied to the design fields, the building sector, and the urban infrastructure. Ethiopia should reconsider its tendency to copy misleading architectural examples from the United States and cities like Dubai, making it dependent upon imported materials and know-how. There is a need to enhance vernacular construction and material knowledge, both of which could be used to overcome the dramatic need for new urban housing. This knowledge must be based on integrative thinking that combines design, construction, building physics, sociology, energy, ecology, and economy. If new methods for low-cost, sustainable double-story building techniques can be found and introduced in African cities, the density of the current urban settlements could be almost doubled, without wasting land valuable for agricultural use.

Sustainable Urban Dwelling Unit (SUDU)

In the summer months of 2010, the Ethiopian Institute of Architecture, Building Technology and City Development (EiABC), together with the Federal Institute of Technology in Switzerland (ETH), built on its campus a double-story Sustainable Urban Dwelling Unit (SUDU). The dwelling was designed according to current urban conditions and needs in Ethiopia. It is a showcase for inter-disciplinary thinking and an experimental laboratory to convince decision makers, economists, environmentalists, urban planners, and architects to rethink traditional building methods and social space requirements, in order to find new ways to build a city. As the example of Tokyo shows, a megacity can be based on double-story buildings.

For less than 1,000 ETB (60 EUR) per square meter, the EiABC constructed the SUDU project as a collaborative process between researchers and students of the ETH in Zurich and the EiABC, under the sponsorship of Addis Ababa University. Students from different backgrounds, cultures, and disciplines cooperated in planning, designing, and building the project in full scale. They also experienced firsthand the network of skills needed to complete such a project and helped to establish interdisciplinary thinking and action. The project represented a test-run between the organizational structures of the ETH, in the field of sustainability. As a result, two departments, the ETH Sustainability and the ETH North-South Center have developed long-term structures to better handle such projects in the future. The ETH plans to use its connections to EiABC and Ethiopia for further research activities.

The need to reduce global emissions, energy consumption, and material waste requires the systematic development of sustainable buildings on both large and small scales. Materiality, social space, water management, waste management, energy production and consumption, operation, and maintenance have to be designed and coordinated in the most effective and efficient way. With the SUDU project, performance standards have been established that emphasize innovation and integrated design.

Ethiopia, once called the granary of Africa, has a rich soil, containing high levels of clay particles. Almost all excavated material in the city of Addis Ababa is a possible source for the material needed to build new structures. The SUDU project used "rammed earth" technology to construct the first level of the building, with a 60-cm-wide wall structure. Using formwork, designed for multiple uses over consecutive layers, loam soil is loaded into the form and densified with small metal ramrods. Each layer is 120 cm high and when the first layer of the formwork is filled, the form is lifted up und filling and ramming can start again. Openings for doors and windows are simply cut out. Using a specialized technique, a small ring beam was constructed on top of the last layer, to ensure the structural strength needed to support the ceiling.

The first ceiling of the SUDU project was done using a tiled vaulting technique, designed and introduced for the first time in Ethiopia by Prof. Dr. Philippe Block from the ETH Zurich. Dr. Block had previously gathered practical experience in similar techniques during the 2008/09 project for the Mapungubwe Museum in South Africa, together with architects Peter Rich and Henry Fagan, along with John Ochsendorf and Michael Ramage as structural engineers. The technique, also known as Guastavino or Catalan vaulting, had already been introduced at the end of the 19th century in many public buildings in New York, such as the Grand Central Station or City Hall Subway Station. The system was patented as "Tile Arch System" in 1885 by the architect Rafael Guastavino, and it can be used to create robust, self-supporting arches and vaults, using interlocking tiles and layers of mortar to form a thin skin. The tiles are usually set in a herringbone pattern layout, sandwiched with thin layers of Portland cement. Unlike much heavier stone construction, these tile domes, or barrel constructions, can be put in place without additional support. Each tile cantilevers out over empty space during construction, relying only on a quick-drying cement, known as "plaster of paris," produced in Ethiopia, to secure it in place. With this technique, no scaffold is needed to construct the ceiling or dome, and only a string-guide system is used to make sure the form is kept in an ideal structural line.

The second floor of the SUDU project was constructed with loam stone produced in a hydraform press, which has an output of nearly 900 stones per day, operated with local know-how and a local workforce. The stones are self-interlocking; almost no mortar or cement is needed to construct walls. The first layer

4: The Hydro-Form press produces loam stones that interlock and therefore are easy to work with.
5: Taking a pressed loam stone block out of the form.
6: Drying loam stones.

7

8

7: The indigenous materials: cactus and loam soil. After 5 days of fermenting, a slime juice results, which has to be filtered for use.

8: In the front corrugated metal roofs, behind it traditional roofing with cactus juice mortar. Cactus juice mortar is 100 percent waterproof.

of stone is put in a loam mortar bed enriched by 5 percent cement, and all other layers are simply placed on top of each other. This technique also allows for additional structural support, if needed, by hollowing out an internal formwork for small columns, which secures the building against lateral forces, since the area around Addis Ababa is seismically active. Again, no additional formwork is needed and a combined technique of interlocking loam stones and the option for a columnar structural support allows for a heterogeneous construction method, that can be custom-tailored to local and regional requirements making allowances for seismic activity.

The roof construction, too, applied the "Catalan vaulting" technique, similar to the ceiling. As the demands of a roof as an exterior element are different from those of a ceiling, it was covered with a special 10-cm-thick waterproof mortar, made of prickly pear cactus juice, salt, lime, and loam soil. Since 2008, this method has also been implemented by the Ethiopian-born artist, Meskerem Assegued, in a project in the village of Aslam, near the city of Dire Dawa, in Easternmost Ethiopia. She investigated the technique in Mexico and brought it back to Ethiopia, where she found historical evidence that it was used for centuries before it fell in disuse and was then forgotten. Because of this loss of knowledge and technique, the inhabitants of the village could no longer repair their roofs. Over the last decades, the roofs were constructed with corrugated metal sheets, producing nearly unbearable interior conditions caused by the almost direct heat transference from the exterior sun-attracting surface of the roof to the interior spaces. As a result of her project, more and more villagers are replacing their roofs, returning to the old techniques and traditions.

Micro-enterprise and know-how developed fast in Aslam and the SUDU project brought the technique to Addis Ababa. The technique uses prickly pear cactus, which are cut into small pieces and left to soak in a barrel of water for 5 days. After this period, the slimy juice is filtered and mixed with salt, loam and lime, and is then ready for use. The Aslam villagers also use the juice to paint all of the exteriors of their homes, thus sealing them against rain. Also, loam stone production was begun in the area with astonishing results in strength and durability. Some walls and roofs of the SUDU project were plastered with the cactus juice mortar; it is easy to handle and produce and no imported materials are required.

The SUDU project uses only 5 percent of the cement that is needed for a hollow concrete block construction, the most common construction method currently in use in Addis Ababa. Local materials such as loam or natural stone, local workers,

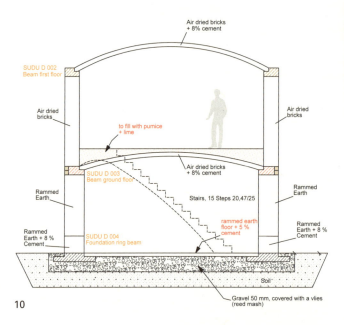

9: Laura Davis on top of a small test vault. Here, already one layer is enough to support the human weight load.
10: SUDU Section.
11: The timbrel vault roof in the making.
12: SUDU Photograph of the construction process with superimposed sections of wall construction details.

Credits SUDU Summer School Project:

EiABC: Herbert Schmitz, Dr. Elias Yitbarek, Tibebu Daniel, Joseph Hennes, Melak Moges, Zegeye Cherenet, Fasil Giorghis, Meskarem Zewdie, Dirk Hebel
AAiT: Getachew Bekele
AAU: Elias Berhanu
SNV: Willem Boers
Department of Architecture ETH Zürich: Dr. Philippe Block, Laura Davis, Dr. Marc Angélil
ETH Sustainability: Dr. Christine Bratrich, Cathrine Lippuner
North-South Centre ETH Zürich: Dr. Barbara Becker, Astrid Smitham, Emma Lindberg
Eawag ETH Zürich: Chris Zurbrügg
Institute for Environmental Decisions ETH Zürich: Dr. Philippe Aerni
Institute for Developing Economics ETH Zürich: Dr. Isabel Günther
and all participating students from ETH and EiABC

and local know-how led to the first case study building in the SUDU project. This can now be used to gather more information, and will hopefully lead soon to an implementation phase, on a larger scale, of the principles and techniques used in the project, and the knowledge gained through their implementation. The project will hopefully push the local industries and small-scale enterprises to rethink the use of construction materials alternative to concrete. Less than 100 years ago, Ethiopia had a tradition of constructing seven-story loam buildings, and it was almost forgotten. New technical infrastructures, in connection with those rediscovered traditional methods, will help to develop sustainable constructions for future generations, in urban as well as rural conditions. EiABC already granted another research project to investigate the possibilities to build a rural counterpart, commencing in 2011.

The SUDU project is a first step towards re-searching, re-applying, and re-inventing vernacular building techniques that fit the Ethiopian context. It is both an empathic response to and the critical transgression of earlier modernist attempts to provide housing models for developing nations, the most prominent of them being Jean Prouvé's *Maison Tropicale*, of which three prototypes were realized between 1949 and 1951 in Niger and in Congo. With this project Prouvé accomplished something extraordinary: the development of a modernist housing prototype, which was able to accommodate the extreme climatic conditions of a tropical context. By virtue of his smart double roof and the elegantly louvered galleries, wrapping the actual living area, the engineer managed to protect the house against direct sun exposure, while allowing the wind to ventilate the spaces naturally. But whereas the project was site-specific in terms of climate, it was thoroughly a-contextual in terms of construction. Its material components were produced in France, and then transported as air cargo to the prototype sites in Niger and Congo. Therefore, the house prototype could never go into serial production in Africa, as all the advanced technologies and materials necessary for its construction were simply not available.

In a tragic sense, Prouvé's *Maison Tropicale* embodies the utter failure of the Western concept of "development aid" which—despite all good intentions—exacerbates the economic dependency of developing nations on 'first world' nations, instead of helping them to sever an umbilical cord that is only vital in the short term, and is fatal in the long run, because it accumulates mountains of debt. With SUDU, we wanted to break with the well-meaning, but ill-fated tradition of giving development aid by way of importing an object, product, or building from a

13: Jean Prouvé, *Maison Tropicale*, Niamey, Niger, 1949. Loading the Houses' construction elements onto an airplane in France.
14: Jean Prouvé, *Maison Tropicale*, Niamey, Niger, 1949. Construction of the foundations.
15: Jean Prouvé, *Maison Tropicale*, Niamey, Niger, 1949. Completed construction.

Western context. With SUDU, we instead want to stimulate the local context and economy to rediscover and re-appreciate its very own building traditions, construction techniques, and locally available materials.

For that reason, we have tried to conceive the project as something that can work as a "prototypology"[2] rather than a "prototype". The modernist notion of prototype is imbued with the belief that there is one ideal model configuration, which could therefore be applied in a serial way in whatever condition. The "prototypology", however, defines a flexible and heterogeneous form of organization, which can be changed and readjusted instantly and serve different contextual conditions. It is a process rather than a product. Ethiopia has the possibility to use such thinking, given the rich and varied local material supply available throughout the country. The Tigray area in the North uses traditional, natural stones and loam mortar, while the southern regions apply bamboo construction techniques on a large scale. All of those materials could be part of the SUDU "proto-typology," and could help to answer one of the most critical questions that Ethiopia will face in the decades to come: How to house 45 million additional people in a sustainable, economical and ecological way, without falling into a complete dependency on the global market?

1.) Official Census of 2008.
2.) I refer to the concept of proto-typology as defined by Andreas Ruby in *The Metapolis Dictionary of Advanced Architecture. City, Technology and Society in the Information Age*. Edited by Susana Cros. Actar: Barcelona 2003. "Just as the prototype anticipates a product yet to be developed, the proto-typology represents a typological configuration in permanent state of evolution. Whereas a conventional typology defines a generic model of organization, which becomes specific through its application, the prototypology is specific from the beginning. On the other hand, it never really becomes generic as it continues to transform itself through the information it receives. As a pliable learning matter it adapts to the changing needs of programs and users. Hence, a prototypology is not a model, but a transient phase of an evolutionary process, and therefore *always ahead of its type*."

About the author: Dirk Hebel is the Scientific Director of the Ethiopian Institute for Architecture, Building Construction and City Development, Addis Ababa, Ethiopia. He has taught and lectured at Princeton University, Syracuse University, the University of Sharjah, and the ETH Zürich. He is principal of DRKH Architecture in Zürich, Switzerland. He previously worked at Diller + Scofidio, where he was the project manager for the BLUR Building, and he was a partner of INSTANT Architects. Their projects included UNITED_BOTTLE, which in 2007 received the Van Alen Institute Fellowship Award, the Red Dot Design Award for Best Conceptual Design and the LANXESS Award Singapore.

future of environmentally-friendly packaging. However, critics argue that corn-based plastics have proven to be biodegradable only in controlled composting facilities and thus are only beneficial if disposed of according to appropriate waste management practices.

Pop-Up Restaurants: Pop-up restaurants, known by various other names, such as secret supper clubs and underground restaurants, are small, privately operated, unlicensed dining establishments run out of people's homes or other non-restaurant locations for paying customers. Said to be based on the family-owned Cuban paladar, pop-up restaurants can include all types of cuisine, atmosphere, and price range, and they range in size from intimate groups to much larger numbers. Secret diners have excited curiosity and interest in an unusual experience as well as the desire for more community, and the opportunity to eat meals with strangers in a stranger's home. Others attribute their popularity to changing economic forces: they offer organizers an additional source of income and participants a unique dining experience as a form of social entertainment.

Portland Cement: Portland cement is the ➝ *matrix material* of concrete that sets when mixed with water. During the setting process, the constituents crystallize and interlock in a way that is still only partly understood. Portland cement is made from limestone that is heated up to 1450° C and then ground. It was developed in Britain and its name is derived from its similarity to Portland stone, a once common building material. In comparison to Roman concrete or ➝ *lime mortar*, Portland cement hardens faster and can take higher compressive stress but is more energy-intensive to produce. (➝ *image 139, p. 240*)

Practical Answers : Practicalanswers.com is a technical information service created and maintained by the charity organization Practical Action, offering free technical construction ➝ *manuals* to people living in poverty. The Practicalanswers.com webpage describes an assortment of small- and intermediate-scale technologies and techniques that can be used to improve the lives of people living in poverty. To share this wealth of technical knowledge and to bring together the knowledge of different people, the site focuses on three main areas: The 'Technical Inquiry Service,' which supplies free technical and developmental information to community-based organizations, NGOs, and development workers, the 'Resource Centers' and the 'Knowledge Nodes,' based within the Practical Actions site, are a collection of appropriate technology and development handbooks, and 'Knowledge Products,' which is a collection of more than 300 how-to manuals, fact sheets, videos, and engineering drawings. Technical briefs, for example, which are downloadable from the website, explain how to build an earthquake-safe shelter in home in disaster areas, how to turn a standard bicycle into a vehicle to transport sick people to a hospital, or how to substitute Portland cement with mixtures that use local materials.

Prefabricated Nature by MYCC: Prefabricated Nature is a prefabricated home built from cement, wood fiber and steel on a seaside hilltop in Cedeira, Spain. Designed by Madrid studio MYCC, the modular home was built in a factory over the course of three months, trucked to the site, and assembled in three days. Prefabricated Nature, measuring 6 m by 3 m, was conceived as a vacation home that would blend in with the surrounding environment of ocean, fields, and farms. The combination of a basic layout with energy-efficient design and technologically enhanced building materials allowed the architects to showcase the potential of modular construction and prefabricated building elements. A prefabricated mixture of cement and wood chips was chosen for lightness and ease of movement but also strength and color integration with the landscape. Corten steel façades on two sides of the home, perforated with images of trees, connect the structure to a local tradition of using the material in boat construction. With its efficient design, use of existing resources, and speed of construction, Prefabricated Nature helps highlight the future possibilities of modular and sustainable architecture and their relationship to the natural environment.

Qanat: A qanat is an old Arab underground water management system. As part of the ➝ *Arab indoor cooling system* it cools air passing through its tunnel system by ➝ *evaporative cooling*. Air drawn by a ➝ *windcatcher* is first led through a qanat to cool down, then through a building's ➝ *shabestan* or a ➝ *yackchal*. Giving off latent heat, air temperatures in qanats can be up to 15 degrees below outside temperature. (➝ *images 135-136, p. 240*)

Quonset Hut: A Quonset hut is a prefabricated, semicircular ➝ *monocoque* structure built from corrugated galvanized steel. The US Navy developed the hut during World War II as an easily transportable building which was flexible enough to be used for various purposes. Quonset huts were manufactured in North Kingstown, Rhode Island, and transported worldwide. Quonset huts were frequently re-purposed after the war, as their durable and simple construction lent itself to civilian purposes as easily as it had military ones. (➝ *drawing 45; image 146, p. 326*)

45: A Quonset hut.

R&D-I-Y: R&D-I-Y (Research and Develop-It-Yourself) is a combination of the concepts of R&D (Research and Development) and D-I-Y (Do-It-Yourself) in which the principles of open source and collaborative innovation are applied to address various issues, particularly in regards to the environment. Popularized by New York artists/designers Britta Riley and Rebecca Bray through the development of their Windowfarms Project, R&D-I-Y takes advantage of web 2.0 technology and online platforms to crowdsource ideas, information, and techniques. The mass collaboration among a decentralized community of thinkers allows for a more rapid and widespread

143: **Round Barn**; An abandoned round barn near Beloit in Rock County, Wisconsin.

144: **Rammed-Earth Tires**; Trash to building material.

145: **Rammed Earth**; House by Roger Boltshauser in Schlins, Austria.

146: **Quonset Hut**; Easily transportable.

147: **Round Barn**; Round barns could be called an architectural fashion.

149: **Reciprocal Frame**; Roof of Ishi Kazuhiro's theatre in Seiwa.

148: **Rammed Earth**; Parts of the great wall in China are made from rammed earth.

150: Rice Hulls: Packed in bags, rice hulls can be used like big bricks.

151: Reciprocal Structures; This structure was built at Kassel University in 2010.

152: Reciprocal Structures; Optimized using a 3D model.

153: Reciprocal Structures; Geometric sketch by Sebastiano Serlio from 1569.

154: Reciprocal Structures: Built structure by Anette Spiro's studio at ETH Zurich.

155: Rammed Earth: Germany's tallest rammed earth building is situated in Weilburg.

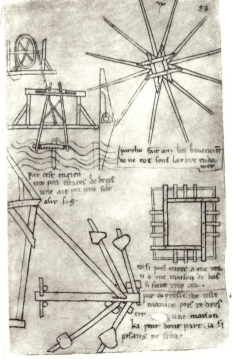
156: Reciprocal Structures: Honnecourt's drawings of reciprocal structures from 1230.

Rammed Earth · Recycled Cities

opportunity for sharing, researching, and testing innovative solutions to environmental problems.
Rammed Earth: Rammed earth is a traditional way of building solid walls using earth, chalk, lime, and gravel. As earth is available on every continent, rammed earth buildings in different variations – made from slightly different mixes – can be found all over the world and in all kinds of climates. Because of their high density and high ➔ *thermal mass*, rammed earth walls are capable of balancing out temperature swings, while their nonsealed surface enables them to store humidity from the indoor air. Basically, rammed earth walls are built by compressing earth within a rigid frame that functions as a formwork. When the formwork is taken off, layers of compressed earth are still visible and give the rammed earth wall its characteristic surface structure. (➔ *drawing 49; images 140-141, p. 240; images 145, 148, p. 326; image 155, p. 327*)

and is loaded by at least one beam) needs to be applied locally to every unit, regardless of its form and size. As the curvature of the structure depends on the dimensions of a single element and its relation to the others, a variation of one beam results in a recursive adaptation of the global structure. Controlling irregular structures has therefore proven to be very difficult. Several research projects working on different topics to revitalize the specific potential of these structures are currently underway, among them one at ETH Zurich, which is developing a digital design tool to generate complex geometries with reciprocal frames.(➔ *drawings 47, 48; image 149, p. 326; images 151-154, 156, p. 327*)

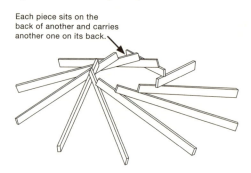

47: A simple reciprocal structure.

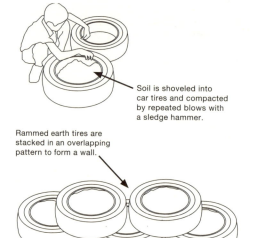

46: Rammed earth tires are easy to make.

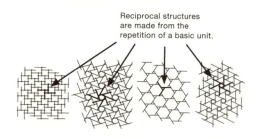

48: Different layouts of reciprocal structures.

Rammed Earth Tires: Rammed earth tires are a construction material made from used tires. Rammed earth tires are common in DIY construction projects because of their ease of use and the abundance of inexpensive used tires. Rammed earth tire construction involves filling tires with a range of organic materials, similar to those used in ➔ *adobe*, ➔ *cob* or classic ➔ *rammed earth* construction. The tires can then be stacked, and optionally, covered with an additional material, such as adobe. The resultant structures have high ➔ *thermal mass* and are waterproof and durable. Rammed earth tires are integral to DIY kit houses, like the ➔ *Earthship*.(➔ *drawing 46; image 144, p. 326*)
Reciprocal Structures: The structural principle of mutually supporting beams in a closed circuit, the reciprocal frame, has been used in countless ➔ *vernacular* buildings and studies of architects in the form of two- and three-dimensional grillages. The principle (one beam is supported by two other beams

Recycled Buildings: Buildings are commonly built for a specific range of programs and uses. However, the demand for these programs and uses can wax and wane over time due to cultural, economic, political or other changes. These changes can in turn change the use of a building or lead to a building being rendered obsolete and subsequently completely abandoned or demolished. When a building can be repurposed, it is recycled on the scale of the entire building. This recycling can result in a use that is radically different to the building's original use, like EM2N's ➔ *Toni Areal* in Zurich, or in use which changes and develops slowly over time like the Porta Nigra in Trier, Germany. (➔ *image 137, p. 240*)
Recycled Cities: Recycling can happen on the scale of the urban environment. Although the process of change and evolution over time is inherent in any

urban form, cities are occasionally abandoned and then rediscovered and reused, or, in the case of the ➤ *Diocletian Palace* complex in Split, Croatia, cities can be built within structures not intended for urban environments, but suitable for rebirth as entire new cities. ➤ *Recycled buildings* are also common, as is the recycling of the components of buildings, known as ➤ *spolia* and ➤ *wa pan.*

Rice Hulls: Rice hulls have recently been discovered as a building material with good insulating properties. As industrial agriculture's second biggest crop and an important staple food crop worldwide, rice is grown in huge quantities. Rice is processed by milling, in two parts, to remove the chaff, and then to remove the husk and germ if white rice is desired. These discarded parts of rice, which are of no or only of marginal nutritional value, are typically a waste product. However, when compressed and packed tightly into bags or casings, they can be used as a building material with an insulation value of R 3-4. Compressed into blocks with a binder they can be made into bricks like the ➤ *Stak Blok*. The nonprofit organization Recycled Rice is currently researching the use of rice hulls in contemporary building applications, and freely disseminates information about methods and techniques of utilizing rice hulls as a building material. (➤ *image 150, p. 327*)

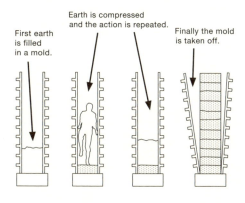

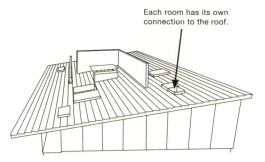

50: An inhabitable roof by Tezuka Architects.

Roof House: The Roof House by Tezuka Architects located in Hatano-shi, Kanagawa, Japan, offers many central living functions on the roof, which is completely accessible. The roof adds 97 m² of living space to the interior space of the house. It is used as a living room, dining room and family space, and it also features an outdoor shower. The house is in a semi-urban context, and all of these uses are fully visible to neighbors. The family had wanted to maximize their potential for outdoor living, and the architects complied with this by creating a house that reconfigures the outdoor space and roof to be the central organizing principle for the rest of the design and heart of the home. (➤ *drawing 50; image 163, p. 332*)

49: Rammed earth walls can be built without machinery.

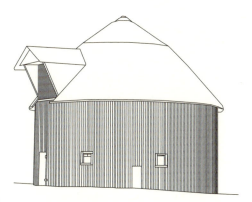

51: Round barns can still be found in the U.S.

Rondavel: A rondavel is a ➤ *vernacular architecture* type from South Africa, Swaziland, and Botswana, among other southern African countries. It is a circular form with an interesting and unique thatched roof. No internal struts are required to support the roof. Wooden poles run radially out from the apex of the roof to the top of the building wall. These poles are supported and reinforced with poles arranged in circular bands, resting on the radial poles. The radial poles support the bands, and the bands support the poles. The poles do not sag because of the bands, which are subject to compression, and the poles do not splay at the bottom because of tension, supplied again by the effect of the bands on the poles. Resembling a ➤ *reciprocal structure*, no additional bracing is needed inside the roof. (➤ *image 160, p. 332*)

Round Barns: Round or octagonal in shape, the round barn was popular in the USA from 1880-1920. Round barns were seen as more efficient than other rectangular barn forms common at the time. The round shape had a greater volume to surface ratio in comparison to a rectangular barn, and therefore less material was needed to construct a round barn. The roof of a round barn was also less materially intensive, and was perceived to be more structurally sound in areas with high wind conditions and tornados. The round shape also al-

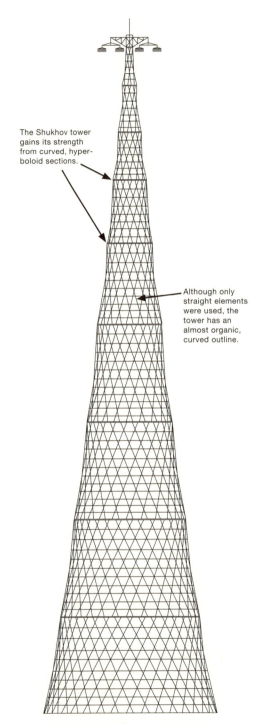

The Shukhov tower gains its strength from curved, hyperboloid sections.

Although only straight elements were used, the tower has an almost organic, curved outline.

52: Diagram showing the basic structure of a Shukhov tower.

lowed farmers to work in an efficient way, encouraging them to make "rounds" of the barn to tend to livestock or other farm tasks, instead of pursuing inefficient work patterns created by a rectangular shaped barn. (→ *drawing 51; images 143, 147, p. 326*)

Rubblization: Rubblization is an onsite building material recycling method which reduces existing concrete to rubble that can be reused for construction at the same location. Concrete rubble can be used as an aggregate material for new concrete or as a high-quality base for pavements. Rubblization saves time, lowers costs and the energy consumption associated with transportation and disposal, and it reduces the amount of mined gravel or other aggregate materials needed. In road construction applications of rubblization, roads and highways can be repaved using specialized equipment that breaks up the existing road, crushes it into smaller pieces and then spreads it as a base for a new pavement. Rubblization can produce pieces of any size depending on the intended end use. Rubblization is a common technique for the refurbishing of airport runways since very smooth surfaces can be achieved.

Rural Studio: Rural Studio is an undergraduate architecture studio at Auburn University, founded by architects Samuel Mockbee and D. K. Ruth. Rural Studio is a design-build based practice and aims to teach students about the possibility of social support and change offered by the profession of architecture through the hands-on design and construction of projects. Rural Studio provides safe, well-constructed and inspirational homes and public buildings for poor communities in rural Western Alabama. Many of Rural Studio's best-known projects are in the tiny community of Mason's Bend, on the banks of the Black Warrior River in Alabama. Since 1993, the program has built an average of five projects a year – typically a house by the second-year students, three larger thesis projects by groups of three to five fifth-year students, and one or more outreach studio-community projects. The projects are funded locally by community groups, and through private donations and grants to Rural Studio. Rural Studio also tries to work with innovative and sustainable materials and techniques and is one of the early adopters of → *papercrete*, a paper-based material for construction.

Sand to Stone: This is a theoretical project by Magnus Larsson in which a wall aims to slow down and prevent desertification. The project stretches across the African continent and is built from solidified sand dunes. Larsson is working on the use of calcite-secreting bacteria to form sandstone from sand. In the Sand to Stone project, the sand that exists in the regions across which the wall will stand will harden into sand dunes, preventing desertification physically as well as providing microclimates to promote the growth of vegetation.

Santorini: The island of Santorini in the Mediterranean is famous for its signature white architecture. This picturesque → *vernacular* architecture is highly tuned to the hot and dry climate on the island. The buildings are white, and by the → *albedo effect* reflect solar gain back into the atmosphere instead of absorbing it. The buildings are also built to have a high → *thermal mass* and most have significant outdoor patio spaces for regular use. (→ *drawing 53; image 170, p. 333*)

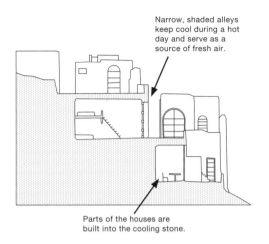

Narrow, shaded alleys keep cool during a hot day and serve as a source of fresh air.

Parts of the houses are built into the cooling stone.

53: Section of a typical Santorini house.

Schlangenbader Strasse Apartments: This complex of 1024 residential units is the largest connected housing complex in Europe, and spans the A104 highway. The complex and highway were planned and built from 1970 to 1980 to combat housing shortages in what was then East Berlin. The construction of the building over the highway alleviates some of the problems of noise and pollution usually associated with an urban highway. The complex is 14 stories above ground level, while the highway sits below the grade of the surrounding streets, allowing through city traffic to remain undisturbed along this 600 m section of the A104 highway. This project is the precursor to projects like the → *Big Dig*, which sink existing highways below street level grade to minimize the disjunction of urban areas by highways and arterial roads. (→ *images 157-158, p. 332*)

Schloss Augustusburg: Schloss Augustusburg, located in Brühl, Germany, has a unique pattern of utilization designed for separate and distinct use by season. The areas of the Schloss designed for wintertime use are located on the upper level, while the areas for summertime use are located on the bottom level. The winter quarters take advantage of passive heating by → *convection*, while the summer quarters benefit from generous windows, → *passive cooling* and → *passive ventilation*. Unique to the Schloss is the added element of room colors by color theory: the winter quarters are painted in warm reds, yellows, and oranges, while the summer quarters are painted in cooler bluish hues. The physiological and psychological effect of these colors on the perception of warm and cool spaces further enhances the comfort provided by the seasonally sensible physical arrangement of the spaces of Schloss Augustusburg. (→ *image 161, p. 332*)

Serious Materials: Serious Materials is a for-profit company that develops and manufactures products and provides services to reduce energy usage in the built environment. The company aims to redesign various aspects of building and construction and reengineer specific architectural elements responsible for considerable carbon emissions. Energy-saving windows help avoid high energy bills spent on heating and cooling, and green drywall production minimizes usage of standard drywall responsible for billions of pounds of CO_2. Through many residential and commercial products, including the installation of energy-saving windows in the Empire State Building, Serious Materials aims to prevent one billion tons of greenhouse gas emissions per year.

Shabestan: The Shabestan is an underground room that can be found in traditional houses, mosques, and schools in hot parts of Arab countries. It is usually the coolest room as cool air from the underground → *qanat* passes through this room first. The Shabestan is used, for example, for prayer meetings or gatherings during hot seasons. (→ *image 168, p. 333*)

Shell-Like Composite Materials: Metallic-intermetallic laminates are → *composite materials*, which, through → *bionic engineering* principles, borrow the strength and structural advantages of seashells. These materials are the research focus of Kenneth Vecchio, aerospace engineer at the University of California, Davis, and have been developed as alternatives to aerospace materials. They are constructed from metals and metal alloys which are then treated and composed in a way that mimics shells, such as that of the red abalone. This is done by copying the extremely thin layers of the shell in titanium and steel. The materials are strong, even in thin sections, difficult to crack, pierce or otherwise penetrate, and they conduct heat. Super-thin layered materials are an important field of exploration for other laboratories and projects as they hold much promise for diverse applications.

Shigeru Ban Building Workshop: The Shigeru Ban Building Workshop was established specifically to work on the planning of the Centre Pompidou Metz. The pavilion that housed the workshop was a temporary structure installed on the roof of the Centre Pompidou Paris. It was built with paper tubes, a building material that Shigeru Ban has experimented with extensively in his architectural projects, most notably in his disaster relief shelters. The Shigeru Ban Building Workshop structure was 34 m long and cylindrical in form, with a diameter of approximately 5 m. The outer shell consisted of a polytetrafluoroethylene membrane, a high-performance material also used in Kengo Kuma's → *Tea House*. The structure was built with a team of students, who also assisted in the planning process for the Centre Pompidou Metz. (→ *image 162, p. 332*)

Shukhov Tower: The Shukhov Tower is a 160 m-high radio tower, designed by Vladimir Shukhov and built between 1920 and 1922 in Moscow. It was built as a → *hyperboloid structure* and is based on Shukhov's long-term exploration into building with these double-curved forms. The structure is ideal for certain uses, and the Shukhov tower benefits from the lattice structure of the hyperboloid because of the lessened wind load on the non-solid surface. (→ *drawing 52; image 159, p. 332*)

157: **Schlangenbader Strasse Housing**; Housing on top of a highway.

158: **Schlangenbader Strasse Housing**; One of the largest housing structures in Europe.

159: **Shukov Tower**; One of the two electricity pylons on the Oka river in Russia collapsed in 2005.

160: **Rondavel**; The combination of a stone house and a smart and simple roof.

161: **Schloss Augustusburg**; The walls of the summer apartment are clad in ceramic tiles in cool colors.

162: **Shigeru Ban Building Workshop**

163: **Roof House**; Maximized outdoor living – the sloping roof functions as extended living room.

164: **Sod and Turf Houses**; The predecessor of contemporary passive houses: high insulation, low maintenance.

165: **Soil Lamp**; Soil lamps power LEDs with current generated from water and minerals.

166: **Social Housing in Mulhouse**; The luxury of a generous, sunlit room between inside and outside is part of every flat.

167: **Solar Tracking Skylight**

168: **Shabestan**; The place to be during the Arab summer.

169: **Social Housing in Mulhouse**; Greenhouse ethstetics.

170: **Santorini**; Verncaular passive solar architecture.

Skyways: Skyways, or elevated walkways that connect buildings, are an alternate means of circulation in urban environments. Predominantly for pedestrian foot traffic only, skyway systems have been built in numerous cities. The largest and most comprehensive skyway project is Calgary's +15 project, currently approximately 16 km of skyways in downtown Calgary. The Minneapolis Skyway System is the longest continuous skyway, approximately 13 km of connected passages. Skyways have the advantage of providing protection against climatic conditions and offering pedestrians an alternative means of circulation. Peter and Allison Smithson have developed a plan for a comprehensive skyway network for Berlin.

Smart Grid: A smart grid is a network of power transmission lines for consumer energy delivery, controlled and monitored digitally. The smart grid allows for two-way communication between consumers of energy and suppliers. Current local grids only allow for one-way communication, from the supplier to the consumer. By establishing two-way digital smart grids, it is possible to adjust energy delivery in relationship to peak use, energy availability, and different sources of energy generation. A smart grid can accept inputs from renewable energy sources, challenging current grids due to variable energy generation. Wind turbines, for example, only deliver energy to the grid when there is sufficient wind to operate the turbines. Smart grids also allow distributed energy sources to be integrated into the larger grid system. The US Department of Energy estimates that, if a smart grid were to replace the current power grid, the energy savings would be equivalent to the elimination of the emissions of 53 million cars.

is a duplex so that all units benefit from a diversity of spatial qualities. Lacaton + Vassal designed the houses to improve on the usual quality standard of social housing projects at the same expense. (→ *images 166, 169, p. 333*)

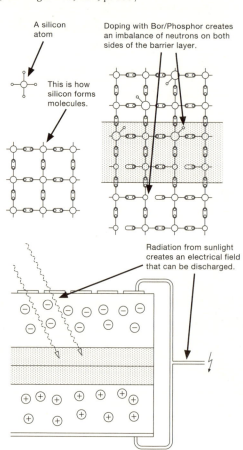

55: Physical operating mode of a solar cell.

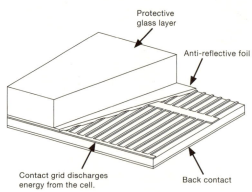

54: The build of a solar cell.

Social Housing in Mulhouse: This project by French architecture firm Lacaton + Vassal is part of a larger social housing complex in Mulhouse, France. Lacaton and Vassal's contribution to the estate of 61 dwellings was a complex of 14 single-family houses. A post-and-beam structure supports horticultural greenhouses at a height of 3 m. Framed with galvanized steel, the walls are made with inset panels of transparent polycarbonate. The → *greenhouses* are partially heated, and partially function as conservatories. Each unit

Sod and Turf Houses: Houses made from sod or turf have been common throughout history in a variety of geographic locations. The houses are constructed from ground that is made firm by organic matter and sometimes compaction, and is commonly cut into bricks, blocks or sheets and used as both a structural material and an insulation material. Though the harvesting of sod and turf is today recognized as environmentally detrimental, the previous building techniques and applications of this organic material are valuable links to a pre-industrial construction past. (→ *image 164, p. 333*)

Soil Lamp: Projects like the Soil Lamp, designed and produced by Dutch designer Marieke Strap, are proof positive that reactive materials present in some soils are capable of generating electrical currents.

Microbial fuel cells utilize metals like zinc and copper in combination with water. The metals are reactive when exposed to water, which generates a small electrical charge. This creates essentially a battery made of earth, almost indefinitely rechargeable with water. (→ *image 165, p. 333*)

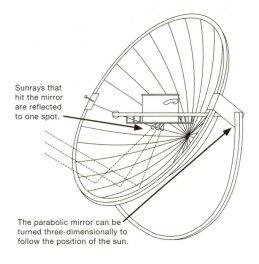

56: A Solar Cooker.

Soil Map: A soil map is the visualization of soil type in a geographically defined area. Soil is classified most commonly by soil morphology, and at the most basic level soils can all be identified according to relative sand, silt, and clay content. Some soil maps also record other soil properties specific to particular uses. Geoscientists, environmental scientists, designers, and landscape architects commonly use soil maps for research and design purposes. Soil maps are useful for agricultural, developmental, economic, and environmental purposes. They provide base-line information important for diverse uses, including agricultural properties, suitability for building and construction, and flood forecasting. Digitized soil maps can be input into → *geographic information systems (GIS)* and combined and manipulated with other data for research and analysis purposes and output into data visualizations in the form of maps.

Solar Cells: Solar cells are devices that utilize the photovoltaic effect to convert energy from sunlight into electricity. When sunlight hits the solar cell, photons are absorbed by semiconductor materials such as silicon. Negatively charged electrons are then jolted loose from their atoms to flow through the material and produce solar energy in the form of electricity. A large grouping of these solar cells can be used to make up solar panels and photovoltaic arrays that can then generate a usable amount of this direct current (DC) electricity for practical use. The current research on solar cells broadly aims to lower costs of solar cells, develop new technologies for solar cells, and develop new materials. Recent technological advances have shown that solar cells can be printed on plastic by standard inkjet printers to produce printable solar panel films. (→ *drawings 54, 55*)

Solar Cooker: A solar cooker is a device that uses simple → *heat transfer* through radiation from the sun to cook food. Most solar cookers use a system of mirrors to concentrate light and heat and make it viable for the temperatures required to cook food. In most cookers, this heat is trapped within the cooker. Solar cookers require no fuel, and are therefore an excellent option in areas with limited resources, or in situations where resource efficiency is necessary or desirable. (→ *drawing 56; image 182, p. 337*)

Solar Ponds: A solar pond is a pool of salt water that can be used as a collector and storage for solar thermal energy. Solar ponds function based on a model of different layers of water that increase in salinity and density towards the base of the pond. Normally, a pond will lose heat energy quickly because warm water rises to the surface, cools, and falls down again in a circular stream that accelerates the process of cooling. In a solar pond of salty water, rays of solar energy warm the water at the bottom of the pond. However, this water maintains high density due to its salinity and therefore does not rise and lose heat. A stable leveling of water temperatures is created, with water at the base that can rise to over 90°C. Colder water on the surface can reach 30°C, which becomes stable in relation to the surrounding air and therefore functions as an insulation layer. The heat trapped at the bottom can be used to heat buildings or water as well as power a turbine or engine. (→ *drawing 57; image 172, p. 336*)

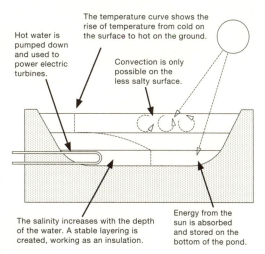

57: A solar pond provides solar thermal energy storage.

Solar Thermal Updraft Tower: The solar updraft tower is a proposed type of renewable energy power plant. Air, heated by the sun, is contained in a large greenhouse-like structure. A large chimney is set into this structure, and → *thermal updraft* causes the air to rise up into the chimney. This air movement pro-

171: **Solar Thermal Updraft Tower**; This tower in Manzanares, Spain is currently in use.

172: **Solar Pond**; This solar pond in El Paso powers part of a food production company.

173: **Stepwells**; Water source and gathering space in india.

174: **Station Z**; The membrane façade is held in place with a vacuum seal.

175: **Spolia**; The Portal of the Basilica dei Santi Giovanni in Venice has Byzantine columns in Greek marble taken from Torcello.

176: **South Asian Human Rights Headquarter**: A brick wall protects the offices from sun and sound.

177: **Stack-Up Factory**; An industrial park on three levels in Singapore.

178: **Stack-Up Factory**; Ramps turn every level in a ground-floor condition.

179: **Straddling bus**; New technology in China.

180: **Structural Brick by Eladio Dieste**; Double-curved roof of the Silo CADYL Horizontal in Montevideo from 1978.

181: **Stockholm Central Station**; Body heat is a renewable and free energy source.

182: **Solar Cooker**; A method of cooking in places without firewood but lots of sun.

183: **Stone Arch**; Renzo Piano is pushing the limits of size.

pels turbines that produce electricity. This new proposal uses the ➔ *greenhouse effect* and wind turbines in a wholly new combination, and the feasibility of the solar updraft tower is currently being researched. (➔ *drawing 58; image 171, p. 336*)

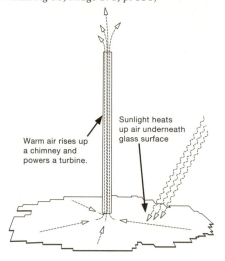

58: A solar thermal updraft tower generates electricity with a turbine.

Solar Tracking Skylight: A solar tracking skylight is a skylight that uses a solar tracking system to follow the sun in order to achieve maximum solar collection. Commonly used with a mirror system to concentrate light into a beam into interior environments, the solar tracking skylight is important in the concept of ➔ *active daylighting*. The solar tracking skylight follows the exact position of the sun throughout the daily and yearly cycles, enabling it to actively collect solar rays. Unlike ➔ *solar cells* the skylight is used exclusively for indoor lighting and not for energy generation. (➔ *image 167, p. 333*)
South Asia Human Rights Documentation Centre: The South Asia Human Rights Documentation Centre, located in New Delhi, was designed by Anagram Architects. The building is built from ➔ *brick* with a sculptural brick sun shutter and façade, or claustra, to shield the building from direct sunlight, while also allowing sunlight through. The claustra also helps to reduce the street noise from the outside, even while the windows of the building are open. (➔ *drawing 59; image 176, p. 336*)
Spolia: Spolia is the reuse of architectural elements or material from old buildings in the construction of new buildings. This practice is common throughout history; as ideologies shifted, raw materials waxed and waned in abundance, and buildings cycled in and out of use. The Roman Arch of Constantine is an example of spolia as the carved relief elements of the arch date from multiple periods in Roman history. Spolia is related to ➔ *wa pan* construction practices in China, as well as being a reuse – differing only in scale – to that of ➔ *recycled cities* or ➔ *recycled buildings*. As spolia involves a certain amount of symbolic content, it is interesting to think of contemporary spolia and what symbolic content, expressive of which ideology, could be reused in the future. (➔ *image 175, p. 336*)
Stack-Up Factories: Stack-up factories are a typology, common in Singapore, which mixes industrial or commercial use with infrastructure. Because Singapore has a limited amount of space for buildings, the stack-up factory developed as a natural response to the inability of commercial or industrial enterprises to have large enough footprints, and as a solution to the problem of increasing demand for space in general. The construction is simple, as the stack-up factory is literally stacked "factory" boxes, one on top of another, connected by ramps suitable for standard 13.7 m container trucks and other vehicles. This model can be used for a range of programs, and levels of stack-up factory spaces have been used as hotels, mills, and other programs. The stack-up factory is an example of vertical densification used for programs that usually boast a sprawling footprint. (➔ *images 177-178, p. 337*)

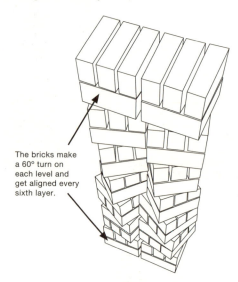

59: Scheme of the translucent façade in New Delhi.

STAK BLOK: The Stak Blok is a construction component made from ➔ *rice hulls* and -straw waste, which is produced in large amounts around the world and usually burned as rubbish. The Stak Blok is an initial attempt to market a prefabricated structural element made from rice straw bio-waste. Stak Bloks are easy to assemble into structures; they are lightweight, have good insulation properties, are seismically strong and are capable of binding carbon. Also, only a small amount of energy is needed in the Stak Blok production process, adding to its appeal as a resource-efficient structural and insulation material. Oryzatech, founded by a group of engineers, is the first company to introduce this building material into the mainstream building material market.
Station Z: The Station Z Memorial by Werner

Sobeck and HG Merz is a large structure located at the Sachsenhausen concentration camp. The structure is partially secured with a vacuum-sealed façade. Station Z is made with steel lattice girders in rectangular box sections, clad with grating and perforated steel sheets. The structure is then wrapped in a glass fiber/PTFE fabric, which is then vacuum-sealed. The Station Z Memorial appears as a semi-translucent box, with a completely homogeneous surface. The structure is 4.1 m high, and is 38 m x 40 m wide and long. The non-articulated, non-ornamented appearance was chosen because of the structure's context at the Sachsenhausen concentration camp, and the structure itself was necessary as a waterproof covering to protect the remains of the crematorium. Because Station Z involves the use of →*air as a construction material*, it can be disassembled completely and easily. (→*image 174, p. 336*)

the station. This heat is drawn from the air and used to heat water by means of a simple →*heat pump*, which in turn helps to heat an adjacent office building. This procedure reduces the heating costs and energy consumption for the office building by an estimated 20% using heat that would otherwise be wasted. This recycling cycle is similar to that proposed by BIG's HySociety project. (→*image 181, p. 337*)

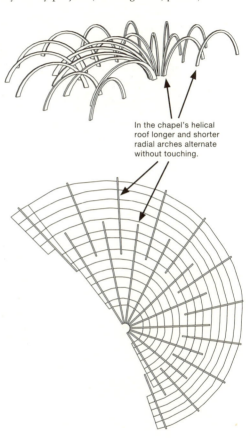

In the chapel's helical roof longer and shorter radial arches alternate without touching.

At a high water level most of the stepwell is underwater.

Low levels are reachable by the help of the stairs.

60: Section of an exemplary stepwell.

61: Structural isometry and plan of Renzo Piano's chapel.

Stepwell: A stepwell is a kind of well for water that is commonly found in India. Generally of a large size, the well works as both a catchment basin for rainfall and access to groundwater. A unique construction allows the water to be reached irrespective of its level in the well. Sequential and continuous steps lead to the bottom of the well, which narrows with each level down, like an inverse stepped pyramid. Although of a utilitarian nature, there are esthetically sensitive stepwells, and most of them also serve as public gathering places because of their comfortable temperatures, as sustained by →*evaporative cooling*. The ability of the stepwell to store a large and fluctuating amount of water is especially important in areas that have to cope with significant differences in water availability, as caused by monsoons or similar climatic events. The fluctuating water level is also well-served by the step system, allowing people, and in some wells livestock, to access the water in any seasonal or climatic condition. (→*drawing 60; image 173, p. 336*)

Stockholm Central Station: This train station, used by thousands of commuters every day, generates excess heat from the passage of many bodies through

Stone Arch: A stone arch is a structure that spans a space while supporting weight, for example, that of a roof. Because all elements of a stone arch hold each other, the building process is a complex one and different solutions have been found over the centuries. Theoretically, stone arches do not need any binder as all parts are under compressive stress that presses them against each other. Gigantic stone arches with a span of 45 m have recently been realized by Renzo Piano in his Padre Pio Pilgrimage Church in Italy. To make sure that each stone stays in place and can conduct the load to the next perfectly, the elements were tied together with internal steel cables. (→*drawing 61; image 183, p. 337*)

Straddling Bus: The straddling bus is a bus deve-

184: **Super Adobe**: This adobe building technique complies with California's earthquake code.

186: **Tensile Structures**: The Munich Olympia Stadium's roof is a huge tent-like structure from the 1970s designed by Frei Otto and Behnisch & Partner.

185: **Tensile Structures**: The first tensile structure erected by Vladimir Shukov in 1895.

188: **Sunflower Umbrella**: At night an outdoor air conditioning system is powered by the solar energy the umbrellas collected during the day.

187: **Superuse**: A platform for unconventional recycling methods.

loped by Huashi Future Parking Equipment in Shenzhen, China. The bus is designed to carry up to 1,200 passengers and straddle two lanes of existing roadway. This allows traffic to flow unimpeded below the straddling bus, and avoids the construction costs associated with building dedicated roadway or railway for similarly sized people-moving options. It is hoped that the use of the bus along fixed commuter routes will decrease traffic, pollution, and other private-automobile-related shortcomings, while minimizing the costs and energy consumption typical of normal buses. The straddling bus is capable of operating on a mixed solar and gasoline power source. (➔ *image 179, p. 337*)

Structural Brick by Eladio Dieste: Eladio Dieste was a Uruguayan engineer and architect famous for both architecture of elegance and beauty and advanced engineering principles. He was the inventor of a vault made from a single layer of ➔ *brick*, constructed as a doubly curved ➔ *thin-shell structure*. Dieste also used brick in unusually expressive geometries, creating fanciful, yet practical and relatively economical architecture. (➔ *image 180, p. 337*)

released by a series of low umbrellas into the air of the plaza, creating a network of lightly air-conditioned spaces. This method of cooling, called "soft conditioning," is not new, yet the application of the umbrella as a shade structure to minimize cooling load and as a renewable power source for the mechanical needs of the cooling system transforms the unsustainable luxury of outdoor air-conditioning into a positive and environmentally friendly form of comfortable climate control. (➔ *drawing 62; image 188, p. 340*)

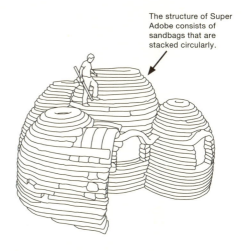

63: Super Adobe building under construction before coverage with clay.

Super Adobe: Super Adobe is an ➔ *adobe* building technique using materials more reminiscent of military operations than building construction. It was first introduced by Nadir Khalili, and the California Institute of Earth Art and Architecture. It utilizes sandbags and barbed wire as structural reinforcement in contrast with traditional un-reinforced adobe techniques. Barbed wire is used as a tensile element. Super Adobe construction can achieve single and double curvatures, arches, and round forms otherwise structurally impossible with traditional adobe. (➔ *drawing 63; image 184, p. 340*)

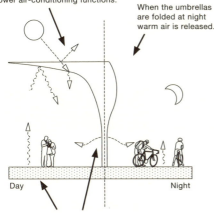

62: Diagram illustrating the working principle of LAVA's sunflower umbrellas by day and night

Sunflower Umbrella: The Sunflower Umbrella project, located in Masdar City, Abu Dhabi, designed by LAVA architects and Transsolar, is an innovative form of climate control for a large public open space, in this application a plaza in a very hot climate. Large devices that have an opening and closing function similar to that of an umbrella or parasol shade the large open space. In addition, when open, the umbrellas use photovoltaic panels to collect energy from the sun to power the chilling of underground water pipes. The water pipes in turn cool air, which is then

Superuse.org: Superuse.org is a website that acts as a collection box for projects and knowledge that relate to recycling and reusing materials. It is an open online forum where any user can submit projects of their own that reuse or recycle. Though Superuse is edited and each project is screened for suitability for inclusion on the website, the content of the website is linked to a crowdsourced and transparent process whereby website visitors can choose to "like" certain objects publicly, raising them by a process of accumulated voting to top positions on the site. (➔ *drawing 64; image 187, p. 340*)

Teahouse: The Teahouse is an inflatable structure by architect Kengo Kuma, located in the gardens of the Frankfurt Museum of Art. It is meant to be used for traditional Japanese tea ceremonies, among other events, but is made from a special translucent high-tech fabric, Gore Tenara, a departure from the traditional teahouse materials of wood, bamboo, and rice paper. The structure consists of two membrane shells, inflated by a pump, and measures a mere 20 m² of interior space. The Gore Tenara fabric is made from polytetrafluorethylene (PTF), which is non-combustible, lightfast, and incredibly strong yet flexible. (→ *image 191, p. 344*)

64: Example of an unconventional idea that can be found on superuse.org.

TED: TED is an organization backed by the Sapling Foundation that arranges conferences that promote "ideas worth spreading" in addition to providing funding and support structures for inventors and innovators. The annual TED conference has been held since 1990, and since 2006 all of the speakers and some related events have been available as streaming video from ted.com. Though TED began in Silicon Valley and has a bias toward technology, the TED platform has been host to ideas from a wide range of disciplines. Kickstarter was introduced to a broad public via the TED platform, as well as the Sand to Stone project.

Tensairity: Tensairity is a structural principle that uses tension-loaded elements, such as steel cables, to augment the structural capabilities of air-filled, compression-loaded structures. This combination of tension- and compression-loaded elements into a single structure allows lighter-weight pneumatics because the steel cables make it possible to construct thinner membranes. Principles of tensairity were used in Werner Sobeck's project at Sachsenhausen to build a large, easily constructed and recyclable structure. (→ *drawing 66; image 190, p. 344*)

Tensegrity: Tensegrity is a term that stands for tensional integrity structuring. A structure built with tensegrity uses a balanced and finely tuned mixture of tension and compression. Elements of a tensegrity structure, composed of cables as tension elements, and rods as compression elements, are used in states of pure compression or pure tension, in combination, which means that the structure can only fail if the cables yield or the rods buckle. Structures must have mechanical stability to allow each member to remain in consistent tension or compression as stress on the structure increases. The placement of the compression and tension elements is such that the tensional forces, which naturally transmit themselves over the shortest distance between two points, span rods in symmetric arrangement and create the compression needed for the structure to function in a balance between tension and compression. The term 'tensegrity' was coined by Buckminster Fuller, and came out of his research and projects like the → *Dymaxion House*, which featured the use of tensioned elements as building blocks of architecture. (→ *drawing 65; image 189, p. 344*)

65: Tensegrity structures can be very light.

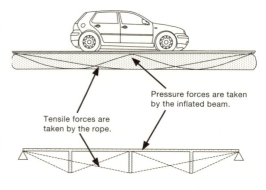

66: Static principle of a tensairity bridge.

Tensile Structures: Tensile structures are built in a way in which structural elements are only subject to tensile force. Simple tensile structures are things like tents. Tensile structures are appealing because of their ease of fabrication, ability to bear loads over long spans and because of their lightweight properties. Tensile structure-based roofing systems are common in structures like sports stadiums, where a large space needs spanning with a minimum of internal columns or supports. Tensile structures rely on strong anchor points to keep them aloft in a stable manner. (→ *drawing 68; images 185-186, p. 340; image 199, p. 345*)

is often restricted by the extreme tractive forces that occur in larger-scale tent structures, but they are a subject of ongoing architectural interest in both tent materials and sophisticated construction methods. (→ *image 196-197, 201, p. 345*)

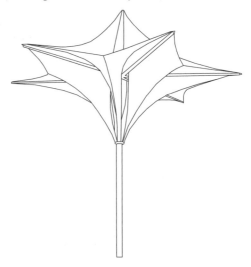

68: Tensile umbrella design by Frei Otto.

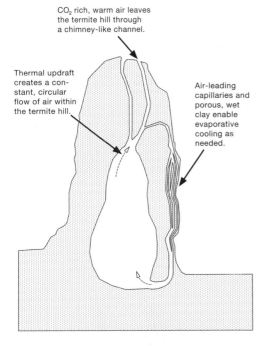

67: Termites use a combination of multiple physical principles to ventilate and air-condition their mounds.

Tent: A tent is a shelter made from fabric in combination with a structural element mostly made from wood or steel. The fabric is suspended or stretched over the structural elements. Most tents can be assembled and reassembled quickly, and are lightweight and therefore easy to transport. → *Vernacular* tent types and forms have been adapted and developed over centuries according to the different climatic circumstances of their area of application and varying programmatic requirements. The yurt is used in colder regions of Asia and is transported only rarely. The American tipi is an example an ultra-portable tent for dwelling, which is light enough to be carried by horses or other livestock. Today, tents are often dome-shaped and made from synthetic fabrics and materials. Larger tent-like structures in architecture use high-tech membranes and structures. Their strength and size

Termite Mounds: Termite mounds, also known as termitaria, occur when a termite nest extends above ground into an elaborate structure that can reach up to 9 m high. Mounds are constructed from a mix of clay and cellulose which, in combination with their spittle and feces, can achieve the strength of sandstone. The termite hill houses the chamber of the queen in the very center, surrounded by chambers for her eggs and sometimes even fungal gardens where termites cultivate mushrooms, their main nutrition. The main task of the termite hill is to create a proper climate. The immense number of creatures living in a termite hill produce a lot of CO_2 that must be drawn out with their ventilation system. In areas like the Australian or African desert, it is also particularly crucial to keep temperature swings to a minimum and provide the right climate for egg production and mushroom growth. To control the temperature and carbon dioxide/oxygen balance, termites use several passive solar and passive ventilation techniques. Termite hills often have high roofs that enable ventilation with the help of the → *thermal updraft*. Also, termite hills are often not perfectly round, but more wall-like and point their narrow surface towards the south to decrease the input of solar heat. To keep even temperatures inside, the → *thermal mass* of the → *adobe* construction of the termite hill is crucial. Small pore-like ventilation holes in the 'façade' of the termite hill draw in air that is 'sucked' out again with the help of the high chimneys. Termite hills work differently in different climates: some mainly have to cool, others, often underground, also use the warmth of the soil against cool desert nights. (→ *drawing 67 image 194, p. 344*)

189: **Tensegrity**; Made popular by the Skylon Tower in London in 1951.

190: **Tensairity**; This construction method combines inflated structural components with tensile elements.

192: **Timbrel Vaulting**; Only minimal scaffolding is needed to build a timbrel vault.

191: **Tea House**; Kenzo Tange's inflated structure is his interpretation of a traditional Japanese typology.

193: **Timbrel Vaulting**; Cuban Arts School.

194: **Termite Mound**; Air conditioning techniques differ from climate to climate and species to species.

195: **Thinshell Structure**; The roof of the Madrid Hippodrome by Aeduardo Torroja.

196: **Tents**; A Samian family and their goathi.

198: **Thinshell structure**; The TWA terminal at JFK, NY by Eero Saarinen.

197: **Tents**; A black nomad tent in Tibet.

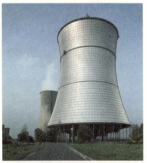
199: **Tensile structures**; Werner Sobek's cooling tower is a thinshell hyperboloid.

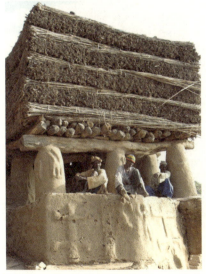
200: **Togu Na**; Built by the Dogon people for community conflict resolution.

201: **Tents**; The Mongolian yurt is insulated with wool.

202: **Toni Areal**: Recycling of an old dairy in Zurich.

203: **Toni Areal**: EM2N are planning to insert an arts school into an existing structure.

205: **Translucent Insulation**: Naked House by Shigeru Ban.

204: **Toni Areal**: The big ramp will be used by pedestrians.

206: **Tire Bale**: One bale is made from up to 100 compressed tires.

207: **Truffa de Madrid**: Anton Garcia Abril developed his own construction method for this project.

208: **Triple Zero**: Werner Sobek's House R128 was built according to his triple zero principles.

Thermal Mass: Thermal mass is the capacity of any given material to store heat. The higher the thermal mass of a material, the greater the amount of heat it can store. Materials with a high thermal mass are important in architecture as they minimize interior temperature fluctuations, also known as the flywheel effect. These fluctuations, the result of solar gain and ambient air temperature, can be evened out by a material with a high thermal mass; the heat from high exterior temperatures can be absorbed by the material and prevented from penetrating into interior building spaces, and then released back into the air as the exterior air cools. ➔ *Adobe* construction has excellent thermal mass.

Thermal Updraft: A thermal updraft or stacking effect is a rising air current. As warm air has a lower density than cold air, it is relatively light and rises up. This effect is used, for example, by gliders, but it is also used in ➔ *vernacular* architecture, for example, in ➔ *windcatchers* as part of the ➔ *Arab indoor cooling system*, and in modern, multilayered façades.

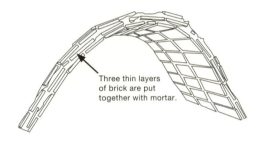

69: A timbrel vault at Peter Rich's Mapungubwe Visitor Centre.

Thermo-Activated Building Components: Thermo-activated building components use the principle of thermal activation as a way of controlling the indoor climate of buildings, using mass to regulate and stabilize temperature and surface area to radiate heat. Thermo-activated building components can be used alone as heating, cooling or insulation systems, or integrated with other kinds of heating, cooling or insulation systems for better efficiency or efficacy. A ➔ *hypocaust* is an ancient Roman heating system that relies on thermo-activation for functionality.

Thin-Shell Structures: Thin shell structures are structures that mimic the curvatures of a shell form to achieve enhanced structural stability in an otherwise thin construction. Thin-shell structures can also be ➔ *hyperboloid*, or ➔ *tensile*. Thin-shell structures made from concrete can span long distances due to double-curved forms needing fewer supports than a typical straight span of the same material and with the same thickness. One of the most famous examples of thin-shell structures is Eero Saarinen's Terminal 5 at JFK Airport in New York. Curved and double-curved structures are utilized today in architecture with increasingly high-tech materials, leading to innovative structural possibilities. (➔ *images 195, 198, p. 345*)

Timbrel Vaulting: Timbrel vaulting, also called Catalan vaulting or Guastavino vaulting, referring to its Spanish inventor, is a method of making self-supporting vaults that require little structural support during construction. Timbrel vaults are made of overlapping layers of tiles which result in a laminated shell-like form that is almost as strong as reinforced concrete. The vault is much thinner and more lightweight than a classic vaulted form, typically constructed using a single layer of thick wedge-shaped stones. The timbrel method uses a quick setting mortar, enabling work on the vault to be done almost completely without scaffold. Though the timbrel vault can be as little as 10 cm, it is possible for workers to stand on top of the vault from day to day as construction progres-ses. The timbrel vault is used in ➔ *Dirk Hebel's SUDU project (essay, p. 315)* with the ETH in Ethiopia, and in the ➔ *Mapungubwe Visitor Centre* in Limpopo, South Africa, a project carried out by Peter Rich architects. (➔ *drawing 69; images 192-193, p. 344*)

Time Banking: Time Banking refers to an economy of reciprocal labor in which people spend an hour a day doing something for someone in the community and in return receive an hour of service from someone else. These hours, generally known as Time Dollars or Time Credits, can cover everything from gardening or care of the elderly to household assistance. Communities in which this is practiced are known as Time Banks, and often use websites to facilitate communication and organize activities. Time Banking provides a platform to connect underutilized resources with unmet needs with the goals of building social capital and recognizing community contributions from all participants.

Tire Bale Construction: Tire bale construction uses bales of tires as a construction element. The bales are composed of about 100 tires, compacted in a hydraulic press which squeezes them down to blocks of approximately 1.5 m by 1.2 m by 0.7 m that weigh around 1000 kg each. They are an alternative to rammed earth tires in the construction of walls as they are less labor-intensive. They can also be used as a material for foundations since they are completely water resistant. Tire bale construction is economical, with one bale costing as little as 5 EUR/7 USD. (➔ *image 206, p. 346*)

Togu Na: The Togu Na is a communal building built by the Dogon people in central Mali. The Togu Na is built from multiple layers of stacked millet stalks. The ceiling and roof of the Togu Na is intentionally lower than the standing height of a person in order to discourage community discourse from becoming heated enough to lead to physical altercations. (➔ *image 200, p. 345*)

Toni Areal: The Toni Areal, located in Zurich, is a former industrial dairy building, which is in the process of being transformed into a building for the Zurich Academy of the Arts and the Zurich Academy of Applied Sciences by architects EM2N. It will be a ➔ *recycled building*: various elements have been changed and new elements added to suit its evol-ving life. The Toni Areal will contain spaces for schools as well as private event spaces and apartments. The ramp of the dairy, formerly used for trucks and other vehicles necessary for dairy functions, has been reimagined as a pedestrian promenade, public space,

Translucent Insulation • Truffa de Madrid

and circulation conduit. (→ *images 202-204, p. 346*)
Translucent Insulation: Translucent insulation is a method of insulation that maximizes intake of solar radiation and minimizes heat loss through the use of transparent rather than opaque insulation materials. Interesting examples for translucent insulation are the principle of → *capillary glass* or the layered façade of Shigeru Ban's Naked House. (→ *image 205, p. 346*)
Triple Zero: Triple Zero is a building concept and set of principles created by architect and engineer Werner Sobeck. Triple Zero buildings use recycled construction materials and can be completely recycled (zero waste), generate their own energy, ideally in excess of the building's actual needs (zero energy consumption), and produce no harmful emissions during any point in the building's lifecycle (zero emissions). Sobeck's own home, R128, located in Stuttgart, Germany, is a prototype for housing that follows the Triple Zero principles. (→ *image 208, p. 346*)

night to prevent heat loss. To keep the Trombe wall from generating unwanted heat during hot summers, shade is created by a cantilevered roof, calculated to cast shade while the sun is at high summertime angles. A vent at the top of the space between the solid wall and the glass wall can let fresh air through. (→ *drawing 70*)

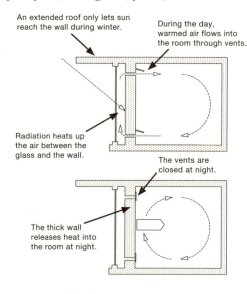

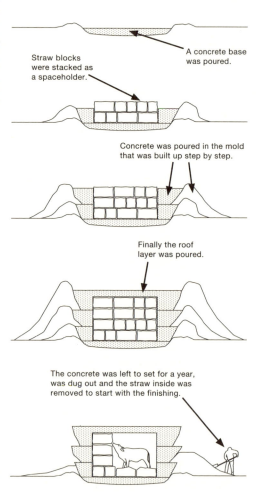

70: A Trombe wall can store and release energy from the sun.

Trombe Wall: A Trombe wall is a passive solar building device, invented in 1881 by Edward Morse and made popular in 1964 by Felix Trombe, that uses solar energy to heat interiors. A Trombe wall functions best in climates with large temperature fluctuations between day and night since one of its functional principles is heat regulation through high → *thermal mass*. A large south-facing glass wall is used as an absorber for sunlight and the heat from solar gain. A second wall with a high thermal mass is spaced apart from the glazed solar collection wall, creating an airspace which traps hot air. During daytime, the first wall absorbs heat, which heats up the air between the walls and the material of the second more solid wall, and this heat is then released into the interior during the night. Vents at the top and bottom of the wall can regulate ventilation but must be closed at

71: Consctruction sequence of Truffa de Madrid.

Truffa de Madrid: Truffa de Madrid, by Spanish architect Anton Garcia Abril and Ensamble Estudio, is a small concrete house in Galicia that was inspired by Le Corbusier's → *Le Cabanon* in Cap Martin. The cast concrete structure was built using a unique technique: concrete was poured into a mold made by a circular earthwork with straw bails stacked in the middle to create a cavity for the interior space. The concrete wall was erected step by step to keep the pressure low on the unique formwork. When the pouring process was finished and the concrete had dried, the house was dug out of its soil mold – like a truffle – and two apertures were created, for an entrance and a window. A cow was then let into the house, to eat out the inner straw, and to use the house as a shelter before human occupation. After a year's time, the inner surface of the house was cleaned and sandblasted. A large window facing toward the sea was set into the structure, a door installed, and the Truffa de Madrid was ready for human tenants. (➡ *drawings 71, 72; image 207, p. 346*)

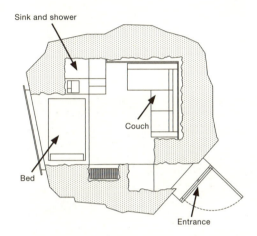

72: The plan of Truffa de Madrid was inspired by that of Le Corbusier's Le Cabanon.

Trullo: A trullo is a kind of stone structure with a conical roof, built with no mortar. The trullo is specific to the Itria Valley region in Italy. The conical roof consists of two stone layers: the interior layer is made from limestone boulders and uses a keystone system similar to that of an arch for structural integrity, the exterior roof layer is made from stone slabs as added protection from water and to protect the complex inner structure of the roof. The walls of the trullo are very thick, and the high ➡ *thermal mass* of the entire construction ensures stable and comfortable interior temperatures through ➡ *passive heating* and ➡ *passive cooling*. The trullo has a somewhat retro-kitsch status in the Itria Valley, and many trulli have been restored and are used today. (➡ *drawing 73; image 213, p. 350*)

Tulou: A Tulou is a type of structure common in the Fujan area of China. The tulou is a large round building, built with a ➡ *rammed earth* outer wall for security. The inner spaces of the tulou are usually built around a central circular courtyard so that the inside of the tulou is open and the outside is closed; typically the exterior wall of a tulou has few openings. The rings of occupied space can be layered in number against the outer wall, and typically vary in height to equalize natural lighting conditions. The tulou was sometimes built on a massive scale. Measuring some 62 m in diameter, the Chengqi Iou consists of four concentric rings of buildings with 288 rooms in the first outer building ring alone. (➡ *images 209-210, p. 350*)

Tussols-Basil Athletic Track: The Tussols-Basil athletic track is located in Olot, Spain. It was designed by RCR Architectes and completed in 2001. The track is set into an area of land left otherwise untouched. This approach is quite unusual as it relies on objects that are set into the landscape, leaving as much as possible undisturbed both physically and esthetically. The track itself is green in color, to help it blend further into the green surroundings. The ancillary support structures, such as the tiered seating, changing and utility rooms, and the toilets are designed so that they are as subtle as possible. The minimal intrusion by three-dimensional elements helps to make the track an elegant – but fully functional – inclusion into the surroundings. (➡ *image 214, p. 350*)

Upcycling: Upcycling is the use of waste material in lieu of new raw materials in production processes. Upcycling aims to convert waste into something of a higher or enhanced quality, or of a more positive environmental quality. Upcycling, unlike recycling, is centered around an improvement of used materials, not just reuse, which is typical of simple recycling. Upcycling is used in ➡ *wa pan* building techniques; this is notable in the upcycling of the materials used to construct the ➡ *Ningbo Museum*. Upcycling is more common in areas with limited resources or access to commercial markets. The ➡ *Jua Kali* craftspeople, featured in the recent book ➡ *Making Do*, about upcycling, are famous for reusing material in their projects and products.

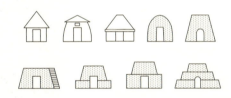

73: Typical trulli come in different, traditional shapes.

Urban Agriculture: Urban agriculture is the practice of engaging in agricultural activities in urban environments. Cities, towns, and other urban situations are not typical locations for the production of crops or animal husbandry. Urban agriculture spans different scales and types of production, from balcony container gardening and henhouse keeping to commercial scale rooftop farms, such as Brooklyn Grange, in New York, a one-acre commercial produce farm. Products for the consumer market, like the ➡ *Beehaus*, enable city dwellers to keep beehives, a form of agriculture that is well-suited to urban environments. Other products for consumers are being introduced onto the market, such as structural soils for green roof agricultural conversions, watering systems, and manuals for easy urban vegetable cultivation. Experimental proposals for ➡ *vertical farms* aim to establish urban agricultural practice on a larger scale and to develop agriculturally self-sufficient cites. This practical and

209: **Tulou**; Arcades face a central, common yard.

210: **Tulou**; A whole village in one building, in reaction to menace from the outside.

211: **Windcatcher**; The key to Arabian passive cooling.

212: **Vertical Farms**; One of many proposals for densified, vertical farming buildings: "Living Tower" by SOA Architects.

213: **Trullo**; A structure completely made of stone.

214: **Tussols-Basil Athletic Track**; Minimally invasive architecture.

215: **VAWT**; The biggest VAWT was built near Quebec, Canada.

216: **Wattle and Daub**; German half-timber houses combine adobe with a wooden structure.

217: **Yakhchal**; Six-foot-walls keep this giant refrigerator cool during hot summers.

218: **Zollingerdach**; An original construction method developed from necessity.

219: **Zeer**; An ancient form of refrigeration based on evaporative cooling is currently a success story in Africa.

220: **Weald and Downland Museum**; The structure was made possible by the flexibility of freshly cut wood.

221: **Weald and Downland Museum**; Bending the roof into shape.

222: **Wall House**; FAR's house in Chile responds to the local climate with layering.

223: **Wall House**; Interior view.

224: **Zollverein School**; Thermo-activated walls as active insulation.

ideological approach is associated with calls for reductions in greenhouse gas emissions caused by shipping and trucking foodstuffs from distant locations, and for a more responsible agricultural practice in keeping with seasonal conditions and local availability.
Vernacular Architecture: The term vernacular architecture is used to describe traditional, often regional construction techniques. ➡ *Vernacular* architecture addresses local needs and circumstances and reflects the environmental and cultural context in which it exists. It is often low-tech but uses resources like energy and available building material in a very smart, sustainable way. This can be explained by the fact that it has evolved over time. Vernacular architecture is a great source of inspiration for architects today because of its sustainability and adequacy regarding climatic conditions and use of material. Inspirational examples include the ➡ *Arab indoor cooling system*, the ➡ *igloo*, ➡ *sod and turf houses* and the ➡ *Togu Na*.

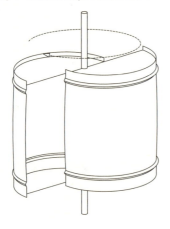

74: A simple version of a VAWT can be built from a halved beer barrel.

Vertical Axis Wind Turbine: Vertical axis wind turbines (VAWTs) are wind turbines with a vertically oriented rotor. Unlike ➡ *horizontal axis turbines (HAWT)* they do not have to be specifically placed in relationship to wind direction, and can operate at relatively low wind speeds. Generally, they do not generate energy in such high quantities as a horizontal turbine but can be used in more flexible applications. (➡ *drawing 74; image 215, p. 350*)
Vertical Farms: Vertical farms are a theoretical agricultural method consisting of farms located in high-rise urban buildings. Using greenhouse practices and agricultural techniques such as ➡ *hydroponics* and ➡ *aquaponics*, these indoor city farms would allow crops to be grown year-round without the need for large land plots. The idea for vertical farms was proposed by Dickson Despommier, microbiology and ecology professor at Columbia University, who developed the concept to include multiple floors equipped with their own watering and nutrient monitoring systems. In theory, vertical farms could increase crop production, conserve resources, and minimize carbon emissions by cultivating plants in proximity to consumers. However, the feasibility and cost-effectiveness of vertical farms have not yet been demonstrated. A number of scientists, architects, and local governments around the world have expressed interest in developing vertical farms or prototypes for actual use. (➡ *image 212, p. 350*)
Wa Pan: A method of building in China that uses recycled parts of old buildings in new structures. This technique, in use for centuries, was recently brought into contemporary architectural discourse when it was used in the ➡ *Ningbo Historic Museum*, in Ningbo, China, by the Amateur Architecture Studio. wa pan is similar to ➡ *Spolia*, the recycling of ornamental building elements.
Wall House: The Wall House in Santiago de Chile by FAR Architects consists of four structural shells, each with different qualities and materials that correspond with use, climate, atmosphere, and structural needs. The innermost shell is a cast concrete structure, designed as a wet space into which the bathrooms and kitchen are integrated. The second shell is like a wooden shelf, used for storage functions. The third shell is the climatic shell of the building: made from highly insulating polycarbonate wall elements for cool winter temperatures, it can be opened almost completely to the outside during the summer months. The outermost fourth shell is a tent-like membrane structure. It reflects about 70% of solar rays and also works as a mosquito net. The fourth shell is made from materials common to greenhouse construction. Each layer has a different spatial interval from the next layer, allowing for spaces to be dimensioned by use. They range from 45 cm to 4 m. The cost of constructing the Wall House was low compared to other residential constructions because the materials were sourced directly from industrial uses. (➡ *images 222-223, p. 351*)
Wattle and Daub: Wattle and daub is a building technique that combines ➡ *adobe* (daub) with a structure made of wood or other natural materials (wattle). Typically, a woven lattice of wooden strips or leaves is covered with a mixture of clay, sand, and water. Wattle and daub has been used for many thousands of years but is still common, for example, in German "Fachwerkhaeuser" for its typical esthetics, or in South American ➡ *Paisa houses*, for its earthquake resistance. (➡ *image 216, p. 350*)
Weald and Downland Museum Workshop: The Weald and Downland Museum Workshop is the workshop building of the Weald and Downland Museum, an open-air museum in Chichester, England. The ground floor of the building is storage for exhibition materials, and the upper floor is workshop space. Designed by Edward Cullinan Architects, the building has a roof made using a gridshell structure. Although the structure is a gridshell, the architects developed a unique construction method, not typical of ➡ *gridshell* construction. Usually gridshells are made to double curve, after assembly of a flat skeleton, from the ground up. However, this requires a great deal of power to deform the structure while also lifting it. Instead, Edward Cullinan Architects developed a method where the shell was constructed at a height of 7.5 m, and then let down to conform to the desired shape, with the curvatures necessary for

the gridshell structure to be stable. This required a certain flexibility of the materials, and so freshly cut wood was used, which was very flexible for a time, and then dried out to be more rigid. Once the form was set and the wood had dried in place, the whole construction was systematically tuned and tightened. (→ *images 220-221, p. 351*)

Whole Earth Catalog: The Whole Earth Catalog was a compendium of knowledge and innovation. Created by Stewart Brand in 1968, the catalog was published intermittently until 1998, with the most intensive years of publication and production from 1968–1972. The catalog featured products intended for creative, ecologically sensitive, and sustainable lifestyles, although it did not offer these for direct sale, as would be typical of a standard catalog. As laid out by Brand, items were listed if they fit the following criteria: 1. Useful as a tool; 2. Relevant to independent education; 3. High quality or low cost; 4. Not already common knowledge; 5. Easily available by mail. The listed items were reviewed by the staff of the catalog and classified into a varying but non-typical structure of item classification. For example, the 1968 catalog used sections like "Nomadics" and "Shelter and Land Use" to organize content.

Windcatchers can be used in three different ways. A windcatcher that is open only to the side that is facing the direction of prevailing winds 'catches' wind from outside and leads it into the building. For changing wind directions, the openings of the windcatcher are adjustable with directional ports. This method does not necessarily cool the interior but relies on a rate of air flow to provide a cooling effect. A windcatcher that is open only to the side that is facing against the direction of prevailing winds creates a suction according to the Bernoulli effect. Warm air is drawn out of the building and cooler air from shadowy courtyards or underground qanats is brought into the building. This technique can achieve cooling by taking in air from cooler places. A windcatcher that is situated in windless regions can create passive ventilation by thermal updraft: warm air rises through the windcatcher that functions like a chimney and makes cooler air from courtyards or → *qanats* flow into the building. (→ *image 211, p. 350*)

Yakhchal: A yakhchal is an ancient Persian type of refrigerator, based on the principle of insulation. During winter, ice was collected in nearby mountains and then brought into the yakhchal that had an underground space and walls at least 2 m thick that were built of a special mortar consisting of egg whites, goats' hair, ashes, and sand that made them impermeable to water and extremely heat-resistant. To add a cooling effect to the mere insulation effect, → *yakhchals* could be connected to the common → *Arab indoor cooling system*, → *windcatchers*, and → *qanats*. (→ *image 217, p. 351*)

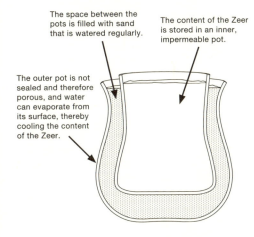

75: The Zeer can also be called 'pot-in-pot refrigerator'.

76: A Zollinger roof under consctruction.

Wiki: A wiki is a collection of linked web pages that can be easily added to or edited. Typically a wiki is used for information sets, though it can also be used for almost any web application. Wikipedia.com, one of the most well-known wikis, is a crowdsource edited and created encyclopedia, available worldwide in multiple languages. Sometimes a wiki can take the form of an online instruction → *manual* for multiple things, like the site howtopedia.com.

Windcatcher: A windcatcher, also called *badgir* (Persian) or *malqaf* (Arabic), is a traditional Arab tower that was used as part of the ancient → *Arab indoor cooling system* and can still be found today. The wind tower is a → *passive ventilation* device utilizing, among other things, the → *Bernoulli effect* and the principle of → *thermal updraft* (stacking effect).

Zeer: The Zeer is an example of a refrigerator that uses no mechanics, only natural → *evaporative cooling*. It is constructed with a small clay pot inside a larger clay pot and wet sand between the two pots and cover. As the water evaporates it cools, and the inner pot becomes cool enough to prevent food spoilage, even in hot climates. It works most efficiently in environments with low ambient humidity. Evaporative cooling for the refrigeration of foodstuffs has been used for centuries. (→ *drawing 75; image 219, p. 351*)

Zollingerdach · Zollverein School

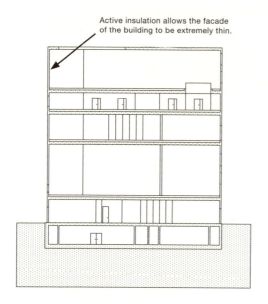

Active insulation allows the facade of the building to be extremely thin.

77: Sanaa's Zollverein School Building has a thermo-activated façade.

Zollingerdach (Zollinger Roof): The Zollingerdach is a roof construction type common in Germany. It uses 40% less material than a standard roof. The Zollingerdach is made from two convex sections, pitched at a steep angle. This form avoids the need for interior columns or other load-bearing structures to support the roof. Each convex section is made from short sections of wood set into diamond shapes, and skinned between each section. This type of roof was easy enough for house occupants to construct themselves, making it less expensive than typical roof constructions. It was invented by Friedrich Zollinger at the beginning of the 20th century, and was inspired by his interest in gridshell structures. (→ *drawing 76; image 218, p. 351*)

Zollverein School: Zollverein School by SANAA in Essen, Germany, is a school built with a special "active insulation" system integral to the building's structure. The school uses → *thermo-activated building components* to achieve a form of insulation that works by virtue of thermal properties instead of specialized materials. The building has an outer thin concrete shell, with a system of tubes, measuring some 3000 m, incorporated into the concrete outer wall which leads water through the façade. This system of tubes and outer shell, in combination with an interior wall, functions like insulation, and keeps the temperature of the interior side of the walls stable. The 28°C water is pumped into the system and up into the building from former mining shafts. This water in the mining shafts has to be pumped out anyway to avoid flooding. The active insulation system works independently of the building's heating, which is a conventional convection heating system, incorporated into the flooring. (→ *drawing 77; image 224, p. 351*)

About the authors: Something Fantastic is a young architectural practice committed to smart, touching, simple architecture. Its principals Julian Schubert, Elena Schütz and Leonard Streich were educated at ETH Zurich and the University of the Arts Berlin. Their book *Something Fantastic – A Manifesto by Three Young Architects on Worlds, People, Cities and Houses* (ISBN 978-3-9813-4361-8) was published by Ruby Press in 2010. Next to Something Fantastic Schubert, Schütz, and Streich operate a creative agency called Belgrad and are teaching at the University of the Arts Berlin.

STIMULATE STAKEHOLDERS

The world is not short of technical solutions to the problems of environmental sustainability, but convincing stakeholders to adopt these solutions is another matter. This is especially true in the building and construction sector, where the complexity of the construction process, the diverse drivers of the many players involved, and the challenges of sustainability requirements are posed to a deeply entrenched status quo, and come together in a tightly coupled system with dynamics that actively discourage meaningful change in construction processes and practice.

The question we need to ask is: How best to encourage behavior change in such a complex environment? Traditional measures tend to be aimed at individual actors, and come as either carrots in the form of financial benefit (e.g. subsidies, tax breaks, reduced operational costs) or increased status and competitive edge (more stars, silver to platinum medals), or in the form of sticks (levies and taxes, fines and regulatory control). These are applied using a range of quantitative performance targets that should, in theory, add up to sustainability. However, these mechanisms are themselves not sustainable because they require constant external intervention. The behaviors encouraged in this way do not arise out of the requirements of the (narrowly defined) system itself, and they target what Donella Meadows[1] identified as the least effective leverage points in a complex system. More effective measures would aim at changing the overall goals of the system, as these arise from a changed paradigm and worldview, and encouraging the ability of the system to self-organize and evolve to support these changed and changing goals.

The global challenges of sustainability, new scientific theories about how the world works, and the technological breakthroughs of the past 150 years combine to bring about a view of the world that sees it as a fundamentally interconnected and interdependent system, one in which conceptual boundaries between economies, nations, disciplines, and the individual and his/her environment are rapidly disappearing. Such a change in worldview, would have at least two implications:

The first lies in the value system that underlies the actions of, and relationships between, stakeholders, including the relationships with voiceless stakeholders, the natural environment, and future generations. This value system is informed by an understanding of an interconnected and interdependent world, one that is co-created through the relationships found in global to local socio-ecological systems, and is shaped by the quality of those relationships. Such a shift in value system will require incentives that expand the notion of enlightened self-interest from the individual to the individual as part of the whole.

The second would be a re-definition of the stakeholders and their roles, one that moves beyond the traditional nexus of built-environment professionals, developers/clients, and government as the actors responsible for creating the built environment. Governments or developers do not drive the rapid urbanisation experienced globally, but instead it is individuals, often poor and marginalised, and their choices that drive this shift. Acknowledging the role of the citizen in creating the built environment, and thus changing the role of the individual, from a powerless affected stakeholder, to a powerful creative stakeholder, will allow the sustainability agenda to harness the incredible energy and power of self-organisation. The tools to motivate change would need to be accessible to these citizens, relevant to their needs and behavioural drivers, and reinforce their ability to self-organize and evolve. Here the technologically enabled phenomenon of our increasingly interconnected and complex social networks can play a huge role in creating awareness, mobilizing action, building a shared vision, transferring knowledge, and ultimately changing worldviews and value systems.

Chrisna du Plessis & Holger Wallbaum

1.) Donella Meadows, *Leverage points – Places to intervene in the system*. Hartland, VT: The Sustainability Institute 1999.

About the authors: Chrisna du Plessis was lead author of the UNEP Agenda 21 for Sustainable Construction in Developing Countries and provided input into several other national and international policy and strategy initiatives on sustainable development, including the Earth Charter. Currently she is on sabbatical at the University of Pretoria where she is writing a book about approaches to sustainability from within an ecological worldview.

Holger Wallbaum is Assistant Professor for Sustainable Construction at the Department of Civil, Environment, and Geomatic Engineering at the ETH Zurich, where this Chair was initiated by the Holcim Foundation for Sustainable Construction in 2004. Holger Wallbaum is a member of the Technical Competence Center (TCC) of the Holcim Foundation. His research at the Institute for Construction and Infrastructure Management (IBI) comprises the development of innovative construction materials and building park modeling, as well as the development of social-cultural and climate specific guidelines and tools for the design and evaluation of sustainable buildings and settlements.

The Empathy Principle

Creating Biosphere Consciousness Through a Communication and Energy Revolution

JEREMY RIFKIN

Human beings have only been on this planet for 175,000 years, which makes us the youngest species on the planet. We are less than one half of a percent of the biomass of the earth, but we are almost six billion strong, and we are using 24 percent of all the photosynthesis of the earth. In 40 years, we will host more than nine billion people. This is just unsustainable, and it is monstrous. The only way to prevent us from devouring our planet is to establish a new kind of empathy that will provide a new social contract.

Two recent events, the skyrocketing and unstable price of oil and the almost complete meltdown of the global economy, signalled the end game of a two-century long industrial revolution propelled by fossil fuels. In July 2008 the price of one barrel of oil hit 147 USD. Commodity prices soared and inflation went through the roof. Basic items became unaffordable, from food in the grocery store to petrol at the pump. There were food riots in 30 countries. Because almost everything we use is based on fossil fuel: fertilizers, pesticides, most of our pharmaceutical products, all of our construction materials, most of our materials for packaging, most of our clothes, our power, transport, heat and light. When the price of oil went over 100 USD a barrel, things began to change. And when it hit 147 USD a barrel, purchasing power plummeted.

Essentially, the engine of the industrial revolution shut down, causing an economic earthquake. The collapse of the financial market 60 days later was the after-shock. Peak globalization for the industrial age has occurred. Peak globalization happened at 147 USD a barrel due to something called peak oil per capita — not to be confused with peak oil production. Peak oil production indicates the point when half of the global oil supply will be used up. After this peak, oil production can only terminally decline. Optimists project this point happening in 2030, others predict it will happen during the next ten years. Peak oil per capita, by contrast, happened in 1979. In that year there were 5.5 barrels of oil available for each person on Earth. Since then this amount has steadily declined. Even though we have found more oil since then, population has increased proportionally even more. China and India, which together make up one third of the world's population, seem determined to use the same centralized fossil fuel based model as western countries for their economic development. Their economies currently have a 10 percent growth rate. Bringing one third of the human race into the fossil fuel age, at a 10 percent growth rate, will push the demand for fossil fuels to unprecedented levels.

As most of these fossil energy sources such as coal, oil and gas will be depleted in the near future, their prices can only go up, but can never significantly go down. Perhaps only uranium may be different, because it is still available in larger quantities, but the sure rise of its processing costs make it as expensive as the other centralized fossil fuel sources. Most technology, the entire construction industry, and all infrastructure are based on those industrial energies. Because we are now at the sunset of that industrial paradigm, the economy can never grow in the same way it did before.

The leaders and delegates from 192 countries came together in December 2009 at the World Climate Summit in Copenhagen to address the entropy bill for the industrial age. Despite the fact that the UN climate panel confirmed that climate change is already taking effect, and despite a dramatic change in the temperature of the Earth that threatens the extinction of 70 percent of the world's species within a century — putting even the human species in peril — our world leaders couldn't come to a deal. The summit broke up in complete acrimony.

Our government leaders were unable to properly address climate change, even though it may be the greatest threat we've ever faced on the planet. The problem lies deeper than something that can be solved with a new economic mechanism to regulate the global economy, or new carbon targets, or a new treaty on climate change. We need to rethink the very assumptions on what makes us human. We are living of a dysfunctional and toxic paradigm about the "nature from the human nature" from the 18th and 19th centuries.

Religion had the final say on human nature for 1,500 years. All the Abrahamic religions—Judaism, Christianity, Islam—taught that people are born in sin and wait for salvation. During the Enlightenment, at the beginning of the market economy and nation-state era, philosophers challenged those beliefs. The political philosopher John Locke postulated that people are born tabula rasa, clean slate, and that the human predisposition is to acquire property with productive labour. Later, the economist Adam Smith added that people are born with a drive for autonomy and behave in their own self-interest in the market. In the 19th century, Jeremy Bentham postulated that people have a drive to seek pleasure over pain. Charles Darwin then theorized that every species has a drive to perpetuate itself. Sigmund Freud reinforced this at the end of the 19th century with the suggestion that people's lives are primarily about extinguishing libido.

The paradigm that results from this thinking is embedded in our education systems, our business practices, and our governing models. But is that what human nature is really about? Are people born inherently depraved and evil? Are we only rational, calculating, detached, self-interested, materialistic, utilitarian, pleasure-seeking, and libido-driven?

In the past two decades, there have been some interesting breakthroughs challenging those embedded notions. In the 1980s and 90s, researchers in Italy studied the phenomena of mirror neurons in macaque monkeys. They studied monkeys opening nuts using Magnetic Resonance Imaging (MRI) brain scans. Specific neurons light up when a monkey opens a nut, and they found that the same neurons light up when it observes someone else opening a nut. Many primates, humans, birds, and other species are suspected to have mirror neurons. The mirror neurons allow a creature to feel what another creature is feeling, as if they were feeling it firsthand. For example, if a spider goes up your friend's arm, you'll have a creepy feeling. If you cut yourself and it bleeds, your friend will probably wince. We take this for granted, but this is a key to how animals socialize. Mirror neurons allow empathy to exist.

THE EMPATHY PRINCIPLE

When a baby cries in a nursery, other babies will cry in response. That is empathic distress in our biology. At about two years of age, children can identify themselves in a mirror. At about eight years of age a child learns about its mortality and where it comes from. This leads to an understanding of the fragility and vulnerability of life. There is an existential sense of the singularity of life that allows humans to empathize with others. This is the key to an empathic civilization, where increasing empathy allows more and more solidarity.

Humans are the most social of all animals. We seek intimacy and universality at the same time. With an understanding of the empathic element of human sociability, it is possible to imagine extending empathy to the entire human family and even to our fellow creatures as part of one extended evolutionary family. That extension and the idea that we live in one indivisible community biosphere is an understanding imperative to the future of our planet.

The great economic transformations in history occur when new communication mediums converge with new energy system. The new forms of communication become the command and control mechanisms for structuring, organizing and managing the more complex civilizations made possible by the new sources of energy.

Hunting and gathering was the energy regime for 93 percent of our history, and oral language was the communication technology used to manage it. Every civilization during this era created some kind of mythological consciousness, empathy extended only to blood ties. People were organized into small migratory hunter-gatherer groups that rarely exceeded 150 or 200 people. Then a paradigm shift happened with the great hydraulic agricultural civilizations. The power of the sun was harnessed to produce barley and wheat as crops, which were then stored as grain. Granaries, roads, and distribution systems were set up. Hydraulic agriculture, as the new energy regime, was complex enough that a communication revolution was required to manage it. Each hydraulic agricultural civilization independently developed written language to manage the new system.

Each of these agricultural civilizations were accompanied by theological consciousness. Mythological consciousness gave rise to theological consciousness. In theological consciousness empathy was extended from blood ties to religious ties. Jews began to see other Jews as extended family. Christians began to empathize with each other, and Muslims with Muslims, etc. Writing, hydraulic agriculture, and theological consciousness allowed empathy to extend to broader domains, enabling solidarity within larger civilizations.

In the 19th century the introduction of print technology ushered in the era of the inexpensive mass-production of printed pages. Public schools and widespread literacy became the norm in Europe and North America between 1830 and 1880. It marked the beginning of the first industrial revolution. The print communication revolution became the management tool to organize coal and steam power, which could not have been managed using codex. Print communication set up a different form of consciousness, more expansive than a single brain. Ideological consciousness arose out of this paradigm change. The Enlightenment was a stand-off between those who believed in ideological consciousness and those who were still steeped in theological consciousness, or even mythological consciousness.

This shift in communication and energy made empathy extend again, to a new fictional division called national identity. The new complex civilizations of the first industrial revolution brought diverse people together, and cities were built vertically, allowing millions of people to live in them. The increase in population and density resulted in disassociation from traditional blood ties and religious associations, and ideological associations based on nationality began to develop. For example, when Italy was formed in the 1870s, the first Prime Minister Camillo Benso, Count of Cavour supposedly said that once Italy was created, the next job would be to create Italians.

This is not completely linear; there have been regressions, and dark periods plagued by genocides and holocausts. However, there is a historical line that can be traced, along which increasingly complex civilizations and more sophisticated energy regimes were created. Advances in communication methods and modes changed consciousness from mythological, to theological, to ideological. In the 20th century, the first generation of electric power, the telephone and telegraph, and later cinema, radio, and television, became the managing communication tools to organize the internal combustion engine—giving rise to psychological consciousness.

Over the last two decades there has been a powerful communication revolution with the personal computer and the internet. This second-generation electronic communication is quite different than the first. First-generation electronic communication worked top-down: telegraph, telephone, cinema, radio, television and were based on a centralized model, managed from above. The second-generation electronic communication is open source, flat, and most importantly, distributed. Today two billion people can send video, audio, and text to each other simultaneously, at the speed of light. This revolution in communication possibilities has been grafted onto the second industrial revolution, based on fossil fuels energy and centralized organisational structures. Now the sun is setting on those old elite energies, and the infrastructure for them is on life support.

Elite energies—oil, gas, coal, and uranium—are elite because they are only found in specific places, in limited quantity. From the beginning they require enormous military investments to secure them, huge geopolitical investments to manage them, and massive infusions of capital organized by centralized financial institutions to utilize them. Millions and millions of people have died in wars over the last two centuries to secure oil, gas, coal, and uranium.

In contrast, distributed energies are found on every square foot of the planet. The sun shines on every part of the Earth every day even if the intensity varies. The wind blows all over the world even if the frequency is intermittent. Wherever we tread, there is a hot geothermal core under the ground. We all generate garbage. In agricultural areas, there is agricultural and forest waste. On the coasts—where much of our populations live—the waves and tides come in every day. People living in valleys rely on the steady stream of hydro energy coming from mountain glaciers. Wherever there is water—rivers, streams, and lakes—hydro energy is available.

Over the last 18 months in Europe, the convergence of distributed Information and Communications Technology (ICT) has come together to manage new distributed energies. When distributed communication organizes distributed energies, there is the possibility for a third industrial revolution to take form. This could lead to distributed consciousness, biosphere consciousness. The European Union has formally committed itself to a five-pillar infrastructure for a third industrial revolution. These five pillars must be laid out simultaneously to create a stable synergetic infrastructure for a new energy regime.

The EU has already committed itself to the first pillar—distributed renewable energies—with its goal of achieving a 20 percent renewable energy grid mix by 2020. Considering that renewable energy is distributed and ubiquitous by nature, the centralized top-down model of generation and distribution doesn't make sense. I'm not opposed to centralized solar and wind, I think they are essential to the transition, but if distributed energies are found in every square foot of the world, why would we only collect them in a few central locations?

Pillar two is based on buildings. Ideally, every existing building in Europe can be partially converted into a power plant, capable of producing excess power and feeding it back to the grid. Accionia has built the first zero emission building in Spain, and Bouyges has a positive power building located outside of Paris. 70 percent of the current building stock will still be here in 2030. So the more improvements that can be made now, the better the long-term outcome. Spreading the idea of dual-purpose buildings, acting as both dwellings and power plants, will boost the European economy, as reconfiguring significant portions of Europe's infrastructure will necessitate the creation of new jobs.

The third pillar is energy storage. Distributed energy is subject to temporal and inconsistent atmospheric conditions, and therefore storage must be established to ensure consistent energy flows. Hydrogen storage might be the best way, but all storage methods—water pumping, fly wheels, batteries, capacitors—are good. When the sun shines on solar panels, generating electricity, the surplus can be used to electrolyze water. The resulting hydrogen can be stored and later converted back into electricity. This idea has been criticized for the loss of power in conversion, but that loss is minute in comparison to the conversion losses with traditional fossil fuels.

Pillars four and five—Smart Grid technology and plug-in hybrid and electric vehicles—are where the communication revolution comes together with the energy revolution to create distributed capitalism and biosphere consciousness.

For 30 years, governments have resisted windmills, solar panels, and other distributed energy sources because it was unclear how they could power an economy. Now there is a clear route to viability. The internet is based on software and hardware that allows us to connect millions of computers around the world. When the distributed computing power is combined it exceeds anything that can be obtained with centralized super computers. This same organizational method and its hardware and software can be applied to the distributed power sources. When millions and millions of buildings are producing power and sharing it across continental landmasses, the power generated exceeds anything possible with centralized coal and nuclear power plants.

If technology similar to the internet is used to help connect energy in the biosphere, biosphere consciousness is possible. If we each take responsibility for our own small swath of the biosphere. there is hope of extending empathy beyond blood ties and religious ties and national association—to start to think as a human family. Our community becomes the biosphere.

When a devastating earthquake hit Haiti in 2010, the first tweets came out in an hour, and the first videos were available online soon after. Within two hours, the whole world had access to immediate imagery. Empathic embrace was possible and happened, because of ICT. When Iran's controversial political elections occurred in 2009, students and others took to the streets in protest. Neda

THE EMPATHY PRINCIPLE

Agha Soltan, a woman attending the protests, was recorded on a protestors' video as she was shot by the authorities and died in the street. Within an hour, the video was on YouTube. Through that and Twitter the whole world learned viscerally about the situation in Iran. People came together in an empathic embrace for the protestors and victims.

Human beings live by narratives. We now know that other species have rudimentary cultures that they can pass down; when geese have to teach their goslings the migration route, they have to pass it on culturally. We know that other animals have empathy and feelings, expressed through play and mutual grooming. But what separates humans from other life forms is the use of complex language in order to express narratives and to communicate.

The third industrial revolution has a logical game plan. Countries and businesses must now consider where they want to be in 20 years. The energy s-curve of fossil fuel is exhausted, it can't be replenished and sunset fossil fuels will not be in use in 50 years. The alternative is to get involved in the sunrise energies and industries of the third industrial revolution, which will exercize a huge multiplier effect that can move the world economy to a sustainable future in the 21st century.

We will not get there unless we have a discussion about human nature and re-think about the human journey. The Enlightenment did it unconsciously; there was a move toward a market economy and a rethinking of the *gestalt*, a new *zeitgeist*, with new temporal-spatial orientation.

We are still saddled with those ideas in our school systems and our business practices today. But it is also important to remember that when we do develop new forms of urban design, architecture, and construction materials, we have to tell a new story on a parallel track. If we are *homo empathicus* as science suggests, we have to prepare our future infrastructure, urban environments, architecture, and living spaces to connect people so that empathy — our true nature — can flourish.

Text documentation by Jessica Bridger

Jeremy Rifkin is president of the Foundation on Economic Trends, a non-profit organization examining trends in science and technology, and their impacts on the environment, the economy, culture, and society. He is a senior lecturer in the Executive Education Program at the Wharton School, University of Pennsylvania. He advises the European Commission, the European Parliament and several EU heads of state. Jeremy Rifkin is the author of numerous books on the impact of scientific and technological changes on the economy, the workforce, society, and the environment.

STIMULATE STAKEHOLDERS

The Settler is King

How to Democratize Home Ownership with Do-It-Yourself Building Techniques

ANNE-JULCHEN BERNHARDT AND JÖRG LEESER /
BeL ASSOCIATES

The Allotment House is a project that explores how lower-income people can become homeowners. The project was originally developed in the framework of the IBA Hamburg 2013 for the urban district of Wilhelmsburg. A dominant building typology in this area is the allotment garden hut, and in the 1970s large social housing complexes were also widely erected in the district. Although the theme of these developments was "urbanity through density," they are neither densely built, nor do they succeed in producing any sense of urbanity. The Allotment House extends the typology of the hut to multi-story housing—a skeleton provides the basic frame, its different stories can be individually filled out, spatially and over a period of time, by the residents themselves, employing self-build methods. The residents can act as settlers, adjusting the open condition of their own dwelling to their personal needs and desires.

Self-determined housing reduces costs and liberates occupants. In modern industrial societies there is a clear need to provide opportunities for large sectors of

1: Allotment house before individual colonization.
2: Allotment house colonized.

the population to buy their own home. The high cost of construction and land in a metropolis like Hamburg exclude low-income groups from this important aspect of civil society. Despite their aspirations, citizens with a migrant background are consequently forced to adapt their housing situation—and with it an important aspect of their life planning—to the facilities offered by rented accommodation. What they are offered imposes passivity. The contrast between their own or their families' background of self-determined housing in their home countries compared with the reality in Germany produces social tension. By lowering costs, the Allotment House project also lowers the bar for those who want to enter the housing market and awakens the potential for self-determined action. By applying their own labor, people can save 30 percent of the construction cost and can take pride in their own work. The ability to exert an influence on their own lives has a liberating effect.

The future homeowners buy a package consisting of a "plot" i.e., the part of the building that corresponds to their unit, which includes the basic structure made of concrete, all additional building materials needed to develop their plot, and a handbook giving detailed instructions on all the steps necessary for the development work.

In warmer climatic zones Le Corbusier's Domino House principle from 1914 has proved its value as a successful construction system for informal housing developments. Aashwa'i in Cairo, polykatoikia in Athens, gececondu in Istanbul, and favelas in Sao Paulo confirm the superiority of the Domino construction principle—and not just from the viewpoint of cost. It is an armature that provides ideal conditions for a mix of functions; a surplus of space creates a flexible basis to be appropriated by future extensions, conversions and adaptations. The open basic structure allows flexibility over a long period of time.

Applying the Domino principle in Germany today requires highly insulated concrete materials in order to satisfy the demands made by highly developed post-industrial societies regarding comfort, economy, and ecology. Monolithic walls of concrete have been a subject of research into building materials since the 1960s. The most recent research work at the Technical University Berlin on reinforced lightweight concrete with an expanded clay additive has led to the development of a new construction material: thermally insulating infra-lightweight concrete. In Berlin, the first building using this material has already been erected by Professor Mike Schlaich, and it achieves a thermal conductivity of only $l > 0.2$ W/(mK).

3

4

3: The basic structure of the allotment house serves as a covered work place for the settlers fitting their own homes.
4: Minimal Fittings turn the basic structure into a fully inhabitable environment.

Pages 371-375: The handbook is a document written by the architects to instruct the settlers on how to build their homes with the construction materials they have received as part of their apartment purchase.

Buildings with a monolithic concrete external envelope meet German enviromental energy saving standards (as defined in the EnEV). The additional cost of a thermally efficient load-bearing structure is more than compensated for by the durability of the material and the possibility to simplify detailing.

The *Grundbau* (basic structure) of the Allotment House has a single staircase serving two units on each floor; the structure is five stories high and offers eight sites for settlers. Each of the four upper stories has two units, whereas the ground floor contains the settlers' private workshops, car parking spaces, the public utilities connection room and the approach to the open staircase. The outdoor space between these individual elements of the skeleton is semi-public. The areas in front of and next to the building are connected to the ground floor spaces and await appropriation. Like the winter quarters of a travelling circus, these areas can be driven over but are not paved or otherwise sealed, so that settlers and vegetation can take over this space and between them negotiate an interpersonal, green neighbourhood.

The settlers acquire a complete kit of building components to build a typical settler's house. This kit contains all the construction material, and a detailed handbook that describes the construction steps that they can carry out themselves, as well as indicating those that must be approved by a specialist.

The organization of the floor plans is independent of the load-bearing structure and the neighbouring stories. All versions of the typical floor plan in the settlers' kit address different housing needs, such as the number of occupants or the kind of life planned and changes of function over the course of time, due to a growing family, the advent of old age, or change of use, for example. A set of functionally neutral spaces is offered with an abundant number of doors. Consequently, the users can employ whatever function they wish. All the rooms are connected to each other; each room has openings to those adjacent. The large number of openings allows the rooms to be grouped as required. For instance: one family may want a large bathroom with a view, whereas another may use this room as a child's bedroom. Each dwelling has two service shafts that are positioned at the intersection of the partition walls and each shaft can serve three rooms. The settlers are free to decide what the rooms will be used for. Flexibility results from use and not only through adaptation. Functionally indeterminate spaces in a floor plan without corridors require the settlers to interpret and conquer their own space. In the 1:50 scale configuration model (contained in the building kit) the settlers can examine which ways of using the spaces work best for them.

Handbook, contents

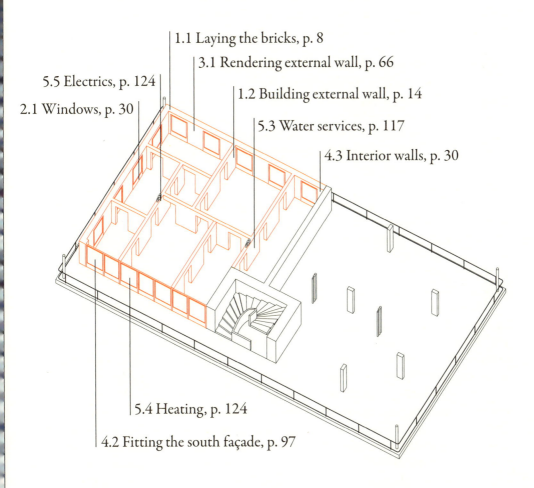

- 1.1 Laying the bricks, p. 8
- 3.1 Rendering external wall, p. 66
- 5.5 Electrics, p. 124
- 1.2 Building external wall, p. 14
- 2.1 Windows, p. 30
- 5.3 Water services, p. 117
- 4.3 Interior walls, p. 30
- 5.4 Heating, p. 124
- 4.2 Fitting the south façade, p. 97

GB
This is the English version of the manual. The manual also appears in ten other languages. Have fun and success in building your owns home!

T
Bu kılavuzun Almanca sürü müdür. El on diğer dillere bölünmüştür belirdi. İyi eğlenceler ve başarı kendi ana binasında!

RU
Это немецкие версии руководства. Руководство состоит из десяти других Языкипоявился. Удачи и успехов в строительстве собственного дома!

List of elements

- (A) Gas concrete blocks, 8 pallets
- (B) Thin bed mortar, 35 bags (25kg/bag)
- (C) Lintel blocks, 9 units
- (D) Air-hardening lime for slurries, 190 bags (30kg/bag)
- (E) Windows, 9 units
- (F) Doors, 16 units
- (G) Gas concrete building panel, 9 units
- (H) Lintel blocks, 9 units
- (I) Gypsum plasterboard panels
- (J) Metal studs
- (K) Sanitary fittings, 1 set
- (L) Heating, heating pipes
- (M) Ventilation system
- (N) Hot-water system

1.1.3 Setting out the corners

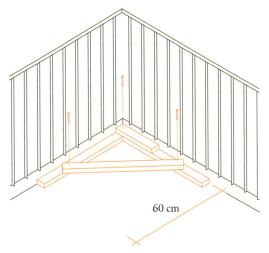

1. The roof battens (2.5/5cm) are laid along the steel edge of the railing as shown and nailed together. It is important that the edges of this construction measure 60 cm.

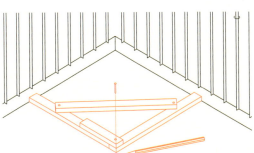

2. The right-angled timber construction is now turned around and again placed in position. The corner point is marked and then permanently indicated by driving in a nail.

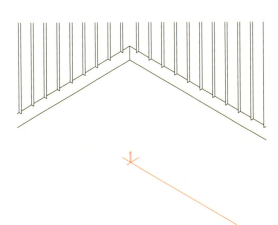

3. The marked point is the outside corber of the external wall. This is where you start erecting the wall. To do this, a bricklayer's cord is stretched to the next corner. If everything has been done correctly this cord should run parallel to the railing. This timber construction is also used later to lay out the corners of the walls at right angles.

1.2.1 Erecting the external walls

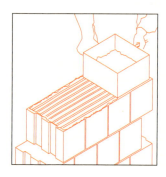

2 The thin bed mortar is automatically applied in the correct thickness (about one millimeter) by using a mortar sledge. The mortar has the right consistency when the furrows remain in place and do not blend into each other.

1 Before the walls are erected bitumen sheeting is glued to the slab along the line of the wall to protect against rising damp. A moisture-resistant cement mortar is used as adhesive.

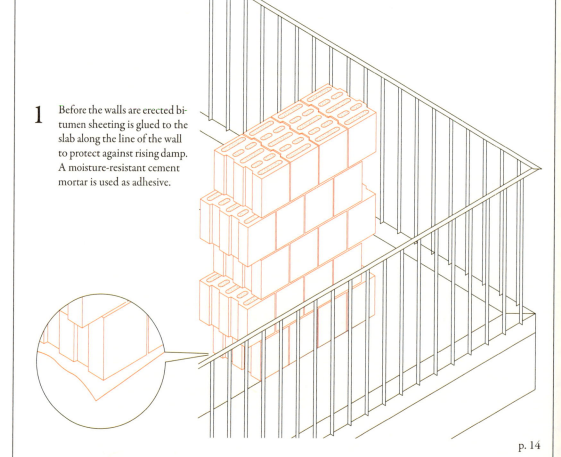

p. 14

2.1.1 Installing the windows

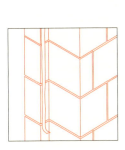 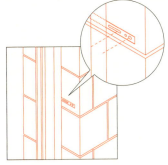 

1 A sealing tape (e.g. Kompriband) is glued to the rebate.

3 The window is screwed to the external wall using window ties.

4 The joint between the window frame and wall is filled with foam or sealed with sealing tape.

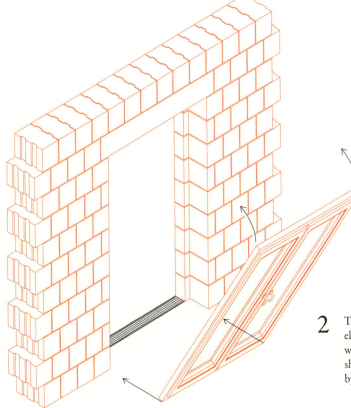

2 The timber window element is installed in the wall opening. The element should be fixed in position by two people.

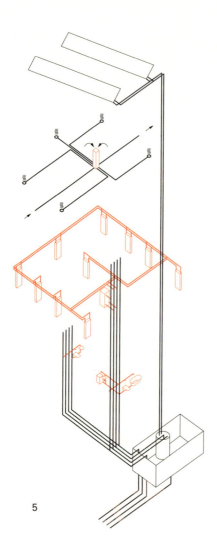

5

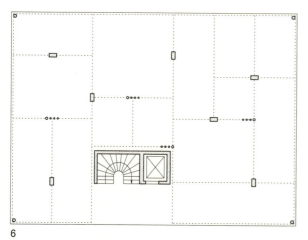

6

5: Building services and plant:
Each plot has two service shafts that house all the services. The insulated wires and pipes run from the utilities connection room, below the first floor slab and through the Allotment House. The settlers develop the infrastructure themselves, using exposed service runs below the ceiling slabs. The service supply shafts are located at the intersection of three rooms, allowing the sanitary facilities, kitchens, and laundry rooms to be flexibly connected to them.
Ventilation plan: An Octopus air distribution system integrated in the floor slabs serves as floor level ventilation. Each room has a ventilation outlet in front of the windows. Individual Multi 100 domestic ventilation appliances with a heat recovery system manufactured by the firm Paul provide an air exchange rate of 0.6.
Heating services: Heating is provided to units by a connection to a central-heating network. There is a central-heating transfer station with a plate heat exchanger and 1500 l heat buffer storage in the public utilities connection room on the ground floor. The heating supply is augmented by a 25 m² solar thermal energy system mounted on the roof that provides up to 16 KW. In summer hot water is provided by this solar system alone – additional district heating is not needed. The settlers connect the full-height tube radiators to the exposed pipe work directly below the ceiling. Cold water is supplied directly; hot water is heated locally in the Danfoss house station from the heating circuit and fed through the plot. This makes circulation unnecessary and meets the most stringent hygiene standards. The billing is based on the amount of heating energy consumed and on a cold water meter. The settlers develop the infrastructure themselves in the immediate proximity of the service shafts.
6: Empty floor plan.
7-9: Possible floor plans with varying apartment sizes:
7: 112 m² and 121 m² apartment.
8: 162 m² and 71 m² apartment.
9: 140 m² and 93 m² apartment.

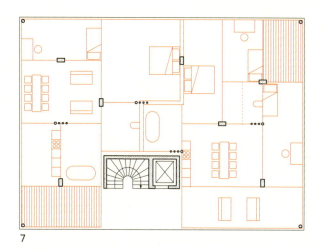

7

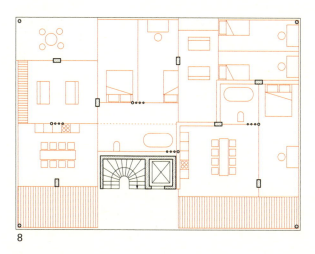

8

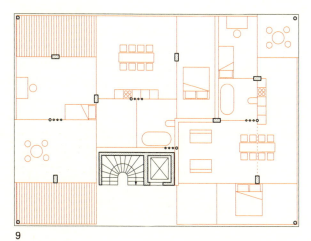

9

Those who wish to do so can ignore the recommendations and the material offered in the building kit and can improvise and everyone has the right to make their own improvements—and mistakes.

Settling is about self-determination on one's own plot. Technical support is required during the building process but neighbors negotiate their particular concerns with each other, as each plot is independent and developments on one plot do not affect the interests of the others. There is a general sense of agreement about the nature of a continuous building process, as all the settlers are self-builders. The Allotment House contains everything needed to build and operate a unit; the settlers can use the workshop spaces on the ground floor from the first day the building is open, and can run their own construction site from there. The Allotment House has railings along the balcony on each story, which makes scaffolding during construction unnecessary; the settlers can carry out their work from the 70-cm-wide strip of balcony.

The building contains eight units. Each unit has a plot size of 158 m^2, with an additional 13 m^2 workshop and parking space. The total cost of each plot is approximately EUR 150,000, all-inclusive, and this works out to be 950 EUR/m^2. Despite this very economical budget, it was difficult to find a financing strategy for the project. The usual procedure of getting a bank loan for each apartment could not be applied in this case, as banks refuse to finance self-build-projects—their loan guidelines only account for completely finished buildings, but to a bank our project is just a half-finished building with a load of construction materials delivered to the site. A possible alternative would have been to create a cooperative to act as the client for the project. However, the critical threshold for such a co-op to work economically is 20 parties, and our project only has eight. A solution began to materialize when we managed to interest a DIY superstore in becoming more than merely a material supplier to the project; they became the investor.

The reason for the willingness of the DIY superstores to get involved was simple. The concept of self-build for multi-story housing creates a high demand for building materials in urban environments, and the Allotment House offers construction suppliers an ideal platform for developing new markets. Manufacturers and retailers have a chance to develop new marketing techniques and get access to low-income customers, who are currently excluded from the real estate market. By using financing models DIY superstores have already introduced, and which have proven to be successful at a smaller scale, the Allotment House will be an exemplary all-in-one solution. The DIY superstore profits from long-term customer contacts and a stable turnover, while the customer has the benefit of access to favourable financing and advantageous quantity discounts. The DIY superstore is therefore investor, loan creditor, and supplier.

In this way everyone gains. Low-income people are given the chance to own their own dwellings as well as the agency to adapt those dwellings to their own standards and needs. The Wilhelmsburg district of Hamburg benefits from the increased engagement of homeowners, and a greater diversity in housing typologies, and the DIY stores gain a new customer base through their direct investment in the Allotment House. The project is also meant as a case-study to examine the feasibility of building customizable living spaces for urban settlers, especially important in the light of the shrinking tax base and therefore uncertain future social benefits and support.

About the authors: Established in 2000 by Anne-Julchen Bernhardt and Jörg Leeser, BeL Associates is based in Cologne, Germany. The office's work comprises 85 projects, with 16 built works, and seven that are in progress. Anne-Julchen Bernhardt is Professor of Building Typology of the RWTH Aachen. Jörg Leeser has taught at several universities in Germany and in the USA.

Governing the Commons in the New Millennium

A Diversity of Institutions for Natural Resource Management

ELINOR OSTROM AND HARINI NAGENDRA

The impact of humans on global environmental change is becoming increasingly apparent, with consequences ranging from impacts on climate change to declines in biodiversity, soil degradation and forest degradation. Governing natural resources sustainably thus represents a major challenge for the future. Given increases in population and in levels of human consumption, we have to develop a diverse and robust set of institutions for the sustainable use of natural resources.

In his influential article in *Science* magazine on "The Tragedy of the Commons," Garrett Hardin presented a logic that he presumed was general and referred to all common-pool natural resources that were not either government owned or privately owned. He envisioned a pasture open to all, in which each herder received an immediate individual benefit from adding animals to graze on the pasture and suffered only delayed costs (with his fellow herders) from overgrazing. Hardin concluded: "Therein is the tragedy. Each man is locked into a system that compels him to increase his herd without limit—in a world that is limited. Ruin is the destination toward which all men rush, each pursuing his own best interest in a society that believes in the freedom of the commons."[1]

Hardin's conclusion was immediately accepted by many scholars. His article is still required reading in most environmental science programs and frequently assigned multiple times during an undergraduate program. In the early days of the scholarly discussion, scholars tended to develop theoretical papers that posited narrowly rational resource users that did not take a long-term view of the problems they faced. Somehow, government officials, on the other hand, were posited as being able to take the public interest into account and develop policies that would avert the tragedy of the commons.

Policymakers tended to accept Hardin's results and thought the conclusions he drew made it obligatory for them to take positive actions to impose policies on the users of pastures, forests, fisheries, water systems and other common-pool resources in their domain. Government officials did not examine whether the users of these resources had developed rules of their own over time, because it was simply assumed that resource users were trapped and helpless. National governments around the world declared that government ownership was the only way to save resources from destruction. Forests in India, Thailand, and many countries in Africa were nationalized during the 1970s and 1980s in an immediate acceptance that this was the only way to avoid massive deforestation. In many instances, these and the related conversion of inshore fisheries policies had the effect of overruling locally developed institutions that were on the ground. In practice, these resources were often converted to "open access" given the lack of administrative follow-up and that local users were told they had no rights. As many of these policies appeared to accelerate deforestation and overuse of resources, a major debate about the best property-rights system for sustainable management of natural resources was initiated.

In addition to the findings that government policies nationalizing forests and other resources did not lead uniformly to a solution, other empirical studies recorded settings where the resource users themselves had developed their own rules that had enabled a resource to be used sustainably over long periods of time— sometimes exceeding a century or longer. The National Resource Council of the US National Academy of Sciences has convened two major meetings—one in 1985 and one 15 years later in 2000—of scholars from multiple disciplines to examine the evidence related to the ability of local users to organize their own rules. Slowly over time this led to the development of a more coherent theory of the commons.

When dealing with a presumption of an impossibility of resource users solving their own problems of overuse, finding a large number of cases where resource users succeed is an important accomplishment. That is exactly what scholars during the last part of the 20th century did. One of the major conceptual accomplishments was the emphatic recognition of the confusion that had existed for some time over the name used for resources and for potential institutional arrangements or property regimes. The term "common property resource" was abbreviated as CPR and widely used across the social sciences for resources such as forests, lakes, pastures, fisheries and irrigation systems. The term confused a resource system that might or might not have a linked property-rights system with a form of institution called "common property." This confused a resource—a common-pool resource—with a property system—a common property regime. The initials, CPR, were used for both concepts.

Slowly, over time, general agreement has been reached that a common-pool resource is one with two characteristics: (1) it is very costly to exclude potential beneficiaries from accessing and harvesting from the resource and (2) the amount of resource flows harvested by one user is subtracted from the quantity available to others. Thus, it shares the first characteristic with public goods (the cost of exclusion) and the second characteristics with private goods (subtractability). A common-pool resource can be managed under any of a broad type of property-rights regimes ranging from:

– Government ownership, where a formal government ranging in size from a local city all the way to national government claimed ownership of the resource and the right to fully determine who could or could not use it and under what circumstances;
– Private ownership, where a single individual or private firm has full claims to determine use patterns; and
– Community or common property ownership, where a group of individuals shares rights to ownership.

A fourth possibility is "no ownership" or "open access," which is what Hardin assumed in his illustrative case. Open access is only one out of four general possibilities that can relate to a common-pool resource.

Evidence from field as well as from research conducted in experimental laboratories around the world challenges the generalizability of Hardin's tragedy of the commons theory. While his theory is generally successful in predicting outcomes in settings where resource users are alienated from one another or cannot communicate effectively for reasons including the size of the group or their total separation, it does not provide an explanation for settings where resource users are able to create and sustain their own agreements to avoid serious problems of overharvesting. Nor does it predict well when government ownership will perform appropriately or whether privatization will improve outcomes. After more than three decades of research related to the possibility that some resource users will self-organize and manage a common-pool resource, while others will not, it is now possible to provide a theoretical argument for the factors affecting the likelihood that the users of a common-pool resource will commit themselves to changing rules from open access to a new set of rules that restricts who can use resource flows and potentially other rules affecting the sustainability of the resource.

Let us assume a set of resource users contemplating a proposed change in the rules related to their use of a common-pool resource. Each user has to compare the expected net benefits of harvesting resource units versus continuing to use no rules or existing rules that are not working well to the benefits he or she expects to achieve with a new set of rules that has been proposed. Each user must ask whether his or her evaluation of future benefits under a new set of rules is positive or negative. If the evaluation of net benefits is negative for all users, no one has an incentive to change rules. One can predict the resource will remain as open-access. If net benefits are positive for some users, each of these users needs to estimate three types of costs:

1. The up-front costs of time and effort spent devising and agreeing upon new rules;
2. The short-term costs of adopting new harvesting strategies; and
3. The long-term costs of monitoring and maintaining a self-governed system.

If the sum of these expected costs for all users exceeds the incentive to change, no user will invest the time and resources needed to create new institutions. No change will occur.

In field settings, not everyone is likely to expect the same costs and benefits from a proposed change. Some may perceive positive benefits after all costs have been taken into account, while others perceive net losses. Consequently, the collective-choice rules used to change the day-to-day operational rules in a group of resource users affect whether an institutional change favored by some and opposed by others will be adopted. One must recognize that not all collective decisions made in the field are democratic or, even if they are democratic, meet all of the conditions leading to stable outcomes. In many field studies, resource users draw on either the accepted rules that have evolved over time in social games or in political games related to the villages where resource users live. It may be that these rules are used as collective-choice rules to decide on future operational rules related to a common-pool resource.

For any collective-choice rule, such as unanimity or majority, there may be a minimum coalition of users (such as a small ruling elite) that agree that they should adopt new rules. If no minimum winning coalition (given the collective-choice rules-in-use) evaluates net benefits greater than the sum of the costs, no new operational rules will be adopted. If a local chief or other notable has dictatorial powers at the collective-choice level, then only this single person has to estimate that the costs of changing a rule are less than the benefits of a new rule. In this case, of course, there may not be widespread benefits for other members of the group. If the group relies on a larger collective-choice rule and if there are several such coalitions, the question of which coalition will form, and thus which rules will result, is a further theoretical issue that is too complex to address in this entry. A similar analysis is also relevant to the continuing consideration of changing operational rules over time.

The collective-choice rule used to change operational rules in field settings varies from an informal reliance on the decisions made by one or a few leaders, to a formal reliance on majority or super-majority vote, to reliance on consensus or close to unanimity. If there are substantial differences in the perceived benefits and costs of users, it is possible that one set of users will impose a new set of rules on the other users. The imposed new rules may then strongly favor those in the winning coalition and impose losses or lower benefits on those in the losing coalition. If expected benefits from a change in operational rules are not greater than expected costs for many users, however, the costs of enforcing a change in institutions will be much higher than when most participants expect to benefit from a change in rules over time. Where the enforcement costs are fully borne by the harvesters themselves, operational rules that provide a substantial benefit to most users lower the long-term costs of monitoring and sanctioning for a governing coalition. Where external authorities enforce the rules agreed upon by users, the distribution of costs and benefits are more likely to benefit a subgroup and may impose costs on the other users.

Conditions that Favor Community Governance

One of the key findings of empirical field research on collective action is the multiplicity of rules-in-use found in successful commons regimes around the world. This has spurred efforts to identify principles of institutional design that characterize robust, long-lasting institutional arrangements for the governance of the commons. To be effective, rules must be generally known and understood, considered relatively legitimate, generally followed, and enforced. Effective, sustainable community management of common property natural resources is also more likely to occur when the boundary of the resource is easy to identify, changes in the state of the resource can be monitored at a relatively low cost, the rate of change in resource condition and in the socioeconomic and technological conditions of users remains moderate, communities maintain frequent social interactions with each other that increase trust within the community (thereby increasing social capital), outsiders can be relatively easily excluded from accessing the resource (preventing large-scale invasion of the resource by outsiders), and rule infractions are monitored and sanctioned. Naturally, all of these conditions will not be present in all field settings—but when present, they do appear to increase the likelihood of successful community management.

Under appropriate conditions, communities can devise appropriate operational and collective-choice arrangements that enable the sustainable use of natural resources. Indeed, this has been observed in field contexts ranging from forests to fisheries and fresh water systems. Just as government ownership does not represent a final solution for the sustainable use of natural resources, however, neither is community management a panacea for all the ills that plague natural resource management. It is difficult to craft successful, sustainable and robust local institutional arrangements by imposing rules from external authorities or through the influx of funds from external agencies. Unfortunately, many policy analysts have not recognized this problem. All too often, analysts enthusiastically propose blueprint, cookie-cutter approaches to community conservation. These approaches are based on relatively simple, even somewhat simplistic models, of what they consider to be "community" management applied across multiple contexts.

In reality, these policy changes are often cosmetic, and lack effective community management. Little recognition has been given to the time needed by a community to develop some of the essential elements of achieving a self-governed or co-managed resource system. The large-scale, rapid expansion of many of these programs has led to problems such as elite capture (especially where the influx of large sums of money has taken place), the "crowding out" of indigenously developed rules that are more appropriate to local context by externally imposed, blueprint rules, increase in social conflict, and a range of other problems. Unfortunately, critiques of these simplistic panacea-like approaches have not yet penetrated policy circles that still recommend simple, uniformly applicable and rapidly scalable solutions to the complex, context-sensitive problems of resource governance.

Much more attention needs to be paid to the need for adaptive crafting of institutions that fit the socio-ecological system of interest. Biophysical scientists have long recognized that ecological systems vary dramatically according to local context. Factors that range from elevation, slope, aspect, temperature, rainfall, soil, and microclimatic conditions all have an impact on biodiversity at a particular location. Policy scientists need to recognize a similar diversity in the institutions that can assist human users to devise arrangements for sustainable management of a resource. Along with encouraging conditions favorable for the success of collective action, learning and adaptation to changing socioeconomic, ecological, technological and policy environments will be critical for the long-term persistence of these solutions in the rapidly changing world of the new millennium.

Governing large-scale commons such as international rivers, the oceans, and the global atmosphere are among the major challenges facing all of us in the 21st century. Substantial progress has been made in developing complex institutional arrangements for improving the ecological conditions of the Rhine River and some other international rivers through initiatives taken by environmental NGOs, local citizens, national governments, and international regimes. The Montreal Protocol on Substances that Deplete the Ozone Layer is a clear example of a successful international regime. We are in an era, however, in which considerable conflict exists among some of the other international agreements such as the Convention on International Trade in Endangered Species of Wild Fauna and Flora (CITES), the Agreement on Trade-Related Aspects of Intellectual Property Rights (TRIPS Agreement), and the General Agreement on Tariffs and Trade (GATT).

Many of the same lessons learned about smaller-scale common-pool resources apply to larger scales—particularly the need to understand that each ecological region is composed of a unique mix of biophysical and social attributes. Similarly, the passage of a formal agreement is not equivalent to the individuals, corporations, NGOs, and relevant governments involved understanding, agreeing to, and following the formal set of rules. Given the growing interconnections among the peoples of the Earth, the coming era is one of great opportunities for creative forms of international governance—as well as one of great threat if the problems associated with diverse large-scale commons are ignored.

1.) Garrett Hardin, "The Tragedy of the Commons." *Science* 162, (1968): p. 1244

This article is held under a Creative Commons Attribution-Share Alike license. It is held online as the following resource: Harini Nagendra and Elinor Ostrom (Lead Author); Peter Saundry (Topic Editor), 2008. "Governing the commons in the new millennium: A diversity of institutions for natural resource management." In: Encyclopedia of Earth. Eds. Cutler J. Cleveland (Washington, D.C.: Environmental Information Coalition, National Council for Science and the Environment). [First published in the Encyclopedia of Earth November 16, 2007; Last revised August 12, 2008; Retrieved August 20, 2010] <http://www.eoearth.org/article/Governing_the_commons_in_the_new_millennium:_A_diversity_of_institutions_for_natural_resource_management>

About the authors: Elinor Ostrom is Arthur F. Bentley Professor of Political Science, and Senior Research Director of the Workshop in Political Theory and Policy Analysis, Indiana University; and Founding Director, Center for the Study of Institutional Diversity, Arizona State University. She is the co-winner of the 2009 Nobel Prize in Economic Sciences, and is the author of several books, including *Governing the Commons*, *Understanding Institutional Diversity*, and *Working Together* (with Amy Poteete and Marco Janssen).

Dr. Harini Nagendra is DST Ramanujan Fellow at Ashoka Trust for Research in Ecology and the Environment, Bangalore, and Asia Research Coordinator at Center for the Study of Institutions, Population, and Environmental Change at Indiana University. Her research examines the drivers and outcomes of ecological change in urban and forested landscapes in South Asia. Her recent co-edited volume *Reforesting Landscapes: From Pattern to Process* was published in 2010 by Springer.

The Promise of Neza

Building a City for 1.2 Million Inhabitants One House at a Time

JOSE CASTILLO

Located only 12 km east of Mexico City's center lies one of the most remarkable urban phenomena of the last half-century. The development of the peripheral city known as "Neza" was started in the mid-1940s, and it is home now to some 1.2 million people. The Mexican government did not plan Neza, nor was Neza organized by professional city planners or architects: Neza was built and transformed by its inhabitants, one house at a time, street by street, operating where developers left off. Neza has developed in little time from wood and cardboard subsistence housing to a complex, vibrant, and viable city.

Mexico City is a city of the 20th century. Though the Aztecs founded it in 1328, and the Spanish conquered and radically transformed it in 1521, it barely grew in size and population until the beginning of the 20th century. At that time, Mexico City had a population of approximately 300,000, which by 1929 had grown to 500,000 in an area of 10 km². By 1950, the population had risen to 3.1 million, and the city occupied an area of 250 km².

THE PROMISE OF NEZA

In the 1950s, Mexico City was on its way to becoming a major capital, rapidly undergoing important social changes that were sustained by a high level of economic growth and an overall process of modernization, which embraced transformations in education, health, and housing for the urban masses. Fueled by rural-urban migration and high birth rates, this massive demographic growth was reflected in the built landscape of the city, in its infrastructure, as well as in its housing.

Mexico City faced two radically different forces in urban development at that time: one was an understanding of the city through modern architecture and planning, accompanied by government-sanctioned techniques to address problems of housing, infrastructure, and services. The second was pervasive informal urbanization, which was gaining momentum rapidly, and was characterized by urban processes that took place outside the "legal" planned and regulated modes of city development.

These two forces were evidence of a kind of schizophrenic divide between the normative practices of urban planning and the reality of the city. During that time, Mexico City produced some of the most heroic, optimistic, and modern architectural and planning projects, resulting in places like the National University Campus and a variety of successful housing projects. For example, the President Miguel Aleman multifamily housing project, built in 1948, helped to establish a benchmark for housing policy, communal living, and scale, with a density of 1000 units in a single block of housing. A few years later, in 1952, the Juarez multifamily housing project placed 1,445 units of housing in a 250,000 m² superblock, and finally in 1963, the Tlatelolco housing project placed 13,000 units of housing in superblocks of 200,000 m², with 60 percent open space. These were all evolving iterations of a model of architectural intervention that become the tool for urban transformation.

During the 1950s and 1960s, the city's mayor, Ernesto Uruchurtu, made urban planning interventions a cornerstone of his leadership agenda. A Robert Moses-esque figure, known as the "Iron Mayor" for his severity, Uruchurtu ruled the city with a combination of populist and socially conservative urban policies that focused on urban growth control, slum clearance, and the construction of large-scale housing, infrastructure, and service projects. In 1958, Uruchurtu implemented a zoning ban on all real estate subdivisions in the Federal District that—by default—translated into a prohibition on low-income housing. Uruchurtu made a point of immediately evicting new informal settlers in the Federal District and steadfastly resisted bringing in infrastructure and services or granting legal land tenure to areas that had been developed illegally.

1: (Previous page) Aerial view of Neza towards the west.
2: Aerial view of Bordo de Xochiaca Avenue facing the east: a mile-long open-air market occupies the median of what used to be the limits of Lake Texcoco.

Within that context one of the most radical and interesting urban phenomena of the last 60 years has taken hold. Ciudad Nezahualcoyotl, better known as Neza, is a community of 1.2 million inhabitants, which has developed informally, or better said, organically, over the past six decades.

Neza is without a doubt the most dramatic example of such an area of organic and informal development. Located 12 km east of downtown Mexico City on the dry bed of Lake Texcoco, its development is intimately related to the drainage of Lake Texcoco in the Valley of Mexico, an operation that started centuries ago with the Spanish colonists and continued well into the 20th century. It was a site that was prone to flooding during the rainy season and to dust storms during the dry season. The development of this vast territory started in the mid-1940s on land with ambiguous tenure, but it wasn't until the 1960s that rapid growth took hold. The receding waterline of the lake continually reconfigured the territory, generating property disputes that remained unresolved for decades.

For many decades, Neza evoked images of chaos, injustice, fraud, despair, vulnerability, crime, and real estate speculation. Neza was—in public opinion, as well as professional circles—the symbol of everything that was wrong with the city. Pollution, environmental decay, and uncontrolled growth all plagued Neza. To its critics, Neza represented bastard urbanization, and was like a cancer that should never have been allowed to grow.

The origins of Neza can be traced to two dominant forces. The first is the rural migration to urban environments and the accompanying demographic changes taking place in Mexico during the mid-20th century: close to 60 percent of the population living in Neza in 1970 had been born elsewhere in the country. The other is the series of disjointed urban policies implemented by the local governments of the Federal District (DF) and the State of Mexico. As a result of rent control policies implemented in downtown Mexico City, added to the uncoordinated policies of the State of Mexico, and the DF's ban on land subdivisions and imposition of growth limits, large masses of residents were forced to move out to the periphery in search of housing opportunities. Neza, with its privileged location just over the state line, was an obvious first choice.

Neza developed through illegal land subdivisions by developers, and through invasions by squatters. Developers appropriated huge tracts of land on the former lake site, through purchases from the government and dubious negotiations, and most of them shirked their legal obligation to provide services and infrastructure. Rather, there was a tacit agreement that the buyers of this "under-urbanized" land, of dubious legal status, would have to fight, negotiate, and self-manage in order to achieve progressive incorporation into a more formal urban regime and independently satisfy their minimum living requirements. Settlers and buyers had to organize into social and civic groups to handle tasks such as the provision of water through tanker trucks, the connection of homes and businesses to the electrical grid, the creation of health and education facilities, and the minimization of damage from flooding. Urbanism was progressively achieved through negotiation with developers and state authorities.

In spite of the fact that much of this urbanization was informal, there was widespread use of drawings and plans for sales and marketing. In some cases these documents show a nuanced comprehension of urban plans, comparable to that of other more formal developers working within the primary land market at the same time. The plans show clear street hierarchies as well as the provision of areas for schools, markets, medical facilities, and open spaces.

The pattern of almost immediate land sales and appropriations, as land was reclaimed progressively during the drainage of Lake Texcoco, points to a rational and almost Jeffersonian subdivision of land. The first operation to transform the territory used an urban grid on two scales: First a maxi-grid, with sections of roughly 1 km^2 to organize the territory into districts, and then a second mini-grid, which arranged each district according to its own distinct logic, with a tight inner structure of roads, blocks, and single-family private lots of approximately 150 m^2 each, measuring 9 m wide at the street edge running 17 m deep into the block. The district typologies varied according to the different developers and to the modality of occupation, either by informal "invasion" or by illegal sale. A typical district has orthogonal blocks ranging from 35 to 40 m in width and from 150 to 225 m in length. The local streets are between 8 and 12 m wide, and the area of each neighborhood is delimited by avenues that are 45 m wide, which is one and a half times wider than the average avenue in Manhattan. At the center of each district, an area measuring 450 m x 125 m is reserved for schools and markets. There are also areas set aside as open space, but for the most part these parcels were eventually built upon, leaving the districts with minimal open public space.

In spite of these plans, architecture and planning decisions were also made at the level of organized groups and individual stakeholders, from the progressive construction of the individual private dwelling to the construction and appropriation of public space and alternative infrastructures. Some of these changes include the development of multifamily households within a single lot, the creation of a myriad of home businesses, and the rise of petty entrepreneurs, as well as the flexible use of the street for alternative forms of public life.

In the late 1960s, a social movement called Movement for the Restoration of Settlers (MRC) was organized by different groups that had been articulating demands and obtaining improvements for many years. The MRC was organized as a response to the unfulfilled provision of essential services, infrastructure creation and delivery by developers. By channeling demands, negotiating with authorities and developers, and articulating protests, the MRC was able to achieve many of the improvements that are visible in Neza today. In fact, it was only in the late 1960s when state organisms, such as Plantecnica and Auris, became involved that small incremental improvements were made in the spatial and infrastructural organization of the settlement. These improvements included bringing in water, sewage, and electrical infrastructure. Ultimately, the MRC was co-opted politically—something common among other grassroots movements in Mexico—initially through an internal division within the movement in 1971, and definitively after the establishment of FINEZA, a trust fund created by the government in 1973 as a response to the urban, political, administrative, and judicial problems that affected Neza. The MRC set a precedent for other grassroots movements striving for urbanism, such as the Movimiento Urbano Popular or the Asamblea de Barrios, and also served as a model for the provision of urban services in most situations of informal urbanization. The MRC was the first group of "bottom-up" planners in Mexico.

The dwellings in Neza were built incrementally over long periods of time, sometimes over four to five years, sometimes over decades. The first settlers in Neza, both buyers and squatters, were involved substantially in the construction of their own houses. Self-build processes were dominant in Neza, at least in the first 20 years of the settlement. In these processes, community members and their kin played an important part in the construction, usually done over weekends or in the absence of other remunerated work.

The early stage involved construction with makeshift materials, including cardboard, asbestos, plywood, and wooden pallets. Most of these materials were recycled from demolitions or even industrial processes. It is no accident that Neza, like other informal settlements, developed close to landfills and waste dumps, and that there is an active secondary market for recycled material in the area around many informal settlements.

The first buildings in Neza were usually small shacks and these tended to occupy the back or central area of the lot, in some cases with a fence or small wall toward the street. In the absence of services, there was no need for a foundation, hard flooring, drainage or piping to be implemented at that stage. The requirement for water was resolved by the use of autonomous tanks provisioned by water trucks. Toilet and bath facilities, when existent, were usually separate from the main structure. At that early stage, the settlement looked a bit like a rural or suburban environment.

As the settlement evolved, individually according to the economic success of each household, the dwelling became more permanent. The first important transition was establishing firm property boundaries through the construction of three-meter-high division walls. This created a kind of "bunker" in which the house could grow. Later on came the replacement of the earthen floor with a concrete slab floor. This proved to be an effective way to deal with the constant flooding of the terrain. Though not necessarily higher, the concrete floor provided more stability and safety and better hygienic conditions for the dwelling.

Wood and cardboard elements shifted to concrete-block and brick structures. In some instances rebuilding meant starting nearly from scratch, but in most cases there was a replacement of the existing housing elements with new ones. When money was limited the blocks were just stacked, notably in the creation of partition walls, but in most cases new walls were built with mortar and reinforced with concrete columns. A basic foundation, just a few inches deep, and a reinforced concrete structure, usually made with small concrete columns and steel rebar, served as an organizational shell within which a house could grow for decades.

The most common building material was concrete blocks. This material strategy proved to be the most cost-efficient way for dwellers to transform their homes from makeshift to permanent: the use of the simple block permitted evolution and allowed for esthetic or functional improvements. The block construction gave a certain security of tenure because the threat of eviction or bulldozing seemed less likely in a sturdy structure. The roofs of the settlement houses evolved from sheet metal to concrete slabs and in recent decades have even been constructed with prefabricated concrete elements. The perception of solidity in the building also creates a perception of security in dwellers.

Horizontal growth came before vertical growth, but in every stage of development rebar steel rods protruded from the walls and through the roof as evidence of the aspiration to grow, and most importantly provide the necessary structural elements to connect the next set of new walls and slabs.

3

3: The free section in Neza's dwellings: each level is evidence of a different stage of construction, material, and even esthetic choices.
4: Diagram showing the incremental transformation of a small shag of makeshift materials into a consolidated mixed-use building.

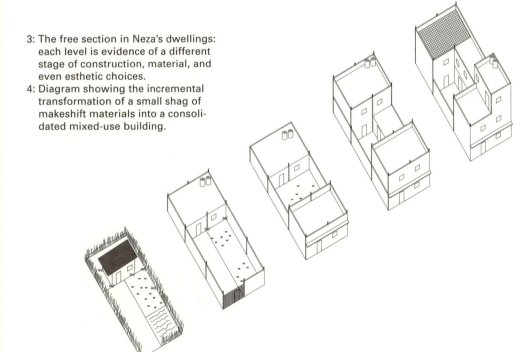

4

6

7

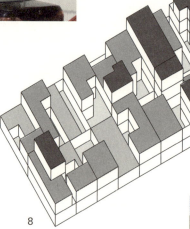

8

9

6: Ground floor dentist's office next to an evangelical church: typical Neza mixture of uses.
7: Classic multi-tenant retail along Neza's main avenues: optical, medical and dental services combined in a single building.
8: Volumetric diagram. More than 75 percent of the lots have two-story structures and 30 percent have three or more stories. Dwelling sizes of 250 or 300 m^2 are possible.
9: The exception to the low-rise development: a six-story building used as a gym and private educational facility.

The small size of the lots, approximately 150 m², meant that only a few types of dwelling could exist, most of them privileging a small courtyard in the central section of the lot. This allowed for both horizontal and vertical growth over time.

The average dwelling tends to leave between 10 and 20 percent of the lot empty, though in some cases some dwellings grew to occupy the total footprint of the lot. Over the decades of development since Neza's beginning, more than 75 percent of the lots have two-story structures and 30 percent have three or more stories. It is not uncommon for dwellings to be over 250 or 300 m² in size. In some extreme cases, properties were "extruded" to five or six stories, the maximum height that the soil type and conditions can bear with a relatively simple foundation structure. These comparatively large structures are always mixed-use, including retail and other commercial space in addition to housing. Differences in the quality of buildings and dwellings indicate where professionals were involved in construction, and where income distinctions began to appear. To this day one can see a certain degree of heterogeneity in the homes in Neza.

The infrastructure in Neza, in a certain way, was more traditional in terms of its provision and construction by the local and state governments. The one significant difference was that it was built post facto. The economics of Neza's grid, the land occupation patterns, and the lacustrine soil were the determining factors for the slow provision of services.

The retrofitting took place according to population density: neighborhoods where the population grew faster got their services more quickly. For many years there was no sewage system whatsoever. The first effort toward sewage handling, during the late 1950s and early 1960s, was to create open-air canals that drained into the lake. A considerable amount of Neza's sewage was being dumped into Lake Texcoco during that time, which meant that the settlement was continuously filled with the stench of putrid water.

In the period from 1969-1970, the first governmental efforts to bring water, sewage, and electricity to Neza were formally started. Before this, less than 15 percent of the dwellings had some sort of contract with the Federal Electricity Commission. A large portion of the districts were serviced with both private electricity and public street lighting, but a few areas were determined to have an insufficient population, so a primary grid was not laid down; instead a few makeshift transformers were installed. Because all of the primary types of infrastructure are threaded through the street, the orderly grid of Neza facilitated a plainly ordered and clean—though expensive—operation. Many of the unpaved streets

10

11

12

13

14

10: The central area of a Neza neighborhood: retail, infrastructure and services.
11: View of a typical Neza neighborhood with consolidated homes and higher car ownership.
12: The exceptional case of a gated cul-de-sac street in Neza with private security.
13: A less developed area of Neza, close to Chimalhuacan: In the absence of cars, the street is used by skateboarders.
14: The intersection of two commercial avenues with a pharmacy and a shoe store.

were finally paved with asphalt or concrete once sewage, water and electricity lines were installed.

In less than 60 years, Neza made the jump from a desolate territory to a city of more than 1.2 million people. Currently Neza is a fully matured city with a high degree of social interaction, plurality, and spatial complexities that other "planned" communities can only wish for. It is possible now to reassess the Neza operating system, and to ask ourselves whether it can actually represent a development model for the city at large. The following is a series of ten short observations on the potentialities, both historical and projected, of Neza.

– Mat City—Morphology vs. Program: Seen from the air, Neza displays the quality of an extra-large mat city: no hierarchies, no verticality. More interesting is the fact that this spatial organization, with its strong urban morphology, as manifested by its clear and severe grid, is countered by an absolute freedom in terms of land use. Neza is the equivalent of a Manhattan grid operating in a Houston (non) land-use plan.

– Open City: Part of the success of Neza can be traced to the fact that, in spite of its size, it still remains an accumulation of neighborhoods, even if most of them house over 50,000 inhabitants. While there are some exceptions, created with private gated streets, Neza remains in general an open city. This is counter to trends in other parts of Mexico City, where gated communities have risen in popularity, both in middle- and low-income developments and in the more typical gated, high-end, exclusive housing. This openness, connected to the original organizational strategy for the neighborhoods, has created a strong sense of identity and community.

– Density: Neza combines a low-rise fabric with a high-density. The density in the neighborhoods is of around 280 inhabitants per hectare, in some of them increasing to over 360 per hectare, which makes it denser than Cerda's Eixample in Barcelona. This is remarkable, especially taking into account that most of the lots contain single-family dwellings with two to three built levels at the most. This is explained by the relatively large size of the families that inhabit the dwellings, as much as by the multifamily household and property conditions on many of the small lots, which is common in Neza.

– On Type: It is clear that the limited variations in lot size and form, combined with the row-house structure, has created a specific type of housing in Neza. It is this same structure that allowed an easy transition from a shack in the back of the lot, made with makeshift materials, to the home built at the front of the property with standard—and in some cases high-end—architectural finishes. If aligning a building to the street was considered "consolidation" a few decades ago, now this consolidation is reflected in the nearly total occupation of the lot by structures and in vertical densification, with up to five stories of mixed-use developments.

– Adaptive Suburban: From its origins as a bedroom community with very little economic activity, Neza has shown an incredible adaptive capacity in terms of growth, household size, type, and use of its lots and buildings. This is evidenced by Neza's transformation over time from a substandard suburb to a huge economic, cultural, and social engine. The constant consolidation and the unfinished condition of the contemporary city is at the core of the recognition that it is probably more important to consider the way cities and communities perform, rather than what they look like.

– Public Space/Public Life: Neza's use of a city structure with a small block size and its absence of "formalized" traditional urban open spaces made the street the default public space *par excellence*. Clearly not only a place for cars to move, the street became the arena for public life, where leisure activities, recreation, economic empowerment and political action take place, even up to the present day.

Jane Jacobs Reloaded: In a similar fashion to Jane Jacobs, the anonymous planners, community organizations, and inhabitants of Neza believed that it was only through autonomy, self-organization, and activism that one could truly resolve the problems of the city, combat authoritarian decisions, and reclaim a legitimate and effective role in the creation of community. Neza is evidence that communities thrive in the spaces between the public and the private, the individual and the collective, the physical grid and the social flow. It is also evidence of the less accepted idea that the constant exposure to those liminal spaces and to the way that conflicts are addressed under such conditions are what construct a productive and thriving public sphere as well as a fertile cultural milieu.

– Neza Unlearned: The recent shopping mall development at the northern edge of Neza, on top of the former landfill, is in a way evidence of the success of Neza, but at the same time it is Neza unlearned; it is an absolutely generic suburban mall, disjoined from the city and unable to provide anything positive to the urban condition of Neza. It's paradoxical that when a large investment project comes about, and formal planning decisions occur, they take the form of an anti-urban model of development.

– The Future of Neza: Construction for a new bus-based rapid transit (BRT), the so-called "Mexibus," has just begun, and this means that many of the neighborhoods of Neza will be within walking distance of public and sustainable transport. The 18-km-long line serving Neza will begin at Pantitlan, one of the most important subway and transportation terminals at the edge of Neza, then bisect Neza and venture into Chimalhuacán, the next informal community, which already has a population of half a million inhabitants. Parallel to the BRT corridor, a new bicycle path will enhance the already dynamic bicycle use in the community. The use of environmentally friendly mobility such as bikes, rickshaws known as bicitaxis, and pedestrian routes has been strong for some years now.

Neza as a Sustainable Future for the City? In many ways Neza represents the future of Mexico City, and maybe even a way of making more sustainable cities in the future. There is no doubt whatsoever that the land where Neza developed was unfit both for agriculture and for urban development. Still to this day, this is evident in the fact that only a few trees are able to grow in the salty soil and only a few buildings are more than four stories tall due to the poor subsoil quality. In any case, Neza's ability to overcome the unfitness of the land makes the development even more outstanding. In the process, Neza created an awareness of the environment and a conscience of how urban peripheries are transformed.

Without ignoring its deficiencies, it is impressive to see how Neza has developed a very distinct and often very successful urbanity. The possible discomfort with the banal, vulgar, generic, and sometimes mediocre qualities of its built environment never detracts from the creative and subversive transgressions that take place there everyday and challenge our fixed assumptions of what a city is and can be. In spite of its visual qualities, Neza has become more complex and diverse, more flexible in land use, and more intense in its economic and social activities as it has evolved over time.

About the author: Jose Castillo is the co-founder, along with Saidee Springall, of arquitectura 911sc, a practice of architecture, urban design, and planning based in Mexico City. His work and writings have appeared in several publications including Praxis Journal, 2G, Domus, Monocle and AD and in the book *The Endless City*. Castillo is a member of the advisory board of Urban Age and currently teaches at the Universidad Iberoamericana and at the University of Pennsylvania.

STIMULATE STAKEHOLDERS

The Mexican Dream

Bottom-up Customization of Generic Tract Housing in Mexico

LIVIA CORONA

In 2000, Mexican presidential candidate Vicente Fox Quezada proposed an unprecedented plan to build two million low-income homes throughout the country during his six-year term. On the eve of his election, Fox proclaimed, "My presidency will be remembered as the era of public housing." To enact this initiative, the federal government agency INFONAVIT commissioned the construction of low-income housing to a small group of private real estate developers. Almost overnight, grids of 2,000 to 80,000 identical homes sprouted up, and they continue to spread in remote rural areas throughout the country.

During the past four years, I have been exploring these developments in my photographic project *Two Million Homes for Mexico*. Through images, films, and interviews, I look for the space between Fox's promises and their fulfillment. In my photographs of many developments built throughout the country, I document the rapid redefinition of Mexican "small town" life and the sudden transformation of the Mexican ecological and social landscape. This type of urbanization

prototype, now prevalent in Mexico, marks a profound change in the shaping of our experience as citizens of a broader world. In my photographs I am particularly interested in the effects of these neighborhoods as a cultural backdrop, and their role in shaping the perspective of the younger generations who grow up within them through key formative years.

President Fox was the first non-ruling party candidate to take reign after 71 years of Institutional Revolutionary Party (PRI) rule, and his promise to build two million new homes for Mexico involved fundamental alterations to pre-existing land titles as well as extensive involvement from a handful of private developers and mortgage financing companies. By the end of his term Fox's goal was surpassed; more than two million new homes were constructed and it is estimated that another four million homes will be built through similar approaches in the term of current President Felipe Calderon.

The land reform began with an overhaul of the system of communal agrarian land titles known as *ejidos*, which had been established in the early 20th century with the Agrarian Reform Act. *Ejidos* gave groups of farmers the right to farm specific plots of land without granting them the option to sell the property. When President Fox took office, NAFTA was in full effect and many Mexican farmers were struggling to compete with low-priced produce imported from the United States. With Fox's new Housing Act, restrictions on *ejidos* were restructured and farmers were encouraged to sell their land to real estate developers who intended to construct the promised housing developments. This farmland was cheap and plentiful, but it was far from city centers and infrastructurally unequipped for the sudden deluge of inhabitants to come. Today, even after the construction of many housing developments, it is still possible to see the *ejido* plots of the past now turned into housing areas in satellite images. From this perspective, the developments can appear like scabs on an agrarian skin though with the straight lined boundaries that the previous agrarian plots required.

While Fox was advocating housing construction and farmers were selling off their land, developers were advertising new housing developments through a loose interpretation of the American dream. Their marketing announced tract homes, cul-de-sacs, and suburban life in the United States. Using model homes, maquettes, radio, and TV spots, they advertised a home purchase option through which Mexican citizens could buy into a modern lifestyle and begin a supposedly new and improved way of life, especially for young couples starting a family. But the advertisements did not mention that the size and construction of this new life would be comparatively small because loans were based solely on earnings, and therefore the homes had to be priced very low. For the developer to remain profitable within this market, the average size of a start-up family home had to be approximately 40 m². Inspite of it, demand for affordable homes was so pressing that families often did not ask important questions such as: Will this home be big enough for me and my two or three children to live in? Will there be an opportunity to enroll my children in the nearby school? Will there be employment options and how long will the commute be?

In a regular city or a rural setting, a home can be an anchor for progress. But the Fox low-income housing archetype removed housing from both urban and rural contexts. Houses are situated in isolated and homogenous suburban conditions. Neighborhoods consist only of homes, a few convenience stores, schools limited to primary and secondary education, a single park with a slide and swingset, and sometimes a soccer field. They are like feral cities—for if new neighborhoods are the natural offspring of a city, these neighborhoods have been separated from their urban mother too early, left to fend for themselves out in the open landscape. Citizens need intact neighborhoods that behave like a community; they can't develop to this status when they have been cut off from communal structures too early.

These new isolated and detached cities are no architectural or urban gesture to integrate the less privileged into the fabric of an existing city. There is also no recognition that the ruling and the working class are in a symbiotic relationship. The working class is relegated to the far outskirts, valuable for the city only during work when they come in to render services. The design of these developments is based solely on profitability for the developer, with almost no consideration for basic tenets of urbanization, leave alone the lives of those who will be shaped by these confined environments.

However imperfect, these houses do represent a certain freedom for some people, and in my interviews with residents, they speak about both positive and negative aspects. Some people express relief upon moving into their own home. A city clerk living in a neighborhood near Merida, Yucatan, told me his new house had given him and his partner freedom to live together on their own for the first time. To maximize space, they had set up the house with hammocks for sleeping, which is common in Yucatan, —yet not part of the "modern" lifestyle as portrayed by the developers—and they enjoyed living away from the city bustle. But most interviews reveal that living in these isolated neighborhoods with minimal services has an enormous and negative social and psychological impact.

THE MEXICAN DREAM

I first noticed these neighborhoods in 2002 when I stayed in one of the homes at a development 65 km inland from Cabo San Lucas. At the time, I was traveling for a book project through many rural areas of Mexico with a group of people who perform dwarf bullfights as the famed Enanitos Toreros de Mexico. The show locations took place mostly in inland farm towns, far from the typical business or tourism routes. In contrast to those places, I found the development outside Cabo San Lucas, the small living space we shared, the window view of endless rows of houses with the exact same design, and the overly close proximity of the units to be very striking. I was interested in the contrast between these new developments and traditional Mexican small towns, where the church, the zocalo, and the city hall remain in the center and the city progressively spreads out in the direction of the four winds. I was also curious to find out how these new development towns compared to Ciudad Neza, a low-income city I had stayed at many times while visiting friends. Located northeast in Mexico's Federal District, Neza was built informally by people who had negotiated their own needs with their neighbors without government regulations or the involvement of developers.

There was no precedent for the scale and repetition I witnessed when driving through these neighborhoods. By the end of 2005, as I continued my travel in rural areas, I saw more and more of these developments sprout up. Reminiscent of Levittowns with a virus, they were established as a result of continually inbred idea configurations that intensified the propensity for urban genetic collapse. San Buenaventura in Iztapaluca: 47,500 almost identical homes. Las Delicias in Tijuana: 20,000. Ciudad Bicentenaria in Zumpango: programmed for 120,000 homes. One developer imitating the other: Casas Geo, Casas Ara, Casas Urbi—the same names throughout the country. The developers' web sites showed that such developments were being built in almost each of Mexico's 31 states. It was possible to locate and purchase an identical house in almost any remote agrarian area.

To get views of the developments from above, but not from the remote distance of satellite images, I rented a helicopter to shoot aerial photographs of a neighborhood of 40,000 homes in Iztapaluca. Before our departure, my assistant and I spent three days in the neighborhood passing out flyers that invited people to step outside of their homes at the time the helicopter would fly overhead. I wanted the photographs to show the people who lived in the neighborhood, as well as their homes, to break any spell of beautiful abstract geometric repeating patterns.

At first, when seen through a camera lens, from a helicopter traveling at a high altitude, the neighborhoods were in fact appealing, like a pattern of biologi-

cal cell structures under a microscope, captivating because of that biophillic way in which the brain can respond to naturally repeating patterns and their subtle deviations. But looking closer, I wondered if the forces that caused this pattern could be considered in accord with nature in any way. Then, when I directed the helicopter to reduce its altitude and zoom in on the neighborhood, the full complexity of the human lives involved became clearer.

The aerial photographs were followed by knocking on doors of houses arbitrarily. I would show residents images made of their neighborhood from above and ask if they wanted to talk about what it was like to live there. I would photograph the people and their homes based on aspects they discussed in the conversations. Sometimes I would shoot individual portraits of a person within his/her neighborhood, other times I would zoom in on physical details of the neighborhood itself. Together with the aerial photos, the images explore the architectural, sociological, personal, and esthetic issues of these developments, and they create a un-linear though numerical act of zooming in and zooming out of something to understand its total scale.

Using principles of symmetry, the homes in these developments are designed to mirror each other, and to create the appearance of a single large home when two or four small homes are combined together. Scale models of the homes used for marketing frequently contain furniture made at a smaller scale in order to make the home appear more spacious. Residents often tell stories about their furniture not fitting in the rooms as they had envisioned. Full-scale model homes are usually constructed at a street corner, or at the edge of a site in order to give the impression of freestanding, sunlit units in an expansive setting. For sites in remote locations, prospective buyers are taken on busses from cities to these future neighborhoods. They are driven through the newly gridded streets and then brought to the model home. The salesperson, as tour guide on this promotional trip, points out where schools and commercial establishments will be built. But they don't reveal that the developer is not responsible for building anything other than the shell of the primary and secondary school, and provide minimal open space. Developers often consider the land between the façade of the home and the street as public space to abide by the minimum requirement set by the government, then don't allow homeowners to expand their homes into this yard. Moreover, they often sell this yard to the homeowner as an assigned parking spot.

The houses in these neighborhoods are constructed in the cheapest possible way. Many of them have only two load-bearing walls, at the front and the back.

Because the houses are built as attached modules, the partition walls between homes are made of Unicel, a panel made of expanded polystyrene foam with a cement coating. The roofs are of a similar construction, with one or two beams supporting Unicel sheets. Because it is so thin, the ceiling often sags, cracks, or leaks, forcing people to redo the roof. This is frequently taken as a chance to add another story to the house since space is always lacking. Construction workers have told me how every centimeter of space is accounted for. A negotiation between neighbors over the exact location of the property line can mean the difference between fitting or not fitting a clothes hanger on the rod of a bedside closet.

To build additional stories, or to make other substantial changes, the house must be structurally fortified from within. This is usually done by a construction worker in an ad hoc manner, with neither engineer nor architect. But if the project is successful, news travels by word of mouth and the worker can find more projects in other homes. Construction work has become an important informal industry in these developments, and workers often rove from neighborhood to neighborhood, doing these ad hoc projects with often only rudimentary tools at hand.

Homes are often turned into small businesses in these developments. These home businesses tend to follow a certain sequence of establishment. The first business to open is usually a mini-market, providing easy access to milk and other basic daily necessities. They are followed by paper stores, which sell the supplies needed by school kids. After the developer's bulldozers pull out of the area, informal shops selling lumber, cement, rebar, and brick open up at the entrance of the development. Informal builders, plumbers, and electricians come into the area as soon as the developers leave. The developers often ignore their own prohibitions on self-built structures, because they have already sold all the homes. They let the plan go wild after their own construction is completed, their profits banked. After the businesses offering essential consumer goods and services have established themselves, some communities begin to develop more sophisticated consumer infrastructure, for instance dry cleaning outposts, ambulance services, day care, and Internet access depots out of their homes. These activities often take place in a very simple and spatially limited way, but they still prove that the community can support self-initiated businesses, and that surplus income spent on these services creates employment opportunities within the community.

Policy makers are reacting very slowly to this situation, but they finally appear to be taking formal action toward promoting a certain level of quality of life in the developments. In January of 2010, an amendment to Article 73,

President Fox's original Housing Act, was passed, which establishes new rules and regulations for housing developments financed with federal funds and for social programs. However, the majority of these types of homes, even though destined for low-income families, are being financed and purchased with private mortgages, so it is unclear how the law will apply to them. In addition, the law does not provide clear directions regarding location for new developments. It appears they continue to be built far from jobs and city centers, thus impeding the quality of family life, forcing residents to spend large amounts of time and money on commuting. An average of 30 percent of the monthly income is spent on transportation to and from work, an amount that frequently exceeds monthly mortgage payments.

With developments being divorced from city life, residents are isolated from the everyday visually and creatively stimulating features that come with living in more varied surroundings. One begins to wonder about the impact on residents, particularly young people who spend their formative years within this setting. The visual impact of these settings in esthetic isolation presents itself in subtle ways. An example is the signs used to announce products for sale. Mexico has a tradition of using handmade signs—not of the minimalist Swiss typography tradition, but with a meticulous one-of-a-kind lettering made with humor and flair. Signs often include an unusual selection of besuited characters: tacos with legs indicate a taqueria, chickens flexing biceps advertize a rotisserie, a couch with smiling lips and eyes announces an upholstery shop. Yet in these new settlements, painted signs appear with stripped-down basic typography, black paint against a white background, with no typographic flourishes or illustrations, no carpentry work or additional material, and no color. Communication is reduced to a dormant visual intent that does not know itself that it is missing.

In some interviews residents reported that their neighborhoods are turning into incubators for antisocial behavior. They are microcosms of what is happening in high-crime cities like Ciudad Juarez. Because of difficult living and working conditions, sometimes parents abandon their homes or both parents are required to be away from home during long work and commuting hours, leaving children to care for themselves from the end of the school day until the evening. This leads to *Lord of the Flies* scenarios, with groups of very young kids roaming the neighborhood without parental supervision for most of the day. With parental supervision becoming an unaffordable luxury, and with limited educational opportunities and few role models, children growing up in these remote neighborhoods face

big challenges and profound long-term consequences, all of which carry over into our life as citizens of the same continent.

Sometimes there isn't even enough room in school for all of the kids in a neighborhood. By law, developers are required to build schools based on the number of acres developed, not the number of homes constructed. They build plain boxes for an elementary school, a junior high, and a high school. They are not required to build cafeterias, auditoriums, or sports fields. Nor are new satellite college campuses planned, so college students must commute, sometimes for three or five hours. This leads to high attrition rates for college students in these neighborhoods. There are few college graduates in these communities to emulate, and therefore little incentive to graduate from college as a means of improving one's situation. So many students go to work at a young age, but there are few opportunities within the communities. Most informal businesses in the neighborhoods are run by the housewife living in the home where the business is located. Other jobs include working at the Oxxo—the convenience store chain that builds the single authorized store in most neighborhoods. A 23-year-old I spoke with told me he had no intentions of wasting his time and money in college, since there were no jobs nearby that would pay him back for his investment. Besides, he added, you'd have to know someone to even get a job interview.

There are also few recreational options in the developments. On weekends in the early evenings, I have seen groups of teenage girls dressed in heels and sequins with carefully done hair. They walk down the streets to congregate with other kids at the periphery of the neighborhood, drink beer bought at Oxxo, and flirt with the boys. They are having these essential adolescent experiences, but at the same time they lack any real place to have them, aside from the fringes of their neighborhoods. Younger girls I have spoken with complained that they do not have space to hang out with their friends. They have no bedroom or space of their own and no acoustic privacy to play or listen to music—their houses are too small, the walls too thin. At the same time they have no after school activities. However, I have begun to see spaces being created within some of the communities that address some of these needs.

One example of this is a do-it-yourself castle in Toluca. The structure was built by a couple that had qualified for a housing loan but already had a house in the city. As an investment, they bought a second home and the remainder piece of land adjacent to it, in a new development outside of the city of Toluca. They originally traveled to their new house to get out of the city and to be near the farmland, which they could see because their property was located on the edge of the development. But they began to realize there was almost nowhere for kids and teens in the neighborhood to gather. The development's high school had not yet arrived—the building was constructed, but the state had not outfitted it with teachers or supplies—so the kids from the neighborhood were bussed to a high school 40 minutes away. The couple came up with the idea to turn their house into a Salon de Fiestas, and to rent it out as an event hall.

The husband designed the castle using a basic CAD program. He told me his design was based on a research process of watching every Disney cartoon movie with a castle in it. He taught himself sufficient Photoshop techniques to design interior banner collages of forests, princesses, and other fantasy characters. The same contractors who do the more basic home renovations in the neighborhood constructed the four-story castle from the husband's CAD design. The original structure of the house is still visible in the structure of the castle.

The couple now rents out the castle for events and as a gathering space for members of the community. It is a strong example of resident-initiated construction of something that has a community function. It is also captivating for me because it challenges these new developments on a number of levels offering an alternative to their monotonous appearance and to limited public and community space. It uses DIY techniques and the local labor market to invent new possibilities in these otherwise sterile environments. And it suggests there might be other layers of esthetics, culture, commerce, social responsibility, and celebration that could begin to grow in these complex and urgent locations.

About the author: Livia Corona is an artist based in New York and Mexico City. Her work presents personal interpretations of various objectives, and considers the interaction of photography with social possibilities. Corona was awarded a Guggenheim fellowship for her project "Two Million Homes for Mexico." In addition to *Enanitos Toreros*, Corona has published *Of People and Houses*, edited by Ilka & Andreas Ruby. Her work exhibits internationally, at locations including The National Museum of Anthropology, Mexico City; and Ballroom Marfa, Texas.

STIMULATE STAKEHOLDERS

Architecture without Developers

Building Groups as a Catalyst for Better Housing

SASCHA ZANDER AND CHRISTIAN ROTH
ZANDERROTH ARCHITECTS

When we came to Berlin as newly graduated architects some 10 years ago, we were fascinated by the numerous empty spaces that existed in the urban mesh of the city. We catalogued these empty spaces and came up with a list of around 1,000 undeveloped sites. A substantial number of them lay in central urban districts such as Prenzlauer Berg and Mitte, which are very popular today. Though we liked the void spaces, we also love buildings and we began to investigate who owned these empty sites and wrote letters to the owners, saying that we had a great idea about what could be built on their site. This was how we got our first commission.

In contrast to the situation today, back then prices in Berlin's Prenzlauer Berg were still very reasonable. All the same, we were surprised when we calculated the profit made by the developer of one of our projects. When we estimated what the costs would have been if we had not involved a developer, we realized that we would have achieved cost savings of around 20 percent for apartment owners.

This is the difference between the production costs and the sales price, which generally represents the developer's profit. Thus, the idea of building an apartment house without a developer seemed highly attractive. One of the inherent problems of developer-built projects is that too many people are involved in the design and in general, the architecture suffers as a result. We were convinced that in attractive locations, such as Berlin's Mitte or Prenzlauer Berg, we could produce better and more affordable architecture than a building developer, if we could determine the framework for ourselves, handle the entire design and construction process, as well as the marketing.

Under our guidance, the apartment buyers become clients by forming a building group in order to purchase the site that we suggest for their particular project. The buyers in turn jointly commission the planning and construction services so that in addition to eliminating the building developer's margin, further savings can be achieved through volume discounts. The purchase price ultimately reflects the actual production costs. To achieve these savings, all those interested in buying take on all the risks of a building client and commit themselves to accepting our design for the structure and façades of the building. Within their own apartments the residents have design freedom. In the interest of a clear separation of responsibility for design, on the one hand, and client care, on the other, we established a project development company known as "SmartHoming," which bundles expertise in the areas of architecture, law, and finance.

Our first building group project was a set of twin towers on Ruppiner Strasse, at the corner of Schönholzer Strasse. It comprises two seven-story buildings, with a total of 12 apartments. Each apartment has a floor area of about $117\,m^2$ and is structured solely from a central circulation core, allowing variety of floor plans to suit residents ranging from a 6-person family to a single-person household. Combining apartments on two floors even resulted in a duplex apartment. For this project we consciously chose a difficult site. It was a north-facing corner site, vacant as the result of war-time bombing, set in a typical Berlin block framework. Given the unfavorable lighting situation, it would have meant somewhat undesirable units if the corner were to be rebuilt to match the surrounding buildings. In order to avoid this and to provide optimal lighting for the apartments by enabling light to enter from three sides, we only developed the areas alongside the firewalls of the neighboring buildings, leaving the corner of the block free, thereby transforming the disadvantage of the corner position into an advantage. At the same time, it allowed us to create an additional public urban square and, in effect,

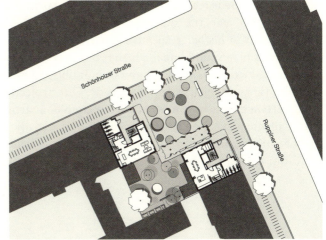

1-2: The twin towers on Ruppiner Straße, corner Schönholzer Straße, Berlin. The site for the project consisted of three lots. By leaving the north facing corner lot empty, every apartment receives light from three sides. Although property of the building group, the empty corner lot was transformed into a public square and is maintained by the tenants of the twin towers.

a lightwell for the buildings. However, the reason that this corner had remained undeveloped for years was because the site was divided up between three different owners: the state, the local government district, and a group of heirs. Before construction could commence the legal framework had to be clarified. These obstacles meant that there was not a lot of competition in acquiring the site and this in turn reduced the pressure on the building group to purchase it immediately. Instead, they could secure an "option to buy" for the site, a kind of reservation, in which the owner commits to not sell the site to another party for a certain period of time, generally one year. Unlike a developer, a building group cannot simply take out a loan when it wishes to purchase a site, as setting up a building group requires a certain amount of time. The option to buy is a way of dealing with one of the main problematic aspects of a building group—the need for a long organizational lead-time—because it gains sufficient time to develop the project and to complete the organization of the building group.

The members of the building group sign a partnership agreement as a *Gesellschaft bürgerlichen Rechts* (GbR, a company organized under civil law), so that they can acquire the site and function as the client. This contract outlines who obtains which apartment, which position the unit occupies within the house, and which share of the total cost it represents. The determination of the ownership shares takes the form of a partition declaration that provides the basis for the apartment owners' association. In formal terms, a building group goes through four stages from the site acquisition to moving into the building. Just prior to the acquisition of the site, the group of buyers constitutes itself as a planning association, and at the start of construction it turns into an association of building clients. After construction is complete it transitions to an owner's association that subsequently takes over ownership of the building. The articles of the partnership agreement regulate this process. Similar to an individual client, the building group also bears the financial risks. However, the total liability of each individual is limited to his/her respective share of ownership. The most important thing—and this may sound banal—is that the sum of all participation costs should cover the production costs. We know of building group associations where this was not the case and which failed as a result. Our projections are always calculated with a certain excess as a buffer if, for example, apartment sizes change in the course of planning, as one does not wish to repeatedly adjust the participation costs. The high demand for housing projects of this kind in central city areas offers additional security. In our second building group project, which we completed in

2008, located at 11 Schönholzerstrasse diagonally opposite our twin tower project, there were 37 reservations for 11 apartments. If somebody had backed out, we would have immediately had a replacement.

In the first two apartment houses we built, before we developed an interest in building groups, our clients simply told us the number of square meters they required and what the building should cost. Of course, that is far simpler than doing a building group project in which all decisions must be made jointly and agreements must be reached between all group members. Despite the greater need for consensus in building group projects, we wish to preserve the amount of architectural freedom that we had in our first commissioned projects. As we are convinced that one cannot design a really good-quality building with 20 people, we propose a deal to those involved in our building group projects. We agree that they can keep the financial gain (which is generally the profit margin that a developer would make in a normal project) and in exchange we are granted full freedom to design the façade and structure of the building. For the interiors of the apartments we then relinquish control to give design freedom to the members of the building group. The possibility for the respective owners—who in our projects are always the actual occupants—to adapt the floor plan to meet their individual needs is a major advantage in comparison to other models of acquiring a home of one's own. We offer a good, solid solution with a standard set of finishes and fixtures included, but if someone is determined to have something exceptional they can of course carry that out. We add 10 percent to our fee for this additional design service, which rarely covers the amount of time and effort involved. In many areas we would like to standardize the options available. In light of the apparently infinite range of building products and appliances on the market, this would be a favor to our clients and would speed up the decision-making processes.

We are not interested in participatory design processes *per se*. What interests us, above all else, is a better architectural result. We don't mean only the apartment and the building but also our contribution to the interface between "public" and "private." The architect and the client have a joint responsibility towards urban space. In this respect the project for the twin towers makes a clear and concrete contribution, by providing a planted urban space between the two buildings, which is paid for and maintained by the building group, but can be used by the public without restrictions. The reasonable price of land made it possible for the clients to leave the corner of the block undeveloped and to make this space available to the public. In contrast, it would be unlikely that building developers

3

4

3-4: The second project for a building group is located across from the twin towers, on Schönholzer Strasse 11. This building—that was built on the empty strip of land along the former site of the Berlin Wall—also benefits from the open corner of the twin tower project.

would have allowed themselves to be deterred from developing the entire area and using the greatest permissible density in order to reap the maximum profit from the site.

In our project BIGyard, located at 5-11 Zelter Strasse, also in Prenzlauer Berg, our contribution to urban space is only revealed at second glance. Two housing blocks enclose a courtyard garden that is 100 m long and 13 m wide — which is exactly the width of a typical street in the historic city center of Berlin. To the rear of the block, the courtyard is framed by a row of three-story garden houses. They have direct access to the garden and balconies with a view of the garden. Their split-level layout allows room heights of up to 4.2 m. The penthouses occupy the top three floors. All have private patios and are reached by two elevators. The garden courtyard is closed off from direct street access by four-story townhouses that face in two directions and are also organized on a split-level system. They have individual gardens and separate entrances off Zelter Strasse. A ground-level garage connects the two housing structures, and the roof of this also serves as the platform for the first floor garden courtyard. The ground floor rooms in the townhouses that face onto the street are suitable for commercial use.

The most fascinating thing about BIGyard is that the 45 buyers involved agreed not to fence off their individual share of the garden in the typical town house manner. Instead, they combined their small outdoor plots to create a far more desirable 1,300 m^2 garden courtyard and this has many advantages, including making it easy for parents to look after their children. Despite the intensive use of this common garden — in the 45 dwelling units there are a total of 112 residents and 40 of them are children — the project combines many desirable qualities of a single family home, such as several floors within one dwelling, terraces, a garage and, in case of the townhouses along Zelter Strasse, access to the dwelling directly from the street. In addition, there is a large communal roof terrace, a sauna, a summer kitchen, and four guest apartments. The savings made by the joint site acquisition, planning, and construction processes meant that the association of clients could afford additional amenities worth 300,000 EUR, and of a kind uncommon and unexpected in a central city area.

Unfortunately, Berlin's borough administrations did not want to have those amenities on the roof of the Zelter Strasse complex. This meant that it took ten months just to have the 300 m^2 roof terrace approved. We had to go first a level higher than the local borough and appeal directly to the Berlin Senate administra-

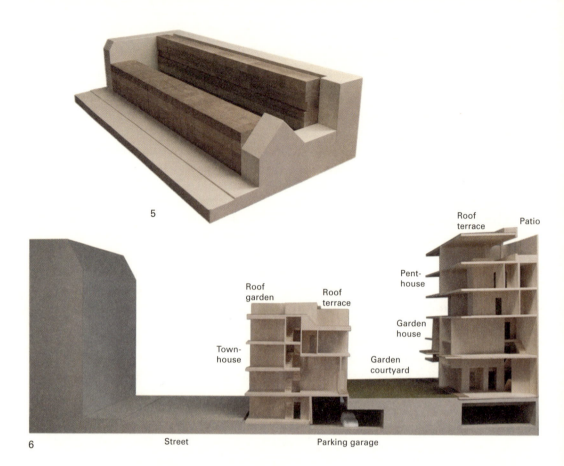

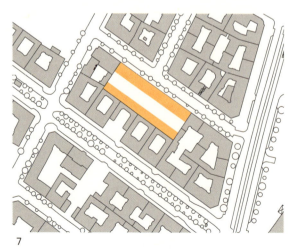

5: BIGyard is a building group project for 45 families composed of four-story townhouses to the street and three-story garden houses with three-story penthouses on top to the rear of the block.

6: On top of the parking garage that connects the front and the rear building, is a big garden courtyard of 1,300 m². Townhouses and garden houses are arranged in split-levels, allowing for room heights of up to 4.2 m.

7: Though integrated into the Berlin block structure, BIGyard offers a way of life that combines urban and suburban lifestyles: it integrates communal facilities, such as a big roof terrace, a sauna, a summer kitchen and four guest apartments, but offers also private street-level access for the townhouses and direct garden access for all apartments except the penthouses, and a car park at street level.

tion, which, incidentally, has been the case with almost all of our projects. We have regularly had to engage in a small war against the authorities, and over the last ten years have had to employ a battalion of lawyers.

However, we are willing to undertake this extra effort because it grants an added architectural value that makes it fully worthwhile. The kind of buildings we can realize this way embody a quality of life which motivates a relatively affluent group of creative people, with an average age of 39 and with, on average, two children per family, to stay in the city. These people might otherwise move to a single-family house in the country outside of Berlin and end up commuting 80 km daily to work, which obviously would have detrimental repercussions from communal, urban planning and spatial planning viewpoints. In this sense, the project expands our ideas about contemporary urban housing. Housing is no longer confined to simply providing accommodation for people. It has more to do with the spatial organization of leisure time spent at home. Ideally, your home makes you feel as if you were on vacation—and indeed the view of the town houses, with their roof terraces laid out in a row, is somewhat reminiscent of a Greek holiday village. Housing should contribute to recreation. In the BIGyard project, housing in a central city location is intended to evoke a somewhat suburban quality of life. A late 19th century apartment cannot provide that; it is large and has tall doors, but no leisure or relaxation areas on the roof.

No building developer would have participated in any one of the three building group projects we have completed so far. In the real estate business housing projects fail because of simple issues, such as an internal bathroom without a window or the lack of a balcony. The concern is never for the overall quality of an apartment. For example: by opting for an internal, windowless bathroom we gain a certain freedom in the floor plan that allows spatial generosity in other places. We did things in this way for the garden houses in BIGyard. The split-level apartments only face in one direction and, in contrast to the townhouses and the penthouses, they do not have their own terraces, but with living rooms 4.20 m high and direct access to the large communal garden terrace, they have other qualities that compensate for the apparent deficits. This is reflected in the price structure within BIGyard: we offered the garden houses for a very low price of only 1,700 EUR/m^2. This was possible only because the owners of the penthouses and townhouses agreed to higher participation costs. Thanks to the size of the project we were also able to cross-subsidize apartments that, although disadvantaged in terms of location within the building, are attractive in spatial terms, through units that have a higher market rating and selling price due to their more attractive location within the building.

Creating reasonably priced living space is an important concern in our building group projects. Our projects are clearly more economical than those built by commercial developers. This means that people earning average incomes, who would otherwise have little chance to enter the housing market, can become homeowners. Despite all of this, we certainly do not reach the lower classes of our society. Our projects create opportunities for the middle-class; generally participants have been young working couples in their late 30s and early 40s, with one or two children. In contrast to many other countries, in Germany it is not usual to own your home, and this is most true in cities, where the majority of people rent and never own. However, the more the viability of the existing state pension system in Germany has been questioned in recent years, the more atttractive home ownership has become as a way to ensure some degree of financial security for one's old age.

In the BIGyard project on Zelter Strasse, this microeconomic principle of cross-subsidizing has not yet led to a socioeconomically diverse mix of residents. This was largely because the generous size and floorplan layout of the apartments was tailored to the needs of families. In our new project at 22 Rigaer Strasse we might actually be able to achieve a greater socioeconomic diversity. In the project we deliberately created and offered apartments of very different sizes: small 1 to 2 room apartments of 55-60 m^2 as well as large family apartments measuring 125 m^2. Small apartments are automatically far more economical than large ones. In addition, we created a large price range, related to the vertical position of the apartment in the building: the apartments on higher floors are more expensive, and those on lower floors are cheaper. This could allow a socially heterogeneous mix of residents to develop. These small apartments are designed in such a way that two adjacent apartments situated on the same floor can be combined to form one large apartment, and then separated again later, depending on the changing housing needs of the occupants over the course of their lives. If necessary, one of the two apartments could even be sold again or rented out.

With a site measuring 8,000 m^2, the project exceeds the usual architectural scale and makes an urban statement. Situated behind the easternmost block of the famous street formerly known as "Stalinallee," designed by Hermann Henselmann and Richard Paulick in the 1950s, the project consists of five freestanding seven-story housing towers. On account of the additive use of the same building

8

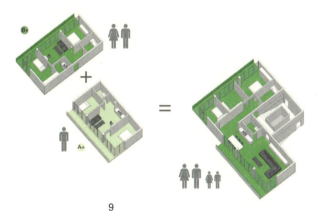

9

8: The building group project on Rigaer Straße, Berlin, consists of five freestanding seven-story apartment towers on a park-like site of 8,000 m².

9: The project offers a range of different apartment sizes: small 1 to 2 room apartments of 55-60 m² can be combined to large family apartments of 125 m². The different apartment sizes and the large price range depending on the vertical positioning of the apartment in the building could allow a socially heterogeneous mix of tenants to develop.

type, the fees of all the engineers and architects in this project are halved. This reduces the total planning costs to such an extent that we can afford to develop the complex with a low density.

In the Rigaer Strasse project, the economic concept goes beyond financing additional qualities through reduced production costs. The penthouse will cost 3,300 EUR/m² which is fairly high for this part of the city. This allows us to offer the apartments on the second floor for 1,800 EUR/m² which is at the lower limit of the range, as normally the prices there range between 2,200 and 3,000 EUR/m². Our tactics in this kind of cross-financing, within a building group project, acquire a certain subversive and ironic connotation: The person interested in buying a penthouse takes the apartment for a fixed price and, despite his/her participation in the GbR, is freed from any kind of cost risk. In return, they contribute a considerable amount of capital to the building group, which enables us to offer apartments for 1,800 EUR/m². With this strategy we can provide a buffer against rising property prices and can extend the price range in two directions in a single project. In a sense we are contesting the market's monopoly in deciding who may live in what kind of apartment. Nevertheless, it would be naïve to believe that, like some kind of Robin Hood for the housing market, we could ever compensate for the major political failures that exist in Berlin due to the complete lack of a socially sustainable housing policy.

As our building group projects have increased in size, we have gradually left the scale of the single building in favor of the neighborhood. Building groups are certainly not the only sensible organizational model. We regard cooperatives as far more worthwhile than associations of apartment owners, as the acquisition of a right of tenancy for life, which can then be inherited by family, means that the mentality of private property ownership does not develop in the first place. This would also remove any motivation for real estate speculation. The problem is that a newly founded cooperative is not as financially powerful as a building group. Old cooperatives have a financial cushion thanks to years of rent payments, which enable them to develop new projects. Newly founded cooperatives, however, must raise the entire budget for the building project from scratch. Even though cooperatives are no longer as favorably treated by the state as in the past, it would make sense to involve cooperatives in building group projects.

Apart from these alternative models, the increasing size of our housing projects also raises the question of their significance for the city district or neighborhood in which they're located. Integrating the kind of additional infrastructural and commercial facilities typically found in a district or neighborhood, such as a shoe-repair shop, a Chinese restaurant, or a newspaper kiosk, would be desirable. Unfortunately the use of the commercial spaces of the townhouses in our BIGyard project is restricted to the residents themselves. The problem is simple: tradesmen and shopkeepers generally do not buy their premises; they rent them. Building groups so far have rarely been able to—or want to—act as landlords.

In the Rigaer Strasse project we want to try to integrate more infrastructure elements than in BIGyard. Apart from the five residential towers in the open space, we also planned a long foundation slab along the street edge. The German supermarket chain Aldi would like to buy this site and erect a single-story building on it, but the town planners will not allow this. We think it would be good to have an Aldi supermarket here, though it would have disadvantages as well as advantages. The main advantage is that people would have a local shop within easy reach of their home and therefore would not have to make a car journey to buy groceries; the disadvantage lies in the esthetic of a typical Aldi store. Our idea is that Aldi would be allowed to erect a single-story building, which is their usual typology, provided that they follow our design guidelines, and only on the condition that the store's roof is made available to the general public as a kind of elevated urban square.

During the past few years this site has been repeatedly occupied by political activists known as "Bambi-Land" and has equally regularly been cleared by the owners. The activists from "Bambi-Land" argue that the city has a responsibility to buy such sites and to make them available to the general public. We can empathize with them and understand this position, but the City of Berlin, whose mayor likes to describe the city as "poor, but sexy", simply does not have 4 million EUR to purchase the site. Aldi, in contrast, would be willing to pay a great deal of money for the site and to create a terrace measuring 2000 m^2 for public use. Aldi's financial strength could allow the creation of very reasonably priced apartments. With project funding and redistribution strategies of this kind, we could also finance social facilities such as children's day care centers and schools—there is a high demand for these in Prenzlauer Berg, which has one of the highest birth rates in Germany. The borough often refuses building groups a building permit for their housing projects on the grounds that there are not enough children's day care centers and schools in the area, yet builds only a few new facilities.

Tactics such as these, where money is taken from one entity involved in the project (without them experiencing it as such) and applied within the same project to something beneficial for the whole, are a means to an end. This allows us to make good architecture and provide affordable apartments in a central city location. One could also see it as taxation of a different kind. In the final analysis, the entity that provides the money also profits. Despite rising land prices we will still be able to achieve a price differential between building developer and building client association for quite some time. But to do this we will regularly have to come up with something new. One way to do this is to investigate areas other than highly desirable boroughs like Prenzlauer Berg. This is not always easy. At the moment, we are designing a project on Adalbertstrasse in Berlin-Kreuzberg. The interested persons who contacted us for the commission think the building we have designed is fantastic, but do not want to live in this marginally gentrified part of Berlin. In ten years time the situation will be different. The value of the residential area between the Spree and the Engelbecken will change completely for the better. A project like this has to be advertised in an entirely different way. Previously we merely publicized our projects on an Internet real estate portal and it was enough to attract interested people; for the Adalbertstrasse project we have engaged the services of a professional real-estate agent.

Naturally, building developers on the lookout for new possibilities for generating profit also continually come up with new ways of doing things. Paradoxically, they are also adopting the building group model. The building projects appear to be building group projects, but because of the involvement of the developer, there is an imperative for the generation of a profit margin, and any cost savings and other benefits are therefore not present. Our theory is that housing concepts become more diverse and experimental through the building group model and after being subjected to five years of scrutiny, this has been happily confirmed.

Interview and text documentation: Julia von Mende

About the authors: Christian Roth is co-principal of Zanderroth, a Berlin-based architecture firm. He studied at the RWTH Aachen, the Academy of Arts Dusseldorf, and the E.T.S.A. Madrid. He has a Diploma in Architecture from the RWTH Aachen.

Sascha Zander is co-principal of Zanderroth, a Berlin-based architecture firm. He studied at the RWTH Aachen, the Academy of Arts Dusseldorf, and the Bartlett School of Architecture at University College London. He has a Diploma in Architecture from the Bartlett School of Architecture at University College London and a Diploma in Urban Design from the RWTH Aachen.

Sustaining what?

The Discourse of Sustainability in Need of Re-invention

CARY SIRESS

Sustainability is the newly ascendant global policy issue of the 21st century. There is hardly a discipline or discourse today that is unresponsive to the cause of meeting present needs without compromising that very capacity for future generations. A reflexive loop is cast. Such an appeal serves to round up—in current terms and under one cause—not only our present, along with all that now exists, but also non-existent trajectories of space and time, including all that *should* come. The sustainability of the present is plotted in terms of some other condition to be, with the way our world is presently constructed held up against one that is better. As clearly circuitous as all of this might seem, we seldom ask why, but quietly assume that the future, by definition the promise of a hereafter, must somehow be better when measured out relative to the moment at hand. Appropriately, and given the rather gloomy diagnosis of our current predicament, the urgency accorded to translating our current way of life into one that can be sustained is fast becoming a bona fide planetary injunction on ways and means, including those that remain to be devised. The mandate of sustainability is therefore predominantly staged as an unequivocal panacea for an admittedly daunting range of political, environmental, and social ills that only threaten to escalate with the worldwide advance of urbanization.

Yet, despite the gravity it sanctions, sustainability is continuously plagued by programmatic ambiguity from any perspective considered. Who decides? Who enacts? Who benefits? For its part in the debate, the city itself tends to confound rather than clarify matters, given that it is frequently bashed and backed simultaneously, cast as both scapegoat and stakeholder. That is, the city is presented as both the main source of environmental degradation and as a vital resource for alleviating this condition. Those prone to dystopian views most often render cities indiscriminately as the chief perpetrator in placing unsustainable burdens on the environment, often forgetting the long history of vilifying the city that, while perhaps initiating necessary reforms in the past, also served in the end to reinforce then existing power interests governing urban society. Yet, such anti-urban bias is met by equally brazen calls at home and abroad for more urbanity at all costs insofar as the city manifests as the most accepted world emblem of all that is modern, and also stages the most lucrative density of channels for capital.

But the loop does not stop here. In many a forum, there is a strong lobby for a consensus among key players in cities, as indispensable to further specifying the provisions of a green turn in urban practice and policy alike, whereas others argue just as passionately that the drive for consensus is ironically the source of ambiguity in the first place. Besides, it is pointed out that agreement, more often than not, only caters to narrow partisan agendas of those served by going green. From another corner, we are reminded that seeking world consensus on what is green amounts to no more than Western shorthand for obliging the rest of the planet to accept *our* view of what counts as sustainable, and usually, to pay a high price for doing so. Such disputes are only intensified by uncertainty concerning how the twin conventions of progress and growth might, if at all, be reconciled with the now obvious imperative for moderating the inflated footprint of human civilization. Add this seemingly implausible balancing act to that of trying to formulate a core set of directives for "sustainable development"—still an oxymoron in its own right—and it is no wonder that, although compelling as a motive for altering our shared means and ends, sustainability remains a blurred project at best.

How could it be otherwise? For no prototype of the finished outcome exists. We already inhabit a thoroughly constructed world. So, there is nothing out there that we can point to as a pure standard of "green" that would ground a collectively sustainable way of life for everything existing today. There is not even a blueprint for what will be collected in realizing said goal, or for that matter, what will be discarded in the process. And if we were ever to accomplish such a task of collection, would all that is gathered be assembled in one or several compositions? But with such queries, we inevitably loop the loop to come upon that familiar bank of the circle once again. Who decides? Who enacts? Who benefits? You would think that having rehearsed such questions over and over in so many guises, we might first take the time to collect ourselves, so to speak, and consider turning that finger back upon ourselves and wonder if we have not been looking (or pointing) in the wrong direction for *the* answer all along, namely, somewhere "out there", be it to *the* Future, *the* Past, Nature, or where you will.

Such an about-face might interrupt our path along the closed loop of sustainability debates, stirring us to begin thinking our constructed environments, if not ourselves, out of servitude to a monolithic Outside. Even if wagered long after the forums have convened, better late than never! Are we not tired of technological disenchantment and being forever distanced by a lifeless techné that makes us less human? Have we not been alienated long enough from that proverbial promised land lost to a time now gone? And, especially today, how much more mileage can we really expect to get from the divide that allegedly privileges us from the rest of the natural, non-human world when it is, after all, the world that we are trying to sustain? Can it be that sustainability, however worthy as a cause, intrinsically boils down to no more than sustaining our disenchantment, alienation, loss, lack, or any other deficit that deprives the human condition? If so, then sustainability as injunction serves to expatriate the majority of our lifeworld by decree of worn-out habit, and everything comprising that world on which we now depend for survival.

It should be clear by now that repeated petitions to an outside become more of a hindrance than an aid to assembling an environmental politics of constructed worlds—one that would draw on our shared condition for insight rather than withdraw from it—in that such petitions foreclose questions in advance which are necessarily collective, and thus political in the broadest sense. When we call out to a primal Nature, for example, this realm is often already held in timeless reserve, making it, in effect, irrelevant and thus unaccountable to decision-making in real time and space. Said realms are locked away as sacrosanct rather than dealt with opportunistically in their construction as such. The loop becomes less blurry. Decidedly cut off from the past, we contemporaries like to think we are impotent when faced, for example, with "Natural Laws," even as we proceed to consult Nature in endless debate loops about our Future, only to exclude it again from the negotiating table. Were we to venture from this fateful circuit, however, perhaps we would risk letting go of our external grounds, those appeals to something beyond us, which categorically either promises salvation or threatens extinction, yet in any case remains immune to negotiation or dispute.

Still in the loop, we must nevertheless face an annoying question: if the global cause of sustainability does not boil down to a hushed inferiority complex about our world standing, then why are we not calling out to our constructed environments for key terms and conditions of becoming credibly and equitably sustainable? We have built them, so why can they not in turn inform us with their amassed material and metabolic résumés? In varying degrees of success, our constructed environments sustain us, so why can they not be afforded a more authoritative stake in the green deals made on their behalf? We survive by artifice, so why should nature not be tested more assertively for its competence as constructive equal along with those other more recognizable, more "human" technologies of production when devising how to construct our way back *inside* to a sustainable coexistence with everything else on the planet?

Of course, this would call for a controversial overhaul of how we view nature, to take just one example. Imagine the scorn or amusement at the very premise that, in place of an eternal static backdrop to human evolution, the myriad collection of environments we attempt to round up with the term "Nature" have in fact co-produced our civilization *and* have co-developed with it. But dispute about the terms of our coexistence is what sustainability is all about, no? And with the world rightly opened to debate, would it not follow that nature is as much co-product of our civilization as its constructs are of nature? This would mean that such qualifying terms as *natural* and *artificial* can no longer be so easily separated from each other in form or content when re-composing ourselves and surroundings, nor can such qualifications be conveniently distinguished by inherent differences in value according to some moral or divine pecking order. Moreover, if the natural and the artificial cannot be separated, then neither can the social and technical challenges that we face in the collectively political project of constructing sustainable environments. For such challenges are wicked problems themselves. They cannot be reduced to singular criterion or values and thus, stun in its tracks again and again any categorical approach aimed at solving them. Indeed, when the environment itself becomes a *project*, the politics of its collection, assembly, and construction are necessarily hybrid by constitution, inseparably natural, technical, social, material, and so forth.

But such an overhaul cannot stop with nature or any other transcendent figure, as this would only revise that nether side of a divide, which remains a black hole for sustainability debates. How we view our built environments will also have to be revamped. This will entail first and foremost diverting more of the time and money spent on speculating about what constitutes a good or green city in abstraction, to understanding what the city is and has become in our time. To mine the city would require an ongoing analysis of forces, processes, behaviors, associations, materials, and any other compound agent generated in, and modified by, the entanglement of heterogeneous environments, including us. To mine the city would be to track translations across different spatial and temporal scales that work to sustain, if only provisionally, the tightly coupled natural-social-technological arrangements that make up our constructed world. To mine the city would be to recognize that cities are already the most prolific test-bed we have devised thus far to collectively engineer artifice in order to survive. Of course, such a stance would leave little room for the hubris of radical breaks, utopian non-places devoid of any resources to sustain them, or the view from a distance of expert systems, and so on. Instead, sustainability would finally have to refer to a view from somewhere on Earth, and the means of life would have to become more tangible as a matter of concern for all. Sustainability, in other words, would have to account for a situated cosmology that hinges on sustaining being *and* being sustained as collective project by warding off the outside. When faced with such wicked problems, it is imperative to know where you stand, for their solutions hinge on first understanding the problems themselves. But if the grass still seems greener on the other side, perhaps it is only because of our continued reluctance to get out of the loop.

About the author: Cary Siress is an architect and a tenured faculty member in Architecture and Theory at the School of Arts, Culture, and Environment of The University of Edinburgh and Visiting Professor at the School of Architecture at the University of Nanjing in China. He is the founding editor of the new journal *Architecture &*. Following graduate studies at Columbia University in New York, he was involved in teaching and research at the ETH Zurich, where he completed his PhD.

IMAGE CREDITS

p. 28: all images © Judy Hill Lovins
p. 38/39: © Zooey Braun
p. 40: 2,3,4 © Zooey Braun
p. 42: 5,6,7 © Roland Halbe
p. 47: © KVA MATx
p. 50-52: all images © KVA MATx
p. 53: 6,7 © KVA MATx,
   8 © Hans-Georg Roth
p. 58: all images © BIG
p. 60/61: all images © BIG
p. 62/63: all images © BIG
p. 65: all images © BIG
p. 87-89: all images © LAVA, MIR VISUALS, Atelier Illume
p. 92: © LAVA, MIR VISUALS, Atelier Illume
p. 129: 1 © Koji Kobayashi,
   2 © C+A
p. 130: 34 © C+A
p. 132: 7 © Koji Kobayashi,
   8 © Sadao Hotta,
   9 © C+A
p. 137: 1,2,3,4 © Rojkind Arquitectos
p. 138/139: 5,6,7 © Guido Torres
p. 142/143: © Paúl Rivera/archphoto.com
p. 149/150: all images © at103
p. 152/153: 15,16,17 © Rafael Gamo,
   18, 19 © Axel Fridman
p. 156: all images © Fito Pardo
p. 158/159: all images © at103
p. 161: 27 © Fito Pardo
p. 166: 1 © Steve Hall/Hedrich Blessing
p. 168, 171: all images © Studio Gang Architects
p. 172/173: 7-10 © Studio Gang Architects,
   11 © Spirit of Space
p. 177: 1 © Lacaton & Vassal Architectes,
   2 © Philippe Ruault
p. 179: 3,5 © Lacaton & Vassal Architectes,
   4 © Philippe Ruault
p. 180/181: 8 © Philippe Ruault
p. 184/185: © Lacaton & Vassal Architectes
p. 186: 17 © Philippe Ruault,
   18, 20 © Lacaton & Vassal Architectes,
   19 © Philippe Ruault
p. 191, 192, 194, 197: all images © 51N4E
p. 198/199: © Jutta Benzenberg
p. 203: all images © Mass Studies
p. 205: 3 © Gaia Cambiaggi,
   4 © Joseph Grima,
p. 208: 5, 6 © Mass Studies,
   7 © Jason Walp
p. 211: 8, 9 © Yongkwan Kim,
   10 © Mass Studies
p. 214: 11 © Mass Studies
   12 © Yongkwan Kim.
p. 218: 74 © Philippe Ruault,
   76 © Lacaton & Vassal Architectes
p. 225: 100 © R & Sie(n)
p. 231: 105, 107 © Oana Stanescu

p. 252: 5 © Gary Anderson
p. 255: 6 © Gregg Brown/Getty Images,
   7 © Richard Rogers
p. 259: 10 © Green Peace
p. 278/279: © Terreform
p. 290: 1 © Ryan Griffis
p. 300/301: 1,2,4,5 © Danny Bright,
   3 © LOT-EK
p. 302/303: 6 © LOT-EK
p. 305: 7,8 © LOT-EK
p. 306: 9,10 © LOT-EK
p. 313: 1,2,3 © Bisrat Kifle
p. 317: 4,5,6 © Catherine Lippuner
p. 318: 7,8 © Dirk Hebel
p. 320: 9,11 © Catherine Lippuner
p. 323: 13, 14, 15 © Centre Pompidou. Mnam. Bibliothèque Kandinsky
p. 332: 163 © Katsuhisa Kida
p. 333: 166, 169 © Philippe Ruault
p. 346: 202,203,204 © EM2N,
   207 © Ensamble Studio,
   208 © Roland Halbe
p. 367: 1,2 © BeL,
p. 369: 3,4 © BeL,
p. 371-377: all images © BeL
p. 390-392: all images © Jose Castillo/ arquitectura 911sc
p. 397-398: all images © Jose Castillo/ arquitectura 911sc
p. 400: © Jose Castillo/ arquitectura 911sc
p. 405: © Livia Corona
p. 408: © Livia Corona
p. 410: © Livia Corona
p. 413: © Livia Corona
p. 415: © Livia Corona
p. 416: © Livia Corona
p. 421: 1 © Andrea Kroth,
   2 © Zanderroth Architekten
p. 424: 3,4 © Andrea Kroth
p. 426: 5,6,7 © Zanderroth Architekten
p. 429: 8,9 © Zanderroth Architekten

All Drawings of the Index © Something Fantastic

DONOR ACKNOWLEDGEMENT

The Holcim Foundation for Sustainable Construction aims to build awareness of the importance of sustainability in construction among professionals and the public. It seeks to globally interlink knowledge and to promote a mindset that views sustainability not only in terms of complex technical challenges, but that also incorporates architectural excellence and leads to a higher quality of life.

The Holcim Foundation conducts activities to encourage innovative approaches to sustainable construction including the Holcim Awards competition and Holcim Forum. To pursue its goals, the Foundation collaborates closely with some of the most renowned technical universities:

Swiss Federal Institute of Technology (ETH Zurich), Switzerland; Massachusetts Institute of Technology (MIT), Cambridge, USA; Indian Institute of Technology Bombay (IITB), Mumbai, India; Universidad Iberoamericana (UIA), Mexico City, Mexico; Ecole Supérieure d'Architecture de Casablanca (EAC), Morocco; Universidade de São Paulo (USP), Brazil; University of the Witwatersrand, Johannesburg, South Africa; and Tongji University, Shanghai, China.

The Advisory Board of the Holcim Foundation ensures that the activities of the foundation remain in line with current interpretations of sustainable construction. Members of the Advisory Board are:

Rolf Soiron (Chair), Chairman of Holcim, Switzerland; Yolanda Kakabadse, President of WWF International, Ecuador; Amory Lovins, Chairman and Chief Scientist of the Rocky Mountain Institute, USA; Enrique Norten, Principal and Founder of TEN Arquitectos, Mexico/USA; Klaus Töpfer, former United Nations Undersecretary-General and Executive Director of the United Nations Environment Programme (UNEP), Germany; Simon Upton, Director of the OECD Environment Directorate, New Zealand/France; and Muhammad Yunus, Founder of Grameen Bank, and 2006 Nobel Peace Prize Laureate, Bangladesh.

The Management Board of the Holcim Foundation determines its strategy and initiatives, provides guidance, and appoints experts who support the foundation's activities. Members of the Management Board are:

Markus Akermann (Chair), CEO of Holcim, Switzerland; Roland Walker (Delegate), Head Corporate Communications of Holcim, Switzerland; Marc Angélil, Dean of Architecture, ETH Zurich, Switzerland; Alexander Biner, Partner of MS Management Service, Switzerland; Harry Gugger, Professor of Architecture, École Polytechnique Fédérale de Lausanne (EPFL), Switzerland; and Hans-Rudolf Schalcher, Professor em. of Planning and Management in Construction, ETH Zurich, Switzerland.

To make the criteria of sustainable construction concise and transparent, the Holcim Foundation and its partner universities have defined five so-called "target issues". They consider sustainability from a holistic perspective:

– Progress: Innovation and transferability
– People: Ethical standards and social equity
– Planet: Environmental quality and resource efficiency
– Prosperity: Economic performance
– Proficiency: Contextual and esthetic impact

The Holcim Foundation publishes compendia of sustainable construction projects, on exemplary buildings as well as from symposia. PDF versions of Holcim Foundation publications are available at www.holcimfoundation.org/publications—including commemorative books on previous International Holcim Forums:

– 1st Forum: *Basic Needs*, ETH Zurich, Switzerland 2004 (ISBN 978-3-7266-0069-3)
– 2nd Forum: *Urban_Trans_Formation*, Tongji University, Shanghai, China 2007 (ISBN 978-3-0002-4878-8)
– 3rd Forum: *Re-inventing Construction*, Universidad Iberoamericana, Mexico City, Mexico 2010 (ISBN 978-3-9813436-2-5)

For further information about the Holcim Foundation and its initiatives, including the Holcim Awards competition and Holcim Forum, please see: www.holcimfoundation.org

The Holcim Foundation is supported by Swiss based Holcim Ltd, but independent of its commercial interests. As a leading global provider of building materials, Holcim Ltd shares responsibility for the future of our planet and society. That is why Holcim produces building materials as sustainably as possible in around 70 countries in which it is present. For many years, the Group has been committed to the sustainable application of its products and has been confirmed as a member of the Dow Jones Sustainability World Index in 2009/2010 in the building materials industry. Holcim has been included in both the Dow Jones Sustainability World Index and the Dow Jones STOXX Sustainability Index since 2003. For further information visit: www.holcim.com